HONOUR THY MOTHER

THE SEARCH FOR JEANNINE DURAND

RICK BOYCHUK

VIKING

Viking
Published by the Penguin Group
Penguin Books Canada Ltd, 10 Alcorn Avenue, Toronto, Ontario, Canada
M4V 3B2
Penguin Books Ltd, 27 Wrights Lane, London W8 5TZ, England
Viking Penguin, a division of Penguin Books USA Inc., 375 Hudson
Street, New York, New York 10014, U.S.A.
Penguin Books Australia Ltd, Ringwood, Victoria, Australia
Penguin Books (NZ) Ltd, 182-190 Wairau Road, Auckland 10, New
Zealand

Penguin Books Ltd, Registered Offices: Harmondsworth, Middlesex,
England

First published 1994

10 9 8 7 6 5 4 3 2 1

Printed and bound in Canada on acid free paper ♾

Canadian Cataloguing in Publication Data

Boychuk, Rick, 1953-
Honour thy mother

ISBN 0-670-85120-5

1. Durand, Raymond. 2. Durand, Jeannine, d. 1968.
3. Murder - Texas - Houston. I. Title.

HV6534.H8B68 1994   364.I'523'092   C93-094957-9

To the memory of
Jeannine Boissonneault Durand
1933–1968

Prologue

February, 1968, Houston, Texas

It was the BB gun, a toy rifle, Gilbert told them. That's why he took the boy out to the Barker Reservoir, he told the deputy at the Fort Bend County sheriff's office.

In the police reports he is Gilbert Pavliska, a thirty-six-year-old grader driver for the Texas Department of Highways. Pavliska is from Richmond, Texas, married to Louise and father to two boys, the youngest being the lad with the new BB gun, seven-year-old Larry.

Sunday, February 11, was a misty, cold day. Gilbert had come home from work that week with a new BB gun for Larry, and all weekend the boy had been pestering him to go shooting. So mid-afternoon, with three hours of light left, they climbed into the half-ton and headed for the Barker-Clodine Road. They bounced over the dike and dipped into the flat, grassy bottom of the Barker Reservoir. Gilbert swung off on a narrow dirt road and parked on the edge of an illegal dump. Folks from Houston—he could hear the hum of city traffic ten miles to the east—drove out there to toss old fridges, crates, junk of all kinds. Larry poured a fistful of BBs into the toy rifle and jumped out of the truck.

"I put him up a can on an old wringer washing machine," Gilbert said.

Larry emptied the gun at the can.

"The boy told me he was hitting it. So I walked over and reached out for the can. That's when I seen the feet. Two blue feet sticking out of a blanket."

Heart pounding in his throat, Gilbert grabbed Larry and hustled him into the truck. They raced home, and when Gilbert entered the house, he says he braced Louise.

"Mother, I think I seen a dead person."

Gilbert made it to the sheriff's office fifteen minutes before sundown. Within an hour police from Houston were crawling all over the site.

The next day, Monday, the Houston *Post* gave the story four inches on the obituary page. "Target Shooter Finds Body at County Dump," read the headline. The story was straight police-desk copy. It read as though it had been written while the reporter was still on the phone with the night duty officer. No frills, no cheap sentimentalizing, no news-room theorizing. The only departure from the "Just the facts, ma'am" format was a speculation on the unconfirmed sex of the victim: "The badly decomposed body of what was believed to be a woman was found in a southwest Harris County dump just before dark Sunday." Gilbert's "two blue feet" had begun to take on the barest outlines of an identity. It would be twenty-two years before the corpse would be given a name.

February, 1990, San Jacinto, California

Her name was Anne Hallberg, but both her parents were French-Canadian. So was Jean Nadeau, senior investigator for the district attorney's office in Riverside County. Nadeau then specialized in political corruption probes and had first met Hallberg in her cubicle at the city of San Jacinto's tax and accounts department. She had reported to the police a number of questionable financial transactions. Her information had been passed on to the DA's office, and Nadeau had conducted the investigation.

Nadeau was grateful for Hallberg's help in the investigation, which led to the criminal indictment of a former senior public official. Nadeau admired the courage it had taken for her to talk to the police. But from the outset the French-Canadian ancestry they shared made their relationship more than professional. It wasn't a romantic interest, but it was a personal one. They were curious about each other, about how they had both become Californians. Nadeau liked Hallberg's tenacity, her wry sense of humour. She admired his *politesse,* the clarity of his thinking. Several months went by, and then one morning out of the blue, Hallberg called with a question.

"How hard would it be to find someone who's been missing for twenty-two years?" she asked.

Nadeau chuckled. "Depends. Who's missing?"

"My mom."

Over lunch Hallberg told the story. Her mother had disappeared from their home in Houston sometime after Christmas of 1967, and they'd never seen her again. She gave Nadeau an account of the disappearance written by her brother Denis and a few notes of her own. Maybe he could help, Nadeau said. He'd see. But he wasn't encouraging. Privately, he figured Anne's mother had walked out on a bad marriage.

To his own astonishment, three days later he was ringing Hallberg at work.

"Anne," he began, hardly able to talk, "are you sitting down?...I think I found your mom." He heard the phone go silent. "She's dead," Nadeau went on. He told her that the medical examiner's office in the Houston area had searched its records and come up with a file on an unidentified woman whose body had been found in a Houston-area dump in February, 1968. He told her that the dead woman fit the general description of her mother. Finally, before ringing off to let Hallberg submit to her grief, he told her the one other thing she needed to know. "She was murdered," he said.

He said that those who have endured some misfortune will always
be set apart but that it is just their misfortune which is their gift
and which is their strength and that they must make their way back
into the common enterprise of man for without they do so
it cannot go forward and they themselves will wither in bitterness.

Cormac McCarthy
All the Pretty Horses

HONOUR
THY
MOTHER

Part One

Home and Family, 1950–1968

For he comes, the human child,
To the waters and the wild
With a faery, hand in hand,
From a world more full of weeping than
he can understand.

W. B. Yeats,
"The Stolen Child"

Chapter One

✦

Pointe Gatineau, Quebec, 1966

Two hours after sunset on a frigid Thursday in January, 1966, more than a dozen Quebec provincial police officers, along with several members of a local police force, surrounded a two-storey house in Pointe Gatineau, a small town that squats along the Ottawa River across the water from the sprawling homes of Ottawa's tony Rockcliffe Park. Several plainclothes officers had been in the neighbourhood for hours, sauntering about in tuques and hockey sweaters, watching the house. At a signal the uniformed officers, carrying pistols, burst through the front door of the house, which was both a home and a printer's shop. The first cops through the door immobilized the occupants with their fearsome, screamed commands, and they threw the owner, twenty-eight-year-old Gilles Paquin, and two companions against a wall.

For the next three hours the police searched the house and shop. By the time they had finished, they had turned up forged car registration forms, forged driver's licences, forged school diplomas, and forged lottery tickets. The next day the local paper, *Le Droit,* played the arrests on the front page with the banner headline: "Half-a-Million-Dollar Racket in Pointe Gatineau; Suspected Forgers Arrested."

At a press conference on the morning after the raid, police officials said that the arrests were part of an ongoing investigation into a stolen-car ring in the region. Otherwise, they were tight-lipped. One reporter, citing "certain sources," said that the police had also been looking for forged money in the printer's shop.

The story kicked the local rumour mill into overdrive, and there was endless speculation within the Ottawa/Hull area about what the police had stumbled on. When Paquin finally appeared in court on the Saturday after the raid, he and one accomplice, Gérard Tassé, were charged with a half-dozen offences related to the production and possession of forged documents. Tassé was an accountant in his late forties, Paquin a small-businessman. The headlines made them out to be big-time gangsters. In person they seemed anything but. Tassé was skinny and long-necked and had a reputation as a little man with a big mouth. Paquin, freckled and red-headed, was nervous and sweaty and was known throughout the community as a decent guy who worked hard for the money he made. More than twenty-five years after his arrest he still marvels at the interrogation sessions he endured in provincial police headquarters in Montreal, where he was accused of having links with the Mafia family that then controlled Montreal's underworld.

Paquin's father bailed them out the following week. The two accused men engaged a local lawyer and began preparing for the preliminary hearing in March. When the preliminary began, the star witness the Crown attorney trundled out, to the surprise of many, was a thirty-one-year-old Pointe Gatineau businessman named Raymond Durand. It quickly emerged that Durand had set up Paquin and Tassé for the bust.

On the stand at the preliminary hearing, Durand, a short, square-faced man with a prominent jaw, testified that he had been working part-time as a private detective for the Pointe Gatineau police for about a year and a half. He said that he had placed an order with Tassé for 150 forged car registration forms and driver's licences and had agreed to pay him fifteen hundred dollars for the lot. The forged documents would be printed by Tassé's collaborator, Paquin. Durand claimed that he had been working with Pointe Gatineau detective Robert Sincennes. He said that, once he made the deal with Tassé, he and Sincennes had called in the auto-theft squad of the provincial police. On the day he was to take delivery of the forms, the police raided Paquin's home and shop.

Paquin, whose house is fifteen blocks from an auto body shop Durand then owned on Michaud Street, was stunned by the testimony. He said later that Durand had approached him about printing up the forms but that he had refused because he didn't trust Durand, whom he described as a "big fat slob with no teeth on the bottom." Paquin said he often saw Durand's car at the Pointe Gatineau police station and wasn't keen to have anything to do with him. So Durand had apparently turned to Tassé, who knew Paquin, and placed his order through the accountant.

The preliminary hearing took the lid off Durand's life. Under questioning by the Crown prosecutor, Marcel Beaudry, Durand described how he had placed his order with Tassé, who, it turned out, had also once worked as Durand's accountant. He described how he had obtained a sample registration form for twenty-five dollars from Tassé and he recounted the calls from telephone booths and the arrangements for the payoff. But when the defence lawyers were given their opportunity to grill Durand, the story got curiouser and curiouser.

Asked by defence attorney Jules Barrière if he was a paid employee of the Pointe Gatineau police department, Durand said, no, his work as a private dick was more of a "pastime." He said he didn't have a detective's licence. He said he undertook investigations for Pointe Gatineau. Then he corrected himself. "Well, not exactly for the town, but for a particular detective. Robert Sincennes." In addition to his "pastime," Durand revealed to the court that he had applied to join the Quebec police force.

Barrière then called to the stand Durand's business partner, Georges Sylvestre, who said he had seen Durand with a .38 pistol and the insignia of the Pointe Gatineau police. He said that after Durand had testified, Durand had told Sylvestre that he had had one of the insignias on him in court and that when he was called to the stand, he had hidden it under a bench. Asked if Durand was a liar, Sylvestre said that his partner had told him "some whoppers."

A second witness, Gaétan Dériger, said he, too, had seen Durand with a pistol and a police badge. He said he had been in Durand's Super Sport Chevy and that Durand had bragged that he wasn't afraid of anything because he had a gun. Dériger said he had thought it was more of what he described as Durand's "bullshit" until Durand pulled out his gun and waved it around. He said that Durand had told him he was a special police officer but that he didn't take it seriously. Finally, a third defence witness, Jean-Paul Lefebvre, said the night of the raid Durand boasted to him that he was a "secret agent" and showed him his .38 and the metal police badge he kept in his wallet.

When the hearing ended, the judge ruled that there was sufficient evidence for Tassé and Paquin to stand trial on the charges. As for Raymond Durand, the Crown prosecutor's key witness, he had been exposed as a liar, a braggart and a bit of a goof. Had he become a stoolie for the thrills, or had he made a deal with the police to save his own skin on some other charge? Three former Pointe Gatineau police officers now say Durand never worked for the force. Sincennes, the detective whom Durand had named as his principal contact, said recently that he has no recollection of Durand ever working with or for him. Another former officer says he recalls Durand once tipped them off about stolen goods that had been cached in a field. They found the goods and staked them out for three days. When no one turned up, they began to suspect that Durand himself had been involved in the theft. The former officer said they didn't trust Raymond Durand and didn't believe him. Yet they were wary of him because, it turned out, he was a good buddy of the Pointe Gatineau police chief, Henri Ferland.

After he had been bailed out of jail, Tassé began investigating Durand's background. In one document Tassé later submitted to the court, he alleged that Durand had sold at least three cars that had been seized by the police and towed to his garage. He named people whom he alleged had seen Durand with blank car registrations before the raid, and he said that Durand was involved in credit-card fraud, the sale of a machine-gun and a variety of other illegal activities.

In another submission to the court Tassé also recounted what had happened to him when he took to the bank a $175 cheque Durand had written to him for the accounting work he had done for Durand's body shop. He said when he attempted to cash the cheque, the bank manager had taken one look at it, laughed and said he "was the sixty-second person to have been fucked by Durand [by writing cheques on that account] since January 1, 1965."

Durand, it appeared, worked both sides of the street. He was nobody's friend but his own. The police and the Crown prosecutor attempted to portray him as a concerned citizen who had willingly collaborated with them. But people who had worked with him or had grown up with him knew another Raymond Durand. Most of them believed that Durand had only just begun to exercise his skills at treachery and betrayal, which had always made him a dangerous person to know. The forgery bust was Durand's first public act. It propelled him to a life on a larger stage. It was a sort of graduation ceremony. Over the next thirty years he would pursue his villainy in Florida, Texas, South Carolina and California. But all the basics he learned in his own backyard.

The city of Hull, which has long been Ottawa's poor stepsister, was Raymond Durand's home town: he had been born and was raised in the Wrightville district, one of the city's oldest working-class neighbourhoods. In 1966, when the forgery bust occurred, Hull was still trying to shake itself loose from its sordid past. The federal government had begun to move large sections of its bureaucracy across the Ottawa River into Hull, and old neighbourhoods were being razed to make way for dull grey office complexes to house dull, grey-suited civil servants.

But when Durand was growing up in Hull in the 1940s, the city was still known as Little Chicago. In the decade after World War II, Hull's population reached fifty thousand. More than 90 percent of the city's residents were French-speaking and Roman Catholic. Hull was a blue-collar city. Across the Ottawa River, the city's residents saw the backside of Canada's Parliament buildings. Ottawa, the city that surrounded the buildings, was mostly English and white-collar.

By contrast, Hull in the 1940s was still an industrial town. Its daytime economy was powered by pulp and paper companies and lumber dealers. At night it became sin city. It was in Hull that politicians and bureaucrats visiting Ottawa sought their late-evening diversions. Well into the 1940s gamblers controlled the nightclubs and the prostitutes. Some cops and municipal politicians were on the take. Corruption was endemic. Liquor laws have always been more relaxed in Quebec than in neighbouring Ontario. Prohibition lasted only about a year in Quebec, while in Ontario it was 1934 before the provincial government eased off and again allowed hotels to sell wine and beer. During the Prohibition years, clubs sprouted all over Hull and with the clubs came gambling joints and prostitution.

Hull's eastern border is the Gatineau River, which tumbles down from the pine and maple forests to the north. Across the Gatineau are a handful of small municipalities—Gatineau, Pointe Gatineau, Templeton—dominated by the stench of sulphur from the mill stacks. In the 1960s they were tough little towns strung out along the river. Once home to *draveurs* who worked the log drives and to mill workers, they gradually became bedroom communities for French-speaking residents of Hull and Ottawa who sought cheap land and housing.

Raymond Durand was the third eldest in a family of eleven children. Nine of the kids were boys. Donat Durand, Raymond's father, was a mechanic at a Hull bus company. He was a hard-working man who rarely spoke to anyone on the street when he was sober. After work and on weekends he would sit on his front gallery in Hull's Wrightville district and empty quarts of Black Horse beer. When the beers did their work, he became quarrelsome and vulgar. His was a classic Jekyll and Hyde personality, one neighbour recalls. "Hey, you fucking Catholics," he'd shout at his most pious neighbours. He often had some choice, ugly words for the widow down the street. "You'd hear him and this other guy on the street shouting at each other until one in the morning," the former neighbour recalls.

There was apparently an even darker side to Donat. Raymond's mother, Marie-Anna, had two sisters who lived nearby. One of the sisters, Simone Massie, said Marie-Anna once confided to her that Donat was, as Simone put it, "a pig with little girls." Not with his own daughters, but with others. Marie-Anna told Simone that she couldn't trust Donat with little girls around. She told Simone that she had had to sell the family's lakeside cottage because she couldn't trust Donat up there on weekends with the kids and their friends.

Marie-Anna Durand ran her house and family from the kitchen in their narrow, two-storey clapboard home on Rouville Street. She was the family's emotional anchor. She indulged and protected her boisterous brood. She was also vulgar. Simone recalls Marie-Anna lecturing her to "keep your little bastards out of my yard." Simone said Marie-Anna could hold a grudge as well. A quarrel that took place when they were both middle-aged lasted twenty-seven years; Marie-Anna refused to speak to Simone for most of the last three decades of her life.

Others who knew Marie-Anna said the most exasperating flaw in her character was the lying. She had a slippery habit of exaggerating the facts to the point that her version of events became bald-faced lies. It was as if she considered reality arbitrary and irrelevant. Truth sprang from the imagination. One neighbour described her as the Ma Barker of Rouville Street. She protected her boys even when she knew they were up to no good. The neighbour says Marie-Anna would tell Raymond, "Don't get caught," not "Don't steal."

The son Marie-Anna openly favoured became a well-known

local clairvoyant, predicting the futures of callers to his radio show. Raymond himself inherited his mother's casual disregard of the truth and, by his teens, had acquired a reputation as an accomplished liar. The lies sprang so easily to his lips that he was, and still is, able to make people doubt what they truly know.

Family members say Raymond was by far the most troublesome of the boys in the family. Conversation among the relatives often seemed to come around to Raymond's latest antics.

"He was always laughing, a comic. But always in trouble. And when he was caught, it was always one of his brothers who was responsible, not him," Simone recalls.

"He detested his father," says Simone, recalling an incident that occurred when Marie-Anna was in hospital and Donat was working the night shift. Raymond took his father's suit and a shirt, stuffed them with rags, tied them all together in an effigy and hung the effigy from the staircase. The other kids raced to the hospital to tell Marie-Anna, and she called Simone to beg her to cut the effigy down before Donat returned from work.

"That was Raymond. Always playing jokes," says Simone, who also describes her nephew as twisted, mean and "as dishonest a person as I've ever known."

A schoolmate of Raymond's describes him as "a detestable, skinny, little liar." He said Raymond was a thief and a hustler. He was constantly scheming, and always had money in his pocket. Asked if Raymond ever played any sports, the schoolmate replied, "The only sport Ray ever practised was masturbation."

The Durands were working class but they weren't poor. They owned their own house and another next door, and they had a summer cottage in the Gatineau Hills to the north, on Lac Clair.

Raymond completed grade six and then dropped out of school. He wasn't yet sixteen. He washed buses at the privately owned transit company that employed his father. His parents insisted that he give them a portion of his pay for room and board. But Marie-Anna complained bitterly that he never did. He was a wild kid, short and thin. He had a long jaw, dark brown hair and an aggressive, magnetic personality. He had an exceptional memory for names, faces and numbers. He knew people all over the city. A brother of Raymond's says that even as a kid Raymond "couldn't sit still for more than two minutes. He was out all the time. My dad would ask why he wasn't paying his room and board and Ray would say that he wasn't working. But he was."

Another brother says Raymond was manipulative. He played people off against each other, lying to one about what someone else had said. Because he did it for pleasure or entertainment and not profit, he could manipulate even people who knew he was a liar and couldn't be trusted. He'd invent stories that were like a sharp dig in the ribs.

That same brother said Raymond was a "joker, a bit of a clown." But behind the good-time-guy façade, Raymond was plotting, thinking through his moves. "He never told us what he was doing. He never confided anything in me. He was closed, alone."

Raymond began dating girls shortly after he turned fourteen. He was only sixteen when he walked into the offices of the Walters Axe Company in Hull and met for the first time a quiet, serious girl with blonde hair and blue eyes who was two years his senior. Her name was Jeannine Boissonneault. He told her he was eighteen and sweet-talked her into a date. More than thirty years later, fate would drag Raymond Durand before the courts to account for his life with Jeannine Boissonneault.

Chapter Two

Hull, Quebec, 1953

The room at the top of the stairs in the narrow, two-storey, wooden house on St Hyacinthe Street was a listening post as much as it was a bedroom. It was Réginald Boissonneault's redoubt, his refuge. He was the sort of kid who was easy to pick on and laugh at. His was a lumbering presence. He was nimble only at avoiding the rough give-and-take of neighbourhood play. He was passionate about baseball and classical music, but feared social contact of any kind. "Friends," he once told an aunt, "they're just trouble." On the rare occasions that he did speak with visitors, he revealed an agile mind that skipped far ahead of the discussion at hand, anticipating responses, side-stepping conversational sink-holes.

He was tall and heavy, with a high forehead and prominent jaw, and his physique only added to the impression that he was always peering into things, watching and thinking but never participating. Neighbours on St Hyacinthe Street in Hull and friends of his younger sister, Jeannine, say that even when Réginald was in his early teens he was heard from but rarely seen. At the sound of a visitor's knock on the front door, Réginald would scoot up to his room. After he completed high school in the late 1940s at a Catholic boys' school, his room became a permanent retreat. A younger cousin Michel Béland recalls that when he visited the Boissonneault household with his mother he would chat with his aunt and uncle for a few minutes, and then climb the stairs to Réginald's hide-out.

"We'd sit there and talk about baseball. It was OK with his mom, my aunt, if I went up there and it was OK with Réginald because I was a cousin. But my aunt was very protective. She guarded his privacy. No one outside the family would have ever been allowed up there."

Réginald's parents, Laurette and Hermas, may have believed that their son was sick but they never sought treatment for him. They believed his ailment was their burden and responsibility, and they accepted it without complaint.

So on that early evening of a sweltering summer night in 1953, when Jeannine brought home her new beau and Réginald says he met Raymond Durand for the first time, what he means is that he heard Durand and saw him from his bedroom window.

"The radio was playing. They were dancing in the kitchen. My parents were in the front room," recalls Réginald, now a portly, balding recluse who pads about his tiny, cluttered apartment just off St Joseph Boulevard in Hull's north end. Boissonneault has never worked outside his home. He kept house and cared for his parents until they died—his father in 1979 and mother in 1983. After his mother's death, Boissonneault made what was up until then the most daring move of his life: he packed everything he owned and moved into a government-subsidized apartment. He lives there today, amid cardboard cartons he has never unpacked. Framed portraits of Mozart, Chopin and Bach grace the walls of his tidy, crowded living-room. Clothes-pins clipped to the bottom of the curtains on his door ensure that passers-by on the outdoor walk-way that runs past the apartment are denied even fleeting glances into his very private life. A lifetime of solitude has made Boissonneault his own best company.

In 1953 Réginald was twenty-two and Jeannine was twenty. She was past marrying age, but Réginald wasn't at all sure about the character of her latest beau: "Raymond was a young guy, skinny," he remembers. "He didn't speak much. He had a car. He loved cars, talked about them, seemed to live for them. He said he was working with his father repairing buses. He seemed too young for her."

But Jeannine was stuck on him. Quiet and shy, she was tall like her mother. Like her brother she had a high forehead and a prominent jaw. If not pretty, she was certainly handsome.

Jeannine had begun studying piano at age six at a nearby convent, and by the time she was twelve she had performed in a recital that was taped and broadcast on a local radio station. She attended a Catholic girls' school and after graduation moved on to a secretarial college across the river in Ottawa. She graduated at eighteen and found a job at Walters Axe, an axe manufacturer on Front Street in Hull. She continued to live at home and began dating boys from the neighbourhood. She had been at Walters Axe about a year when Raymond Durand dropped by the office one day to pick up an order for his employer. He caught her eye and drew her into a conversation. They were discreet when they began dating; it took Jeannine a year before she worked up the nerve to bring Raymond home to meet her parents.

Within their working-class neighbourhood, the Boissonneaults were an exceptional family. At a time when families of twelve and more children were the norm, Laurette and Hermas had two. Jeannine's best friend from across the street, Rollande Guenette, came from a family of thirteen. She remembers the Boissonneault home as an oasis of calm. The Boissonneaults were, in terms of income, working class: Hermas was a clerk in a hardware store and Laurette a seamstress for a tent manufacturer on Bank Street in Ottawa. They lived in rented houses all their lives. But they always found the money for Jeannine's piano lessons. Laurette herself was an accomplished pianist, and the piano in the front room was always in tune. Hermas was reserved and soft-spoken to the point of silence.

Laurette was the dominant force in the family. Born in Hull, she was the second oldest in a family of twelve children. She had married at twenty-two and lived by a rigid moral code. She never gossiped, refused to indulge with the neighbours in idle chatter about who was doing what to whom. She lectured her children on respecting other people's privacy and didn't discuss with others details of her own family life. She never spoke with outsiders about Réginald's pathological shyness, never considered his condition anything other than a family matter. Laurette's sister, Berthe Laframboise, a nun who left her order in 1975, recalls that the Boissonneaults minded their own business and kept to themselves. "Laurette was very elegant, very distinguished and never spoke unless she had something to say," she says.

Laurette's husband and son rarely asserted themselves. She took it upon herself to be the spokesperson for the family, responsible for charting the household economy, dealing with the landlord, orchestrating their engagements in the rituals of their faith. They were Roman Catholic, parishioners in good standing.

Jeannine was ever the dutiful daughter, always deferring to her mother's strict principles. Dating Raymond may have been Jeannine's first gesture of independence. Raymond was French and Roman Catholic and came from a working-class family in a nearby neighbourhood. He was always respectful of Laurette, and he never, for as long as he knew her, ever addressed her as anything other than Madame Boissonneault.

Despite the outward similarities between the two families, the Durands and the Boissonneaults were as different as fire and ice.

To a teenager without the pluck of Raymond Durand, the two-year age gap between himself and Jeannine might have been unbridgeable. But for Raymond it was a minor challenge. The greater the barrier separating him from his ambitions, the higher his flights of fancy. Sooner or later everybody who gets to know Raymond comes to realize that nothing he says can be trusted. But before that realization strikes, most people find his story-telling and his charms compelling. So it was with Jeannine. He told her he was eighteen, and it was his own mother who finally admitted to her, more than a year after they had begun seeing each other, that Raymond had lied about his age.

Wherever the two of them went, Raymond would make himself the centre of attention. For a lonely, shy girl from a family with a father who rarely spoke and a brother who seemed to be patterning his life after the Boo Radley character in *To Kill a Mockingbird,* Raymond must have seemed like just about the most exotic man in her universe. He was hard-working. When he wanted something, he went out and got it. He was never still, never alone, never in a quiet contemplative mood. Nobody can ever recall Raymond reading a book, listening without interruption to others, or pursuing a quiet hobby.

He was a one-man circus. Like a stage performer, he needed an audience. What mattered was whether he had those around him in his thrall. Except when he was running a con, he never gave much consideration to what people thought of him afterwards. He didn't care. For, as Jeannine was to discover much later, Raymond had nothing but contempt for those stupid enough to believe his stories.

Jeannine was the opposite. She had one close friend, spent a great deal of her time alone, read, and played the piano for her own enjoyment and sometimes for the pleasure of others. She had internalized her mother's strict moral code and, like her mother, had an extraordinary ability to deny or ignore breeches of what she considered acceptable behaviour. She saw what she permitted herself to see.

Yet, at the same time, she felt vulnerable and stifled by life at home. People were talking. She was well past the age when girls were supposed to be married and starting a family.

Hull, like most of the province of Quebec, was then a closed and ethnically homogenous community separated from the rest of North America by the great barrier of language. For those who were part of the community, it was familiar to the point of intimacy. But for those like Jeannine who didn't conform to the norm, it could be oppressive.

Jeannine must have been haunted by her mother's favourite phrase, an expression that could have served as the Boissonneault family motto: "What is everybody going to say?" Although the family minimized contact with the world around them, they were obsessed with what others thought of them. They invested a good deal of emotional energy in appearances, in maintaining the reputation of the family.

Jeannine knew her mother would consider it scandalous for her to marry a boy two years her junior. So she didn't tell her. She had fallen in love. Raymond had transported her, in her imagination, from a strict, emotionally forlorn home to a life with a hard-charging young man to whom anything was possible. Life with him, Jeannine must have thought, was going to be an adventure, not a burden.

For Raymond, Jeannine had qualities that he associated with social success. She was an attractive and educated woman earning her own living. He admired the fact that she played classical piano. She was a woman of quality, and he'd never known anyone quite like her before. Jeannine thought for herself, didn't interrupt him when he was blabbing on and knew how to do more than just make babies. She believed in him.

He was still a short, skinny teenager when he met Jeannine but he felt old beyond his years. He needed people to take him seriously. Marrying an older woman who was anything but frivolous made him feel older.

They became engaged in the summer of 1954. They were to marry that fall, on October 30, the day after Jeannine's twenty-first birthday. The night before the wedding Madame Boissonneault chanced across Raymond's baptismal certificate, which Jeannine had left on the top of the piano.

"My God," she cried. "Jeannine, you're robbing the cradle. He's only eighteen. He's just a boy."

Despite her entreaties, her pleas for her daughter to reconsider—and she most certainly asked, "What's everybody going to think?"—Jeannine stood firm.

"Mama, I love him" was her simple reply.

The wedding photos show them standing on the church steps, Jeannine as tall as her new husband. They look tense, as if they were at the centre of a fragile alliance between two families that would never understand each other.

Réginald, of course, decided at the last minute that he was too ill to attend the celebrations.

After the festivities Raymond and Jeannine Durand found a small apartment on Guertin Street in Hull. Jeannine continued to work as a secretary at Walters Axe. She spoke almost no English and kept to herself. She didn't make friends easily and had neither the inclination nor the need to engage in conversational chatter. People who knew her well say even in company she seemed to feel no need to keep a conversation afloat. For Jeannine silence wasn't a social gaffe but a condition in which she felt completely at ease.

At the outset they complemented each other. She was a calming influence on Raymond, his home base. What Raymond did for Jeannine was the reverse; he introduced her to the social life of their community. He took her to restaurants, to parties, introduced her to summer-cottage society around the hidden lakes in the heavily wooded Gatineau Hills. She was never the life of the party and she didn't drink—unlike Raymond's crowd—but she went along for the ride. Always more of an observer than participant, she trailed along in Raymond's wake.

Raymond drifted from job to job. The Hull directories for the 1950s show Raymond employed at four different companies as an unskilled labourer and later a mechanic. Family members remember his being employed at another two firms. The job that they remember his holding the longest was with Frazer Duntile, an Ottawa/Hull company that made concrete blocks and sold crushed stone, concrete and sand. He worked in the body shop, repairing and painting the company trucks. Once he had picked up the basic skills of an auto body man, he moved across the river to Percy Carrière Auto. He had decided he would be an auto body painter. He was a quick study and he worked at taking the dents out of damaged doors, cutting away rusting quarter panels, sanding, priming and painting.

Auto body men are the cosmetic surgeons of the auto trade. In short order Raymond learned to transform a beat-up old rust bucket into the object of other men's desire. He discovered that a car with a leaking transmission, cracked engine mounts, rattling tie-rod ends or crapped-out engine could be palmed off on even the most discerning buyer if all its dents had been pounded out and it was given a brilliant coat of paint. He had found his niche. Raymond had always been car crazy, had always considered a man's car to be the most visible manifestation of his social station. In the 1950s, when car ownership was becoming commonplace, Raymond understood both that many families took pride in just having a car parked within view of the front window and that few men had sufficient mechanical skills to assess the running condition of a used car.

Raymond's auto body skills became his passport; he could ply his trade anywhere. In another age he would have been a cunning horse trader, feeding old nags grain to give them shiny coats, poking pepper under their tails to make them perky.

While he was working for Percy Carrière he was always on the look-out for a newer, better car for himself and a sucker he could unload his old one on. He bought and sold cars as easily as other men change their minds.

Within five months of their marriage Jeannine became pregnant and quit work. Raymond was now carrying the load financially. Jeannine withdrew into their apartment, playing piano, keeping house and talking on the phone with her mother. Jeannine's loss of an income marked the beginning of a disastrous change in their relationship. Now he controlled the purse-strings. Whenever she needed anything, she had to ask him.

From the day they married, Raymond had never been able to completely dominate Jeannine, largely because he never really understood her. She had private places to which she would retire, emotional hide-outs. Her music was one of those places. Raymond considered her piano-playing a skill that could and should be used to impress, a means to an end. It never occurred to him that music allowed Jeannine to express what she couldn't communicate verbally. Music was her first language, and she used it to tell herself and others about the joy, the pain and the loneliness of life. Without music, Jeannine became a virtual mute.

Raymond couldn't dominate the conversation when Jeannine spoke to him and others through her music. The longer they lived together, the more agitated he became by her relationship to her music. Eventually he couldn't stand being in the same room when she played. Jeannine's Aunt Berthe recalls the burning jealousy she saw in his eyes once when Jeannine sat down at the piano and everyone in the room turned to listen to her play.

Having no access to their money made Jeannine more dependent on Raymond. She may not have resented it—passive, silent acceptance was how Jeannine responded to many of the forces that hemmed in her life—but she began to see how arbitrary and petty he could be in his exercise of that new power. He begrudged her money for even the smallest and most basic household needs.

Jeannine gave birth to her first child, a blond, blue-eyed son, on December 30, Raymond's twentieth birthday. They named him Denis, and he was destined to be the only person Raymond Durand couldn't con, the only person who wouldn't ever forget Ray's sins.

Chapter Three

+—❈❈—+

Pointe Gatineau, Quebec, 1959

When Denis was old enough to climb out of his crib, Raymond and Jeannine rented a small bungalow on Michaud Street in the village of Pointe Gatineau. The rent was cheap and they remained in that house until Denis started school.

Raymond returned to Frazer Duntile and was made foreman of the paint shop. But he had decided he was going to start out on his own. He had his eye on a couple of lots just up the street from the rented house. In March, 1958, he put a hundred dollars down on a lot at 44 Michaud Street and, according to a brother, began filching the materials he needed to build a house. When he had slyly removed from the Frazer Duntile yard enough concrete blocks and cement, he brought his brothers over and they threw up the ugliest house on the street. They dug out the foundation by hand to the sound of Roy Orbison on the radio. Denis remembers sitting on the steps of the rented house listening to Roy while his father did the spade work on the foundation. The house was a rectangular box with a flat roof, no larger than any of the bungalows on the street. From the front, it appeared to have two storeys. But the bottom floor was simply an unfinished basement. The main floor had a kitchen, living-room, bathroom and two bedrooms. Around back, Raymond dug out a slope that would allow him to drive a car into the basement. If there were zoning regulations, they didn't mean anything to Raymond. He had decided that he would set up a body shop in the basement and that the family would live in the upper floor.

Looking back at it now, the idea seems pretty boneheaded. He built a shop in the basement and used it to hammer out bent and twisted car bodies, weld new parts in place and remould, sand, prime and paint vehicles. Meanwhile, Jeannine lived upstairs with Denis and a baby, Anne, born in January, 1959. The hammering, the stench from the welding, the dust from the sanding and the toxic odours from the paint must have rendered the upper floor virtually uninhabitable. But that was Raymond. It'd be quiet when *he* was upstairs.

Still, it was their own place, Jeannine had a piano in the front room, and there was plenty of space for the kids to play outdoors. From the beginning Jeannine had her hands full. She not only cared for the kids but fixed lunches for Raymond and whomever he happened to have working for him and did all the books for the business.

A year after the family moved in Ray added a much larger shop on the back of the basement floor. The garage under the main house remained his paint shop. The addition, which was large enough to hold four cars, was used for body work and for prepping cars that were to be painted.

Roger Prud'Homme, who still lives on Michaud Street, remembers Raymond Durand as a hustler and a self-centred, big-mouthed, fat man. Raymond had ballooned from a skinny teenager to a two-hundred-pound lug. Still only five foot six inches tall, he waddled around his lot, jabbering and shouting orders. More than thirty years after he had last seen Raymond, Prud'Homme still remembered tools—a saw, a mortar pan—he lent Raymond that were never returned. "That's the kind of guy he was. He came first."

Although Jeannine was known to everybody on the street—and Prud'Homme still has grainy black-and-white photos of her with Denis on a tricycle, and of Jeannine standing next to an old Ford— she made no real friends. People liked and respected her for the way she treated her kids, for her evening piano recitals and her gentle nature. But she wasn't the type to dawdle over coffee in a neighbour's kitchen.

For the kids, Michaud Street was the happiest time of their childhood. Denis had playmates all along the street. Pointe Gatineau was a small town—its population then was about three thousand— and everybody knew everybody else. Property was cheap, and despite the fact that you could see downtown Ottawa, it was like living in the country. Maple forests descended from the Gatineau Hills to the north and surrounded the town. There was a pulp and paper mill just outside the town limits but the smell of sulphur from its stacks was no worse in Pointe Gatineau than in Hull or even in Ottawa. Both Jeannine and Raymond warned Denis against playing down on the river and against straying too close to the mill. But there was too much happening on that river to keep a boy away. Every spring entire forests were floated down the Gatineau

River to the mills. Denis was often along the river with his friends, watching the *draveurs* chugging about in their little tugs, following the progress of the log booms.

Anne, too, remembers the happy times on Michaud Street. Her earliest memories are of life in that house. She recalls her grandpa Durand visiting with a gift of rabbits, the vanity her mother set up for her in her room. The only memory she has of her mother losing her temper was the time a neighbour boy offered Anne a cookie to pull down her pants. It seemed like a fair exchange until Jeannine happened on the scene and ordered the boy out of the yard.

The house on Michaud Street was ideal for Raymond. It was on the edge of town; behind the house was an empty field. Beginning with Michaud Street, all his life Raymond would live in that indeterminate zone between city and country. He sought out places where there weren't many prying neighbours, where he could bury his sins and waste, where he wasn't among the ploughed fields and barns of industrious farmers nor among the neatly trimmed lawns of orderly minded suburbanites. His activities conformed to none of the neat zoning categories of urban planners and property tax appraisers.

For the first three years or so, Ray's Body Shop was a back-lot operation. Officially, he was working for somebody else—Frazer Duntile or as a mechanic for Bruce Coal Co. It wasn't until 1963 that he began openly operating and advertising the services of Ray's Body Shop.

As his business expanded at Michaud Street, Raymond Durand revealed himself to be a cheat and a thief. Those who had grown up with him knew that he was a pathological liar and that he was utterly insensible to the feelings of others. As he matured, those qualities became his principal income-generating skills.

Men who worked for Raymond in his body shop or simply crossed trails with him in the early 1960s say he was enterprising and persuasive. He launched his body shop business by visiting used car lots and offering to repaint clunkers. A quick paint job for a modest fee could boost the resale value of even the sorriest wreck. Raymond was soon painting ten to twelve cars a week from a number of used car lots.

Most body men consider work for used car lots to be a mug's game, the sort of work you chase only if it's the slow season and there isn't anything else going. Used car dealers tend to chisel and complain about price. They want a paint job that looks good and costs as little as possible. They expect rapid turnaround and pay for only the cheapest materials and paint. For a body man who takes pride in his work, used car lot owners are welcome only in times of financial distress. But for Raymond used car dealers were ideal clients. Shoddy work didn't bother him in the least. He didn't have all the proper tools anyway. So if all the client wanted was an overnight paint job to hide the rust temporarily, Ray could do that. He came to specialize in body work that would last a month. Former clients and employees recall the time Ray plugged a hole in a car door with a wooden shingle. He riveted it in place, smoothed it over with body putty, primed and painted it, and the door looked like new. Three weeks later the guy was back. He'd been hit in a fender-bender and the shingle had come off, revealing Ray's handiwork.

By the early 1960s Raymond's biggest client was a used car lot in downtown Ottawa, run by André Paquette, a man who billed himself as the King of the Automobile. Paquette was a sandy-haired, cigar-smoking, bilingual businessman who ran one of the busiest used car lots in the city. He drove a Cadillac, wore natty suits and hustled cars day and night. Everybody knew Andy Paquette.

One of Raymond's brothers says Paquette's people delivered cars to Ray's shop at all hours. The deal was that those cars got priority. Ray turned them around overnight in most cases. Paquette, who still lives in Ottawa, remembers Raymond as loud and rough, a man whose word was worth nothing. He said he eventually cut Durand off, but the facts suggest they stuck with each other to the bitter end.

In the summer of 1963, a couple of months after Raymond's father died, one of Paquette's employees delivered a 1962 Chevrolet Impala to the body shop for a paint job. The car was delivered on a Friday. Raymond painted it black on the Saturday and on Sunday drove it to his mother's house. She was looking for a car. She'd come into some insurance money after Donat's death and had asked Ray to help her find a car. She wanted the Impala as soon as she saw it. So on Monday, after Raymond had delivered the car to Paquette's lot, he took his mother to meet André and she paid cash for the Impala.

During those years—from 1960 to 1964—neighbours on Michaud Street say there was a lot of traffic in and out of Raymond's shop, lots of coming and going late at night. From cops to local hoods, all sorts of characters were seen there. Some of the characters, it seemed, just needed a place to park a car for a couple of hours. One of Ray's brothers recalls a guy driving into the shop with a half-dozen bullet holes in the trunk of his car. When they opened the trunk to begin working on the holes, they discovered it was full of guns. They puttied over the holes, touched them up with paint and out the car went the next day. Ray's clients knew, said the brother, that Raymond would keep his mouth shut and mind his own business.

In the shop, with his customers and employees, Raymond worked every hustle he could. A former employee says they had an arrangement whereby he would get a percentage of the weekly take after expenses had been deducted. He said he quit after it became clear that Ray was routinely adding zeros to his expense receipts. A twenty-dollar receipt for paint purchased would become two hundred. Even then, he wouldn't pay his suppliers. The employee says suppliers often showed up with overdue bills. Once an angry creditor refused to leave, insisting that he knew Raymond was in the shop. While the employee held him off, Raymond slithered out a back window.

As Raymond's business began to expand, a rumour began to circulate that he was part of a stolen car racket. It wasn't surprising that rumours would circulate about Raymond. He was known everywhere and seen everywhere. He always drove a new car—a luxury sedan or a red convertible. He began to be seen around the nightspots with other women.

Raymond not only liked to be seen with women, but he had a habit of bragging about his conquests. A former employee at the body shop recalls that Raymond once told him he was going to pick up a girl-friend that evening and have sex with her in his car in the field behind his house, within sight of Jeannine's bedroom window. Just to make things a little riskier, Ray had asked the employee to work late that night on a job and he told him to keep an eye out for him: he would flash his headlights after he'd had an orgasm. Sure enough, after dark there was Ray parked with his girl. And just as he had promised, he flashed his lights to signal his sexual triumph.

Ray wasn't a heavy drinker—nobody can recall seeing him drunk back then. He was a pill-popper. Goofballs, a high-octane mixture of prescription stimulants, were his favourite. He loved to party, dance and eat in the best restaurants. He always had a fist-sized roll of cash in his pocket, and when he was on a spree, he picked up the cheque.

At home and in the shop he was another man. He made Jeannine plead with him for every cent, peeling off a twenty for groceries only when he absolutely had to. He complained about the smallest expenditures for the kids.

Some months after he had arranged for his mother to buy the Impala, Ray had his first brush with the law. The Ottawa police had begun investigating the registration of a number of cars that had been sold by Paquette. One day in the spring of 1964 two detectives arrived at Ray's mother's house and asked to see the registration for her car. They examined the serial numbers and announced that it was stolen. They removed her plates and called for a tow truck to take it down to the police impoundment lot. Madame Durand protested. She told the detectives that she had purchased the car from Paquette, had paid cash for it and that her son Raymond had painted it two days before she bought it. They listened with interest, took notes and ambled off. As soon as they left, she called Raymond to complain. He rushed over and called Paquette from her house.

According to Durand family members, Paquette wheeled over, cigar glowing red hot. "Don't worry, Mum. We're going to fix you right up," he assured the distraught woman. He asked her what kind of car she wanted, and when Madame Durand replied that she wanted the same make and model, he got on the phone and located another Impala at a lot in Alfred, Ontario. He negotiated a deal and told Raymond and his mother that they could drive down to Alfred the following day and the car would be waiting. Then Paquette casually hopped into his Caddy and cruised off.

The next day Raymond, his mother and a brother drove to Alfred and picked up the Impala. She was happy but Raymond was worried. Later that week police detectives descended on Michaud Street with a search warrant. They went through the shop, examining the cars, the parts and Raymond's books. But he was clean and they departed without any evidence that Raymond was anything more than the innocent painter of a stolen car.

Paquette was in a much deeper puddle. The Ottawa police spent months investigating his operation and eventually uncovered a sophisticated car theft ring. One of the cars they later recovered had been boosted in Ottawa at 11:30 P.M. one day and was sold at an auction in Toronto at noon the following day. Russell Berndt, the Ottawa police detective who ran the investigation, said cars were stolen in Ottawa and Montreal and sold in cities all over Quebec and Ontario. Paquette was arrested and charged with five counts of possession of stolen autos, one count of stealing a car himself and three counts of fraud. He pleaded guilty to the possession and fraud charges, and the theft charge was dropped. He was sentenced to two years less a day on each count and was out in fifteen months. By then he had lost his car lot and his reputation.

Paquette's bust put Raymond in contact for the first time with the provincial and municipal police forces. The encounter fed his rich fantasy life and aroused his appetite for intrigue. Raymond has a gift for sensing the weaknesses of others and for making his lies speak to those vulnerabilities. Now he created a new persona for himself. He told people he was a cop. Over the next forty years the background of that cop changed as circumstances dictated. At times he was a Royal Canadian Mounted Police homicide detective, at others a Montreal motorcycle cop, a sly and slightly crooked provincial policeman, an investigator and a beat patrolman. He used the persona to intimidate, to run confidence scams, to charm his sexual prey or just to impress the most casual and fleeting acquaintances. None of this meant that he respected the police. He was just as contemptuous of cops as he was of anybody else he encountered. He saw them as eminently corruptible and amazingly easy to dupe. He learned how competition among police forces—the Pointe Gatineau police, the Hull police, the RCMP, the provincial police—hampered investigations and created rivalries that blunted the effectiveness of even the best-run organizations. Much of this he learned right in the village of Pointe Gatineau.

Sometime in the early 1960s Raymond befriended Pointe Gatineau police chief, Henri Ferland. Ferland was a former wrestler and the son of the Hull dog catcher. He was a hard-drinking brawler who used his authority to obtain free lunches, drinks and whatever else solicitous citizens wished to offer him in return for his favour. He had a half-dozen officers under his command and the bulk of their work in Pointe Gatineau consisted of breaking up fist fights and ticketing speeders. He spent a good deal of his time in one of the local bars and was in the habit of ordering one of his officers to drive his wife, in a patrol car, to and from her job in Hull.

Whatever they had going between them, Raymond and Ferland kept it to themselves. Officers who worked for Ferland at the time say Ferland, Durand and one other cop formed a little clique that no one else was allowed into. Raymond's car became a fixture in the police parking lot, and Ferland's car was often spotted in Raymond's yard. Denis and Anne have vivid memories of the shiny police car that was often in the driveway.

Now that he was friends with Ferland, Raymond began flashing a Pointe Gatineau police badge and a pistol similar to the one carried by the police. He claimed he was a detective.

After Paquette's arrest Raymond also expanded his business interests. He bought a tow truck and obtained regular work from the Pointe Gatineau police. He hooked up with a neighbour who was also a car salesman, Georges Sylvestre, and together they bought a gas station and set up a used car lot in Hull. They planned to buy used cars, do the mechanical work at the gas station, the body work and painting at Ray's shop and then sell them on their own lot. Raymond and his partner made regular trips to Montreal and Toronto to buy used cars, taking along a carload of buddies to drive the vehicles back to Hull. For a time they made good money, and Sylvestre says he thought they were on a roll. Sure, Sylvestre says, he had doubts about Raymond, but his partner always had a quick answer for everything.

Sylvestre says he once sold a local man a car and the buyer agreed to pick it up the following day. When he arrived, he discovered the expensive tires that had been on it had been replaced by a set of bald retreads. Sylvestre rushed down to the lot to cool out his angry customer. He pulled Raymond aside and asked what had happened.

Raymond laughed and clapped Sylvestre on the back. "It's nothing," Sylvestre says Ray told him, "Don't worry. I just lent a guy the tires. He had to go to Montreal. We'll get them back." Sylvestre says now, when he thinks back on it, it seems pretty foolish to have believed such a lame story. But, he says, that's the way Raymond was. You knew he was bullshitting you but he was so engaging, so convincing, so dismissive of even the most blatant evidence of his dishonesty, that you believed him.

Sylvestre says there were many similar incidents. He had a 1962 Chevrolet convertible that was all chrome under the hood—chrome alternator, valve covers and manifold. He took it to Montreal and was in the middle of talking a browser into buying it, bragging about the chrome, when he popped the hood to display the wares. He said he crumpled in embarrassment. Raymond had pulled all chrome parts off and had replaced them with the cheapest used ones he'd had at hand. "I lost four or five hundred dollars on that deal," Sylvestre recalls.

To illustrate how brazen Durand was, Sylvestre tells a story about the time a doctor brought his car in to Ray's Body Shop for some bodywork. He insisted to Ray that he wanted all the work done with lead and not Bondo, a plastic auto body filler that had recently come on the market. The old lead technique was time-consuming but enduring. Lead would be melted onto the dented area or around the piece of metal that was being used to cover a hole. It would be shaped with a wooden block and, when it cooled, filed to an even finish. Raymond assured his customer that he used nothing but lead. A day later while he was working on the doctor's car, the doctor dropped into the shop, followed by Sylvestre, who was on an errand. While Sylvestre watched, the doctor walked over to look at Raymond at work and noticed, on the floor, a plate with a lead-coloured substance on it. He asked, "Don't you have to heat it?" and reached down to touch it. Raymond shouted at him, "Goddamn, don't touch. You'll burn yourself." The doctor pulled back just in time, red-faced. He chatted for a bit and then left. As soon as he walked out of the shop, Raymond picked up the substance on the plate and, with Sylvestre looking on with mouth agape, casually tossed it to him. Sylvestre jumped back, and the goop fell to the floor. The crazy bastard, he thought, until he saw Raymond laughing at him. It's the new metal-coloured Bondo, he told Sylvestre between guffaws.

At the gas station Raymond was equally flinty and, because he had more contact with the public, even more predatory. Marcel

Legendre, a mechanic who did car repairs at the station, says he couldn't believe how dishonest Raymond was with customers and employees: "One time this guy came by with a load of fabric in his car. A salesman, I guess, for a textile manufacturer in Montreal. Ray bought the whole load off him. I think it was worth about two thousand dollars. He gave the guy a check and signed it as Mr Brown. The next day the guy came back looking for Mr Brown, the boss. Everybody said, 'There's no Mr Brown here.'"

With the income from the body shop, gas station, car lot and his tow truck, Raymond accelerated his spending on the good times. Jeannine's cousin, Jocelyne Béland St Louis, recalls that during those years she baby-sat Denis, Anne and the third baby, Marc, born in September, 1962: "They went away a lot for the whole weekend. They'd leave on a Friday night with another couple, Ray's brother and his wife, and they'd come back on Sunday night. They went to Montreal—to hockey games. The kids were good, easy to take care of. But the house seemed like such a sad place. Only Anne's room seemed happy. Jeannine had made a pretty vanity for her."

Those weekends trips—to resorts in the Laurentians north of Montreal, to Montreal and to the Carnival in Quebec City—were all at Ray's expense. He treated and they went often. When the outings began, Jeannine enjoyed herself, laughing at Raymond's jokes and antics. She never drank—the smell of liquor made her queasy. She wasn't amusing company, but she was kind and thoughtful and was easy to be with.

During the summers, Durand loved to be on a lake. After their marriage they used Durand's father's cottage on Lac Clair. But in the early 1960s they acquired a cottage on a tiny island just off-shore from Donat's cottage, but on the opposing side of the island so they couldn't see Donat's place. They bought a boat, and Denis learned to water ski at six years old. They spent all their summers there, free of the muggy nights in Pointe Gatineau. Durand and his brothers had for years used their father's cottage for parties, and they had fond memories of the good times there.

But before his death, Donat had lost his own place for reasons that are not clear. Marie-Anna told her sisters that she sold it because she couldn't trust her husband there. But the place was never sold. Donat had leased the land from the government and perhaps the lease was up. Whatever the case, a Hull man who owned a neighbouring cottage began using it, and it appeared that he was going to acquire it. Raymond hated the neighbour and decided the cottage was not going to fall into his hands. So one summer night he rowed to shore with a can of gas, doused his father's place, a cottage that he and his brothers had helped build, and set it alight. Durand later told family members that when he jumped into the boat to row back to the island he scraped his shin on the dock. He hadn't thought that the blaze would light up the whole lake. He said he felt that a spotlight was on him all the way across. Durand bragged about setting the fire, and in later life even told Denis about it, laughing at how close he came to getting caught.

As Raymond's little business empire grew, friends say, it became evident that Jeannine took less and less pleasure in her husband's company. Part of the growing distance between them was created by Raymond's treatment of the children. He barely tolerated them, never indulged their hurt feelings and never took the slightest interest in their activities. When he was home—and increasingly he was out day and night—he had no patience for the kids. At lunch one day, with a visitor at the table, he watched Denis flood his plate with ketchup and then lost his temper. Seizing the bottle he poured it over Denis's head. Jeannine's response was to comfort Denis.

"Leave him alone, Raymond," she pleaded. "It will pass."

From then on Raymond called Denis "Ketchup."

There were plenty of playmates for the kids along Michaud Street. The river was close by, and the yard was big enough for pets and hammer-and-nail projects. As the eldest, Denis has the clearest memories of the street. But even by age five, a rowdy and happy kid, he feared and mistrusted his father. All his memories of his father are about disappointment or of being coaxed into violating his sense of fairness.

One summer evening, Denis remembers, he rushed into his dad's shop in tears. He had been racing soap-boxes on wheels with the other kids on the street. A bully had bashed into his soap-box from behind and busted it. There'd been some pushing and shoving and he'd run home crying.

"Stop your goddamn crying, Ketchup," his father had growled at him. "I'll make you a real go-cart, one with a motor in it. We'll do it in the shop."

Denis remembers he grabbed at that promise, clutched it tightly, made his father repeat it. He instantly imagined what it would look like, where the motor would go, the old car seat he could use, how he could paint it, the helmet he'd wear. He'd ride it to school. The guys would be climbing over each other to be his best friend, he imagined. They'd beg him for rides.

He'd sprinted out and bragged about it all afternoon. Told the guys he and his dad would do it right in the shop downstairs, that his dad had it all figured out, all the stuff they'd need. Then they'd paint it in the body shop.

He'd coasted on that promise for weeks, bugged his father for months about it. Then winter came. Raymond had never even begun assembling the parts, had never had the slightest intention of building the thing for him.

Denis remembers, too, how the yard around their house was littered with shards of metal, scraps that his father had just tossed out of the shop when he had completed a job. Jeannine accused Raymond of carelessness.

"Raymond," she'd say, "why do you just throw the scraps around like that? Think of the kids."

One Sunday they had come home from the cottage in the early evening. It was muggy and hot, and Jeannine had taken out the hose to water her flowers. Denis says he was teasing her. She sprayed him and it felt so deliciously cool that it had become a game, sprinting in and out of his mother's range. Until he landed a bare foot on a dagger-sharp piece of metal. He screamed, and blood had poured out of his foot. His mother carried him to the house. When his blood soaked the towel she had bound around his foot, Denis remembers crying and his father shouting, "Stop your whining. You'll be OK."

Finally, Denis remembered, his mother had screamed at his father, who had reluctantly driven Denis to a clinic to have his foot stitched.

Denis remembers another time when he had a toothache that had hurt so much that he had finally told his mother. She made an appointment with the dentist and his father drove him. By the time Denis had climbed into the dentist's chair he was shaking. His father didn't bother hanging around. He left Denis and strolled across the street to the police station to see his buddy the police chief. The dentist came in, gave Denis a shot of anaesthetic and told Denis to wait in the hall. When no one was looking, Denis crept out and hid in the car. The dentist had looked all over and finally called the police station. When Raymond had jumped in the car to see if Denis had gone home, he found him and cursed him roundly. He swore about the money he'd wasted, Denis recalls.

Perhaps the most difficult element of his father's character for Denis was his wit. Ray was a natural mimic and joker but all his routines had a mean edge to them. Denis remembers he could never resist laughing, but afterwards he always felt badly about having done so.

Jeannine hated it when Raymond made fun of people. Denis knew that, and he knew how much it hurt to have his father make fun of him.

Denis remembers the time he felt the most badly about laughing was when GaGa Patate brought his chip wagon into the shop for a paint job. Everybody knew him; GaGa sold French fries near the bridge across the river to Hull. He had been there forever with his hunchback and the same question for everybody: "What size you want?" Denis, his uncles and his sister were all in the shop one day when his father put GaGa's hat on, climbed into the wagon, stuck his head out the serving window with his back all hunched and said: "What size you want?" He imitated GaGa perfectly. They were all laughing so hard that they didn't see GaGa walk in. Denis heard GaGa's cry of anguish before he saw him. He was screaming that he wanted his wagon, he was going to get the work done somewhere else. It took Raymond the longest time to cool GaGa off. He told him, "GaGa, I was just trying it out."

Jeannine, the kids remember, was everything their father wasn't. She was patient, affectionate and protective. "She was a real mother hen," said a woman who often saw Jeannine with the kids. "She didn't want anybody teasing the kids or making fun of them." And she grew to resent Raymond's habit of tagging everybody, including the kids, with a nickname that made them feel small and stupid. Anne was Little Runt. Réginald was Big Dummy.

Anne and Denis remember their mother as a calming presence whose lap was always beckoning. In the evenings she'd put them to bed and leave the bedroom door open. Then she'd sit and play them a good-night tune. They remember that whenever she learned a new piece of music, she would call her mother, place the telephone receiver on the piano and play it for her. All the neighbours on Michaud Street enjoyed her music as well. At night they'd sit on their porches and listen to her playing Mozart to her kids.

Jeannine didn't mind weekends at home and came to prefer the company of her kids to weekend outings with Raymond and the other couple.

Jocelyne Béland St Louis says Jeannine was often deeply unhappy when she did accompany her husband and that she didn't consider the weekend excursions a relaxing adventure. She seemed to depart with great reluctance and to consider the trips an unwelcome duty.

It was not only Raymond's treatment of the children that Jeannine had begun to dislike. She discovered that he was dishonest in business and was a pathological liar. She continued to defend him to her parents, even telling them about his financial accomplishments, but she did once confide to her family that she was no longer doing the books for the business. She wanted no part of his crooked deals.

And so Raymond, always a skirt-chaser, began spending more time and money on other women. Now he often didn't come home at night. It took Jeannine a long time to recognize that he was philandering, but eventually she did and it became a source of many quarrels. Raymond would endure no criticism from Jeannine, however, and at some point he apparently began slapping her around. Jeannine's uncle had a milk route that included 44 Michaud Street. One day he arrived to hear Raymond shouting and Jeannine crying. He left the milk on the table and tiptoed out. The next time he saw her she was wearing sunglasses and wouldn't look at him. Denis recalls he grew so frightened by the quarrelling that he would cover his head with his pillow whenever he heard a fight about to ignite.

Denis remembers the first time he heard his mother say that his father was chasing around. Whenever his dad would jump in the car, she would say, "Raymond, take Denis with you. Take him along." So Denis would spend hours just sitting in the car, parked in front of an apartment building in Ottawa or another one in Hull. Somehow Denis remembers knowing that his father was visiting another woman. He remembers that he often asked himself what he was supposed to tell his mother. He feared what his father might do to him if he ever did say anything, but he hated himself for keeping his dad's secrets. When his mother asked him where they had been, Denis remembers he would just say that they had been at a car lot or that they'd had to get some car parts in Ottawa. Denis knew that his mother had figured it out because she didn't press him for the details.

Every time Denis and his mother passed the apartment in Hull that Raymond used to visit, she would look over at it. Denis remembers pretending not to see the hurt on her face. Whenever she was hurt like that, she played sad music on the piano at night. "Get into bed," she would say, "and I'll play for you." But when she played the sad music, Denis thought about sitting in the boiling hot car waiting for his father, and he felt all tangled up inside.

Chapter Four

Hull, Quebec, 1966

Pointe Gatineau police chief, Henri Ferland, was among the dozen officers who raided Gilles Paquin's printing shop on that cold night in January, 1966. Ferland was evidently involved in the planning of the raid. Yet Raymond Durand, his good buddy, never said anything about working as an informant for Ferland; he said he was working for one of Ferland's detectives, Robert Sincennes, who denied that Durand had ever fed him any information. As usual in matters involving Durand, the truth is that only he knew what he was up to.

After the preliminary hearing Durand told family members that he was going to be paid forty thousand dollars for his testimony and that he was going to use the money to make a new life. But police officers in the Ottawa area say that story was a fantasy. They say that back in 1966 the only force in the country that would have had that kind of money to spend on an informant would have been the RCMP and that the Mounties might have been willing to pay an informant forty thousand dollars for a murder investigation, but they would never have handed that much cash to a rinky-dink hustler like Durand for turning in a small-town forger.

Aside from the looming forgery trial, which was scheduled to begin in the spring of 1967, Durand had problems at home. He had taken out an eight-thousand-dollar mortgage on his house in March, 1965, to invest in a new business with his friend Georges Sylvestre. At first they had made money. But Durand had spent it much more rapidly than he had made it, and by Christmas of that year he was in serious financial difficulty. He had fallen behind on his mortgage payments, had mountains of unpaid bills from suppliers and, after it became known that he had snitched on Paquin and Tassé, business began to dry up at the body shop and garage. His intrigues were catching up to him. He was a friend of the cops and of members of the criminal subculture. Now neither side trusted him. He still had his pal Ferland, but by mid-1966 the writing was on the wall for Ferland as well. He had alienated most of the department, and the city council was discreetly probing his activities. Within a year that probe would lead to a full-blown judicial inquiry and Ferland's suspension without pay.

Despite his mounting financial difficulties, Durand partied and chased skirts with great vigour. He had seemingly insatiable appetites and enormous physical energy. He was rarely at home.

Jeannine had never set foot in the body shop at home, but as their financial difficulties mounted, she began running errands for Ray and the boys at the gas station. Mechanic Marcel Legendre says she became the company gofer. Perhaps she was attempting to establish a greater presence in Raymond's life. One day, alone in the car, Jeannine was approaching an entrance to the recently constructed Macdonald-Cartier Bridge when a front wheel came loose and she lost control and slammed into a concrete pillar. The car was totalled but she was unhurt. The next day, Legendre recalls, Durand told the guys at work: "How's that for being unlucky? The wife wasn't even bruised." Legendre says today that his recollections of the accident are a bit hazy, and, to be fair to Durand, it sounds like the sort of crack that might have been made for a laugh. But Legendre says he retains to this day an impression of Durand as a cruel man who hadn't been joking when he said he was unlucky.

Two months after his testimony at the preliminary inquiry Durand was in bankruptcy court. During the months that he had been cruising around in his Super Sport Chevy with a pistol in his pocket and a police badge in his wallet, bragging that he was working as an investigator and snitching on Paquin and Tassé, he had been sliding into bankruptcy. Now, the list of his assets and his debts revealed just how much his pursuit of a fantasy life and good times had cost. Asked in one of the bankruptcy forms to explain what had caused his businesses to fail he wrote simply: "Too many debts, not enough revenue." He said he had known since November, 1965, that he was in trouble.

So, at thirty-one years old, he lost everything: the house that he had built, his body shop, gas station and interests in two other companies. His debts totalled more than forty thousand dollars, his assets about seven thousand. He owed money to six finance companies, to auto parts suppliers, to other car dealerships, to the company that delivered his gas, to an advertising company and to the hardware store where his father-in-law worked.

For Jeannine and the kids, the bankruptcy brought to an abrupt end life on Michaud Street. A quarter of a century later the children would remember it as the only happy period of their childhoods.

Denis's memories of that summer are all tied to a sunny day near the end of the school year. He was trudging home from classes, Anne trailing behind as usual, and his friend Beaver Bélair was dancing alongside, taunting him. "Your dad's ban-krut," Denis remembers Beaver telling him. Denis had no idea what it meant, but his ears burned with shame. He knew that if Beaver knew, the whole town knew. It was something Raymond had done.

Denis was ten years old that summer. He feared his father but that wasn't so unusual; so did a lot of boys he knew. Denis says he thought of himself as a normal kid from a normal family. He spoke only French. Within his world, he was snuggled deep in the bosom of the majority. He played hockey in the winter and summered at the lake. He was surrounded by a large extended family of grandparents, uncles, aunts and cousins.

The bankruptcy changed everything. For years afterwards Denis thought all the family's troubles were caused by that ugly word that Beaver had taunted him with, a word that sounded like it had been broken in half. *Ban-krut.*

In early summer the finance company foreclosed on the delinquent mortgage, and the family was obliged to move. But the bankruptcy was the least of Durand's worries. Now increasingly fearful of the enemies he had made by informing on Tassé and Paquin, Durand relocated his family to a rented house on Bernier Street, in Hull's north end.

After the move, Denis recalls, his mother seemed so unhappy. He remembers the day she put all the kids in the car and drove around Hull. How his heart jumped when she parked outside the apartment building that his father used to go to! They sat there and waited. Denis didn't say anything. He says he couldn't figure out what she was going to do. Was she waiting for Ray? Was she going to talk to the woman? Would she ask him to go in and ask for Ray? He says he wanted to cry. He sensed that his mother was aware of the secrets he was keeping but he knew she wouldn't ask him to betray his father.

Denis had become his mother's best friend. He took on chores

around the house and helped with Anne and Marc. He could make
her laugh as Raymond once could. At night, Denis remembers,
he'd be in bed and he'd ask her if she could bring him a glass of
water. She'd bring it and he'd try to make her laugh because he
knew she had her false teeth out. She'd cover her mouth and say,
"Denis, don't make me laugh." It was a game they played.

When school started, Denis remembers, the hard times took hold.
There was no money, and his father was rarely at home, day or
night. They never had any visitors. Everything seemed to be in
limbo. He assumed they were waiting for something. Denis got a
paper route and began delivering *Le Droit*. He gave all the money
he made to his mother. One afternoon a couple of guys whom
Denis had met came by and asked him to go to the movies with
them. He said he couldn't go. Jeannine heard and said, "Why can't
you go?"

"We don't have the money," Denis told her. He thought she was
going to cry.

She held him and said, "I have money." So he went to the
movies.

The bankruptcy may have been traumatic for Jeannine and the
kids but for Durand it appears to have been a sort of liberation. He
had once seen an episode of "Les Plouffe," a popular television
series, in which one of the characters vacationed in Florida. That
television program had a great impact on him; friends recall he was
always going on about how he was going to live near the beach in
the sun.

Like many residents of Hull, Durand grew up speaking only
French. By his early twenties, however, he had picked up a basic
working knowledge of English. Today he is still virtually illiterate
in English and has a noticeable French accent, but by the fall of
1966 he was confident enough of his ability to speak English that
he decided to cross the river into Ottawa for work. He had become
too well known in Hull. He snagged a job in the paint shop of one
of Ottawa's biggest car dealers, Campbell Motors. The showroom
and body shop were downtown, but the paint shop was in the west
end on Scott Street. His boss, the foreman, was a fellow francoph-
one.

Despite the bankruptcy, Durand managed to buy on credit a new
car, a Beaumont. It didn't matter how broke he was, Durand

refused to be seen driving a clunker. With the car he was back on the prowl, looking for opportunities. Neither the bankruptcy nor the preliminary hearing had apparently shrivelled his fantasy life. In the 1967 Hull city directory, which lists the name, address, phone number and occupation of all heads of household, the entry for Raymond Durand at 3 Bernier Street shows his occupation as police chief.

At Campbell, Durand sized up the situation pretty quickly. He got one of his brothers a job in the shop with him and, shortly afterward, was accused by the foreman of stealing paint. According to a co-worker in whom Durand confided, Durand responded by hauling material from the shop to the foreman's own garage and then calling the police. When Campbell management learned of the situation, the foreman was fired. Durand felt emboldened and set his sights on another target.

From time to time Durand would deliver freshly painted cars to the lot downtown. When he did, he always took the time to chat up the buxom, red-headed switchboard operator, Patricia Holben. He told his brother that she was having an affair with a senior executive at Campbell and that he was going to have her himself.

A cheerful, salty, heavy woman, Holben was then living with a civil servant named Albert Dudley, who worked for the Department of Defence. Before she had gotten the job as receptionist at Campbell, Holben had been a waitress at a café next door. A hairdresser named Lucille Savage, who knew Holben when she worked at the café, said all the Campbell men would have lunch there. Holben always laughed and shared dirty jokes with the boys, said Savage. "Guys would hit her on the butt," Savage says. "She was quite sure of herself. She seemed to be a happy person. She didn't wear much make-up, wore a uniform. Sometimes her hair would be blonde, sometimes auburn."

Savage describes Dudley as comfortably middle class and deeply in love with Holben. In the city directory they were listed as husband and wife. However, Holben's relatives say they were never married. Savage said Holben and Dudley had a beautiful apartment furnished with antiques on Frank Street in downtown Ottawa.

Durand told a family member that to impress Holben he was going to buy a new, luxury car. First he talked one of his brothers into buying his Beaumont. The brother was told he could just assume the payments and he did. As soon as the papers were signed, transferring the loan to the brother, Durand bought on credit a new, red Buick LeSabre. It was a huge boat of a car, a top-of-the-line Buick. Immediately afterward, his brother discovered that Durand hadn't made any payments on the Beaumont.

By that fall Holben had fallen in love with Durand and had walked out on Dudley. Apparently the then 220-pound Durand had literally charmed Patricia into leaving Albert Dudley. They got an apartment together, and soon Durand was spending more time with her than at his own home. He bragged to a co-worker that he was shacked up with Patricia Holben, but his colleague just laughed, thinking it was another of Durand's lies. So one afternoon Durand took his co-worker to an apartment near the shop. He opened the door with a key, walked into the bedroom and opened the closet. "Whose clothes are these?" he asked.

"Pat's."

"And whose are these?"

"Yours."

At about this time Durand began telling Jeannine that they were going to move to Florida, that it was no longer safe for them in Quebec. He explained his absences by telling her that he was working nights to earn the money for the move.

On a warm, sunny day late that autumn, Jeannine's cousin Jocelyne Béland St Louis, who often baby-sat for Jeannine and Ray, bicycled over to Bernier Street to visit Jeannine. She hadn't baby-sat for the Durands in months, and she decided to drop by to see how they were getting on in their new place. She found Jeannine deeply depressed, sadder than she had ever seen her. While the children played in the backyard amid the maples shedding their brightly coloured leaves, she and Jeannine sat on a swing and talked. For the first time Jeannine took her cousin into her confidence. Béland St Louis remembers Jeannine was crying as she talked.

"Raymond wants to move to Florida," Jeannine said. "He's gone, and when he finds us a house we will move. It could be tomorrow. His brother will take us part of the way. I don't want to go."

Part of Jeannine's unhappiness may have been her discovery that she was pregnant for the fourth time. But she was also desperately broke, often barely able to feed the kids. She was too proud to ask her parents and entirely dependent on Durand's sense of responsibility. She felt vulnerable and afraid.

It is unlikely that Durand had actually left for Florida. He was certainly back at Bernier Street for Christmas. It's more likely that he was living with Holben and had simply told Jeannine he was in Florida.

Although Pat Holben appeared jolly to many, she apparently was pursued by inner demons. That fall Durand called a relative in a panic when he discovered Pat on the floor of the apartment they were sharing. She had slit her wrists. Durand, apparently more concerned about the pickle he was in than his mistress's condition, asked his relative for help. Call an ambulance, he was told. He did and Holben recovered in the hospital. Durand never explained what had happened and never talked about it again. The other evidence that Holben had troubles of her own comes from Nancy Granger, then a seventeen-year-old who filled in for Holben on the switchboard at lunch. Granger says Holben used to lunch with Durand at the café and that she'd frequently have to walk over to tell her lunch hour was over. Granger says her last memory of Holben is that she used to cry a lot: "I see her at the switchboard with tears on her face."

Shortly after Christmas, Holben began sanding trucks in the shop with Durand, working late into the night. Durand was painting the trucks so fast that he began delivering them downtown before the paint had dried. He was being paid for the number of vehicles he painted, so the more rapidly he worked, the more money he made.

One Friday night he collected his pay and his brother's as well, and walked out of Campbell's without a backward glance. He had convinced Holben to move to Florida with him and start a new life. Neither of them gave notice, and nobody knew where they had gone. Durand took Holben's winter clothes and told her he'd give them to a sister. He dropped them off with Jeannine and told her he'd be in touch. Then he picked up Holben and they cruised south in the big, red Buick. When they coasted to a stop the next day they were in Fort Lauderdale, Florida.

Chapter Five

Fort Lauderdale, Florida, 1967

A t first Fort Lauderdale was a clean break for Raymond Durand. Nobody knew him and he was free to remake his identity. He had discarded his home town, his language and his culture. He had parked his family in quiet isolation. Since his skills were portable, he had had no difficulty finding work in a body shop.

Raymond and Pat rented a furnished, air-conditioned house together. Pat found a job in a cafeteria so they weren't short of money. Whenever Ray felt it was time to send a few dollars home to his pregnant wife and three kids, who were still living in the house on Bernier Street, he'd work late painting cars for three or four days. He had the stamina of a bull.

They spent their free time on the beach. Ray loved to ogle the women. He had a thing about big breasts. Pat was no beauty—she had a hard face and long, straight auburn hair then—but he was crazy about her breasts, which spilled out of the yellow one-piece bathing suit she wore. He'd sit there in the sun, drinking beer, swimming, working on his tan, commenting on the beauties that strolled by. He fancied himself a good-looking guy. He had a buzz cut, a decent set of false teeth, a hairy chest. He had a fair-sized spare tire around his waist, but he believed that his charm made up for the extra weight.

When Ray left Canada, he had told his brothers and other family members that his life was in danger because he had crossed some big-time mobsters in Montreal. That may or may not be true. What is certain is that he was fleeing both creditors and the courts. He owed money for the new car he had bought, and he was expected to testify at Tassé's trial in the late spring of 1967. Paquin was to go to trial later. But Ray had decided that he'd done his bit and wasn't going to wait around to repeat what he had already said at the preliminary hearing.

About a month after Ray and Pat settled into their new life in Florida, Ray made a lightning trip back to Hull to move Jeannine and the kids over to Ottawa. It's not clear what prompted him to return, but the instructions he left, warning Jeannine and the children not to contact anyone in Hull, suggest he was concerned about their safety. Perhaps he felt his enemies were closing in. A brother and another relative say that from the moment he left Campbell Motors, they began receiving calls, asking where Raymond had gone. People were looking for him.

The move to Ottawa meant Denis and Anne had to go to an English-speaking school even though they could neither speak nor understand the language. The apartment Ray rented for them on Carling Avenue, in Ottawa's west end, was tiny and there was no phone. Ray said they weren't to call or visit any of the family. Nobody was supposed to know where they were. They were in hiding.

The night they moved into the apartment Denis remembers he was in bed and he heard his parents arguing.

"You stupid bitch," his father screamed. "You don't put money in an envelope."

She said something like, "Raymond, why are you leaving me with this hanging over my head." Denis had seen her put a wad of twenties in an envelope. His father had given her the money. After the fight he heard her leave. He thinks she went out to mail it. Denis thought that his father owed the money to somebody and that he wasn't going to pay it.

At school Denis struggled with English. He was terribly lonely. The only money he remembers they had came in airmail envelopes. Once again he got a job delivering newspapers. All his newspaper money he gave to Jeannine for milk and bread. She was tired a lot, and her belly was beginning to swell. But the hardest part was not seeing anyone. Jeannine didn't call her parents. Denis says they didn't see any of their uncles or cousins. The winter seemed to go on forever. To Denis it felt as if they were frozen in time, living in that apartment in a strange city among people they couldn't understand.

After moving Jeannine and the children, Ray raced back to Fort Lauderdale.

Years later Pat said that at this point she had no idea that Ray was married and had kids. She said one day, after they had been in Florida for months, he told her about Jeannine and the kids and said he wanted to bring them to Florida. Pat says she was stunned but didn't think she had any choice in the matter. Here she was, living illegally in the United States, having burned all her bridges behind her, in love with a married man whose wife was pregnant. So she stuck with him and agreed to a plan Ray suggested: he would introduce her as his boss's wife. She evidently hoped—and perhaps Ray gave her reason to hope—that he would eventually divorce Jeannine.

After he had told Pat about Jeannine and the kids, Ray rented a small house for his family on the outskirts of Fort Lauderdale near factories and railroad tracks. Then in early April he obtained a classy, red Thunderbird convertible. (One of his brothers later said it was a rented car.) It was the sort of car that turned people's heads. He drove it north to Hull, where he immediately sold it to an old acquaintance for fifteen hundred dollars cash. Two months later the man who bought it was having his hair cut one morning when he saw two men in suits examining his Thunderbird, which was parked in the street. They were waiting for him when he stepped out of the barber shop. They introduced themselves as RCMP officers and said they had been searching for the car. The man explained that he had bought it from Raymond Durand. They seized the car and shortly after formally charged Durand with selling a U.S.-registered vehicle in Canada. They were never able to find him to advise him of the charge.

With the money from the sale of the Thunderbird, Ray bought airplane tickets for Jeannine and the kids.

Denis remembers the leaves were just budding out and the snow-banks shrinking into the shadows of tall buildings when he saw his father climb out of a car one day. It was early spring, 1967. Raymond swept into the apartment and announced they were moving to Florida.

His father told him that Florida had palm trees, beaches, the ocean, but Denis didn't believe him; he didn't believe anything his dad said anymore.

The next day they went shopping for suitcases. With Denis by her side Jeannine chose a checked suitcase that folded in half. She told Denis she could hang her clothes in it and they wouldn't crease. She always wore skirts and dresses. Denis says he can't recall ever seeing his mother in slacks. She also bought a blue suit-case for the kid's clothes. That night they packed, and the next day they took a taxi to the airport, the whole family. It was the first time Jeannine and the children had been on an airplane. Denis remembers coming in for a landing and seeing the blue, blue ocean and the sand. It looked like a postcard. He remembers wanting to be happy but thinking about school and wondering where they were going to live. He says he was frightened that it was going to be another one of his dad's fairy-tales that was going to turn out to be a nightmare for everybody

The summer that the family moved to Florida, the United States was being torn apart by race riots and opposition to the Vietnam War. All across the country hippies were trekking to San Francisco for what would become known as the Summer of Love.

In Fort Lauderdale, Ray settled in for his own summer of love. He moved his family into the tiny, dark house he had rented for them. Unlike the place he had rented for himself and Pat, this house was not air-conditioned. They suffered in the heat, often unable to sleep at night. Jeannine was now six months' pregnant.

Why Ray bothered to bring Jeannine and the kids down to Florida after he had settled in with his mistress is a mystery that puzzles Denis and the other children to this day. He and Jeannine had not been getting along, and he barely tolerated the kids. It may be that he felt a sense of responsibility for them. It may also be that the truth is a story he once told a brother. He said he believed that it was going to be easier to obtain status as a legal immigrant in the United States with a wife and kids. He may have been misinformed about U.S. immigration law, but if he really believed that, it would explain the reason he went to such lengths and expense to move the family.

Shortly after Ray moved his family from Ottawa to Florida, Corporal Yves Chalifoux of the Quebec provincial police began searching for him. He had been detailed to serve Durand with a subpoena to testify at Tassé's trial. The Crown attorney was getting nervous. His star witness had disappeared. Chalifoux talked to Georges Sylvestre, who told him that he had heard rumours that Durand had fled to Florida and was working as an appraiser at a garage. Chalifoux found Albert Durand, one of Raymond's brothers, who said Raymond had called from Florida but hadn't given him an address. Then Chalifoux looked up Jeannine's father, Hermas Boissonneault, who said he had been looking for Jeannine for more than two months. Hermas said he too had heard that the family had moved to Florida but he had no idea when they had left or where they were living. If Boissonneault was being truthful—and there is no reason to think he wasn't—that means Jeannine hadn't contacted her parents after Ray moved her to the apartment on Carling Avenue. Whatever Ray had told her, whatever reason he had given her when he had warned that she shouldn't contact anyone back in Hull, it had been sufficient to make her obey. During those winter months that she had lived in poverty and loneliness on Carling Avenue, pregnant, with the kids struggling in an English school, she had not once called her mother or father. She had suffered in absolute silence.

Several days after the family flew to Fort Lauderdale, Ray brought Pat to the house and introduced her to Jeannine and the kids as Pat Anderson, wife of the owner of the body shop where he was working. Jeannine spoke very little English and Pat spoke no French at all. Still, they managed to communicate and Pat became a frequent visitor to the house. To the kids she was Aunt Pat. Denis, Anne and Marc liked her. She played with them, bought them things, took them out occasionally. Ray was rarely around. On most nights he did not come home, and when he did, it was only to dash out again a short time later. If Jeannine and the kids expected he would introduce them to the pleasures of Florida, they were soon disabused of that notion. They were on their own. He never took them anywhere, except for a couple of visits to the beach.

In early May Corporal Chalifoux managed to locate Durand. He had obtained a letter Durand had written to his brother Albert in which he boasted that he had a five-bedroom house and a good job. He suggested Albert join him, and wrote that he could get him a job in the same body shop. Working with police in Fort Lauderdale, the Quebec police and the Crown prosecutor contacted Ray. He refused to return. Since apparently they couldn't extradite him, they applied to the court for permission to seek his testimony in the United States under a rarely invoked judicial procedure. Crown prosecutor Maurice Chevalier had Durand subpoenaed and then made arrangements for the trial judge, court reporter, defence attorney and himself to fly to Miami to hear his testimony. At 11 A.M. on May 26 at the Main Post Office Building in Miami, Durand repeated his testimony and was then cross-examined by the defence attorney, Jules Barrière. Once again Barrière asked Durand whom he was working for and whether he was to be paid. Durand was as slippery as soap on tile.

"Well, I am expecting something, yes, from the case which I am not sure, though," he said when asked about payment.

Had he been offered money?

"Every weekend I was working with Mr Sincennes with the Gatineau police, but I was never offered to be paid."

Yet he believed he deserved something?

"All that I did, I think it was just."

He also said that he had discussed with the provincial police the possibility of a job on the force. Then, under Barrière's questioning, Durand related a bizarre story of how he had taken a cheap used car to a guy in jail. Durand got the prisoner to sign over to him his car, which the police had seized and was in storage in Durand's garage. In return, Durand paid the prisoner with the used car and anted up the money for his fine to get him out of jail. The hapless con later discovered the beater that Durand had palmed off on him didn't have any registration documents. The way Durand told it, the problem was a misunderstanding that he fixed by writing to Quebec for the proper documents. Barrière apparently had information to the contrary, but he eventually gave up all hope of getting a straight story out of Durand.

After his testimony Durand was apparently free to go. He was in the United States illegally, working without papers, and yet it appears he wasn't questioned about his immigration status.

The judge, lawyers and court reporter promptly flew back to Hull to complete the trial. Some weeks later Tassé was convicted and drew a two-month jail sentence. Paquin went to trial later the same year and received an even lighter sentence. He was given one day in jail and a five-hundred-dollar fine. The Crown appealed Paquin's sentence but it was upheld. Despite the evidence against them and the nature of the crimes, the two men were punished by nothing more than a slap on the wrist. It must have been humiliating for the prosecutor and the police. They had invested a great deal in the case, had publicized it, had gone to the expense of chasing down a witness in Florida, all for the sake of a two-month sentence for the man who had served as an intermediary. The actual forger had walked away with a fine and a couple of hours in a cell.

Raymond Durand may have taken the biggest lumps of all in the entire affair. He had become known as a stoolie and, according to what he told family members, lived in fear of retribution for some years afterwards.

As it happened, Durand's departure for Florida also coincided with the launch of a judicial inquiry into Henri Ferland's conduct as police chief in Pointe Gatineau. During the inquiry Ferland was described as a drunkard who was once seen passed out in his car in front of the police station, an open liquor bottle lying on the back seat. His officers testified that they saw him drunk in public on many occasions, once showing up wobbly-legged at the mayor's residence to take charge of an investigation into a break-in. They said he routinely ordered them not to charge people arrested for fighting or other infractions at the local bar that he drank in. Reports of any incidents at or near the bar were to be put in a sealed envelope and addressed to him.

The inquiry suggested that Ferland was, at best, a drunken incompetent and, at worst, a crooked cop who could be counted upon to fix a ticket or provide protection for a favoured bar owner. But such was the prevailing public morality that the judge who presided at the inquiry concluded that it was no crime to take an occasional drink or for a police chief to exercise his discretion in deciding not to charge someone. When Pointe Gatineau council members received the report, they concluded that the judge's interpretation of the evidence had been exceedingly generous to Ferland and they voted to dismiss the chief regardless.

Now settled in Fort Lauderdale, Jeannine had three children racing about the house, no piano to console herself with and her husband's mistress as her only visitor. Did she know Pat was having an affair with Ray? Pat has said Jeannine didn't know and the children believe that to be the case as well. In any event, she must have been suspicious. She was never introduced to Ray's boss, Pat's supposed husband. And Ray often didn't come home at night.

Jeannine wrote to her parents from Fort Lauderdale, sending them pictures of the family with Pat, whom Jeannine described as a friend. Despite the apparently cheery tone of the letters, Jeannine wasn't happy. She was having a difficult pregnancy, and the heat didn't make things any easier. She was also hard pressed to keep the kids occupied. She knew no one and had very little money. Still, she was resourceful. One day Denis came home from exploring the neighbourhood with an armload of fabric scraps he had picked up behind a nearby garment factory. Jeannine became excited and asked him to get more. She got the kids working on projects in the house, and she herself began working on a patchwork comforter.

Meanwhile Ray was up to his usual high jinks. Jeannine was alarmed when he was taken by the police to Miami, but he came back boasting that he had obliged the whole court to fly down just to listen to him. He later told another relative he had spent an evening drinking with the judge and lawyers, and he once told another relative that he had been paid an additional twenty-five thousand dollars for his testimony.

Shortly after that incident he came home one day with his hair dyed red. As usual, he had an outrageous lie ready. "I was in the sun tanning and it just turned red," he told Jeannine. By an interesting coincidence, his hair was now the same colour as Pat's. Denis remembers hearing his father and thinking both that he'd have to be careful not to stay too long in the sun because he didn't want red hair and that his father was lying.

In mid-June, Jeannine entered Broward County Hospital to give birth to her fourth child. Pat moved in to care for Denis, Anne and Marc while she was in the hospital. Jeannine's admittance records show she was five feet, three inches tall, had upper and lower dentures, wore a gold wedding ring and spoke little English.

Jeannine gave birth on June 16 to a healthy, blonde, seven-pound girl. The records indicate Jeannine weighed 186 pounds when she entered the hospital. After giving birth to a seven-pound baby her weight was recorded as 181 pounds.

After the birth her doctor recommended she undergo a bilateral tubal ligation. The hospital records simply state that the reason for the tubal, which would prevent any more pregnancies, was "too many children." So the day following the birth she was wheeled back into surgery, a three-inch incision was made below her navel and the attending surgeon performed the then-standard Pomeroy procedure. He cut through each Fallopian tube, sliced out about one inch and then took the two tube ends and placed them together lengthwise like two index fingers pressed against each other. He

tied them together with catgut, which would dissolve in approximately twenty-one days, and then stitched up the incision.

When Jeannine entered the hospital and Ray told the kids that
Aunt Pat would be staying with them, they were thrilled. Aunt Pat
had an easy laugh and, unlike their mother, loved to go places and
do things. She swam with them at the beach and played with them.
Denis, in particular, liked the way she talked back to his father. She
was a big woman, solid, not as tall as Jeannine, but she had a confidence that made her seem more substantial.

Aunt Pat was to sleep in Ray and Jeannine's bedroom. The first
couple of nights Denis saw his father make up a bed for himself on
the sofa. But a couple of days later, in the early hours of the morning, Denis got up to go to the washroom and saw the sofa hadn't
been slept in. He figured his father was sleeping with Pat and he
knew that was wrong.

That discovery filled Denis with confusion. He loved his mother
but couldn't tell her. He liked Aunt Pat but says he was frightened
by her dishonesty. What if her husband found out? Denis wondered. He spent days wandering around the neighbourhood thinking about what to do. He thought about his mother in the hospital
with the baby, about what would happen when she came home.
Maybe his father and Aunt Pat were just sleeping together until his
mother came home. Then Aunt Pat would go back to her husband.

He hated his father for the lies. After he figured out what was
happening with Pat, Denis couldn't stand talking to Raymond. He
wanted to smash his face in. His thought his father was making
trouble for his mother and for Aunt Pat. Raymond didn't seem to
care about the baby. He didn't care about anyone but himself.

When Jeannine was released from the hospital, weak and in considerable pain, she insisted that the baby, whom they had named
Martine, be properly baptised with godparents. Durand agreed and
called his father's brother, Robert Durand, to ask if he and his wife,
Claudette, would be Martine's godparents.

Robert Durand had never been particularly close to his nephew,
but they had become friendlier in the final year that Raymond had
spent in Hull. Robert, who is no more than a decade older that
Raymond, says he was surprised by the call from his nephew but
agreed to the request immediately. Raymond offered to fly the
couple down. Robert saw it as a free trip to Florida, and although

he didn't trust Raymond, he didn't dislike him. He and Claudette found a baby-sitter for their three kids, who are almost the same ages as Raymond and Jeannine's oldest three children, and flew south.

When they arrived, Ray met them at the airport and told them they could stay with him and Jeannine in the children's bedroom. In the first few days Ray took them and the kids to the beach, introduced them to Pat and made them feel welcome. He took Robert down to the body shop where he worked. Together they made the arrangements for the christening.

Robert says Ray boasted to him about forcing the court to take his testimony in Miami: "He said it was a real party. He took them all over. He was frightened of going back to Quebec. He was also scared of being discovered in Florida."

Robert says Raymond never talked about who was after him or why, but it was clear he was nervous, worried that if the Quebec police could find him, others could.

While he and Robert were out running around, Claudette was stuck in the hot little house with Jeannine and the kids: "It was so hot in that house you couldn't sleep," she says. "I was there all day with Jeannine and she didn't talk. If she said one or two words all day, that would be it. She was in pain. She talked to the kids though. I think she was afraid of Raymond. As soon as he got in the door, he'd start a fight with her and then he'd walk out. He was looking for an excuse, I guess. He'd say, 'How are the kids?' And she'd talk about the children and he'd start arguing about what the kids were doing or had done. He didn't come home to sleep at night."

Claudette also remembers how tender Jeannine was with the children: "Jeannine was an angel with the kids. She didn't talk loud. She'd say try this. She'd never shout, she was patient, she'd sit with them and talk with them if they got in trouble. She never went out, not for groceries, nothing. I guess she was afraid so she didn't want to talk."

Four days after Robert and Claudette arrived, Martine was baptised at a nearby Catholic church. Pat had been invited as well and served as the *porteuse,* the person who carries the baby for the mother. Following the christening, Raymond suggested they spend the day at the beach. Claudette remembers that Raymond didn't want Jeannine to come along. In perhaps the only surviving photo of the outing, Ray, Pat, Claudette, Denis, Anne and Marc are sitting on beach chairs beneath a yellow canopy. They are surrounded by coolers and sparkling sand. The ocean is visible behind them. Anne, impish and then eight, squints at the camera, and Denis, a lanky eleven, sits behind her, looking doubtful. Pat is beside them, big-chested, tanned, a thin smile on a face that looks as if it has seen its share of pain and suffering. And beside her is Ray, big-bellied, brown, a banana in his hand, and little Marc looking up at his daddy.

The day after the baptism Ray announced he had business to attend to. He told Robert and Claudette that they would have to leave several days before they had planned, and he bought them first-class tickets for the flight back.

At the same time he told Jeannine that since there was no French school in Florida for the kids, she should return to Quebec and wait for him. He was heading to Louisiana, and as soon as he found a place where the kids could go to school in their own language, he would bring them down.

Denis was elated by the news. It seemed unlikely to Denis that his father would find a French school in Louisiana and so he dismissed from his mind the long-term plan and focused on the return to Hull. They would live with his grandparents, the Boissonneaults. They had a small place and Uncle Réginald was a bit odd, but Denis was eager. He could look up his friends, could go to school in French, and his dad wouldn't be around bugging him.

Robert and Claudette and Jeannine and the children returned to Ottawa on the same flight. Robert and Claudette were met by a relative. They noticed that Jeannine had been held up by the immigration authorities and that Jeannine's mother was there to meet her. They assumed the delay wasn't serious and didn't see the point in waiting so they left without saying goodbye. They never saw Jeannine again.

Chapter Six

Hull, Quebec, Summer, 1967

It was late when Jeannine and the children arrived in Ottawa. At the immigration desk Denis stood beside his mother as she explained that Martine had been born in Fort Lauderdale. Denis wondered why his mom was nervous. Through the open doors he caught a glimpse of his grandmother, Laurette Boissonneault, waiting. But there was a problem with Martine, and it seemed to take forever for his mother to straighten it out with the immigration people.

When they finally made it into the waiting area, his grandmother hugged him and the other kids. They climbed into a taxi, Denis in the front seat. During the half-hour ride across Ottawa to Hull, his attention drifted from the sights to the conversation going on in the back between his mother and grandmother. At one point he heard his grandmother say, "What is Raymond thinking of? Where are you going to stay?" Denis felt a sudden buzz of alarm. Maybe his grandmother didn't want them at her place. It had never occurred to him that she wouldn't. He couldn't think of any other place they could go. Maybe to the home of his Durand grandparent, but would his mother want to live there?

Denis's panic subsided when he saw the taxi pull up in front of his grandmother Boissonneault's house. At least, he remembers thinking, they could stay here tonight. He had forgotten, though, how small the house was. There were only two bedrooms upstairs, a toilet and sink but no bath, and a living-room and a kitchen downstairs. Inside, his grandfather and Uncle Réginald were waiting. His grandfather seemed older and a sore under his eye that Denis remembered seemed to be getting bigger. Réginald scared Anne and Marc.

His grandmother and his mother made beds with quilts on the floor in the living-room. Martine slept in a little basket near the stove. The rest of them slept together. Jeannine seemed exhausted. He thought she'd be happy to be back and staying with her family but she seemed tense.

They spent the whole summer there, sleeping in the living-room. Denis was content living in Hull in his mother's old neighbourhood. They had no visitors, never looked up any of their Durand relatives. One day Denis spotted an uncle of Raymond's entering a house across the street. When he told his mother, she ushered all the kids into the house. They sat in the front room while their mother peeked through the curtains. When Ray's uncle had departed, they were allowed to go out again. For some reason she didn't want anybody to know they were back. Another time Denis ran into a neighbour from Michaud Street. He chatted with the neighbour and told him they were back and living with the Boissonneaults. When he got home and told his mother, she was angry.

"You shouldn't have told them," she lectured. "Don't tell anybody we are here." Denis assumed his father was hiding out from someone, so he kept his mouth shut after that.

Denis liked his grandfather. He would stand by the kitchen table and roll the old man's cigarettes for him. His grandfather's affection for him drew him out of his melancholy moods. The old man was so calm and was silent as a mouse.

His mother warned Denis and the other kids not to bug Réginald. Denis found him easy to ignore. Anne and Marc, though, lived in terror of their uncle. They'd hear the floor-boards creaking when he walked around upstairs and thought it was creepy that he spent his days up there by himself. They both skittered behind their mother's skirts whenever Réginald came down.

It was hot that summer, and Denis was relieved that his father wasn't around crabbing at him. He felt free to run around till sundown, and he didn't always have to baby-sit the little ones. His grandfather would give him change for an ice-cream cone from time to time. He was happy, and he knew that, even if they couldn't stay with the Boissonneaults forever, this place, this neighbourhood, would always feel like home.

Jeannine lived for the daily mail. She'd check the mailbox two or three times a morning. She was broke and didn't like having to depend on her mother for money. It hurt her pride not to be able to help out with household expenses. Two or three times that summer, Denis remembers, there were letters from Raymond with money in them. And occasionally his father would call, always late at night. Denis would be in bed on the floor and hear his mother murmuring into the phone.

Denis wasn't sure that his mother knew where Raymond was living. The letters she wrote him at first had been sent to Florida. But by late summer she wasn't writing any more. There were only phone calls. Since it seemed she could reach him when she wanted to, maybe she had a number for him. Where was he living? Had he found the French school? Would they have to move that fall? Denis tried not to think about it, but as summer slid along he found himself worrying about it more and more.

From the moment of their arrival Denis knew there were tensions between his mother and her parents. She had never criticized Raymond to her parents. She defended him. She had married Raymond over her mother's objections, and now her pride precluded her from acknowledging that she had made a mistake. Not that there was much she could have done about it even if she had decided to end the marriage. She had four kids, and her parents couldn't possibly support her and the children. She was strapped financially. And if she did leave Raymond, it would be a scandal. Divorce was unthinkable. The Church considered it a sin, and it would have set the neighbours' tongues wagging. If only to protect her mother's reputation, Jeannine wouldn't consider such an option. Denis could hear, in his mind, his grandmother asking: What would everybody say?

Denis felt his mother's uneasiness. He sensed her struggling through every day while the unanswered question—If Raymond is such a success, why can't he take care of you?—weighed heavily on her. She looked tired and beaten. She was still in pain from Martine's birth and the tubal ligation and she was nursing the baby.

By late summer Denis felt the tension mounting within the house. None of the adults ever raised their voices; they were all polite to each other and respectful, but he sensed that, underneath, hard feelings were taking shape. One night at the dinner table at the end of the summer a quarrel exploded without warning.

"If he wasn't so selfish, he would have given us his room. Martine and I could have slept up there," Denis remembers Jeannine saying with hurt in her quavering voice.

Réginald was shocked. Denis knew Réginald had suffered because of their presence in the house. He had lived alone with his parents since Jeannine's marriage. During the day his parents went out to work and Réginald had the place to himself. He needed his privacy. Jeannine and the kids had turned his world upside-down.

Denis wasn't surprised when he heard his grandmother defend Réginald. "That's his room; he has a right to it; he needs his own place," he remembers her saying. It was as if she was defending both Réginald's needs and her refusal to accept that there was anything wrong with him. What really hurt Denis was not his grandmother's defence of Réginald's needs but her advice to her daughter: "Jeannine, you're married. Your place is with your husband."

Jeannine received the remark like a slap in the face. Denis knew she had toiled all summer under the weight of that unspoken thought. Anger flashed in her eyes. Just as she was rising from the table, tears began to flow.

Suddenly Hermas Boissonneault raised his voice: "He should have given her his room."

The room went silent. No one had ever seen the old man angry. Jeannine was the first to react. She pushed back her chair and strode out the door. It had been a brief quarrel but Denis could see it had stunned the family. The Boissonneaults had had to acknowledge the existence of feelings that were less than charitable. They'd lived by a code that prized family unity, love and respect for each other. Now they had permitted themselves to express anger towards each other and they all felt wounded. Jeannine felt hurt that her mother had sided with Réginald; Réginald was probably hurt by his father's criticism. In another family such an exchange might have been easily forgotten. For this family, the hurt lingered. Laurette Boissonneault was to regret for the rest of her life what she had said in a moment of anger.

Denis remembered they had finished their dinner in silence. After cleaning up, his grandmother had turned to him and told him, in a low voice, "Denis, go find your mother."

Denis remembers sprinting out into the muggy night. It was still light out, and he wandered up and down a half-dozen streets. It was dark before he spotted her, standing alone and motionless in front of the Cinéma de Paris. She was crying quietly when he walked up and took her hand.

"Denis, what are we going to do? Why is your dad dragging us all over?" she asked, while the tears continued to roll down her cheeks. He wanted to cry himself, couldn't stand seeing his mother so vulnerable, so close to the edge. Finally, though, she composed herself. She had allowed a lifetime of feelings to leak out and it had been cathartic.

"Look, Denis," she said. "Here's where I went to the movies when I was a little girl." She began talking about her childhood. She told him about memorable movies she had seen and then, taking him by the hand, led him through the neighbourhood. She pointed to playgrounds and houses of friends, and she talked about how happy she had been. They stopped and she bought him an ice-cream cone. Just him and his mom. He couldn't remember it ever having happened before, having his mother all to himself. She made him feel that she needed his advice and depended on his good judgment and help.

Finally, they turned home. As they entered the door, his grandmother beckoned. "Jeannine," she said, "it's all arranged. You will take Réginald's room."

"No, Mama," Jeannine had replied. "It's too late. We can't stay here." And that was that. No amount of pleading or apologizing would get Jeannine to change her mind. Secretly Denis had hoped that his mother would just forget it all and that they would go on living there, but he feared the worst.

And sure enough, only a few days later, he heard his mother talking on the phone with his father. "Raymond, we cannot stay here any longer." And then several days after that they were loading all their stuff into a taxi. It was midnight. His grandparents and Réginald helped them wedge everything into the cab. His grandmother kissed all the kids. She was crying. He heard his mother promise to write, and then they drove off into the night. It was a long ride. Denis kept asking where they were going, and his mother said Dorval airport in Montreal. But where are we flying to? "God only knows," she said.

At the airport, Denis helped with the luggage and kids and then followed his mother to the ticket counter. She was given tickets and assigned seats.

Then she turned to Denis. "Houston, Texas. That's where we are going. Texas."

She hadn't known, Denis thought. Dad just told her to go to the airport. He didn't even tell her where we were going to. Houston. Texas. Denis became excited. Cowboys. Horses. The old west. Then he wondered: are there French schools in Texas?

Chapter Seven

+—❀❀—+

Houston, Texas, Fall, 1967

Jeannine and her children flew into Houston's Hobby Airport in mid-afternoon. When they stepped off the plane, they were hit by a wave of hot, moist air. It was early September and summer wasn't yet over. Jeannine couldn't believe the heat and the vegetation. It was what she imagined the tropics would be like. It certainly wasn't what she expected of Texas.

Houston, then one of the most rapidly growing cities in the United States, lies just east of Galveston Bay, which empties into the Gulf of Mexico. Once a water-logged, low-lying patch of mosquito-infested salt marshes, creeks, bayous and sloughs, it has grown since its founding in 1863 to become home to one of the busiest ports in the country and to be considered its oil capital.

In the late 1960s Houston, whose population was then 1.1 million, was also known as an exceedingly violent city. By 1969 it had been cited as having one of the highest per capita murder rates in the world. Texans are wonderfully hospitable people who are justly proud of the state's reputation as the heart and soul of the southwest. But Houston is something else again. The city is a volatile mix of staggering oil wealth and chilling poverty, which engulfs entire inner city neighbourhoods. Most of the wealth is in the hands of whites, and most of the hardships that accompany poverty are borne by the city's large black and Mexican-American populations. The violence that was tearing at the city in 1967 when Jeannine and the children arrived and is still shredding the city today is about race and class. In 1967 the local jails were filled with poor, dark-skinned people, and the police force was manned by whites. In the newspapers, blacks were still called Negroes. In the streets, Mexican-Americans were spics.

For those who could afford it in Houston that year, a new Mustang cost $2,280, an electric washer $148 and a cotton Oxford shirt a mere $3.99. The starting salary for an engineer was $11,000. That summer crowds were lined up at the cinemas to see *Bonnie and Clyde* and Clint Eastwood in *The Good, the Bad, and the Ugly*.

At home, television offered "The Flying Nun" and "The Rat Patrol."

When Ray and Pat arrived in Houston they had settled in Bellaire—the name may have misled Ray into thinking that it was a Cajun district. In fact, it was an established, white, middle-class neighbourhood of bungalows and oak trees dripping Spanish moss fifteen minutes southwest of the downtown core. They had rented an apartment in a complex with a pool. Ray had almost immediately gotten a job in the paint shop of Sam Montgomery Oldsmobile. He was now going by the name Ray Holben. On some nights Pat worked with him sanding and detailing cars.

Before Jeannine's arrival Ray rented a furnished, three-bedroom bungalow on Beech Street, just a few blocks from the apartment he was sharing with Pat. The house had an attached garage, a large oak in the front yard and was just around the corner from Maud W. Gordon Elementary School. High above the school playground was a water tower with "Bellaire" written on its side in huge black letters.

Ray met Jeannine and the kids at the airport. On the drive to Bellaire, with Denis listening intently from the back seat, he told a whopper so audacious that it took his son's breath away.

"Jeannine," he said, smacking his forehead, "you'll never believe what happened. I was driving to Louisiana to find a French school for the kids and who do I run into on the highway but Pat and her husband. They were on their way to Houston to open a body shop, so I came down here with them and got a job in their new shop."

Denis couldn't tell whether his mother believed that story or not. He certainly didn't. He kept his mouth shut though. Inside, his guts were churning.

During the ride, while the kids gazed at the city zipping by, Ray also made a number of cutting remarks about Réginald. Jeannine had evidently told him of the quarrel, and Ray blamed Réginald for forcing them out of the house. He called him Big Dummy. And he made fun of Jeannine's father, who feared doctors and dentists and continued to cover with a Band-Aid the growth under his eye that had proven to be cancerous.

"Your father is so stupid he thinks he can stop the cancer with a Band-Aid," he told Jeannine with a sneer.

When they arrived at the bungalow on Beech Street, Jeannine and the children discovered that it was sparsely furnished but comfortable. The one real comfort was a rocking chair that Jeannine liked to sit in. One evening Anne jumped on the back of the chair and it flipped over with Jeannine still in it. Anne was horrified at what she had done, but Jeannine displayed her usual calm and didn't show any anger. "Please be careful, Anne," she said as she righted the chair. That simple remark stuck in Anne's memory. Years later, she remembered flipping over the chair and how, when her mother was upset she didn't shout, she cried. And when she cried she got a little dent in her chin and an otherwise invisible red birthmark on her forehead would surface.

They all liked the new neighbourhood. Jeannine made a playhouse in the backyard for the kids although it was mostly Anne who played in it. She put a little table and chairs inside and made it her home. The kids were shocked when they discovered there were no French schools and that they would have to go to school in English. Denis was eleven, going on twelve. His father just dropped him and Anne off at Maud W. Gordon school one day and told them to go on in. Denis was placed in grade five instead of grade six. He was humiliated but realized that he couldn't cope with grade six. His teacher devoted extra attention to him, however, and within a matter of weeks he was speaking English with a Texas drawl. Anne was put into grade three, and Marc remained at home with his mother and Martine.

Once again, Ray was rarely at home, day or night, and there was little money for extras. As soon as they had unpacked, Ray brought Pat by and she re-established her friendship with Jeannine. Once again she was introduced as Pat Anderson. Pat came by often and Jeannine valued her visits. She was lonely and knew no one else on the street. She spent her days at home, speaking only to the kids and to Pat when she came by. Ray had decided not to install a phone at the house so Jeannine felt doubly isolated. Her parents couldn't call her, and she had to drag the kids along whenever she wanted to call her folks from a pay phone.

Once Denis and Anne began speaking English, they became more autonomous. Denis joined the Boy Scouts and got to know some of the boys in the troop. Jeannine had to badger Ray for weeks to come up with the money for Denis's uniform and dues but he eventually did. Anne played by herself in the backyard. Like her mother, she was always in dresses or skirts. She pretended she was a mother herself. She worried about the feelings of others, was always thinking of others, and shared her treats. Like Denis, she found school hard.

Denis, Anne and Marc became fonder of Aunt Pat. She arrived one day with new bicycles for all of them and would occasionally take them out shopping. Anne remembers having fallen asleep one afternoon on the living room floor during one of Pat's visits. When she awoke, she found Pat had taken Denis and Marc out shopping and she cried inconsolably for hours. She was angry with her mother. Pat would occasionally take them to her apartment so they could swim in the pool, and the kids felt she was a genuine friend. Anne remembers Aunt Pat always had a little gift for them when she came over. "I loved her," she says.

The most distressing part of life in Bellaire for the kids was not their father's frequent absences but the fighting that occurred when he was home. The fights filled Denis, in particular, with dread. He felt some responsibility because the quarrels were often about the kids—not exclusively, but often enough to fill him with anxiety. He also heard his father trying to convince Jeannine to begin using a new family name, Holben. Denis couldn't understand why and neither could Jeannine. "Why?" she'd ask Ray. "That's not our name. Why should I use it?" She refused despite the fact that he had begun using it himself. Although the kids had been registered in school under their real names, everywhere else Ray introduced himself and his family as Mr and Mrs Ray Holben and kids.

The new bike gave Denis mobility, and he explored the neighbourhood on it. By accident one night he discovered his father's car at Pat's apartment, and after that, he saw it there often. He figured they were sleeping together again, and now he was certain that Aunt Pat didn't have a husband. It all fit. His father didn't work at a body shop owned by a Mr Anderson. He worked for Sam Montgomery Oldsmobile, a large, established dealership.

Seeing his dad's car at Aunt Pat's wasn't nearly as disturbing, though, as seeing the car at home. Denis's guts would knot up as soon as he rounded the corner onto Beech and see the car in the drive. He knew they would be fighting. It was becoming worse all the time.

One night, lying in bed, he had heard Jeannine shout, "Stop, Raymond, you're hurting me." He knew that his father had hit her and it terrified him.

But the fighting didn't occur just at night. One evening his parents quarrelled, and Jeannine stomped out the door. Denis jumped to his feet. Where was she going? His father put them all in the car and went after her. They found her walking down a street several blocks from home, sobbing. His father pulled alongside, opened the passenger door and, still coasting along, shouted at her to get in. She shook her head. He pleaded, and finally she relented and got in. The children were speechless with fear.

One night Jeannine called her parents. She had sent pictures of herself and the kids and the new house. She had written that everything was fine, but on the phone she sounded depressed.

According to Laurette's sister Berthe, who was told about the call, Jeannine asked what the weather was like at home.

"We've just had our first snowfall and everything is white and clean," Laurette answered. Jeannine answered questions about the kids and then asked to speak to her father. She asked him how he was feeling, said she missed home and hung up. The call worried her parents.

Around the same time the family gathered for dinner one night, and while they were eating, little Marc blurted out his discovery of the day.

"Mom, I saw Dad on top of Aunt Pat today."

Ray gave his son a sour look. "Marc, you don't say those things," he lectured. Jeannine stared at Ray but didn't say anything and the moment passed.

Now Christmas was approaching and it didn't look as though it was going to be a festive one. If Jeannine hadn't known before about her husband and Pat, she knew now. She didn't confide in anyone, but she did have a revealing talk with the only person she trusted, Denis.

One day shortly before Christmas, she told Denis that what she wanted more than anything else was a piano. She asked him to let his father know, to tell him that that was the only gift she was keen to have for Christmas. Her request suggests she had reconciled herself to her situation, that she was willing to continue their life while he maintained a mistress. She hadn't banished Pat from the house; on the contrary, they continued to see each other. Maybe Jeannine considered it a relief that Ray had someone else willing to satisfy his sexual appetites. It certainly wasn't in her nature to confront Pat and there is no evidence that she ever did. As usual, Jeannine was probably more concerned about the children than herself. Perhaps she believed that if Ray continued to support them, she and the children would be left to themselves. And maybe in her mind that was the bargain. If she had the kids, a piano and money to live on, he could do as he wished, spend every night of the week at Pat's if he felt like it. As far as she was concerned, there really wasn't any other option. She had no way of moving back to Canada. She was either too proud to ask her parents for help or convinced they couldn't raise the money anyway. And even if they did move back, where would they go? She hadn't worked since Denis's birth, and she still had a baby at her breast. Everything must have seemed well beyond her control. She was living illegally in the United States. Therefore, even if she had spoken English well enough to seek help locally, where could she have gone for help? A more worldly woman might have considered turning herself in to the immigration authorities and asking to be deported. But Jeannine had neither the social skills nor the knowledge of how things worked in the big city to allow her to consider, much less pursue, such a solution. And so, resigned to her fate, she began to prepare for the holidays. One of her first acts was to invite her husband's lover over for dinner on Christmas Day.

Jeannine's request for a piano must have been revealing for Ray. Pat wasn't working, so clearly Ray was supporting two households on his wages. Naturally, he was chasing all the angles. Pat said later that he was bouncing cheques at the time. Still, he must have resented having to bear the financial burden of two places. The fact that Jeannine wanted a piano must have made it clear to Ray that she wasn't planning to leave. So what were his plans? And why did he keep insisting that Jeannine begin using the name Holben?

On Christmas morning Jeannine discovered that her wish for a piano had come true, sort of. The gift was not from her husband; it was from Pat, and it wasn't a piano but a toy electric organ that could be held in the lap. Denis saw her disappointment. But Anne was delighted. She had been given a tea set for Christmas, which she promptly set up on her table in the playhouse. But she was even more enthralled by the organ. Her mother taught her how to turn it on and began to teach her how to play.

Pat came over in the afternoon of Christmas Day. Although she didn't have kids and wasn't married, her circumstances were remarkably similar to Jeannine's. She, too, was living in an unfamiliar city. She had no friends in Houston, no job, no legal status in the country. Both women were entirely dependent on Ray, who they knew was a pathological liar, philanderer and thief. It's no wonder that the two women felt an affinity for each other and that Pat often bought the children gifts and Jeannine her Christmas present.

Given Jeannine's nature it is not likely that they ever sat down and had a frank discussion of their predicaments. Jeannine would never have initiated such an exchange, and Pat had no interest in doing so. Whatever degree of sympathy and affection Pat felt for Jeannine, it seems insignificant compared to the hard-hearted deceit she practised every time she walked in the front door of the house on Beech Street. She continued to dupe Jeannine, a woman whose affection she had earned. To do so, either Pat lived with guilt for what she was doing, or she rationalized it, justifying her behaviour to herself by holding the victim of her lies in contempt.

The contempt is what Denis saw. He remembers his mother basting the turkey in the kitchen that Christmas Day while his father and Pat winked slyly at each other in the front room. Denis was the only one who noticed. The three other kids had a happy Christmas. The troubles of the adults around them had not yet intruded on their lives.

Five days after Christmas, Jeannine baked a cake for Raymond and Denis's birthdays. Raymond was turning thirty-two, Denis twelve on December 30, 1967. They waited all afternoon for Raymond, then finally, in the early evening, Jeannine gave up. They cut the cake and Denis blew out his candles. It wasn't his happiest birthday. His mother was upset. His father hadn't even phoned to say he wasn't coming home.

Between Christmas and New Year's Day Jeannine managed to call home six times. Réginald remembers only that she made the calls. He has no recollection of plans Jeannine might have been making, any emergencies or distress signals. Just that she called and talked to the family. Looking back now, the calls seem strangely suggestive. What was she trying to say that drove her to phone home so often? Was she trying to repair damage that had been done to fragile family feelings by the quarrel? Was she just lonely or so sickened by the deceit in her own home that she had to talk to someone, even someone in whom she couldn't bring herself to confide? Was she opening the possibility of her return somehow? Jeannine wasn't given to small talk. There was a compelling reason for those calls. Their frequency suggests she was desperate. But for what? Perhaps she herself couldn't articulate what she needed or feared. She loved her mother but her mother's rigid sense of propriety had always stood between them. Maybe those calls were Jeannine's attempts to bring herself finally to tell her mother that the marriage to Raymond wasn't working, that he was just plain no good. If that is the case, she didn't succeed. Her mother said later that she had no idea how bad relations between Jeannine and Raymond had become.

In the end, no one will ever know what Jeannine tried to say in those phone conversations. After that last call on New Year's Day, neither her parents nor her brother ever heard from her again.

Part Two

Years of Doubt, 1968–1991

There is confusion worse than death,
Trouble on trouble, pain on pain

Alfred, Lord Tennyson,
"Song of the Lotos-Eaters"

Chapter Eight

Houston, Texas, 1968

One morning about a month after Christmas, Denis woke and stumbled into the kitchen for breakfast. He found Aunt Pat sitting at the kitchen table with a cup of coffee.

"Where's Mom?" he asked, bewildered.

"Your dad took her to the airport last night. Her mother's sick. She's gone back to Canada to take care of her."

"How long will she be gone?"

"Your dad said about two weeks."

Since his father wasn't home, Denis assumed he had gone to work. He was more annoyed than disturbed by his mother's sudden departure. She hadn't even said goodbye. He liked Aunt Pat but he was uneasy about her moving in again. And he assumed she would be moving in. Martine was only six months old and would need a full-time baby-sitter. Denis was surprised his mother hadn't at least taken Martine with her, but he knew that Aunt Pat adored the baby and would take good care of her. Pat held Martine whenever she was at the house. She cuddled her and cooed over her blonde curls and made her laugh. Denis thought that Aunt Pat had convinced his mother to leave the baby with her.

Denis pondered all this over breakfast. It was a Saturday so there was no school. When Anne awoke, she, too, asked about her mother, and Pat explained again. Anne shrugged it off and went out to play. Aunt Pat had promised to take them swimming in the pool at her apartment. They left later in the morning and had lunch at Aunt Pat's and swam. Afterwards, Denis went out by himself. He had his bike, and for some reason he can no longer remember he ended up at his house. He was inside in the hallway walking towards the door—he thinks he must have been leaving—when suddenly the door opened, and his father struggled in with two suitcases, one of which was the checked foldover that his mother had bought before the move to Fort Lauderdale.

"Hi dad. Is mom gone?"

"Yeah, your grandma's sick."

"How long's she going to be gone?" Denis asked over his shoulder as he headed out the door.

"Maybe two weeks."

Ray joined the family later that afternoon at Pat's apartment, and that evening they all returned to the house. Pat slept with Ray that night, and the next day they announced that they were all going to stay in an apartment in Pat's building. The move was hasty. Denis remembers seeing Pat stuffing all his mother's clothes into large garbage bags. Then Pat moved her stuff from her apartment, which only had one bedroom, into the new apartment, which had two. Ray told the kids that the move was temporary, that'd he'd found a new house.

A week later they moved to the new house on Holly Street. It was sixteen blocks south of their place on Beech. It was another bungalow, slightly larger than the first place. He told them they would be going to Paul W. Horne Elementary School, whose playground was visible through the oaks across the street. He showed them the public swimming pool two blocks from the house, a pool with three diving boards. He promised to buy a pool for the backyard of their new house and said the boys would have one bedroom and the girls another.

When the children had made their first move in the summer of 1966, they had been traumatized. Since then they'd lived in Ottawa, Fort Lauderdale, Hull and now in Houston. They'd become accustomed to the constant packing and unpacking. Moving three times in the first few months they were in Houston was a bit more than they were used to but they didn't question it. And once they'd unpacked on Holly Street, they sensed they were going to be there long enough to get to know the neighbourhood.

Denis worried about his mother but he hadn't panicked. At the end of two weeks he had asked his father if his mother was coming back that day, and Ray said she had been delayed because Grandma Boissonneault was still ill. At four weeks Denis got the same response. Again he was more annoyed than angry.

What irked him more was the new routine that had been established in the house. He treated it as temporary but sensed that Pat didn't. She was strict about meals, forbade any snacking in between and didn't permit the children to rummage through the fridge for something to eat when they were hungry. She scolded

Denis for the amount of sugar he used on his cereal, and when he ignored her, she told his father. Denis began to dislike Pat for ratting on him.

One evening as he was passing the bedroom, he saw Pat take the electric gizmo his mother used for removing facial hair and throw it in a trash bag. If Mom finds out, Pat's gonna catch it, he thought.

Denis also noted that his father was around more than ever and that he and Pat were drinking heavily. Denis had only seen his father drunk once before, years ago in Gatineau, and Anne had never seen her father stumbling drunk. Now though it seemed that they were emptying a bottle or two of whisky every night. The more they drank, the more surly and grouchy they became. Denis knew enough to stay out of his father's way when he was in an ugly mood but he didn't see why he should tiptoe around Pat when she was hung-over. She was a temporary resident and she'd better not forget that, he thought.

Pat evidently viewed things differently, however, and soon the epicentre of family conflict was the relationship between Pat and Denis. She'd nag, he'd talk back to her, and she'd explode. She expected kids to do what they were told and to do it in silence. She'd once heard Ray call Denis a big dummy and now she began calling him that as well. Denis took that as a declaration of war. When Mom comes back, he thought, that bitch will never be allowed in this house again.

Gilbert Pavliska walked into the Fort Bend County sheriff's office at 5:45 P.M. on February 11, 1968. He'd found a body. He thought. Deputy Sheriff Robert Madeira questioned Pavliska, and then he and the department's identification expert, Buster Dennis, ushered him into a patrol car and they set off, following Pavliska's directions. He steered them onto a dirt road that led into a remote area known as the Barker Reservoir. When torrential rains hit low-lying Houston, a network of concrete-lined bayous funnels the runoff into the Barker Reservoir, which is simply rolling, grassy parkland several miles square surrounded by dikes. For most of the year the interior of the reservoir is dry. It's flat and windswept, covered with tall grass, shrubs and short bush.

When they arrived at the scene, Madeira and Dennis left Pavliska standing on the road and, in the gathering darkness, walked over a ditch and forty-three feet into the underbrush. There, in an unsupervised dump surrounded by brush, an old fridge and a cast-off wringer washer, they found a body neatly wrapped in a bluish-grey bedspread. A finger-thick cotton rope had been carefully wound around the shoulders, the waist and the knees. Madeira and Dennis confirmed only that it was a body, then they retreated from the bitter cold to the warmth of their patrol car. Both officers had realized that they were now in Harris County, just outside the limits of their own jurisdiction. Madeira radioed his office to call in the Harris County sheriff's department, the thirteenth largest police force in the United States. It administers the county jails and polices a huge area encircling metropolitan Houston.

The Harris County sheriff's office records show the call came in at 6:09 P.M., and several units were dispatched. Night had fallen. At the wheel of one of the units that responded to the call was Detective Johnny Klevenhagen, who was working on a number of homicides of juveniles whose decomposing corpses had been found in fields within the county. By the time Klevenhagen arrived, five other officers, plus Madeira and Dennis, were on site. Ted Walsh, of the medical examiner's office, was en route. Madeira and Dennis departed soon after, leaving Pavliska with the Harris County officers.

The officers began a detailed examination of the scene and body, which appeared to be that of a white female with brown hair. Photos were taken of the body and the surrounding area.

The body was lying on its right side in a slight foetal crouch. A small, white towel was found under the head. Decomposition had set in, suggesting the body had been there for some time. The investigating officers later noted in their report that "Portions of the upper left leg appeared to have been eaten away by varmints." They searched for a weapon but found nothing that seemed likely.

Once the search was complete, attendants with the Belfort Ambulance Service put the corpse in a body bag and drove to the medical examiner's morgue in downtown Houston.

Klevenhagen asked Pavliska to get into his patrol car, and they headed downtown as well. In the headquarters of the homicide division of the Harris County sheriff's department, a detective took Pavliska's statement. According to Klevenhagen, the investigator on duty had doubts: why did a guy drive fifteen miles to take his

kid target shooting with a BB gun? Why not do it in the backyard?
No kid in Texas would have waited for his father to take him to the
countryside to shoot a BB gun. Most kids would have grabbed the
gun, stuck a target on the garage wall and fired away. We weren't
talking about a shotgun here or even a .22. Pavliska was asked to
explain.

"Our houses are real close together. The neighbours don't care
for no shooting," Pavliska says he told the sceptical police. "I work
for the highway department and I take a short cut through the reservoir. That's why I know that road's there. I'm a graderman."

The investigator wondered if Pavliska himself had been taking a
load of trash out to what was an illegal dump and simply didn't
want to say. Maybe he was just scrounging. Whatever. Convinced
that Pavliska was telling him everything he needed to know, the
investigator allowed the graderman to return home. Pavliska had
been up most of the night, and it was almost dawn when he walked
in his front door. His worried family had waited up for him.

At 9 A.M. next morning, the corpse, which had been given identification number 68-500, was wheeled into a hallway of the medical
examiner's morgue in the basement of the Ben Taub Hospital. It
was Monday, and there was a queue of bodies on stretchers in the
hallway waiting for probing by the staff pathologists. The tag
number on the body found by Pavliska indicated that this was the
five hundredth corpse that had entered the medical examiner's
morgue in the first six weeks of 1968.

The autopsy was performed by the associate medical examiner,
Dr Robert Bucklin, who was then conducting seventy-five to
eighty autopsies a month. Speaking into a microphone situated
above the partially decomposed body, Bucklin noted that the body
was clothed in a pair of white panties, a white half slip, black bra,
green skirt and yellow and green striped sweater/blouse. He
removed a wedding band from the ring finger on the left hand. He
observed "defects" on the head and left cheek, lip, right arm, fore-
arm, hip and thigh where "the body had been devoured by animals." The face was swollen, discoloured, the eyes protruding. The
person might still be recognizable by a loved one but it would be
difficult to be certain.

Bucklin noted the presence of full upper and lower dentures with
no identifying inscriptions on the dentures, and reported the body

weighed 144 pounds and was 67 inches in height. He said the eyes "appeared brown" and that the hair was dark brown, six inches in length. He discovered and described a "healed three-inch scar below the umbilicus."

Bucklin then cut the corpse open and examined and weighed all the organs. He noticed nothing out of the ordinary. There was no indication of disease or deformation. He reported the presence of food fragments in the esophagus, some food material in the stomach. He took samples and wrote out a request for toxicological tests to be conducted on the samples for the presence of alcohol, barbiturates and narcotics. (The test results showed no trace of narcotics or barbiturates in the blood of the dead woman but did confirm the presence of alcohol, which forms in the body during decomposition.)

Bucklin examined the uterus, ovaries and oviducts and noted signs that the woman had borne children. And then, in one of his concluding observations, he noted that the "ovaries and oviducts were normal." His examination had been thorough and complete and professional despite the condition of the corpse. Decomposed corpses are always a challenge, and this one was no less so. Bucklin had tried to be as accurate as possible, confining himself to descriptive precision. He had noted the presence of "a healed three-inch scar below the umbilicus" but saw nothing inside that explained it. If it was a surgical scar, what had the operation been for? Had he searched for an explanation or had he simply ticked off a routine checklist of things to be done? Whatever the case, when he had completed the autopsy, the scar remained unexplained, and he had made an unequivocal note on the condition of the oviducts. He saw no sign that the woman whose body he had just examined had ever had a tubal ligation.

An examination of the bones revealed that ribs one through six on the left side had been fractured in both the front and back. In addition, Bucklin described a two-inch depressed fracture on the top of the skull, which had split open the entire brain cavity.

When he had completed the autopsy, Bucklin and his boss, Dr Joseph Jachimczyk, the Harris County chief medical examiner, concluded the report with a legal summary statement on the cause of death. "It is our opinion that the decedent, UNKNOWN, came to her death as a result of a skull fracture and subdural haematoma, due to blunt trauma to the head, homicide."

Tuesday, the day after the autopsy, both Houston dailies carried follow-up stories on the body in the dump. The stories were short and placed deep inside the papers. With the front pages that week occupied with news of the Tet offensive in Vietnam and a bizarre tale about a quarrel over three cents' worth of gas that had left one man dead and two others, one of them a policeman, badly injured, an unidentified body wasn't big news. She was white and in her thirties so the story had potential. But no one had reported her missing and she had full dentures. She didn't sound like a bank president's wife.

The *Post* ran its story next to the television listings with the headline: "Body in Dump May Be Victim of Bad Beating." Quoting Bucklin, the paper said the woman had been dead for about ten days. He described her as white, thirty-five to forty years old, five feet, seven inches tall, 144 pounds with brown hair and wearing a size 18 skirt. He said she was not wearing shoes or socks and had a wedding ring with alternating sections of white and yellow gold.

The *Chronicle*'s story was even briefer. "Dead Woman Had Skull Fracture," read its headline, which was stacked on the obituary page beneath the daily reports on the weather and the tides. The *Chronicle* said the woman's skull had probably been fractured by a blow from "a blunt instrument." What the police and medical examiner's officer were saying, with that familiar phrase, is that the weapon could have been anything from a rock to a chair leg.

One morning six weeks after Jeannine's departure Denis was playing ball with Anne in the driveway. It was a Saturday, and Ray and Pat had taken the baby with them to buy groceries. Anne was on the lawn and Denis was near the curb. They still spoke to each other in French. Anne was studying his face and suddenly told him:"You know, Denis, Mom is not coming back."

Denis froze. "What?" he cried.

"Promise not to tell, OK? Pat told me Mom is not coming back. She said Mom doesn't love us."

Tears poured down his cheeks. "That's not true, Anne. It's not true," he told her, slumping to the ground, sobbing. He couldn't stop crying, couldn't make Anne believe that it couldn't possibly be true. Their mother loved them; it was a betrayal even to think otherwise.

Finally he picked himself up, angry at Anne for believing what Pat had told her, angry at Pat for saying it, angry at his father for bringing into their house a woman who wished to push his mother out. He didn't for a moment believe that Pat had told the truth. He was no longer sure what was going on, but no one would ever convince him that his mother didn't love him. He'd ask his father. He'd force him to tell what was going on.

That afternoon all the kids went out for a ride with their father. Pat remained at home. The little ones were in the front, and Denis was in the back seat on the passenger's side. They were passing the new Astrodome when he finally worked up the courage to ask.

"Dad, when's Mom coming back? Pat says she's not. Why did she say that?"

Inexplicably, Denis's questions provoked his father. "Shut the fuck up about your mother," he screamed while swinging his powerful right fist, his working hand, at Denis in the back seat. "She's not coming back. Pat's your mom. You call her mom from now on. She's taking care of you and she's your mother."

Raymond's fist missed, but Denis cried so hard he could barely see. He couldn't stop, couldn't restrain himself from accusing his dad of lying. The other kids huddled in the corners for safety, the car swerved as Ray glanced behind to connect once, just once, with his fist on his goddamned kid's head. Then, suddenly, Ray stopped. Denis sat in the back and cried quietly. Ray drove and cursed him for a bit and then gave up. He threatened to beat him, but even that wasn't enough to stop Denis from crying. So he ignored him. "Let the cry-baby cry," he said with a sneer.

Mom wasn't coming back. Denis felt the bottom had dropped out of his life. The day after the fight with his father the whole family drove to the beach at Galveston for the day. It was cool. Pat, Ray and the baby sat at one table on the beach and made Marc, Anne and Denis sit at another twenty feet off. Ray got a barbecue going and grilled chicken parts for the kids. They had to walk over and get them and then stay out of Ray's range. They spent the whole afternoon there, huddled against the cold. Denis later thought of it as the saddest day of his life. He was miserable and couldn't stop thinking about his mother. Where had she gone, and why?

Over the next few weeks he came to the only conclusion that made any sense. His father and mother had fought. She'd gone back to Hull to get away from him for a couple of weeks. And as soon as she'd left, Ray had moved so she wouldn't be able to find them and he could live with Pat. He imagined his mother returning to Houston to the empty house on Beech. They were only sixteen blocks away but she'd never find them. From that point on, Denis snuck back to the old house whenever he could. He'd pedal over and sit on his bicycle at the corner and look for any sign that his mother had returned. He couldn't bring himself to knock on the door and ask the people who lived there if they had seen her. He was scared his father or Pat would find out. And, anyway, he wasn't sure that she had returned. He wanted to believe it but he just didn't know. He was as terrified of that possibility—the possibility that his mother had left and wasn't coming back—as he was of his father and Pat. What he really wanted, what he imagined, was that he'd be sitting there on his bike one day and his mother would come walking up the street and he'd shout, "Mom," and she'd rush over and hug him as she used to. That scenario became a fantasy that he retreated into whenever he was in trouble with Pat or his father.

At home the new regime became law, and Pat became mom to all the kids but Denis. Pat would rise in the morning and begin drinking before noon. Whisky. She'd be pickled by the time the kids came home from school. She'd grudgingly whip up some food for them—invariably Kraft dinners—and then send the kids off to bed at 8 P.M. She and Ray would sit up and drink, and sometime late in the evening, they'd grill a couple of steaks and have their dinner.

Pat, the children quickly discovered, was mean as spit. They had to brush their teeth exactly as she told them or take a slap to the back of the head. While eating, one hand was to remain on the lap and God forbid if they ever put a stray elbow on the table. They couldn't drink anything, not even water or milk, during their meals. Only when they had cleaned everything from their plates could they ask for a glass of milk. The boys were not welcome in the house until Ray came home from work. Denis and Marc would come home from school, drop their school stuff off and be marched out the front door. They spent many afternoons standing across the street waiting for permission to re-enter their own house. On weekends, Denis, Anne and Marc would be given a sandwich each in the morning and sent out to the park for the day. They'd be alone all day. It was too cold for other kids to be in the park. They became closer during those first weeks at the house on Holly Street, real friends.

When they were home, they did all the chores. Denis was responsible for the lawn and the trash. He washed the dishes and Anne and Marc dried. Pat, it turned out, was neurotic about dirt. Anne was made to wash the floors and dust almost daily. If any of the kids broke any of the rules, Pat would strike out. She slapped them hard. At first she singled out Denis and went after him for the most insignificant of reasons. Later she took her anger out on Anne and Marc as well.

Anne felt as if she was "in hell, pure hell." She lived in terror of Pat. She couldn't figure out why Pat had suddenly started hating her but she believed that the woman she now called mom did hate her. She thought it might have been something she had done but couldn't figure out what. She became timid and compliant, doing exactly what she was told without complaint. At night she'd huddle in the corner of her bed, shaking. She couldn't stop shaking. She'd pray for her real mom to come back. She was too frightened to say anything to her father, to ask him about her mother. He never beat her, but she felt that he was the one in control.

After Pat told Anne that her mother didn't love her and wasn't coming back, Anne felt responsible for what had happened. It was something she had done. At first she couldn't figure out what it was. Then she remembered the time she had flipped over the rocking chair with her mother in it. Her mother hadn't shown any anger but she had probably been furious. And she remembered how angry she had been with her mother when she had wakened from a nap and found Pat had taken the boys shopping without her. At first she was unsure of the connections between those incidents and her mother's disappearance but time made her certain. She had driven her mother out. She was a brat and her mother had finally just left her. She never told anyone that it was all her fault, but she thought that the others suspected the truth. There were days when she felt so much anguish inside that she wanted to lie down and never wake up again.

Anne had noticed, too, what had happened to Marc. He had been a normal kid, happy and talkative. Now he and Denis were inseparable but Marc had become a cringing, timorous little thing who couldn't look anybody in the eye. At dinner he'd sit with his head down, and he'd slink away as soon as he was finished. She felt sorry for him, sorry because he was so unhappy and sorry for Denis because he was often in tears.

The baby, Martine, was Pat's pet. Six months old when Jeannine had departed, Martine became Pat's baby. Pat indulged her and made sure that Anne attended to the baby's needs. Pat wasn't keen on changing diapers so Anne did most of the feeding and changing. Anne was also the one obliged to take Martine out for walks. But when visitors were over, Pat clucked over the baby like a proud mother, telling everyone that Martine's blonde curls were from her side of the family.

When Officer L.E. Shipley arrived for his shift that Monday morning, February 12, 1968, at the Harris County sheriff's office, he discovered he had been assigned to a new case. Lieutenant Joe Thorp had been on the scene the night before when the body was found in the dump, and he left a note requesting Shipley to join Deputy Eddie Knowles at the morgue for the autopsy at 9 A.M. Knowles was to take possession of the clothing, towel, bedspread, dentures and ring and to get fingerprints from the body. Knowles also took thirteen colour photos of the corpse, including several of the face that would be used for identification purposes.

Shipley concentrated on making careful notes of anything he thought he'd need later in the investigation. He filed his report at 11:40 that morning, as soon as he had returned from the morgue. Shipley was observant and methodical. He noted that the body had been covered with a chenille bedspread and that the rope around the body had been knotted under the left armpit. A second rope had been knotted behind the knees and both ropes had been tied together.

Shipley's notes and the photos show that whoever tied those ropes had taken his or her time. They had to have rolled the body into the bedspread and lifted it several times to wind the rope around it. She was a heavy woman; somebody had exerted him or herself.

The wound to the head, Shipley noted, had probably been made with a flat, blunt instrument. Only one blow. Were the six ribs that had been broken in back and in front fractured after the blow to the head? It wasn't possible to say. Bucklin informed Shipley that it would have taken considerable force to have broken the ribs in back and front.

The morgue photos suggest that the blow that killed the woman came from the front. The wound was at the top of the head, just above the forehead on the left side. It appeared that her assailant had been facing her and had been right-handed. Either that or she'd been on the ground and the killer had swung the weapon downward. Either the blow had been delivered with great power, or the weapon used had been heavy; the wound showed that the weapon had torn the scalp and had left a hole in the skull about the size and width of the small finger on a man's hand. The blow had also caused fractures that radiated from the hole itself.

Although Bucklin had described the woman's hair as dark brown, Shipley, in his report, described it as reddish brown. He concluded his reporting by noting that Knowles had taken the white cotton face towel that had been found underneath the woman's head. He stated that he would contact the Houston police homicide department with a description of the woman.

While Shipley was observing Bucklin at work, officers J. Conley and R. L. Foudray, who had also been on the site the night before, had returned to the scene for a more detailed search in broad daylight. Thorp had asked them to look for envelopes or other trash that might be traced to the person who had dumped the body. They turned up three envelopes with names and bagged them as evidence. One was addressed to a Mrs P.D. Bevis and bore a Bellaire address, a second had the name Debbie Hooker on it and a date—7-10-67—but no address and the third was for Christine Gardner, Tax Assessor and Collector, Big Lake.

While they were searching the area, a man who gave his name as Joe George pulled up. They questioned him, and he told them that he drove through the area every morning to check on his cattle in an adjoining field. He told them that he had seen a late model blue Chevrolet parked just past the dump on the Clodine-Barker Road the Thursday before at about 3 P.M. He said he thought he had seen a woman in the car along with a man but he wasn't sure. Conley

and Foudray also talked to Ruby Seymour, the maintenance foreman of the Addicks-Barker dam, who also showed up while they
were searching. Seymour told them he passed the site twice a week
and that he would have seen the body had it been there the last time
he had gone through. He told them he hadn't noticed an ice box
that had been near the body the last time he went by. He couldn't
remember exactly the day he had last gone through but believed it
was the latter part of the previous week.

That afternoon Bucklin called Shipley and told him he was certain that the blow to the head had been the cause of death. The two
men then discussed the operation scar that they had noted below
the navel. Bucklin said he couldn't figure it because, as Shipley
noted in a report he filed at 2:12 P.M., "the deceased did have all her
organs."

The last thing Shipley did that day was to track down Knowles
and examine more closely the clothes the woman had been wearing. He made notes as he looked over the garments, but he didn't
find much. He was looking for a laundry tag, but there weren't any.
He noted that the bra was made by Vogue and was size 38, and that
the skirt and blouse were both size 18. Neither, he said, had brand
names on them.

The following afternoon Shipley was given a report by
Lieutenant D. Brock, which appeared, at first glance, to have
resolved the identity of the dead woman. On the day before,
Shipley had had his department send out a description of the
deceased to the FBI, the Texas Rangers and all other police departments in Texas. Early that morning Brock had taken a call from
Detective Cantrell of the police department in Grand Prairie, Texas.
Cantrell said he was searching for a missing woman named Retha
Nell Gilbert, forty-four years old, who was last seen with her husband John Gilbert, a twenty-five-year-old white male. Gilbert had
returned to town alone on February 9 and was promptly arrested
for drunkenness, disturbing the peace and resisting arrest. He had
apparently "lost his mind" and had been committed to an institution in Terrell, Texas. Cantrell had talked to Gilbert's mother, who
said her daughter-in-law wore a wedding band very much like the
one the woman in the dump had been wearing. Cantrell also
reported that Retha had been wearing a knit green skirt the last
time she was seen and that she had false teeth, uppers and lowers.

Shipley, who had now been joined on the case by his partner, J.R. Hutchison, called Cantrell and learned that Retha Gilbert had left her husband in early January and spent two weeks at the YMCA in Dallas. She had returned to him on February 4 and they had gone out for a picnic. That night they had gotten into a nasty quarrel and she hadn't been seen since. Gilbert had been arrested four days later and transferred to the Mental Validation Ward in Dallas. The dates made it seem unlikely that the woman in the dump was Retha Gilbert—she had disappeared February 4, while Bucklin had estimated that the body had been there for ten days prior to its discovery on the eleventh. Nonetheless, Shipley and Hutchison played out the lead. They contacted the Dallas police who sent a couple of uniformed officers to talk to a former neighbour of Retha Gilbert's. The neighbour described Retha as five feet, four inches tall, 110 pounds, size 34 bust.

In the meantime, Shipley fielded a call from a Clara Wilson who said the dead woman might be her niece, Jean Lieb, who was thirty-one years old and white. Wilson was taken to the morgue and shown the corpse but she said she wasn't certain it was her niece. She left assuring the investigators that she'd track down her niece's dentist and call them back. She did call later that afternoon and said it had all been a mistake. The police report noted that Wilson said while she was making her way home from the morgue "she had located her missing niece working at a Shamrock Service Station on Almeda Road."

At 5:30 that afternoon, Shipley and Hutchison concluded that the corpse found in the dump was not that of Retha Gilbert. They had talked again to the Dallas police who had interviewed Retha's minister. He described her as a 105-pound woman with dirty blonde hair. The Dallas police had also learned that Retha had phoned her attorney on February 6 and had told him that she was headed for Massachusetts.

The next morning Shipley and Hutchison found themselves without fresh leads. They decided to go back over what they had. They obtained the dead woman's effects and once again conducted a detailed examination of them. The blouse, they discovered, did have a tag in it. It had been manufactured by Gia Knits of New York City. And in the skirt they turned up a manufacturer's label that showed it was a product of White Stag Industries of Edmonton, Canada.

Shipley knew that on a recent murder case Klevenhagen had tracked down some clothing through a manufacturer. He asked Klevenhagen for contacts, and Klevenhagen passed on to him the names of several buyers he knew in local department stores. The buyers told them neither Gia Knits nor White Stag was sold locally.

Shipley called Gia Knits in New York and got a Mr D. Okum on the line. Okum explained that his company distributed its merchandise in the northern part of the United States and in Canada.

Meanwhile, Hutchison paid a visit to Maurice Levit of Levit's Jewellers who examined the ring they had found on the body. Levit told Hutchison it was maybe twenty-five to thirty years old and that there was no way of positively identifying it from any markings made by a jeweller.

Now, because of the tags in the clothing, they figured there was some sort of Canadian angle. But what? The FBI and the Texas Rangers had reported back that the woman's prints didn't match anything they had on file. Maybe she was Canadian? They prepared a complete file—the offence report, all the photos, the prints and the notation about the White Stag label—and mailed it, special delivery, to the director of criminal investigations, RCMP, Ottawa.

Chapter Nine

Big Thicket, Texas, 1968

Anne coped with the loss of her mother by being helpful at home and at school. She thought she wasn't a good person and so she worked at becoming one. She habitually thought of others first; she was an earnest if not brilliant student, and she was quick to spot someone else's hurt feelings. Privately she felt as if someone had drained the vital fluids from her life.

More than anything else she just wanted to be loved, to be hugged by someone who loved her. Pat never held her and neither did her father. The kids had all grown closer since Jeannine's departure, but Pat constantly conspired against them, pitting Anne against Denis and Marc. Pat began to keep Anne in the house with her, telling her, "Don't go with that big dummy brother of yours." At first, Anne read this as a sign of affection. Since it made her feel that she was wanted, she responded with loyalty to Pat. She was the first to begin calling her mom. But Pat didn't answer Anne's loyalty with warmth. She was a sharp-tongued drunk who cursed everyone, even, Anne noticed, Raymond. When he would stay out late, Pat would call him a bastard to his face the next day. Pat suspected him of seeing other women, and her suspicions made her wild with jealousy.

And so after a brief romance with her new mom, Anne devoted herself to the boys. Denis and Marc didn't always want her around and they weren't very considerate of her feelings but they loved her, she knew that. And her father too. He didn't often pay attention to her but he was her dad. She had always been his favourite. He often told her she looked like one of his sisters. As for the baby, Anne as well as Denis and Marc began to resent the way in which Ray and Pat fawned over her. It was as if she was the only kid who mattered.

Slowly life took on a new shape. The gaping hole that had been left by Jeannine's departure repaired itself until there was but one tiny aperture left. It was almost unnoticeable. Occasionally, though, Anne would be out somewhere and she'd hear a few notes of a piece of music that her mother had played and she'd be paralysed. That tiny aperture would open up and all the memories would come flooding back. She'd remember sitting on her mother's lap, feeling her warmth and her smell and the strength of her hands. She wouldn't cry though, wouldn't let herself. Denis cried all the time. But not Anne. Nobody could hurt her as much as she had been hurt by her mother's departure.

Unlike Anne, Denis couldn't suppress his feelings and his memories. Jeannine had been his friend as well as his mother. She'd discussed things with him, solicited his opinion, made decisions with him. She'd also protected him from his father. He didn't for a moment believe that she had just left or that she didn't love him and the other kids. He knew that his father had somehow managed to separate Jeannine from her kids. He also believed that Pat had helped. They were clearly in love and had wanted Jeannine out of the way. The question in Denis's mind was whether his mother would be resourceful enough to find her kids and take them from Ray. He knew she'd be desperate and determined. But she'd have to be more than that. She'd have to figure out how to find them. Denis thought she'd need money and help. She didn't speak English well and was too shy to go knocking on doors asking after them. If it were up to him, he thought, he'd begin at the school. He'd ask where the kids had transferred to.

Denis spent as much time as he could at his new school. He hated going home. Pat walked around all day long with a glass with ice in it. She smelled of liquor and was glassy-eyed and nasty most of the time.

What made Denis even angrier than the drinking, though, was the fact that Pat kept all the kids in a state of near starvation. Denis was constantly hungry. So were Anne and Marc. They could never have seconds at mealtimes, and she rarely allowed any kind of snacks. The meals were either tuna fish or Kraft dinners. He came to hate both and to this day cannot eat tuna fish. What made it worse was that they'd get up in the morning after a party, and the kitchen would be stacked with dirty dishes and evidence that Ray and Pat and their party friends were eating well. Anne and Denis would have to clean the entire kitchen. Occasionally they'd manage to filch some left-overs. Later he discovered Pat kept a supply of frozen chicken pot pies in the freezer and he'd steal one every now and again and eat it, still frozen, on the way to school. He blamed Pat for his constant, gnawing hunger and his father for allowing her to starve them.

On weekends Ray began taking Denis along to help him out at the body shop. They'd drive down Saturday morning and work in the shop till early afternoon. While his father was painting, Denis would sand and tape. They spoke French when they were alone together, and there were times when Denis felt they were really father and son. At lunch-time his father would give him the money for three chili dogs, two orders of fries and two soft drinks.

One Saturday, Denis had just finished eating his chili dog and fries and was sitting, staring at his dad when Ray said, "Hey, are you still hungry?" Denis was taken aback. His father seemed genuinely concerned. He always remembered it as a tender moment. "Next time," his father told him, "get yourself two chili dogs, too." Starved for affection, that modest offer wiped away a lot of pain for Denis. Pat hated his guts, but on some level, his dad still loved him. And, he realized, he loved his dad. Now that he was old enough to work alongside him, there were things he could learn, things they could do together. It was confusing because he also hated Ray and what he had done. But then there'd be these moments when he was just his dad. Denis tried whenever he could to speak French to Ray. It angered Pat, but he felt that the language and the work helped them connect in a way that nothing else did.

Ray bought a pool and set it up in the backyard with lights, a deck and chairs. As soon as the weather permitted, Ray and Pat began throwing weekend pool parties for people they had met along the street. The parties got pretty wild. One of the spotlights shone right into Denis's bedroom window. He looked out the window one night and saw his father and Pat and several other women all naked in the pool. Anne saw it as well. The adults were drinking, barbecuing steaks and splashing around. Denis was embarrassed by it all and hoped that none of the neighbours could see. He knew his father didn't care what anybody thought.

Another time Denis arrived home, heard some banging in the garage and walked in to find his father with a sledge hammer pounding away on the passenger-side quarter panel of Pat's car.

"They're not gonna pay," he was screaming. "They'll pay now. They'll see."

Pat was beside him, grabbing at him. "Not in front of Denis," she said.

Denis figured it was some crooked insurance deal. It's always something, Denis thought.

The best thing that happened to Denis that winter, which helped him cope with the hunger and loss, occurred one night when he attended a meeting of the Boy Scout troop he had transferred into. He was alone and lonely, and another boy his age had seen him standing by himself and had walked over and said, "Hi, I'm Jack." Jack was there with his stepfather, Keith, and it turned out they lived on Holt Street, a block from Holly. Denis and Jack became fast friends almost overnight. Jack was an only child. His real father lived in another state. His mother, Evelyn, was sweet and pleasant and made Denis feel welcome in their home. Jack's house became a second home for him. Occasionally, he'd invite Jack to his place, and Pat would be on her best behaviour. Anne liked Jack. Pat was forever telling the kids to hurry up and once she told Jack, "Shake a leg there, Jack." He'd stood on one leg and shook his other leg. Anne laughed till she had tears in her eyes.

Jack's friendship eased the loneliness. As soon as he felt Jack was a true friend, Denis confided that Pat wasn't his real mom. He never told him what had happened to his real mom but it was important to him that Jack understood that Pat wasn't his flesh and blood.

Denis and Jack became avid Scouts together. They went on outings with Jack's folks and were occasionally treated to meals in restaurants by Jack's stepfather. Pat and Ray were delighted. Denis was out of their hair. Denis was drawn to his friend's house by the food that was always available and by the love he felt there. Here were decent people who felt and showed affection for each other. Here was a real family. The more time he spent at Jack's, the more embarrassed he was by his father and Pat. Sometimes when he felt overwhelmed by those feelings, he'd jump on his bike and ride over to Beech Street and watch the old house. Why couldn't his mother figure it out? he wondered. Maybe she was just earning the money to bring them back to Hull.

At the end of the first week on the case, Shipley and Hutchison devoted almost a whole day to chasing down information on the towel that had been found under the dead woman's head. Local linen services told them it was a basic hand towel used by doctors, barbers, motels and so on. That didn't give them much. Maybe she'd been killed in a motel and wrapped in the bedspread. They could make the rounds of the motels with pictures of the bedspread. There were a hell of a lot of motels out there, though. They'd think about it over the weekend.

The following week they took a call from an Inspector Renshaw of the RCMP in Ottawa. Nothing on the prints, he told them, but he'd passed on the file to Superintendent Pritchett in Edmonton. Pritchett would have someone follow up the White Stag lead and call them back.

The same day Conley and Foudray turned up a promising lead. A Mrs Frances Green had called to say she might have information pertinent to the case of the woman in the dump. Conley and Foudray had visited her and taken down the details. Green said she read the story in the paper about the body in the dump and that the description fit a woman named Helen she knew. Green said she last saw Helen and her husband Billy on December 18 at 2 A.M. when Helen had come over to say she was moving to Austin. Green said Helen seemed upset and that Billy beat her frequently and had once threatened to kill her. Green then showed Conley and Foudray a 1959 Pontiac that was still parked in the driveway of the apartment the couple had been renting. The car was filled with clothing, utensils, pillows, canned goods and folding chairs. Green said all the items in the car belonged to Helen. The officers took the name of the owner of the apartment and then swung by Poor Joyce's Lounge, where Green said Helen had worked. They found the lounge closed so they returned to the office and filed a detailed report for Shipley and Hutchison. The following day, Hutchison called the Austin police and gave them Helen's particulars. Within a couple of hours they had tracked her down and reported back that she was working as a waitress at the local Holiday Inn and living with Billy at his mother's place. Helen said she planned to return for the Pontiac.

That afternoon Shipley answered a call from Corporal J.W. Clark of the RCMP in Edmonton. Clark said he had checked with White Stag and had been told that the company had accounts with twelve hundred firms, all of which were in Canada and the Bahamas. The company did not export to the United States. Clark added that he had checked the missing persons file and had come up empty-handed.

One day that spring Anne saw Pat lying on her back on the floor in the bathroom of their house, naked but for her panties. Anne remembers she had red liquid coming out of her mouth. She remembers her father throwing his weight against the bathroom door and finally wedging it open. Pat was inside. The red stuff looked like blood but she heard someone—who?—say it was iodine. Anne was chased off to her room, and nobody in the family ever spoke about the incident. Was it a suicide attempt? Anne believes it was but can't remember why or who might have told her. Was it a snatch of conversation she had overheard?

Anne lived in such terror of abandonment that all her memories are fragmented. She saw and heard things that sank without trace into her unconscious. Snippets of her life just disappeared. They were all down there, fermenting, making her a little bit more frantic every day. Outwardly she appeared normal, maybe a touch hyper. Underneath, she felt her life was a bottomless black pool that would one day drag her under.

Early that spring Ray was listening to country music on a local radio station when he heard an advertisement for a jamboree and land sale in Big Thicket. The ad promised there'd be a barbecue, a country music band and cheap resort lots for sale. On the Saturday of the jamboree Ray got the family in the car and headed east out of the city on the Liberty Freeway. It was a two-hour drive deep into the piny woods of east Texas. The jamboree was to promote Big Thicket Lake Estates.

The Big Thicket area is a swath of wet, hot, snake-infested forest 125 miles wide that extends all the way to Louisiana. The forest is a mixture of pine, hickory, elm and southern magnolia. Scattered throughout the woods are small towns, sawmills, revival meeting tents at crossroads, barbecue joints and unpainted wooden houses with galleries and rocking chairs out front. Trucks laden with logs as wide around as the truck wheels themselves rumble down the roads.

Ray, Pat, the kids and hundreds of other eager families streamed into Big Thicket Lake Estates that Saturday. The radio promos had portrayed the development as a luxurious country retreat with all the amenities. What the eager visitors discovered was an untamed world made accessible by narrow roads that had been hastily bull-dozed through the forest. There were hundreds of heavily forested lots for sale but they came without electricity or water. At the heart of Big Thicket Lake Estates was a small artificial pond where prop-erty owners could swim if they didn't mind the water moccasins.

At the entrance to the development was a restaurant with a half-dozen tables. Out back, under a pole roof, was a juke-box and dance floor and bandstand. The sides were open to the woods. Ray pulled up to the restaurant and let the kids stuff themselves on bar-becue. Then he got a map and drove up and down the tiny dusty roads that had been carved through the woods. The lot Ray bought for $160 was up a side-road cut between towering magnolias and pines. The earth was crimson-coloured, and the road was often washed out or cut by deep ravines created by the pounding rain.

If Ray was looking for a hide-out, Big Thicket Lake Estates was made to order. It was difficult to find, marked only by one fading sign, and once inside the development visitors could easily get lost in a maze of roads that led into cul-de-sacs. Few of the lots were ever occupied; most remained primeval forest.

Ray decided that he and Denis were going to build a house on the lot, which was solid forest. To build they'd have to drop six or seven pines that were at least three feet in diameter.

By spring they were driving out every weekend. Ray toppled three pines, rolled them parallel to each other, slid concrete blocks under them and they became the foundation of the cottage. As soon as he and Denis had laid down the floor of the house, Ray erected a tent on the platform. The children and Pat cleared the thick, tangled underbrush. They created a yard to let sunlight penetrate the forest canopy. Martine picked up a poisonous coral snake one day, attracted by its pretty colours. Critters of all kinds lived around them—armadillos, bobcats, possum, deer and every kind of snake imaginable.

Every Friday right after school Ray would load the car, get the kids and Pat in and head to Big Thicket. They'd stop in a lumber yard in Liberty and pick up the supplies they needed. They'd hammer and saw all day Saturday and Sunday, and at nights Ray and Pat would drink themselves stupid. Denis worked like a mule, and Ray appreciated his endurance and counted on his help. Denis sometimes resented his father's bossiness but he felt useful and close. They'd speak French together all day, and Denis learned something about carpentry. One day his father was working with a chain-saw when it slipped and cut him to the bone near the knee. He looked at Denis and, gritting his teeth in pain, told him to fetch a bottle of vodka and some rags. Denis ran for the supplies while blood poured from the wound. When Denis returned, Ray poured a slug of vodka on the cut and, with sweat dripping from his brow, bound the wound with the rags. He teased the kids all night that he was probably going lose his leg, and they cried with fear. He never bothered to have a doctor look at the cut, which left a jagged scar on his leg.

Another weekend they were barbecuing dinner one night after a long day of work. Denis got into a quarrel with Pat. It escalated and Denis began crying. Pat and Ray were drunk.

"You guys don't love me," Denis sobbed. "Why don't you let me go live with Mom in Hull?" He retreated into the tent with Pat cursing him. He curled up on his sleeping-bag, feeling sorry for himself. Outside he could hear Pat calling him names. "How did you get a big dummy like that for a son?" she asked Ray.

He was drunk and reflective. "Look," Denis heard him answer. "He's my first born. He was a son. Born on my birthday. I was so proud of him. We loved him. But he turned out like the Boissonneaults. He's a dummy like them."

Pat's rage intensified. "Well I'm going to go in there and beat your big dummy," she declared.

Denis went silent and heard his father say, "Maybe you should watch out, Pat. Maybe he'll beat the shit out of you."

That's it, Denis thought, he doesn't care. She comes in here and I'm going to hammer her. He clenched his fists and waited. Outside, Pat heard what Ray hadn't said and decided to confine herself to flinging a few more curses at Denis. After that night, Pat was careful with Denis. She abused him verbally and emotionally and would slap him in the face but she seemed to be frightened of him. She must have seen the hatred burning in his eyes and sensed that if he ever exploded, he wouldn't be able to stop himself.

By the time school was out Denis and his dad had put up a thirty-by-thirty-foot cottage with plywood walls. Inside were a kitchen,

bathroom and three small bedrooms. Shortly afterward, they abandoned the house on Holly Street and moved out to the woods.
There, Denis felt, they were completely isolated. They had no
phone, no electricity and no neighbours.

On the last day of February, Hutchison took a call from a Mrs E.
Smith that seemed promising. Smith had a dramatic story to tell.
She said she had been in the Candlelight Lounge on Spencer Road
about ten days before the story appeared in the paper about the dead
woman in the dump. She and the owner of the lounge, Lois, were
alone. It was early on a Saturday. A couple entered and asked if
they could join the two women. The newcomers introduced themselves as Bobby and Buddy Geer. After a couple of beers, Mrs
Smith said she got up to go to the washroom and was joined there
by Mrs Geer. As soon as the door closed on them, Mrs Geer said,
"Remember my name, Bobby Geer," and she spelled it for Mrs
Smith. She said she had been married to Buddy for only three
weeks and that he had threatened to kill her several times. She said
they were living at the Bayshore Motel on Highway 146. They
returned to the table, and when Lois, the owner of the lounge, rose
to go to the washroom, Bobby Geer followed her and repeated the
same information. A couple of hours passed and finally Buddy Geer
said, "Let's go." Mrs Geer looked at him and said, "I'm not going
with you. You're going to try and kill me." Geer walked over to her,
picked her up and carried her outside to their Oldsmobile. Smith
said he then "stood her on the ground and she started slinging her
arms and [Geer] struck her several times real hard and then picked
her up and threw her on top of the Oldsmobile station wagon and
then opened the door, pulled her from the top and threw her inside
and drove away." Smith said the Bobby Geer fit the description of
the dead woman perfectly, right down to the dentures.
    Hutchison immediately got on the phone to the Bayshore Motel
and spoke to Mrs Cook, the manager. Mrs Cook said, "No, Mr and
Mrs Geer are no longer living at the motel." They'd moved, she
said, to the Colonial Oaks Apartments. She gave Hutchison their
apartment number and said that Bobby was a hairdresser and had
just done her hair. Mrs Cook added that she had seen Bobby and
Buddy the night before and she assured the investigator that "they
are both very much alive and fighting."

Shipley and Hutchison had now been working on the case for more than two weeks. Nobody had reported a missing person fitting the dead woman's description. They'd diligently chased down every lead, every call. Detective Klevenhagen, who has since become the sheriff of Harris County, says that at this point they sat down and talked about what they had. "We had good identifiers. If somebody had reported her missing, we could have identified her from what we had. But there were no missing persons fitting that description."

Klevenhagen says they all knew the Canadian angle was important but had no idea what it meant. Was she visiting from Canada? Had she recently vacationed in Canada and bought the skirt there? Was the skirt a gift? Did she buy it in a used clothing shop?

"It was cold enough around the time she was killed so it made sense that she was wearing heavy clothes. But the clothes were not that much heavier to indicate that she had just come from Canada," says Klevenhagen. "There were a jillion possibilities. We wore the phone out calling Canada to find a missing person from up there."

That year, 1968, Harris County and Houston police conducted 252 murder investigations that concluded with arrests and charges. Klevenhagen says he alone was carrying four homicides at the time. Those numbers don't include the murders they were not able to solve, like the killing of the well-dressed white woman in her thirties whose life had ended with one savage blow to the head, whose body had then been trussed up, transported to a remote site and dragged forty-three feet from a vehicle into a brush-covered field where animals fed on her corpse.

The local media had dutifully reported the story and the Harris County sheriff's department had conducted a thorough, professional investigation. They'd come up with nothing, not even a name to attach to the corpse. It seemed that most of the leads had involved men beating on their wives. It was like some sort of national blood sport. If they had been able to identify the dead woman, the chances were that a trail of blood would have led right to the person who had slipped the wedding ring on her finger. It was time to move on. There were other bodies turning up every day, bodies with names whose killers were still on the loose. It was not as if the local media had been hounding the sheriff's department to solve the mystery of the body in the dump. Perhaps if the newspapers had devoted a couple of feature stories to the case, the investigation might have been prolonged for another week. Still, it might not have made any difference. So Shipley and Hutchison were reassigned, and the investigation was suspended. The file remained open and would be reactivated if any new information turned up.

Some weeks later corpse 68-500 was taken from the morgue and put into a simple wooden casket and transported to Harris County Cemetery, the county's potter's field. The cemetery, at the corner of Oats and Beaumont, two hundred yards from the asphalt of the Liberty Freeway that runs east from Houston towards Big Thicket, is well groomed and surrounded by mature poplars and pines. A full-time caretaker cuts the grass and trims the lilac bushes. There are no gravestones in the cemetery, just a long, narrow strip of concrete at the head of the plots with tiny metal plates attached to it. Each plot is marked by a two-inch-square plate with a number on it. Cemetery records show the autopsy number of the body buried in each plot. Corpse 68-500 was buried in the fifth plot, Row I, Section C, just across from the section reserved for babies. Within a couple of years all that was visible of the plot was a slight depression in the rolling, clipped lawn.

When the body was lowered into the grave, there was no funeral, there were no visitors, no flowers to mark the passing of a woman who had been somebody's daughter, maybe somebody's sister, certainly somebody's wife and, from the evidence of the autopsy, mother to more than one child. Twenty-two summers would pass before a lone visitor with a lifetime of sadness in his eyes would arrive one bright May morning when the lilacs were in bloom, make his way to the foot of that long-forgotten grave, assure himself that he had the right plot, slump down beside it, whisper, "I found you," and cry his aching heart out.

Chapter Ten

Big Thicket, Texas, 1969

R ay continued to work in Houston after the family moved to Big Thicket. He had acquired a black Lincoln Continental, which he used for the two-hour commute between his job at Sam Montgomery Oldsmobile and Big Thicket Lake Estates. All summer long he made improvements to the property. He brought in electricity. He paid a local man to dig a well. Long after it had been completed, the man continued to drop by, asking to be paid. Ray kept putting him off and, in the end, never did pay him.

Pat and the children spent their days in the cottage in their own little clearing in the forest. The nearest neighbours were a Hungarian couple who had a place two lanes over. During the week, visitors were few and far between. Denis got a dog and a .22 rifle and with Marc in tow spent days wandering through the woods or hiking down a gas pipeline right-of-way that ran near their property. He came across a bobcat one day and fired at it but it bounded off. He built a trap and caught an armadillo.

On weekends other families would come out and camp on the lots they had purchased. Then there would be other kids around to play with. Often there'd be a country band at the restaurant, and Denis would hike over on Friday afternoons to watch them unload and set up. He developed a passion for country music. Merle Haggard. Buck Owens and His Buckaroos. He'd sit behind the drummer at night and follow the beat with his hands. He was a mimic, and soon he was "tawkin' lak a geud ol' countra boah." The first country song he learned—"Momma Tried" by Merle Haggard—seemed to echo some of his own hurtin'. To this day, listening to the songs that he first heard that summer brings back the loneliness, anger and fear he experienced at Big Thicket.

Ray fell in love with country music as well. Denis remembers his father humming the lyrics to Merle Haggard's "Branded Man," a song that tells the story of a man who can't escape his own past.

Denis maintained contact with his friend Jack, and that summer Ray drove him into Houston and he spent two wonderful weeks at

Jack's house. Jack's stepfather had two lawnmowers and the boys set themselves up as lawn contractors. Up and down the streets they'd go, Denis knocking at one house, Jack the next. If they got work, one would cut the front lawn, another the back. They used some of the money they earned to accompany Jack's mother to bingo games. A couple of times during those two weeks Denis managed to slip away and check for his mother at Beech Street.

At the end of the two weeks they bought themselves boxes of .22 bullets, and Jack returned with Denis to Big Thicket for two weeks. They spent their days in the forest with Denis's rifle, hunting, talking about music—Jack was crazy about the Beatles. Some days they'd wander down for a swim in the lake. Or they'd make a raft, run it down a creek and try their luck at fishing.

Ray had gotten into the habit of bringing home every week two cases of liquor: a case of vodka for himself and a case of V.O. for Pat. He drank vodka and orange, she took hers straight on the rocks. A bottle a day.

That fall Marc started school. All three kids took the bus together to Hardin School, a half-hour drive from the cottage. They had to hike out to the bus stop near the entrance to the development.

Denis liked Hardin School. His difficulties with English were behind him, and he felt comfortable with the work. He joined the track team and the football team. He was tall enough but thin as a rail. One day the football coach told him, "You got to put some meat on those bones, son." Denis seized the moment and asked the coach if he could write a letter to his mother telling her he had to have two sandwiches in his lunch instead of one if he was going to stay on the team. The coach must have felt sorry for him. He wrote the letter, and Denis got a two-sandwich lunch from then on.

Despite his contentment in school Denis was lonelier than ever that fall and winter. His best friend was in Houston; there were no more dances, and folks didn't come out camping on weekends during the winter. Things got steadily worse at home. Some days at school he'd go to the library, pull out an atlas and chart a course for Hull, Quebec. He imagined himself hitch-hiking north to the Canadian border, making his way to Hull, walking up to his grandmother's house and into his mother's embrace. He imagined her living there. She'd have a job, she'd be overjoyed to see him. It would be a great adventure and would show his dad he was no big dummy.

Anne, too, was lonely and starved for affection. She had a warm-hearted and sympathetic teacher at school. Anne had once seen the teacher hug a little girl who was in tears. More than anything else Anne longed for someone to just hold her. One day she marched up to the teacher in tears and told her that someone had stolen her Vicks nasal tube. It was a lie but she just wanted to be taken in her arms. The teacher held Anne until the sobs subsided.

At nights Anne would dream of having her mother back. Life with Pat and her father made her so unhappy; some days it was unbearable. At school she got to know other girls, and hearing them talk about their lives made Anne wonder what was wrong with her own family. Why are we so different? Why isn't there any love? Why is there so much hatred? And why is Pat always trying to separate us kids?

Pat kept Anne within sight and away from the boys as much as possible, and eventually her attempts to split up the kids altered the family dynamics. One Friday night Denis whispered to Anne that he and Marc were planning on going fishing the following day. He wanted her to come along and she was keen to go. He had a couple of dollars he had earned somewhere and they agreed that he'd buy some snack food for the excursion. Pat overheard the conversation. Anne approached her later to wiggle out of their routine Saturday grocery shopping trip.

"Mom, I don't think I'll go shopping with you tomorrow," she said before Pat cut her off.

"Anne, you come with me. Don't go with the boys. Little girls shouldn't be with boys all the time." She was being stupid about it and Anne knew.

Ray happened to be home as well, and when he heard Pat trying to talk Anne out of the fishing trip, he stomped over to her and screamed, "Why are you trying to separate my kids?" He was furious, but Pat held her ground.

"I just don't want her going with those little fuckers," she replied.

Ray turned to Anne. "What do you want to do?"

"Go fishing."

"Then you go," he said, and he and Pat quarrelled about it for the rest of the evening. It was clear to the children that he took their side, and they loved him for it. When their mother had been around, she protected them from their father. Now, they drew closer to him because they felt he protected them from Pat's hatred.

One day Anne was going somewhere in the car with her father when, out of the blue, he told her, "You know, your mom tried to throw you in front of a car." Anne just sat there, silent, listening, wondering. "Yeah," he continued, "she was in a mental institute and then a prison." She had never heard the story before and couldn't remember anything like that ever having happened. She didn't believe it, but she was confused. She knew her father was always telling lies, and she wasn't about to tumble for what might be just another fib.

The Christmas of 1969 was bleaker than any they'd ever had. The forest seemed to have closed in on them. Denis's moodiness was broken Christmas Day when he discovered he had been given a pair of cowboy boots. All the boys wore them and he fell in love with those boots. But Pat decided he couldn't wear them to school. There were fights about it but she was adamant and Ray backed her up. So he kept the boots in large wooden shoe box his father had built and mounted on the outside of the cottage. The box had a heavy lid on it and was designed to prevent the dog from running off with everyone's shoes. One day that winter Denis was walking up the road towards home, just back from school, and he saw, to his horror, his dog had one of his boots in his mouth. Denis shouted and ran after him. The dog crawled under the cottage with the boot. Denis dropped his books to wiggle under after him and saw Pat standing there laughing. He banged his head under the cottage, and when he had finally retrieved his boot, it was in shreds. He crawled out in tears.

Pat sneered at him. "That'll teach you to put your boots away," she said. He looked in the shoe box and saw his other boot there. He couldn't have left one out. How had the dog gotten in? It was Pat, she had given the dog the boot.

"You fucking bitch," he shouted at her, staying out of her range. They cursed each other until she told him he could damn well stay outside until his father came home. It was ten o'clock before he saw his father's car's headlights. As soon as Ray drove up, Denis told him what had happened. They walked in together, and Pat laid

into Denis for cursing her. Ray looked at them both and sent Denis
off to bed without dinner.

By spring Ray had stopped working at Sam Montgomery in
Houston and had found a job at a body shop in Beaumont, a half-
hour from Big Thicket Lake Estates. That summer he moved the
family to a rented house in Beaumont and leased the cottage to a
Mexican family. By September, though, they were back in the cottage and Ray was out of a job. He began driving the school bus the
kids took. He did odd jobs during the day. Then the dam that had
been built to create the lake at the heart of Big Thicket Lake
Estates broke, and what had once been a swimming hole and fishing pond with houses all around it became a dry mud hole. Now
they had to walk a half-mile from the broken dam to the cottage;
there was no way to drive across it. Eventually repairs were made
so they could drive over the busted dam but the lake was never
refilled.

Soon after they returned to the cottage Denis was walking by
himself one day, day-dreaming, when he suddenly realized that he
was day-dreaming in English. He felt his old identity was slipping
from his grasp. He used his French so rarely that he didn't even
think in it any more.

At first the kids were thrilled to have their father driving the bus.
He'd park it in the yard, and Denis would sweep it out. But the
thrill soured quickly for Denis. There were blacks living on the bus
route, and a unspoken code obliged them to sit at the back of the
bus. One day a little black boy who was being teased walked up to
the seat behind the driver, crying. "Mr Durand, they're calling me
nigger." With Denis and the other kids watching, Ray glanced back
at the boy.

"Shut up, nigger, and get to the back of the bus," he barked at the
kid, loud enough for all to hear. Denis cringed, feeling the little
boy's pain. He couldn't believe his father's cruelty.

Their second Christmas at Big Thicket was as cheerless as the
first, but by then they knew there wouldn't be another. Ray had
decided that they were leaving Texas. He sold the cottage to a man
he had worked with at Sam Montgomery Oldsmobile, traded the
Lincoln for an Oldsmobile station wagon and rented a U-Haul
trailer. A couple of days after Christmas they loaded the car and
trailer and locked the cottage. It was night and the kids had no idea

where they were going. Ray just told them to get in the car and he pulled out.

They cruised through a snowstorm in New Mexico, and Ray laughed at all the cars that had skidded off the road. "The stupid fuckers," he told Pat. "They don't know how to drive in the snow. I do. I spent twenty years driving in snow as a cop in Montreal."

In Arizona they were in a restaurant and spotted two stars of the television show "Hee Haw." Ray urged Denis to get their autographs but Denis was too timid. Anne finally jumped up and was back in a minute with the signatures.

They were on the road for Denis and Ray's birthday on the thirtieth, and they were still on the road on New Year's Day, 1970. Early in the new year they drove into Los Angeles. They camped out in a motel, while Ray looked for work.

Two weeks later Ray packed them up again, and they headed south to San Diego. He knew it was a stone's throw from Mexico and he apparently liked the idea of living that close to the border. The day they arrived he rented an apartment in a run-down wooden complex on Bunker Hill Street. There were two buildings with four apartments in each. He moved the family into one of the apartments and secured a job as the caretaker for both buildings. Within a week he had talked himself into a full-time job as a body man at Guy Hill Cadillac, a large dealership within walking distance of the apartment. It was a modest start but he had dangerously large ambitions.

Chapter Eleven

San Diego, California, 1970

Mission Bay Drive skirts the northwest corner of Mission Bay, an M-shaped inlet off the Pacific Ocean, fifteen minutes from downtown San Diego. A thin finger of land closes off most of the bay from the ocean. Along the outside of the finger is Mission Beach, a gently arcing stretch of dun-coloured sand that separates the pounding ocean from crumbling, fifty-foot-high cliffs. When Ray, Pat and the kids arrived in San Diego in January, 1970, surfer dudes would be out every morning riding the curls at Mission Beach. Up above the beach, coffee houses and nightclubs catered to the bohemian and hippy set.

San Diego, like most of the United States at the time, was in the midst of a great cultural upheaval. The nation's youth had been politicized by the Vietnam War and alienated from the mainstream by the madness of suburban consumerism. The kids were into drugs, music and sex. Ray loved being down on the beach. The scene there fired his imagination. He'd long ago acquired a taste for mood-altering pills and was aggressive in his pursuit of sex. He couldn't sympathize with the rejection of consumerism, though. He'd come out of poverty and aspired to a comfortable middle-class existence. There was poverty in San Diego but there was also great wealth. He knew where he wanted to fit in.

He got hipper—his hair trailed over his collar, he grew a moustache, bought a pair of flared trousers—but only enough to obscure his alien origins. He was thirty-five now, a fan of country music, father of four kids and totally apolitical.

The kids were just as enthralled by San Diego as their father. It was exotic and balmy. It wasn't a hardship to be outdoors all day long. Pat would give them each a sandwich in the morning and chase them out of the apartment. Denis, Anne and Marc discovered Sea World on Mission Bay and found a way to sneak in the back without paying. They saw the porpoises perform so many times they could have taken over from the trainers.

Eventually they were all enrolled in school, and life returned to what constituted normal for the family. Pat was still at home all day with the baby. She was still drinking a bottle a day and, it seemed to the kids, getting meaner. Her concern appeared to be directed not so much towards the health and welfare of the children as towards her need to control them. The less control she had over her own life, the more she sought to dominate the children. She had no money of her own, no job, and no legal status, but she did have responsibility for four children and, perhaps most bitter to her, a lover with a roving eye. What enraged her more than anything else was the children's disobedience. Where once she confined her attacks on the children to slaps, increasingly there were kicks and punches as well.

Ray scared them as well, but he was a bit more predictable. If they obeyed the rules, kept out of his hair, did what he told them, he'd treat them half-decently. They could joke with him, sometimes persuade him to take them places. He was strict but Marc and Anne never took that to mean that he hated them.

Denis was another matter. He often despised his father and felt that Ray wanted him to be someone he wasn't. Ray was always urging Denis, now fourteen, to chase the girls. "Be like your dad," he'd say to Denis on the beach. "Go hustle those girls." Denis was too shy and tongue-tied to strike up casual conversations with girls he didn't know. And he was sickened by his father's attitude towards women, his assumption that sex was the only reason you'd ever befriend a woman. He also hated Ray's habit of commenting on people's looks. He'd see a woman in the street and tell her in French, "My God, you're ugly." He'd be smiling when he said it so the woman would be confused.

Still, however much Denis disliked his father, he thought of him as an indestructible force. He was his dad; a kid didn't have any choice in the matter of who his father was going to be.

Pat was another matter. There were no shared memories with Pat. And she was closed about her past. She never talked of her family or her background. They knew from Ray that she had sisters and brothers and a father. And they knew that she had been in an orphanage and foster homes. And once she had told them about long walks to school and beatings for taking apples from a tree. Beyond that, she was an unknown. There was a hardness at her core that didn't permit her to indulge in sentimentality, that denied her the capacity to trust others. She was suspicious by inclination. There was no getting a story by her. Even Ray, an accomplished, professional liar, had a hard time making her believe his tall tales.

Just down the street, almost directly across from Mission Bay itself, was Guy Hill Cadillac, then the second largest Cadillac dealership in San Diego. Ray got himself a stall in the body shop and soon everybody knew him. He was fast and friendly and knew what he was doing. He was the kind of body man that dealerships love. He worked so quickly that he made his employers good money.

Fred Angelo was then a mechanic at Guy Hill. He got to know Ray and lent him $150 shortly after he arrived. "He was broke and, oh, he had a way with words," Angelo recalls.

At the apartment block, Ray collected the rent and was responsible for maintenance. Almost as soon as the family had settled into the new routine, Ray began calling his uncle Robert Durand in Hull. He wanted to know what was happening up there, who was saying what about him. In one of the first calls Robert told him he was out of work. The concrete company he had been with for years had closed down. Ray immediately suggested he come down to San Diego. He said he could get Robert a job in the body shop with him. Robert didn't take the offer seriously at first, but it got him thinking. He'd always dreamed of living in the south of the United States.

Robert and Claudette were the only folks from back home who had had a glimpse of the life Ray was making for himself. They'd seen Ray splitting his time between Pat and Jeannine and the kids in Fort Lauderdale. They knew he was much more fond of Pat than Jeannine. They also knew that Jeannine and the children had returned to Hull, but then they'd heard that she had moved to Houston. When Ray told them he was calling from San Diego, they were curious. He told them about the move and said that he was living in an apartment with Pat and the children. Robert can't now recall if he asked about Jeannine or if Ray volunteered the information, but in one phone conversation Ray said that Jeannine had thrown herself in front of a car with the baby in her arms. He said she had become hysterical and had to be hospitalized in an insane asylum. Robert and Claudette were shocked but not at all surprised. She had been so unhappy when they had last seen her. They didn't inquire further but assumed she was in an asylum in San Diego.

The next time he called, Ray told Robert that he could obtain a green card for him—Ray had somehow gotten a green card for himself in the name of Ray Holben—and he'd secured a job for Robert in the body shop. Robert couldn't believe it, but the more Ray talked, the more he made it seem like the move would be a piece of cake. Robert discussed it with Claudette and they decided to plunge into what they believed was going to be a great adventure. They realized that the transition would be difficult because their children didn't speak English. Both Robert and Claudette understood English but neither of them spoke it fluently. They decided that Robert would fly down first for two weeks to check it out. He'd call once he got there, and if he gave her the green light, she'd pack, they'd sell the house, pull their three children out of school and move. So Robert flew to Los Angeles in March, and Ray met him at the airport.

Ray had decided that Robert would move into the apartment above the one he was living in. At the time the apartment was occupied by a sailor and his wife. As Claudette later learned, to get the sailor out, Ray stole his pay cheque from the mailbox, tore it up and then told the owner of the apartment building that the sailor hadn't paid his rent and was trashing the place. The sailor apparently had no idea that Ray was behind his eviction because the day he left he came downstairs to say goodbye.

While he was conspiring against the sailor, Ray took Robert to Guy Hill. He had talked the service manager into letting Robert work with him as his assistant.

Once Robert had convinced himself that the move was possible and had been given his green card by Ray, he flew back to Hull to help Claudette with the final preparations. They sold the house, their trailer, car and all their furniture. They had fifteen thousand dollars cash, which they agreed would be a safety cushion, plus several thousand dollars that they would use to buy a car and furnish the apartment. They flew down together with the three children and moved into the apartment.

The two eldest children, twelve-year-old Luc and ten-year-old Luce, were enrolled in the same school as Denis, Anne and Marc. Claudette, like Pat, remained at home with her baby, eighteen-month-old Robert, Jr. The women saw a lot of each other but

Claudette didn't much like Pat. She thought she was mean to the kids.

"Pat would say to them, 'Eat your goddamned food and get out.' She was like a prison matron," Claudette remembers. She saw that Pat was drinking heavily and that Ray was both drinking and taking goofballs.

One day shortly after their arrival Claudette was alone with Pat and casually asked her if the children missed their mother. Pat, she remembers, immediately stiffened with anger, pointed a finger at Claudette and said, "Don't you ever mention her name again or else." After that exchange, Claudette said, Pat didn't speak to her for a week. "She looked threatening. She scared me," Claudette says. Shortly after, Ray came up to Robert and Claudette's apartment and tore the phone off the wall. Claudette believes he didn't want her making phone calls to Quebec.

Claudette also remembers how hungry Ray's children were. Two days after their arrival she bought some hamburger meat, set up a barbecue and began making burgers for the kids. "Ray came crashing through the screen door and grabbed the barbecue and threw it over the fence. He said, 'You mind your own business.' He didn't want me feeding his kids. He was crazy, wild, stoned on goofballs."

Despite Claudette's misgivings, she and Robert forged ahead. They got a bank account and bought furniture. One day at work, during a conversation with Fred Angelo, the talk turned to cars. Angelo said he had a used 1959 Cadillac for sale. Since Ray had recently bought himself a 1960 gold-coloured Cadillac, Robert decided he'd splurge and do the same. He got a good deal from Angelo and felt everything was working out. He had a green card, a job, an apartment and now the kind of car he'd always imagined himself owning.

Robert and Ray were in Ray's Cadillac soon after, returning from the bank, when Ray suddenly asked Robert how long it would take for a body to decompose. Years earlier Robert had worked as an embalmer in Hull, and he knew a good deal about the decomposition process.

"Depends where it is," Robert replied.

"How would a corpse be identified?" Ray then asked.

"Oh," Robert replied, "teeth, scars, tattoos. That sort of thing."

"And how long would a corpse be kept?"

"Depends," Robert answered, thinking Ray was asking how long a corpse would keep after it had been buried. "It could be kept for a long time, depending on soil conditions."

Meanwhile, at work, Robert quickly picked up some basic skills. But, as Angelo remembers, there were concerns. From the time of Ray's arrival tools had started disappearing. Eventually, management came to suspect Ray. And Angelo hadn't got his $150 loan back and began to wonder if he ever would. Then one day Ray brought a little Ford station wagon into work and offered Angelo a deal. He said he'd do a bit of body work on it, then give it to Angelo for the $150 he owed him. Angelo agreed and, shortly afterward, sold it for about $200. He was relieved he'd finally gotten his money back. Then a police detective showed up one day and asked him about the car. Angelo told him he'd got it from Durand, who wasn't in that day. The detective told him that the car's registration papers didn't match the vehicle, that the papers were for a car that had been towed from the parking lot of an apartment building on Bunker Hill. Angelo told the detective that Durand was the manager of the apartment in question. The detective took notes and left. Angelo says he can't remember what happened afterwards. He isn't certain but he has a vague recollection of Durand being fired shortly afterwards because Guy Hill management finally decided he was responsible for the tool thefts.

At about the same time two men knocked on Pat's door one afternoon and announced that they were immigration officials. When they asked to see her papers, she said she had none. They told her she'd have to leave the country and gave her two weeks to pack and move. Then they climbed the stairs and repeated the routine with Claudette, who remembers the two men were polite and sympathetic. "They said we could come back if we filled out the right papers," she remembers. While they were talking to her, Ray and Robert arrived. They were all ordered out of the country. They were stunned and angry. (Robert remains coy about whether he knew the green card Ray had given him was legal or forged.) Somebody had informed on them. The immigration officers returned two days later to make sure they were packing and getting ready to leave.

Both families packed and sold what they couldn't take with them. It was the end of March. The day they moved out, Ray collected the following month's rent from all the tenants and pocketed it. Then the two families pulled out in the Cadillacs. The plan was that they'd check into a motel for a couple of days. Ray said he had to get some work done on his car. They rented adjoining rooms at the Swinger Motel in El Cohon, and Ray asked Robert to lend him his car so he could drop his Cadillac off to have the mechanical work done. Robert agreed and handed Ray the keys. Pat drove Ray's car, and Ray followed her in Robert's. Robert, Claudette and the kids settled in for the night.

The next morning they noticed that Ray, Pat and the kids hadn't come back the night before, and they started to get a little anxious. They had hidden their fifteen-thousand-dollar stash in their daughter's suitcase and had left it in the trunk of the car. That afternoon Claudette called their bank. She wanted to close their account. She told them they were leaving the following day and asked for her account balance. The clerk told her the account was empty. Claudette was stunned. By her reckoning, there should have been more than fifteen hundred dollars left. She insisted that the bank was in error, but when the clerk checked, the balance was indeed about zero. A cheque had been drawn on the account just the day before for fifteen hundred dollars. Claudette, now certain that an error had been made, said they hadn't written a cheque for that amount. So the clerk got a copy of the cheque, which had been cashed at that branch. With Claudette listening, her heart in her throat, the clerk said, yes, Robert had written a cheque for fifteen hundred dollars to a Raymond Durand. It was, said the clerk, for the purchase of a Cadillac.

Now certain that Ray had cheated them, they called the police and reported what had happened. They said they had been deported and that Raymond Durand had emptied their bank account, had made off with their Cadillac, had their suitcases and the money they had hidden in them and even their credit card. Robert made out a formal complaint at the police station. When he returned, they sat down and reviewed their predicament: they had thirty-eight dollars cash and the clothes on their backs, and they were facing a deportation order. They'd been told to be at the Canadian border by April 15. They were devastated. They were told the city's welfare agency might help so they contacted the agency and were given food and some clothing and two dollars cash. They had enough money to pay for their room for a week. They visited the bank and insisted that the cheque to Raymond Durand was a forgery. The bank eventually covered part of the theft. Then the police called and said they had found Robert's Cadillac abandoned in the city. Robert and Claudette rushed to the lot where it had been towed and discovered that the only suitcase missing was Luce's, the suitcase containing the money.

With the recovered car and the money they'd managed to get from the bank, they packed quickly and headed north. It took them five days to make the border crossing at Buffalo, New York. They were beside themselves with grief and anger, and both Robert and Claudette almost suffered breakdowns on that seemingly endless drive with three kids, one of them still in diapers.

Back in Hull they rented a place with the assistance of the provincial welfare agency, bought furniture at the St Vincent de Paul Society store, and Robert began looking for work. He was the first to break down. First he was hospitalized and then Claudette, both with stress-related disorders.

"I almost went crazy," Claudette recalls. "We got back and had no house, no clothes, no furniture. Then Ray's mother told everybody that we were liars, that Ray wouldn't have done such a thing to us." Now retired, Robert and Claudette live in a mobile home in a trailer park near Hull. It still hurts them to talk about how their trust was betrayed.

Robert eventually found work, and they went on with their lives. In the months after their return, though, Robert wanted vengeance. He visited the RCMP and told them that Ray had stolen everything he owned, that Jeannine had disappeared and that Ray had been asking questions about corpses. Robert told the officer he talked to that Ray had probably killed Jeannine. The officer told him there wasn't much he could do, that the theft had occurred in San Diego and that it was a matter for the local police. As for Jeannine, it appears that nothing was ever done. Maybe the officer thought Robert was exaggerating or that the case was out of his jurisdiction or that surely someone had filed a missing persons report—or maybe he was just lazy and disbelieving. Whatever the case, Robert was sent home.

Robert also visited Ray's mother and told her the story but she defended her son and later called Robert a liar. He looked up

Jeannine's aunt, Berthe Laframboise, who at the time was still a nun. He told her that Ray had said that Jeannine was in an insane asylum. He recounted the story of what Ray had done to him and said he suspected that Ray had killed Jeannine. Berthe contacted her sister, Jeannine's mother, and they weren't quite sure what to make of the story. At the time in Quebec, Catholic religious orders administered many hospitals and psychiatric institutions. Berthe told Laurette that she knew nuns in most of the asylums in Quebec and would check with them to see if Jeannine had been committed to one of them. Berthe began calling friends in the institutions, asking them to verify whether a Jeannine Boissonneault or a Jeannine Durand had been admitted. It was a long shot because Berthe knew that Jeannine could have been committed anywhere in the United States. Her search of Quebec institutions proved fruitless. When she reported back to Laurette, they weren't sure what to do next.

By this time Robert felt that he had done everything possible to alert the right people to the truth about Ray. He was bitter and angry, particularly at Ray's family. After it was all over and Robert had accepted the fact that he had ignored the warning signals and let his pursuit of his dreams blind him to the truth about Ray Durand, his credit-card company tracked him down and presented him with his unpaid account. Ray had used Robert's card to pay for gas and food all the way north to the Canadian border. That hurt, Robert remembers, that really hurt, looking at the meals and gallons of gas that he had bought for Ray as he took a leisurely drive up along the west coast and into British Columbia.

Denis remembers they were in the Cadillac and heading north out of San Diego. His father rolled down the window as they passed the motel where Uncle Robert and Aunt Claudette were staying. He had Robert's car keys in his left hand, and he flung them over the car, across the highway. "There's your fucking keys, Robert, you prick," he muttered and rolled up the window. Denis had no idea what was happening. They were moving again but he had no idea why or why his father was angry with Robert. He knew better than to ask questions.

The kids all sat in the back and watched the scenery. They drove through California, and Denis remembers the redwoods. Anne remembers somewhere along the way they spent a night in a motel and Pat showed her some new clothes they had got for her. She was thrilled because Pat never bought her clothes. Did she recognize them as Luce's? "Maybe," she says now. "But I didn't care. They were new clothes and they were beautiful."

They drove north through Oregon and into Washington. There was a ferry ride to a place called Victoria. It was in Canada. At the other end, waiting for them, was an old man with a glass eye and a woman with a claw-like hand. They got out of the car and Pat brought them over.

"This is my dad, kids. Your grandfather. Say hello."

Chapter Twelve

Victoria, British Columbia, 1970

Pat's father was a one-eyed war vet who lived in a small, run-down house and worked as a labourer on Victoria's waterfront. Nothing was ever said about Pat's mother but the woman who lived with her father now was evidently his second wife. Denis and Anne liked her; she was kind and welcoming. She had a deformed hand, and Ray would make fun of her behind her back. They had three daughters—one of whom was younger than Denis—who were Pat's half-sisters. Pat had never met them before.

They spent two weeks with Pat's family in a rickety house next to a creek on what Denis remembers as the outskirts of Victoria. The children had no idea where they were and didn't care. They were weary of being uprooted every few months, weary of making and losing friends, trying to catch up in a dizzying succession of schools. "Grandpa" was decent to them but they hated the charade. He evidently believed they were Pat's kids, and they were too frightened of Pat to set him right. Martine and Anne shared a room with Pat's half-sisters; Marc and Denis slept in a second bedroom, and Ray and Pat bunked on the sofa. When they finally moved on, it was to a duplex on Shearwater Street. It felt like coming into sunlight.

The kids were old hands now at cracking new neighbourhoods. They made friends quickly, and one of the first kids they met was Lori Wells. Lori was fourteen that spring when she says she saw a new family moved into a duplex across the street. Lori's father, Robert, was a truck driver for a janitorial supply company. He was an organized, fastidious man who kept his tools in order and his lawn neatly clipped. Her mother, Mary, worked as an order clerk for the same janitorial supply company and was devoted to Lori and her sister, Bobbi.

The new family intrigued Lori. They had arrived in a gold-coloured Cadillac with fins on the back. And they had kids. She says she noticed first the tall, blond boy who was tanned and lightly freckled. He was cute and terribly shy. He had a sister who was skinny and a real live wire. She had freckles and long brown hair. First chance she got, Lori introduced herself to the boy. He had a Texas drawl and gave some words a slight French pronunciation. His sister Anne was the same age as Bobbi. There was a cute baby, too, and a tiny boy with a brush-cut.

Lori discovered that the family had just moved from California. She met Denis's folks and saw something of how they lived. She was struck by the fact that the kids did all the chores around the house and by how strict their parents were. After every bath, the kids would have to scrub down the tub. "They were quiet, hesitant kids. I had never been around kids like that. They were so afraid that they wouldn't say boo," she says.

Lori was keen to have her parents meet Denis's folks, Ray and Pat, and she eventually arranged an introduction. Her father and Ray hit it off. On weekends her parents would cross the street for a drink with the Durands and a late barbecue. Lori remembers being amazed at how often the Durands ate steak. And they were boozers. Lorraine says her mother rarely drank, and she had never seen her tipsy. But once, after an evening with the Durands, she remembers her mother came home a little shaky on her feet.

It was near the end of the school year but the Durand kids were immediately enrolled in Lori's school, and she saw a lot of Denis and liked him. She didn't know what to make of his father, though. One day she was walking up the drive with Denis and saw Ray on the porch with his elbows propped on the railing. As Denis and Lori approached, Ray said something in French to Denis. Denis didn't answer and looked embarrassed. Lori remembers thinking, That remark was about me. Otherwise, why would he have said it in French. She suspected it was rude. "He was a spooky guy. The kids didn't like being around him," she remembers.

Denis and Anne remember how easily they adjusted to the new climate, the new home. Summer was coming and they remained outdoors as much as possible. And it was at Shearwater Street that Anne overheard a telephone conversation that was to haunt her ever after like some unnamed, faceless terror. It was night. She was in bed, but got up to go to the washroom. She heard her father on the telephone. He said, "Madame Boissonneault" and Anne froze. She realized immediately that he was talking to Jeannine's mother.

"We're fine. Jeannine and the kids are just down the street," she heard him say.

What was he talking about? Why was he lying? Anne asked herself. Now she was terrified that Pat would overhear.

"Yes, we're in town. We'll drop by later in the afternoon, as soon as Jeannine and the kids return."

Jeannine's not here. We're not in the same city as my grandmother, Anne thought, now frantic. Why was he lying? She couldn't begin to understand what he was doing. Whatever it was, it scared her to death, although she couldn't say why. She loved her father. He protected her from Pat. Anne couldn't understand the call and couldn't bring herself to acknowledge its chilling implications, so she buried all knowledge of it. It had never happened. She'd be a fully grown adult before she had the courage to unpack that memory and tell someone about it.

Anne now often heard Pat call her "my kid." Whenever Pat said it, Anne felt a little jolt of confusion. "I felt I was living somebody else's life," she said years later. "It wasn't me. I wasn't happy. It wasn't a life. It was existing."

She didn't want to be like Denis, who was always fighting with his father. She felt sorry for him but felt there was too much hatred and anger in the family. It made her sad to see Denis crying and asking about Jeannine and being told that she had left because she didn't love him. But she couldn't take on those battles. She wanted peace not more war.

By the time summer rolled around, Ray was involved in a new business. He had found a job in a body shop that specialized in custom paint jobs—laces, candies, pearls and some "real psychedelic stuff," as Denis remembered. Most of the trade was motorcycles. Denis met the owner and helped out in the shop on weekends. One Saturday before school was out he was working, and he and the owner stepped across the street for a chocolate milk. While they were sitting over their drinks, the owner looked at Denis and told him, "Your dad's a prick." Denis reddened but didn't protest. It was true. He knew they weren't getting along so it was no surprise to him that, when the holidays started, the owner was gone and the place had been renamed Ray's Kar Kare. Ray was in charge.

Victoria was beautiful in the summer. It was cooler than San Diego but it was along the ocean and the houses were tidy and brightly painted. The first time that Denis saw the provincial legislature building, he thought of Ottawa. He was happy to be back in Canada.

Denis hadn't forgotten his mother but she'd been out of his life now for two and a half years, and every physical trace of her had disappeared. She had left behind things that would never be erased, though, intangibles like Denis and Anne's appreciation of music, their shyness, their moral sense. She still inhabited a corner of the lives of her two eldest children but they'd got over the initial shock of her disappearance.

Denis and his father still fought but the fights didn't have the edge of viciousness to them that quarrels with Pat did. Denis got a glimpse of the depths of Pat's anger towards him one night after he and Ray had a shouting match. Ray had chased Denis out of the house but he was drunk so Denis ran around to the back of the house and slipped in the back door, into his room and hid in his closet. He had just made it into the closet and was crouched in a corner behind his clothes when Pat entered the room. She was drunk and made right for the closet. He figured he was done for. He saw her legs when she opened the door and was about to shove her out of the way and dodge past her when he realized she hadn't seen him. While he watched her legs and listened, she took a pair of his jeans and ripped the pants from knee to cuff. There had been a small hole at the knee of the jeans and they had recently fought about his wearing them. He had disobeyed her so she was destroying the jeans. Now they were unwearable. Denis slept hidden in the closet that night, too frightened and wounded to emerge.

They started a new school again that fall, and in November Denis fell madly in love with a girl in his grade eight class. He had first noticed her in his homeroom. Her name was Gayle Wigmore, she had shoulder-length brown hair and greeny-blue eyes and he thought he'd never before seen anyone as beautiful.

Gayle, who still lives in Victoria, knows the precise date that she fell in love with Denis. She recorded everything in her diary. On November 12, she wrote, "Denis Durand is really smiling and winking at me" in math class. And the following day: "Walked out of math class today and I asked him for his picture. He said he really likes me. Oh boy, I'm on cloud nine."

Gayle is the only child of Bill and Grace Wigmore. Bill is an engineer who then worked at a nearby military base. Her mother,

Gayle says, was a "real milk-and-cookies mom" who made her friends feel welcome and was happy to feed them all. Denis, she remembers "had blond hair, he was skinny and tall. And he had a very gentle face. He was quiet and that's what attracted me to him."

Later that week Denis walked Gayle home from school and met her mother. Gayle says her mother was charmed by Denis and remembers him to this day as "a really nice, decent kid."

"My mom says that, of all the boys I dated, Denis was her favourite," says Gayle. "He was very quiet. He didn't really have any friends here except me." She remembers Denis was always drumming on the furniture, working out the beat to songs he had heard on the radio.

Gayle became Denis's soul mate in the way that Jack had been in Houston. She was a companion, and she helped dissipate the cloud of loneliness that hovered over him. He was embarrassed by Ray and Pat's drinking and carrying on, and he was reluctant to bring her home. He didn't want her to know that he was the son of a thief and a drunk and a pill-popper and all the rest of it. When he did talk about his father, he told Gayle that his dad owned a body shop, that he was a businessman. He told her about his sisters and brother. Gayle eventually met them and she remembers how they looked up to Denis and how protective he was of them.

Denis loved visiting the Wigmores. They seemed so rooted in who and what they were. Gayle had been born in Victoria, as had her parents. Gayle was surrounded by uncles, aunts and cousins. Her place was everything that Denis imagined a happy home should be. Gayle's parents were thoughtful of each other and enjoyed seeing their daughter happy. They were stable, respected. Denis longed to be part of such a normal, happy family.

Gayle's affection for him was healing. It made him feel human and boosted his sense of self-worth. For both of them, it was their first glimpse of love. "He made a deep impression on me," she remembers.

Denis never did tell Gayle anything of his family's travels. When she asked, he simply told her that his father moved a lot looking for new work. A lot of it he didn't know himself. He had never been told why his father had left for Florida in the first place. He believed that Ray had been on the run, that he had crossed the wrong guys and somebody wanted to kill him. And the truths that he did know were embarrassing. He was a proud, sensitive teenager without a great deal of self-confidence. Like his mother, he considered family matters to be state secrets. His father's beatings and Pat's drunkenness filled him with debilitating shame. He lived in constant fear that people he knew and respected and, in Gayle's case, loved would find out about his sordid family life. He felt as if he was leading a double life. There was the Denis who was known at school as a well-mannered, likable boy, polite to his elders, a cool guy with his peers, a romantic figure to his girl-friend. Then there was the Denis at home who was known as the big dummy, who couldn't do anything right, was always in trouble with his folks. The Denis at home was such a worthless person that Pat couldn't resist slapping him whenever she felt the urge. "You're like the Boissonneaults," his father would tell him. "You'll never amount to anything."

That fall Ray and Robert Wells struck a business agreement. Ray had talked Robert into investing in Ray's Kar Kare. He was to become a partner. Robert mortgaged his house and borrowed some money from a finance company. He gave Ray about seventy-five hundred dollars cash and then signed a personal guarantee for another three thousand that Ray had borrowed. It was a giant leap for Robert. His house was his only real asset and he'd never been in business before.

Almost immediately after Ray's partner joined the firm, the Durands moved from Shearwater Street to a bungalow on the outskirts of the city. Anne later remembered it looked like a doctor's house. They furnished the place on credit. Once again the children were obliged to change schools. It was a particular hardship for Denis because he was no longer within walking distance of Gayle's place.

They celebrated Christmas in the new house. Ray and Pat had frequently asked Denis why he never invited his girl-friend over, and Denis had shrugged them off for months. Now, he decided, he'd take the plunge. He invited Gayle over for dinner on New Year's Day. His father had invited a young man he had met, Cookie, a sailor, who lived just down the road with his girl-friend. Denis fretted for days that Pat and Ray would get drunk and embarrass him. On New Year's Day he and Ray drove over to pick up Gayle. Gayle remembers Ray was jolly, always laughing. Pat, she says, "cooked the toughest roast beef I've ever eaten." Gayle remembers having a good time, dancing with Denis's father to music on the record player. The next day, she wrote in her diary: "Denis has a real nice family."

Immediately after New Year's, Ray told Robert that he had to make a quick trip to Ottawa and asked if he could borrow Robert's credit card for gas in case he had trouble. That night Ray brought his friend Cookie over and told the kids they would be staying with Cookie and his girl-friend for a few days. Then Ray, Pat and Martine drove off in the Cadillac. The kids were elated. It was party time. Cookie and his girl-friend were friendly and affectionate. Anne was so starved for attention that she told Cookie's girl-friend that she thought she was starting her period. That caught her a hug and sympathy and a helpful talk.

The children had no idea where Ray, Pat and Martine had gone, but they assumed they would be back in a few days. Then one morning they woke up and Cookie told them there was no more money and that he couldn't take care of them any more. He told them to pack and that he would take them to their grandfather's place. They were shocked but quickly gathered everything they needed and rode to the Holben place in silence. The old man greeted them at the door, and Denis heard him tell Cookie, "It's OK. I've heard from them. The kids can stay here."

That night Denis was in bed when he heard a knock on the door. The old man answered the door. It was Robert Wells. Denis heard Robert say, "Where is that son of a bitch. He cheated me out of all my money." Denis crept to the door of the bedroom and opened it a crack. Robert was in tears. He'd never seen an adult cry before and it made him want to cry himself.

Holben told Wells that he had no idea where Ray had gone. He couldn't help. Eventually Wells left, crushed.

As Lori remembers it, her father went down to the body shop one morning after Ray had left for Ottawa and found the place had been cleaned out. He was left holding the bag for the loans Ray had made at the bank and for all the charges Ray ran up on his credit card. By the time he realized he had been had, the kids had moved from the big, white house. Wells found them at Holben's place but soon after they disappeared as well. He had been completely taken in by Ray and had been skinned for virtually all his modest life savings.

Chapter Thirteen

Ottawa, Ontario, 1971

When Denis, Anne and Marc were ushered aboard a twin-engine airplane at Victoria airport on January 22, 1971, they hadn't the slightest idea what they were headed into. Their bags contained nothing more than their favourite clothes and their toothbrushes. There were no mementos, gifts, sleep toys or baby pictures nestled in among the packed clothing. They had moved so often, often so rapidly, that not a single artefact of their past remained. They had left their maternal grandparents' home in Hull on a muggy summer night almost three years earlier. Their world had been transformed since then. They had lost their mother, and since her departure the only people they had seen from their old life were Robert and Claudette and their kids. They had learned a new language and used their mother tongue so infrequently that it now took a conscious effort to speak French. In all the houses they had lived in since then there wasn't a teacup or chair or painting or photo album that they could point to and say, "I remember that from Pointe Gatineau." The past seemed irretrievably lost.

When they boarded that airplane in Victoria they knew all Pat's dishes and the household effects that had been assembled since Holly Street had been left behind. They thought it would all be shipped out to them and that they would be staying with some friend of Ray or Pat's until their stuff arrived. Who, they didn't know. It didn't bear thinking about.

They flew to Vancouver, and when they landed a stewardess met them and escorted them to another gate where they waited for another plane. Hours later when they arrived in Ottawa, their father was waiting and they slid into the Cadillac and drove to a small house, this one inhabited by a man who appeared to be a friend of Ray's. Outside it was polar-bear cold and the snow was piled shoulder-high. Denis knew they were in Ottawa but he has no recollection of being immediately stunned by the import of that. They were in a suburban neighbourhood on the southern edge of the city and it looked like any suburb in any city.

Denis still believed that his mother had come back to live with her parents and hadn't been able to find them again. Now, when he thinks back on it, he can't explain why he didn't immediately connect Ottawa with Jeannine. He has no memory of being angry with her for not being able to find him and the other children. "It's stupid," he now says with a shrug, unable to fathom why he can't remember being filled with anticipation when he flew into the city. He was fifteen, and the geography of the area was a puzzle. He was fearful of talking about or even thinking of Jeannine around Pat and Ray. That part of his life was taboo. He can't remember thinking about his mother the night of his arrival or, indeed, for the first week or so. He was back with Ray and Pat and that in itself took some getting used to. Was Ray still worried about his enemies? He was well hidden in a quiet suburb but there were a lot of ghosts in the Ottawa/Hull area for Ray Durand.

They spent about a week in that first place, a stranger's house. Denis can't remember what it was like but he does recall it didn't last very long.

January 28, 1971

Dear Gayle,

Hi! We had a nice plane ride down here. It's very cold down here. I got a cassette recorder. I went to a fishing derby. When I got here we went skidooing. It sure is fun. It sure feels good to speak French again. But I would rather be with you....

Say hi to your mom and dad. Write to me at 2848 Grandeur, Ottawa.

Love,
Denis

By the time Gayle received that letter Denis and his family had moved to Grandeur Avenue along the river in Ottawa's west end. They were now staying with Pat's brother, Harold, his wife, Barbara, and their four boys. Harold was a Korean War veteran who had a wooden leg, a direct manner and was a year older than Pat. In the late 1950s he had been a truck driver for Frazer Duntile and he'd met Ray then. Harold says Ray and Pat appeared unexpectedly on his doorstep in January, 1971: "They had no furniture, dishes, anything. But they had money. Ray always had money. Ray said they'd had to leave the U.S. because of the Vietnam war. He didn't want Denis to be drafted." They needed a place to stay for a few weeks so Harold offered to put them up.

"Ray treated Denis like shit," Harold recalls, remembering how appalled he and his wife were by the Ray's meanness. "All those kids had to toe the line or they wouldn't even get fed. Ray and Pat would eat steak and feed the kids macaroni."

Denis was about the same age as one of the "cousins," Derek, and he discovered that both Derek and one of his brothers, Michael, were in the cadets. When Derek suggested he come along to a meeting, Denis jumped at the chance. They took a bus on a frigid evening after dinner and alighted in the city centre.

They were walking to the cadets' meeting, and Denis was shivering with cold, when he noticed a tower with a clock in it. A block farther on he saw the tower was part of a massive Gothic stone building with two wings. Parliament Hill. He'd felt a mounting sense of anticipation since his departure from Victoria. He knew that his grandparents lived in Hull and he'd always believed that his mother was with them. But now, for the first time, it struck him just how close he was to her. He remembered the view of Parliament Hill from Hull. It sprawled on a hill high over the river. Now he was seeing it from the front. His mother was just on the other side of the tower, across the frozen river.

He couldn't believe it, couldn't believe he hadn't realized before just how close he was to seeing her again. He wanted to scream, to cry and to sprint over there right then. Despite the arctic cold, he felt a comforting warmth inside. He was almost home. His odyssey had ended. He'd never leave here again.

His mind was racing so fast that evening he couldn't focus on what it meant to be a cadet. He joined the cadets during the meeting but he didn't really give it much thought. He was too busy pondering his discovery.

By now all the kids knew better than to utter Jeannine's name in the presence of Pat or Ray. Whenever Denis fought with his father, he knew that the moment he said her name, the fight would take on larger dimensions. Those would be the nights that Denis would end up making a dash for the door before his father took a swipe at him. So he knew that if he was going to contact his grandparents, he should proceed by stealth.

Denis's middle name was Hermas, and he knew that he had been named after his grandfather. And he knew his mother's maiden name was Boissonneault. His father had slagged him often enough for being a Boissonneault that he couldn't have forgotten the name if he had wanted to. He couldn't remember what street his grandparents lived on but knew it was in Hull. He decided to phone them the first opportunity he got.

His dad had found a job as an insurance appraiser with Collision Appraisal Services so he was gone most of the day. But Pat was around. For one reason or another—Denis says he was scared, the house was always full, he panicked at the thought of what he was going to say to his mother—the right moment was a long time in coming. They had been in Ottawa two weeks before an opportunity presented itself. One Friday night in early February, Ray and Pat announced that they were leaving for the weekend. They were off to the Carnival in Quebec City. All four kids were to stay with Harold and Barbara. Denis watched them drive off, sucked in his breath and decided that the following day he would embark on what would turn out to be the most fateful encounter of his life.

On Saturday morning he slipped out of the house, a dime clutched in his fist inside his mitten, and he began searching for a phone booth far enough from his house that he could be certain he wouldn't be seen. It was cold and the snowbanks in some places were above his head. Finally, he spotted a booth. He entered, picked up the white pages and turned to the B listings. Sure enough, there was a Hermas Boissonneault but it was on a street whose name he didn't recognize. Mutchmore Street. Still, it was in Hull. Trembling now, he slipped the dime into its slot and dialled the number. A woman answered. He thought he remembered the voice. He searched desperately for the French words. He groped and finally issued a tentative, "Grandmama?"

He had barely uttered the word when he heard sobbing on the other end of the line.

"Denis? Denis? Let me speak to your mother."

It was his grandmother. He recognized her voice, understood her French. He replied in a mixture of French and English.

"No, Grandmama, she's not here. She's with you, isn't she?"

At that, both of them burst into tears. When she was able to talk again, she asked, "Denis, where are you?"

When Denis explained that he was in Ottawa, she pleaded with him to take a bus to her place. She gave him directions, told him what buses to take and how to find the house. He hadn't thought to put a pencil or piece of paper in his pocket so he struggled to remember it all. Denis left the phone booth after promising to come over first thing the next morning, a Sunday. He was dizzy with his discovery. For three years he had dreamed of walking into his mother's embrace in his grandmother's house. Through the worst of times, when Pat beat him and hunger gnawed at his stomach and his father ridiculed him for his crying and his melancholy dreaminess, he had imagined that there was an alternative. He hadn't for a moment doubted that his mother would welcome him and the other kids and take them to live with her if only he could make his way back to Hull. It was like a medieval quest where, by his own ingenuity, overcoming all adversity, he would arrive, triumphant, to claim his mother's love. What he hadn't imagined was that she wouldn't be there. Now, suddenly, he was confronted with the news that his mother had never returned to her family in Hull. What was he to make of it?

The following morning he told one of the Holben boys that he was going over to Hull for the day. He took a bus downtown and then, uncertain, transferred to another bus heading across the broad, ice-encrusted Ottawa River. He got off on Marengère Street in Hull, but couldn't remember the street name his grandmother had told him to look for. He hadn't a cent left in his pockets and began to worry that he would have to walk all the way back to Ottawa. He thought he'd probably freeze to death on the walk. He wandered for an hour in the bitter cold until, quite by accident, he came across Mutchmore Street. That rang a bell in his memory. He remembered she said it was the house with a red mailbox. He walked the entire length of the street but none of the houses had a red mailbox. Puzzled, he retraced his steps and noticed, on a corner, a big, red Canada Post mailbox. He raced up the stairs of the house behind it and knocked on the door. The door swung open and out of the steam created by the contact of warm and cold air, there emerged the tall, bespectacled, grey-haired woman he remembered as Grandmama.

She hugged him and cried and he cried and she brought him into the tiny, warm house with a piano in the front room. Waiting inside was his grandfather, the sore on his face larger than ever. Uncle Réginald was there, too, now balding and stouter than he remembered. And his great aunt Berthe. They made him tell and retell, in his halting French, the story of Jeannine's departure and where the family had been since. In turn, they told him that Ray had come by some weeks earlier when only Hermas and Réginald had been home. He had told them that Jeannine and the kids were living in Vancouver. He had given them a phone number and a Vancouver address but there was no Jeannine at the phone number he had given them and the letters Laurette had sent to the Vancouver address had been returned, unopened. They told him that they had received a number of phone calls from Ray over the past three years. He had always said Jeannine was out somewhere and that they were all doing fine and that she would call. But she had never called. Then they told him what Robert had told Berthe, that Jeannine had been put in a mental hospital. Denis told them he knew that his father had cheated Robert. He said he couldn't believe his mother had gone crazy.

Over lunch they discussed and quarrelled about the meaning of the information Denis had brought, conversing in a French spoken so rapidly that Denis couldn't follow. Denis had told them that they had all been using the name Holben in the United States, so Berthe decided she'd visit the asylums this time and check for patients named Jeannine Holben. Laurette suggested that Jeannine might simply have become so fed up with Ray that she had slipped off and entered a convent.

Later, when Denis and his grandmother were alone in the kitchen together, they fell silent. Denis felt there was something she wanted to tell him.

Finally, she said, quietly, "Denis, you remember the night we quarrelled...."

Denis looked at her. How could he have forgotten. He still harboured a grudge against Réginald. He blamed his uncle for forcing them to leave. He'd heard his father say so many mean things about Réginald that he half-believed them himself.

"You know, Denis, we never wanted Jeannine to leave. I didn't know how bad things were with Raymond. If I had known, I would never have suggested that her place was with her husband."

Denis saw that his grandmother was consumed with guilt for that one sharp remark. It was clear, too, that she wasn't sure that Jeannine had ever really forgiven her. As Denis listened, Laurette explained that after they had left, a letter Jeannine had sent to Raymond in Florida had been returned, unopened. Laurette had readdressed it to Houston but again it had been returned. She had then held onto it for months. Finally, when she hadn't heard from Jeannine for an unbearably long time, Laurette had committed what she considered a gross breach of good manners and had opened the letter. She never showed it to Denis but she made it clear that the letter had revealed to her that there wasn't much left of the affection Jeannine had once felt for Raymond. Laurette wouldn't permit herself to reveal the details of the missive. But Denis wondered what his mother had written. Had she told Raymond that she knew about his relationship with Pat? Had she said she didn't want to live with him any more? Had she thrown in a line about how uncomfortable she was living with her family? Had Laurette read something in the letter that led her to believe that Jeannine was upset with them? Whatever it was, Laurette was paralysed with uncertainty. She couldn't be sure that her daughter wasn't still upset with her. At the same time, she couldn't believe that Jeannine would have left her children. And why had Raymond lied to them? The way Laurette saw it, only one explanation fit the facts. Jeannine had left Raymond. She couldn't take it any more. She knew he'd never let her leave with the children, she couldn't bring herself to return to her family, and so she had simply entered a convent. Only a life devoted to prayer and to the love of God would allow her to live with herself once she had abandoned her children. As for Raymond, he had been so embarrassed by the fact that his wife had rejected him that he had lied about it. Laurette knew Jeannine wasn't mentally unstable. Therefore, Jeannine had to be in a convent.

Laurette lived within such a small, orderly universe that she could not imagine other, more bizarre possibilities. She had never been the victim of random crime, had never been in a traffic accident. She had protected and sheltered her children from the vulgarities of life. The central struggle of her existence had been against poverty. She hadn't emerged triumphant from that struggle but she could claim the satisfaction of a draw. By dint of hard work and watching her pennies she had always managed to pay the family's bills and make a weekly contribution to her parish church. She missed Jeannine's company but believed she would be happy in a convent. Laurette could imagine how comforting the daily rituals in a convent might be for Jeannine but she couldn't imagine the geography of her daughter's life. When she considered the physical surroundings of Jeannine's monastic existence, she saw only a void.

Denis, the Boissonneaults and Aunt Berthe spent the entire afternoon mulling it over together. Denis hadn't planned to stay for dinner but he couldn't resist a decent meal. Before he left that night Laurette promised him that she would come to Harold Holben's and confront Raymond. She would insist that he tell them what he knew. As for the business about going to the authorities for help—an idea advanced by Hermas—Laurette said that was out of the question. What would happen to the kids? she asked. Regardless of what she thought of Raymond Durand, Laurette couldn't ignore the fact that he was the father of her four grandchildren. During the day-long talk with Denis she had been careful not to criticize Raymond. She had even reproached Denis for some of his comments about Ray. "He's your father," she told him several times. She may have been desperate for news about Jeannine but she couldn't abandon herself entirely to her feelings. There were social conventions to be respected. Above all, she didn't want a scandal. "What will everybody say?" she asked the others. It wasn't just the neighbours she was thinking of. It was Jeannine, too. What if Jeannine didn't want to be found?

It was dark by the time Denis began making his way home on the bus. He hadn't meant to stay so late. As he approached the Holben house, he saw his father's car parked on the street. They were back. His stomach sank. He braced himself for a fight. When he walked into the house, there was only one light on in the living-room. It seemed everyone had gone to bed. Denis took off his boots, hung up his coat and walked into the living-room to find his father sitting on the sofa, under the light, with a Consumer's Distributing catalogue on his lap.

"Where've you been?" he growled.

"Just out for a bus ride."

"You're lying. You were in Hull. You went to see your grandparents. I know."

Shaken, Denis denied it, but soon his father was shouting at him. Finally, he didn't care any more.

"You said Mom came back to her parents' place. Well, she didn't. Where is she? Why won't you tell me? You lied to Grandmama. You came back with her suitcases. What did you do to her?"

Ray didn't bat an eye. Denis had seen it before. His father would be in the tightest situation imaginable and he'd stroll out of it with a series of lies so brazen they would work. Now, Ray shrugged it all off, accusing Denis of lying, the Boissonneaults of distorting his words. Soon they were screaming at each other. Denis had lost a great deal of his fear. The visit to his grandparents' house had given him the feeling that he now had a home base, that someone, finally, was on his side. His fears weren't imaginary; his father really was a liar. He told himself that if things got out of hand with his father, he would run off and live with the Boissonneaults. They would protect him. They certainly loved him.

As the quarrel raged, Denis also began to see that his father wasn't about to bare his soul. Suddenly, Ray lowered his voice and began working to persuade Denis that the Boissonneaults were bad people, that they couldn't be trusted. Then he pointed down at the catalogue. It was open to a page on which drum kits were displayed. Pointing at one of the drum kits, he made his pitch.

"I'll buy you these drums if you promise never to go over there again," he offered.

Denis was stunned. It was such a transparent ploy. His father was attempting to buy his loyalty. If he had had doubts before he walked in, now there were none left. He was certain that his father was concealing a vital piece of information about Jeannine. He'd have to find a way to get it out of him. Ray wasn't going to volunteer it. So Denis opted for a temporary truce.

"OK, dad," he whispered. "OK." And he stumbled off to bed.

By the time Laurette made her way over to the Grandeur Street address Denis had given her, the family had moved. It was a Sunday night and no one answered her knocks. She was exhausted by the fruitless effort but perhaps also a little relieved. Laurette was in her early sixties, her husband was dying of cancer, and she was still supporting her family, working as a seamstress for a tent manufacturer in Ottawa. A hole had been torn in her life and she didn't know how to repair it. She didn't know whether her daughter was beckoning to her or not. And she was frightened of Raymond Durand. She had never before encountered a man with his charm and his malevolence. He had always treated her with the utmost respect, but now, perhaps for the first time, she saw how empty his gestures had been. He had lied to her for a reason that she was unable to discern. He frightened her. Was he protecting Jeannine or himself?

Laurette had lived all her life in a small, French-speaking community that reinforced her sense of place and identity. Her job, her church, her family and her music defined the boundaries of her world. She had never travelled, wasn't well read and was completely overwhelmed by the times. She saw the long-haired young people in the streets and heard some of their music on the radio and listened to the warnings of her parish priest about the evils of drugs. She must have felt that her world was fading and a new one was being born, a world that she'd never understand and couldn't imagine wanting to be part of. All the changes seemed to be emanating from the United States. It was such a big country, such a vast place to lose yourself in. If Jeannine was down there somewhere, Laurette couldn't imagine how she could possibly find her. There were hundreds of thousands of small cities and towns that Jeannine could have fled to.

Her last link with her daughter was her grandchildren, the only grandchildren she had. When Denis had visited, she had pleaded with him to bring his brothers and sisters over so she could touch them, hold them, maybe catch a glimpse of Jeannine in them. Denis's visit had left her with mixed feelings. The news he had brought was distressing but he looked so much like Jeannine. He had her blonde hair, her high forehead, her gentle nature. She had to see the others.

That spring Denis, Ray and Pat attended a Durand family gathering in Hull. Midway through the party Denis stepped outside for a breath of fresh air, realized he was only a couple of blocks from the Boissonneaults' place and decided to duck over there for an hour. No one noticed he was gone. At the Boissonneaults', Denis asked his grandmother why she hadn't come to talk to his father. She explained that she had. He gave her the new address and pleaded with her to try again. Laurette wanted to know about the little ones.

She was desperate to see them. Denis said he'd try to bring them over but he worried that Marc would blab to Pat and he knew that Anne would be too scared.

A week later Denis talked Anne and Marc into taking a walk with him after school. It was a good half-hour hike to the tent manufacturer on Bank Street where Laurette worked. They trundled down the sidewalk, bundled up against the cold. Finally they arrived outside a two-storey building. Denis looked up at a second-floor window and saw his grandmother at her sewing machine. They stood there until she glanced out at the street and saw them. Her face lit up and she held out a finger to say, just a minute. By now Denis had told Anne and Marc whom they were going to visit. Marc was scared but not as much as Anne was. She couldn't stop shaking. She wanted to leave right then and there and pleaded with Denis to take them back home. She was furious with him for bringing her along.

Finally Laurette came out, rushed over and hugged Marc and Anne. She couldn't stop crying. She led them to a restaurant and got a booth. Anne sat in a corner, unable to speak, shaking with fear. Laurette bought them all soft drinks and kept caressing Marc and Anne. She saw how frightened Anne was and said to Denis in French, "Look, she's so scared." She assumed Anne couldn't understand but Anne remembers sitting there amazed that she understood perfectly what her grandmother was saying. Later, going home, Anne's fear mounted. She told Denis that she thought her grandmother was nice but she was certain Pat or Ray would find out. But neither Pat nor Ray did.

Denis was emboldened by the success of his expedition and decided to take Anne to his grandparents' place in Hull. He thought taking Marc might be too risky. A couple of weeks later Denis talked his father into allowing Anne and him to go to a movie downtown. His father dropped them off and agreed to pick them up after the film. As soon as Ray drove off, Denis told Anne they were going to take a bus to Hull. Anne refused. She whimpered that she was afraid. Denis had to drag her onto the bus. But she calmed down once they were in Laurette's kitchen having a snack. They stayed for an hour and a half and left with change jingling in their pockets.

Back in Victoria, Robert Wells brooded all winter about Ray's betrayal. In the spring his wife told him to go and do what he had to do. So Robert got on an airplane, flew to Ottawa and somehow managed to locate Ray and Pat. He hired a lawyer and filed a lawsuit against the two of them for breach of contract and breach of trust. In his statement of claim, Robert said that he had mortgaged his home, guaranteed bank loans Ray had made, emptied his own savings account and lent Ray his credit card to become a partner in Ray's Kar Kare. He said Ray either never invested any of the money in the company, or, if he had, he then withdrew it for his own use. Robert claimed Ray owed him more than twelve thousand dollars plus the costs of the legal action. Ray arrived at work one morning at Collision Appraisal Services and discovered a bailiff waiting for him. He was served with legal notice of the lawsuit. Ray responded by hiring lawyer Gary Schreider to defend him.

Cadet meetings were every Monday night. Denis would skip every second meeting and spend the evening with his grandparents. He got to know Réginald and realized he couldn't hold a grudge against him. It wasn't his fault that he felt trapped in his room. If anything, Denis felt sorry for him.

On some nights his grandmother would be out, and he'd chat with Hermas, who was in declining health. The cancerous mole on his face was slowly killing him. Unlike Laurette, Hermas was willing to entertain darker suspicions about what had happened to Jeannine. With Denis close at hand, he'd theorize.

One night, to Denis's astonishment, Hermas told him: "I think he killed her. If I was younger and in good health I'd go down there and find out what happened. I think he tied a stone around her and drowned her in a lake. There are lots of lakes in Texas. Was there one near where you lived?" Denis told him about the lake at Big Thicket and the old man nodded, as if to say, *See, I told you.* Denis didn't contradict his grandfather but he considered the old man's macabre theory nothing more than morbid speculation. Denis now had no idea what had happened to his mother. He knew his father was hiding something and he figured Pat was in on the secret. He couldn't for a moment believe that his father had killed his mother. But he was willing to believe the worst about Pat.

In the early 1960s, when Pat had worked as a waitress, she had met and occasionally gossiped with a hairdresser named Lucille Savage who worked across the street. After her return to Ottawa she ran into Lucille one day. They exchanged pleasantries and Lucille happened to mention that she and her husband, Maurice, spent most of their weekends at their cottage on Lac Champeau. "Come on up sometime," Lucille told Pat. It wasn't a specific invitation but a vague remark made to be polite and ease out of a conversation. Not long after, Lucille, a petite, jittery blonde, and Maurice were relaxing one Saturday at their cottage deep in the Gatineau Hills when a gold Cadillac pulled up and the driver leaned on his horn. Lucille rose to see who was making the racket and saw Pat climb out of the car. Pat waved her over and introduced her husband, Ray Durand. A polite hostess, Lucille invited them in. More than twenty years later, she still regrets having done so.

Maurice, a short, muscular and friendly man with prominent incisors that give him a Dracula-like grin, has also never forgotten the moment Ray Durand walked into his life. "He didn't even know me when he walked into my cottage and yet he said, 'Hello, Maurice. Remember me. We used to go to school together. You have a brother, René.' I never went to school with him. He must have heard about my brother from my wife. He took over the place that weekend. He was going to buy the whole lake. He was driving that gold Cadillac, smoking a cigar, had a pocket full of money."

Maurice was no shrinking violet himself. He had been a top salesman for a chain of health clubs and knew something about hooking a sucker. Once he'd bet some fellow employees that he could sell a club membership to the next person who popped his head in the door of the health club he was then managing. It was ten minutes to closing time, and when the door opened, in walked four people in search of a restaurant. Maurice sold them all family memberships and won the bet. Now he was taking a breather from the health club business and looking for a new line of work.

Maurice remembers being completely bowled over by the power of Ray's personality. "That guy had very strong magnetism. He was a jolly person and people fell for that. If he could have used his magnetism in the right way, he could have been very successful."

Ray, Pat and Maurice partied all weekend. Lucille, who wasn't much of a drinker, stood by bewildered. Lucille now owned a hairdressing salon and had a clientele that included Prime Minister Pierre Trudeau and a half-dozen members of his cabinet. She was hard-working and serious-minded and maintained her good looks by keeping fit and tanning almost daily in her bikini. Ray set off alarms for Lucille. He was aggressive, vulgar and looked at her in a way that made her uncomfortable.

When the weekend ended, Ray and Pat drove off, much to Lucille's relief. But Ray was back that same week. He had spotted a cottage for sale. He arranged to live in it rent-free all summer on the strength of a promise that he would buy it in the fall. They lived up at the lake all summer and Ray devoted himself to scamming full-time.

Maurice started chumming around with Ray and saw him in action. He couldn't believe how outrageous Ray was. "I remember sitting with him in a restaurant, and he said he had to sit with his back to the wall because the last time he had been careless a guy had busted a bottle over his head. He said he used to be with the police. He said once he was investigating a theft from a grocery store in Gatineau. He chased the thieves and saw them throw a bag of money out of the window. He kept after them and caught them and then later he went back and found the money. He kept the money but his superiors suspected him and he was fired."

Ray also told Maurice about Florida. He said he fled to Florida "because he was hiding out from some guys from Montreal. He said he had to dye his hair red and give testimony in Miami."

The more time Maurice spent with Ray the more he learned of his relationship with Pat and the kids. He once asked Ray how long he had been with Pat, and Ray had told him five or six years. He said his first wife had run off with her uncle. He said he thought she was in a mental institution or something.

All Maurice remembers of the kids is that Denis's hair was getting long and he wasn't keen to be up at the cottage. Anne was skinny and had freckles. They did all the cleaning at the cottage, all the dishes. Martine, he saw, was treated differently: "Pat cared for her more than for the others."

Lucille remembers how mean Pat was to the kids: "Denis was shy and he looked deprived. I remember trying to talk to him. Denis did not mix. He looked scared. He didn't socialize. Anne was pitiful, so tiny. Pat would make Anne wash the floor, do the dishes. Anne and Denis did the chores. You could tell they weren't loved. Marc was even more pitiful. It was the little girl who looked loved. She was doted on. She was beautiful, had ringlets. Pat dressed her up so nice. Pat was always kissing her, hugging her. She would sing to her. She was a doll. She reminded me of little Shirley Temple compared to the others."

Denis spent the first half of the summer at cadet camp in northern Ontario. He and his grandmother Boissonneault wrote to each other. He sent her pictures and told her how happy he was. The camp was a much-needed break from Ray and Pat, and it infused Denis with self-confidence. He came back feeling competent. He had made friends and had earned the respect of the camp leaders.

The night he returned on the bus his father was supposed to meet him at the station. But Ray wasn't there so Denis hiked over to the Boissonneaults with his kitbag on his back. He had dinner with Réginald and his grandparents and then set out for the cottage on Lac Champeau. He hitched a ride and ended up walking the last ten miles. He arrived in the early hours of the morning, completely exhausted. His knocking woke his father, who told him he had forgotten what day he was supposed to pick Denis up. Before he drifted off to sleep he heard his father say that he had found a job for him for the remainder of the summer.

Shortly after Denis's return, Ray launched another con. He had done some body work on Maurice's car and had discovered Maurice's bank book in the glove compartment. Maurice, he learned, had a nice pile of savings in the bank. So shortly afterwards he made a pitch to Maurice. He told Maurice that he wanted to set up a company called Auto Appraisal and Checking Service.

"The idea was," Maurice remembers, "we would save insurance companies money. When a car had been repaired and the insurance company was about to pay, Ray would check to see that the parts that the body shop said had been installed had actually been installed. The insurance company would pay us a percentage of the money we would save them. Ray said, 'You come and I'll introduce you as my partner.' I did go around with him—met insurance company officials. He was received openly. They were all in favour. They said, 'You guys will have a big battle with the body shops.' The insurance companies were in favour but the body shops would be opposed."

Maurice bit hard and agreed to put up the money for the venture. "We opened an office on Rideau Street in Ottawa. I paid the rent,

signed a lease, hired a secretary, furnished the office, put in parti-
tions." Maurice also had stationery and business cards printed, got
phones installed and agreed to pay Ray wages until they had a
stream of income.

That first month Maurice remembers spending days sitting in the
office waiting for things to happen. He was sitting at his desk one
day when the phone rang and the caller asked for Mr Côté. "I said,
'Mr Côté?' And Ray started waving at me from the other side of
the room. He took the phone."

Apparently, Ray had an accomplice who had gone to a finance
company to borrow two thousand dollars. He told the finance company that he was employed by Auto Appraisal and Checking
Service and that his boss was Mr Côté. When the finance company
official phoned to check the borrower's references, Ray answered
and said he was Mr Côté.

"So Ray gets on the phone," Maurice remembers, "and says,
'What? He's asking to borrow two thousand dollars? He didn't say
anything about it to me. Don't lend him the money. If he wants
money, I'll give it to him. Tell him to come to me.'"

Ray then sat back and let the finance company official convince
himself that he had to make the loan. As Ray later explained to
Maurice, the finance company official told him, "Well, he's signed
the papers so I'm going to lend him the money." The con worked
so well that Ray repeated it a number of times.

Maurice was opposed to Ray using the company for his cons but
Ray always managed to allay his fears. He made it sound like a hell
of a good joke played on people who deserved to take a hit now
and again. Still, Maurice was getting nervous. Ray didn't seem to
be digging up work for them.

At home, relations between Denis and Ray were worsening.
Twice Ray had found Denis walking down a street in Hull near the
Boissonneaults' house. He didn't fly off the handle but he wasn't
happy about it.

For most of July and all of August Denis worked in a body shop
in Hull earning twenty-two dollars a week, fifteen of which he had
to give to Pat for room and board. That didn't leave much for other
expenses but Denis managed. And Ray told him that he could keep
all of his last two pay cheques to buy clothes for school. In early
September, Ray took Denis to the Giant Tiger store on Eddy Street

in Hull. When they were inside, Ray asked Denis how much money he had. When Denis replied that he had less than twenty dollars, something snapped in Ray. He began screaming at Denis, who bolted for the door. They ran into the street, Ray aiming kicks at Denis while they shouted at each other. It was a no-holds-barred fight so Denis threw Jeannine's name into it. When they finally wore themselves out, Denis was bruised but nothing was broken. Ray was rattled, though. He got Denis into the car and drove him to his mother's place on Rouville. He walked into the house with Denis in tow and asked his mother to take care of his son because he had had it. He pointed at Denis. "You'll live here now."

Marie-Anna agreed. She had a big house and took in boarders. She liked Denis, and Ray had said he would pay for the boy's room and board. Denis was relieved. He wouldn't be constantly fending off blows, and there was a school nearby that he could attend. He'd miss his brother and sisters, but he could visit them and they'd come by, he was sure, to see him.

With summer over, Ray and Pat and the kids moved back to a brick house in Hull they had lived in briefly in June. They were likely not even unpacked when Ray delivered the *coup de grâce* to his prey.

"One day I came into the office," Maurice remembers, "and Ray had his head in his hands. I said, 'What's wrong?' He said, 'I'm pulling out. I'm leaving.' I said, 'Why?' He said, 'The only thing I ever wanted to own has been taken from me. The cottage.'"

By now Maurice was alarmed. He could see his investment disappearing. Ray told him that he needed forty-five hundred dollars by noon the next day or he'd lose the cottage.

"I said, 'I'll get the money,'" Maurice recalls. He offered to lend Ray the money he needed. The following morning, Maurice withdrew the money from his account and accompanied Ray to a notary to close the deal. "Ray talked to the notary and then he came to me and said, 'He can't see me now.' He said, 'Go and eat, Maurice, and I'll pick you up at one-thirty.' I waited and I waited and then I called the notary. He said, 'Ray was here at eleven and the papers are all signed.' I think he bought the cottage for two thousand dollars and sold it the same day for eight thousand dollars. So he walked away with my money and the profit from the sale of the cottage."

When he figured out what had happened, Maurice phoned Ray at
the brick house Ray had been renting. The owner of the house
answered. "He asked me if I was a friend of Ray's. He said that Ray
had stolen his two snowmobiles, his boat and most of his furniture."

Maurice said he never bothered going to the police. "What did I
have? I had no proof. I couldn't back anything up."

After Ray disappeared, Maurice shut down the office. The telephone company made him cover the calls. Ray's long-distance bills
for one month came to something like six hundred dollars, Maurice
remembers: "About a week after, I was driving from the lake and I
saw papers blowing on the road. I stopped and they were our office
files. Ray had thrown everything in the ditch by the side of the
road."

Meanwhile, back in Ottawa, Robert Wells's lawyer had obtained
a judgment against Ray but couldn't enforce it. He couldn't find
Ray. The lawyer Durand had hired had reported to the court that in
early September he had told Ray on the phone that he hadn't been
properly retained. Ray had promised that he would drop by the
office the following day. He never did, and when the lawyer called
Ray's house, he discovered the phone had been disconnected. The
lawyer petitioned the court to be allowed to remove himself as the
attorney of record.

When Robert Wells discovered that he had won the suit but had
lost the war, he flew back to Ottawa. He knew Pat's maiden name
was Holben so he checked the Ottawa phone book and found a
Harold Holben. He showed up at Harold's door and asked for Ray.
Harold remembers Robert as tall and grey-haired and upset. He had
no interest in protecting Ray and was willing enough to give
Robert Ray's address. But the weekend before he and Barbara had
taken a drive to see Ray and Pat and had found their house empty.
They had moved again. Robert eventually flew back to Victoria
empty-handed. He had not only been skinned by Ray but had
wasted money on a lawyer and two trips to Ottawa. His daughter
Lori says he never really recovered psychologically from the blow.
He died several years later, still pained by the memory of how he
had been talked into gambling away his only wealth.

On Rouville Street, Denis was timid at first but grew to feel
comfortable with his grandmother Durand. She prepared nourish-
ing lunches for him, made him feel like her own son and promised

that he could live with her as long as he wished. He told her of his father's lies about Jeannine. She offered him sympathy but nothing more. He wasn't far from the Boissonneaults, and although he was emotionally closer to them, he realized that there wasn't room for him in their small house.

Denis enrolled in a technical school in Ottawa and received a government grant to pay for some of his school expenses. He used some of the money to buy himself a set of drums, which he kept in his grandmother's basement. He practised down there whenever he had time.

Late that October, Denis returned from school to find his grandmother Durand sitting in the kitchen with a letter in her hand. "Sit down," she said, "I have some bad news. Your father has left. You will live with me now for good."

Chapter Fourteen

San Diego, California, 1971

Anne remembers the nervousness that was visible on her father's pudgy face as they approached U.S. immigration in the Toronto airport. She heard him tell the uniformed officer that they were headed to Los Angeles for a two-week vacation. They had a mountain of luggage with them and Anne thought for sure the officer would call Ray on the lie and send them back. And what if he asked her some questions? Would she know what to say? She felt her knees shaking. The wait was nerve-racking. Finally, though, they were all waved through, and Ray and Pat and Anne, Marc and Martine made their way to the departure lounge.

Denis wasn't coming with them. He had moved out about a month before. Anne remembered one day he had come up to the cottage on the lake and the next thing she knew his stuff was gone and he wasn't living with them anymore.

"Why?" she had asked her father.

"He's a trouble-maker and he doesn't love us and he doesn't want to be with us any more," Anne remembered her father had told her.

They had all gone over to her grandmother Durand's for dinner once and Denis was there. They didn't talk much but she saw his room and realized he was living there. He seemed happy and at home. She was envious but upset, too. She felt abandoned by her older brother. She'd always looked up to him.

That night grandmother Durand had served them homemade soup. Anne enjoyed the meals there. Her grandmother fed them so well. She envied Denis that, too. After the meal her grandmother had left the room to fetch something and Ray had walked over to the trash can and plucked a can from it.

"Look," Anne remembers him telling Pat. "She always says she makes homemade soup. It's Campbell's." He laughed and held up the can for all of them to see. Anne was shocked both by her father's disrespect and by her grandmother's deception.

That was the last time Anne was to see Denis for three years. She thought about him often and was, for the longest time, deeply unhappy about his departure from the family. She withdrew even farther into herself. Now there was no one to share secrets with. She had been terrified by the trip to her grandmother Boissonneault's but amazed by Denis's courage. She remembered how badly she had wanted to hug her grandmother Boissonneault and how she had held back because she was frightened and knew she wasn't supposed to be there. She remembered how angry her father had looked when he had told them that they were not to go to Madame Boissonneault's place. She felt a little kernel of strength inside that came from the knowledge that she had visited her grandmother despite her fear and despite the warnings.

She was twelve now. Although she would be a teenager within a few months, she was still desperately skinny, still badly dressed and still as timid as a six-year-old on her first day of school. Her father told her she looked like a Durand, like one of his sisters. She had a cute little nose and brown eyes and a mischievous look. She carried a heavy load on her shoulders. She still believed that something she had done had caused her mother to leave. She wouldn't listen to Denis's wild talk that her father had done something to Jeannine. Deep inside she felt that if she were a better person, Pat would like her and her father would love her more and treat her better. And her mother would come back.

They flew into Los Angeles and within a day or two had made their way back to San Diego in a new car Ray bought. Ray found them a flat in the Diana Apartments on Claremont Drive, five minutes from their old place on Bunker Hill Street. Anne entered grade seven at Einstein Junior High School. This time when she registered for school, her father put her name down as Anne Holben. The Durand part of their lives disappeared completely. They were known as the Holbens.

At school, despite all the moves, Anne had managed to maintain her grades. She was an average student. She made friends but never talked about her home or her family and envied other girls she saw who had nice clothes and chattered about their rooms and families.

At home she worked like a beast of burden. Every morning before school Pat would make her clean out the fridge, dust the whole apartment, vacuum the rugs and wash out the sinks. Pat was neurotic about cleanliness. If the cleaning wasn't done to her exact instructions, she'd grab Anne by the hair and slam her against the wall. She was getting rougher with Anne all the time.

Anne shared a bedroom and a bed with Marc. One night she was sound asleep when she felt herself being pulled. She woke to find Pat "just beating the crap out of me. I just lay there and cried. She was just hitting me, hitting me, calling me a stupid bitch. Marc, I knew, was awake. I remember him putting his hand on me. She was drunk. She looked like a witch as she was hitting me. Her hair was all pulled down. She had these black glasses on. She just looked like a mean witch. She was wearing a nightgown that went below her knees. It had a purple tie and shiny material on the outside."

Pat broke Anne's nose during that beating. The next morning, when she woke, Anne found her face was swollen.

"My dad said, 'What happened to you?' I said 'I fell.' And Pat looked at me as if to say, If you say anything I'm gonna beat the crap out of you again. I knew if I said anything, I would get it. I think Dad knew but he didn't want to face up to it. He didn't say 'Where did you fall?' I felt if my father loved me, he'd make it stop. So I dressed up and went to school. I told everybody that I was running and fell."

Although she managed to keep up in school she didn't like going. "I hated to go to school. Pat always made me wear clothes that were outdated. Like three years before. I looked awful. I didn't have a nice haircut. I was very shy. I had friends, girls who were nice to me. They came from happy homes. I used to love going to their homes because I could eat. And I would eat until I made myself sick. Reese's Peanut Butter Cups. There was a little store just up the street. My girl friends would buy them for me."

"My girl-friends' parents were so nice. I wished I had parents like theirs. I remember once my girl-friend was riding my bike and I was sitting on top of the handlebars and a car hit us. The car stopped and I went flying over the hood. The driver said, 'Are you OK? We'll take you home.' And I said, 'No, please, please don't take me home.' I thought it was my fault and that Pat would beat me because I got hit. I never told them. I was scraped up pretty bad and I told them I fell off my bike."

Not only was Anne terrified of Pat, she was convinced that she hated them: "I don't know why she hated us. I thought she was a wicked woman."

Like Denis before her, Anne once got a secret glimpse of Pat's hatred. The kids were all obliged to leave their shoes outside by the door before they entered. One day Anne saw Pat drop into the trash can Anne's favourite pair of shoes. Pat didn't think anyone had seen her. Later that same day when Anne asked Pat if she'd seen her shoes, Pat gave her a blank look. "No," she replied and turned away. Anne seethed inside for days afterward. That incident and the broken nose made her desperately lonely. She longed to meet someone she could trust.

Back in Hull, Denis found it hard to relax, but one day, talking with his grandmother, he blurted out just what was bothering him. He felt both abandoned and fearful that his father would swoop down one day and pluck him from his grandmother's and the old nightmare would return. She felt sorry for him and was reassuring.

"Denis, you will live with me as my son. Raymond will not take you from here if you don't want to go."

That remark changed everything for Denis. He felt a sense of security that he hadn't known since childhood. And he began to settle into a routine. Marie-Anna apparently enjoyed his company. He helped with the dishes, shovelled the snow in winter and every night joined her in the kitchen for an evening snack, just the two of them. He became deeply attached to the old lady who had reared eleven children and outlived a husband in that house. He felt connected to a family, a community. The only disquieting note in those first few months was the memory of his mother. He had told Marie-Anna the whole story and she had looked shocked but accepted it as fate, a state of affairs she could do nothing about. She made no suggestions and offered Denis nothing more than her sympathy. He was frustrated by her passivity but was so grateful for the home she had made for him that he didn't have it in his heart to be angry with her.

January 20, 1972

Dear Gayle,

Hi!...You asked about my parents. To tell you the truth I don't ever see them anymore. They don't live in Touraine [the location of the last house Ray had rented]. They left me all by myself. But I work after school. So I pay room and board. It's a pretty lousy thing to do to your son....
Love, Denis

Shortly after he began attending technical school in Ottawa, Denis found work in the evenings as a janitor. He'd come home from school, have a bite to eat, then head back across the river to wash floors, clean ashtrays and tidy up in commercial buildings in Ottawa from 6 to 10 P.M. With the money he made he bought a bike and he always had a few bucks in his pocket for snacks and movies. He had his drums in the basement, and he practised till he could play well enough to begin jamming with other musicians. Eventually he was able to get up on a stage and play a dance in a Legion hall with his buddies.

After years of coping with the unexpected, with rapid, late-night moves, he craved routine. At his grandmother's he got just that. He was only sixteen but he felt like an adult. Without anyone nagging him, he voluntarily adhered to a fixed schedule that permitted him to fulfil all his obligations. He wrote to Gayle and told her he was five feet, ten inches tall, and weighed 155 pounds and had had his teeth fixed. Years of eating candy had given him a mouthful of cavities. The dental work gave him a brilliant smile. He felt good about himself, and it showed in his heightened self-confidence. He found he could talk to people without stammering or flushing bright red.

Denis also got to know some of his father's brothers and was welcomed into the fold. Ray's youngest brother, Serge, still lived at home. Another brother, André, lived across the street. And upstairs, in a separate apartment in his grandmother's large house, the brother who was closest to his father in age lived with his wife and a boarder. That brother, Michel or Le Gros (which translates roughly as Fatty) as he was known, lived on welfare, kept a couple of nags at the local harness racing track and used his boarder, a younger man who was mentally handicapped and was receiving monthly social assistance cheques, as a combination servant/labourer. Michel has a large, bald head that remembles a brown egg and shifty eyes. He carries a great deal of fat on his chest and belly. Michel's wife, Estelle, was and still is an attractive blonde who had once been his stepdaughter. Michel had been married to Estelle's mother, Pauline Filion, but had eloped with Estelle before she was sixteen. Exactly how old she was at the time of the elopement is a matter of some dispute. What is known is that she was young enough that the police were called and Michel was obliged to lay low until she came of age. And if all that weren't complicated enough, Michel's own daughter by Pauline boarded downstairs with his mother, Marie-Anna.

It took Denis a while to wrap his mind around all the tangled relationships. (For one, Michel's wife and his eldest daughter are half-sisters.) But they were a fascinating bunch and he became friendly with them all. And for a sixteen-year-old boy, Michel was a pretty interesting specimen. He didn't have a regular job but he had plenty of hustles. Some weekends Denis would accompany Michel to the track to help Michel's labourer clean out the stables. He was sure his horses were going to make him a bundle, and he bragged about them endlessly. Other times Denis would see Michel out with the labourer selling apples that they had picked in heaven only knew whose orchard. Michel even drove a taxi, and on Saturday nights he'd occasionally give Denis a couple of bucks to ride along. Whenever he got a call to pick up a customer in a rough bar, he'd send Denis in after the fare.

Michel often spent his mornings reading the paper. One day he saw an advertisement in a lurid, weekly crime tabloid that set his pulse racing. "Need help finding lost relatives?" the ad read. "Call us." The phone number in the ad was for the news-room of the tabloid, which was published in Montreal. The paper evidently used the ad as a means of generating story ideas. Since Michel had often talked to Denis about Jeannine and he knew that Denis was desperate to find her, he told Denis about the ad. They kicked the idea around for a few days until Denis agreed. Michel called the paper and sketched in the story for them. The reporter he talked to said he'd come up first thing in the morning with a photographer. Almost immediately afterward Marie-Anna tumbled to the plan and had another son call the paper back to tell them not to bother coming. She was furious with Michel for his meddling and assumed the second call had nixed the idea.

But the next day the reporter and photographer showed up anyway. With Marie-Anna hovering in the background, fretting, the reporter heard Denis's story and Michel's embellishments. When the two were finished, the reporter said they should all go to the police station and let them hear it as well. So the whole group trooped to the nearby Quebec provincial police detachment. En route to the police station, the reporter nudged Denis and told him that his father had probably killed his mother.

At the police station, with prompting from Michel and the reporter, Denis repeated his tale for Corporal Meloche. While he was talking, the photographer fired off a roll of film of Denis and the police officer. Meloche told Denis that he was too young to file a complaint, that he should either come back when he turned eighteen or get one of his grandmothers to come in and make a formal complaint.

Denis raced home only to have his grandmother Durand refuse, saying she would sign if his grandmother Boissonneault signed. Denis knew she was upset. She and another uncle berated Michel for stirring up trouble that would reflect badly on the Durand family.

Soon after Denis went to the Boissonneaults' and told Laurette the story. She was scandalized.

"Denis, what about the children?" she asked him. "What will happen to them if your father is taken away?" She refused to draw the police into what she considered to be a private, family affair. No amount of pleading would change her mind. Denis was bewildered. She apparently was still not certain that Jeannine hadn't disappeared of her own volition. Before Denis left, she reminded him that there was someone within the family who could help if they needed the police. She was referring to her nephew, Michel Béland, the son of her sister.

A dark-haired, square-jawed, six-footer, Michel Béland was Jeannine's cousin. He was about ten years younger than her and had memories of visiting Jeannine at her cottage. He had been at her engagement party and had last seen her with Ray at his wedding in 1965. Michel had joined the RCMP two years before his marriage and by 1972 was posted in Montreal. He knew that Jeannine was missing and had often told his mother he'd be glad to help but that he wouldn't do so unless Laurette asked him to. He was uneasy about the fact that she had not gone to the police but felt that he had to respect her wishes in the matter.

Some weeks after the newspaper reporter and photographer visited, the tabloid played the story on the front page with a photo of Denis, looking both innocent and sorrowful, holding a picture of his mother. Next to him they ran, in quotes, the headline "MA MERE A ETE ASSASSINEE" (My Mother Was Murdered). Inside, the paper carried two full pages of photos and copy, badly written and incompetently researched. They basically took Denis's words, revved them out of the range of possibility into the red-line zone of tabloid certainty, and set them in type. Denis was alarmed that they had attributed to him the notion that his mother had been murdered but he was pleased that the paper had taken him seriously. He didn't know it then, but he later learned that one of his uncles was in contact with his father and had told him about Denis's visit to the police and had sent him a copy of the paper.

As it happened, on the very day that the story appeared, Michel Béland was crossing the country by train. He had just been posted to the RCMP's training base in Regina. He was to work there for the next two years as an instructor. He had obtained a copy of the paper before he had boarded the train, and as he read it, he felt a sense of relief. By coincidence, he knew Meloche and assumed that an investigation would be launched. Finally, he thought, somebody is going to unravel this mystery.

April 22, 1972

Dear Gayle,

My father called a couple of weeks ago to join him in Houston. I told him no because I am doing fine here; so he said then I'll send you fare by plane and you can come down and see me this summer. I said no, because I have other plans this summer (like going to Victoria, B.C.). My pictures are all over the papers here because I am searching for my mother that I haven't seen for almost five years. As you know, the lady who was over at my house the day you came to see me wasn't my mother. Some reporters came over to our house and they took pictures of me. And they asked questions and they published so don't be surprised if you see any of that stuff on the papers in B.C. It's supposed to be all over Canada.
Love,
Denis

Chapter Fifteen

San Diego, California, 1972

Ray Durand turned thirty-five three months after his return to San Diego. He had put on fifty pounds since Fort Lauderdale but still had the swiftness and agility of a much thinner man. Everything he did, he did to excess. He drank too much, ate like a glutton, chased and propositioned women regardless of the setting and circumstance, worked like a man possessed and partied with the zeal of a Roman senator. His English had improved but he still had a French accent. He had talked himself into a job at Bay Ford on Mission Bay Drive not five blocks from Guy Hill Cadillac. There, one of his co-workers called him Frenchy one day, and Ray adopted it as his new name. He liked the sound of it. To co-workers at the body shop, to people he met, he introduced himself as Frenchy Holben. Even Pat began calling him Frenchy. The new identity was a caricature of the original and it was disarming. People felt that he was a guy who wouldn't take offence if they made a crack about the French or foreigners, that he wasn't sensitive about his ethnicity. He could take a joke and was clearly trying to fit in.

Making people feel at ease suited Ray's predatory purposes. He wanted his victims completely disarmed first. He came across as a harmless, good-time fellow, a joker and a party animal who spoke understandable but mangled English.

Several months after his return to San Diego, Ray began working as a body man at National Paint, a body shop that specialized in rapid turn rounds. He was to remain at National Paint for the next eight years.

Daniel Knight, a burly man with a slow walk and a patient, reflective talk, hired on at National Paint some time after Ray started. He recalls Ray's "exceptional skills as a body man. He was a flat rater. He could take a job that would require ten hours and do it in four or five. He was very fast, very clean. Anybody he worked for liked him because he made them a lot of money. But then anybody who worked for him didn't like him. He's a chiseller, always figuring a way to belittle his employees and not pay them. Or pay them very little."

Daniel, who is now part-owner of a truck body shop in the Los Angeles area, says National Paint was "a good-running, high-volume shop. They advertised in the paper—fifty dollars of free body work with a paint job. And three different grades of paint job. The offer of free body work was a good lead to get customers in to sell them a lot of body work. Almost all cars need body work by the time they need a paint job."

As soon as Ray came into enough money, he moved the family from the Diana Apartments to a house on Cameo Lane with orange trees in the backyard and an above-ground pool. He bought a small motor home and often spent weekends with Pat and the kids at Butterfield Country, a camping and recreational area just outside San Diego. From the outside they appeared to be a comfortable, middle-class family.

Martine, a pretty blonde girl with a high forehead, started school when they lived on Cameo Lane. Marc, by then nine, had his father's looks and energy. All three children spoke English only. Martine had memories of Denis but knew almost nothing of her background. When she was old enough to wonder about it, she asked Pat where she had met Ray and why they didn't have any wedding photos. Pat told her that they had met at an office party and that they had lost all the wedding pictures. Curious and not at all satisfied by Pat's answers, Martine began pawing through Pat's things when she could.

Pat never beat Martine as she did the others. They were close, and Martine resented her father's abuse of the woman she believed was her natural mother. She remembers Ray telling Pat, in front of others, "You're so ugly and stupid." She remembers him pushing her around. As she got older, she felt sorry for Pat.

Unlike Denis and Anne, Marc and Martine grew up without a moral compass. Before her disappearance, Jeannine had passed on to her two eldest children a sense of right and wrong. They grew up steeped in the Catholic notions of guilt and sin. But Marc and Martine acquired none of that moral absolutism. The only parents they ever knew were slaves to greed and their own insatiable appetites. As they grew, Marc became much like his father and Martine like Pat. By the time he turned thirteen, Marc had Ray's irrepressible charm. He could talk to anyone, seemed like a hell of a nice guy, had a terrific sense of humour and was handy with his hands. Unlike Denis, Marc needed no encouragement from Ray to talk to the girls. He was sexually precocious. He also inherited Ray's compulsive disregard of the truth. Talking to Marc is like entering a hall of mirrors; everything is distorted or conveniently rearranged.

Martine was emotionally closer to Pat when she was a child and took on a great deal of Pat's temperament. She might stretch the truth to extricate herself from unpleasant situations but she wouldn't do it for the simple pleasure of confusing others. Her blonde good looks attracted attention and affection of the kind that wasn't ever showered on her brother. She was the favoured child and became accustomed to having things done for her and having people care for her because of her beauty.

October 14, 1972

Dear Gayle,

Right now it is 3 o'clock in the morning. I just took a hot bath and I am writing to you in bed, (that is why I am writing a bit crooked). The reason I am feeling good awhile ago is because I just came back from a party which we were playing at....

Would you believe that I cannot drink beer yet and I don't smoke. My grandmother hopes I will always stay like that.

I miss you very much and I am going to dream about you tonight. I might be calling you before long so be ready. Gayle, I want to say something to you. I love you with all of my heart. xoxo

I haven't heard from my dad and brother and sister. It has been a year since I have seen them. I miss them very much, I get lonely sometimes and I go and walk by myself in the woods behind our house and I think about things (life, you, my brother and sister). I love my brother and sisters and sometimes I just want to cry. I also love you...

If Lori Wells tries to get you to tell her my address [tell her] I don't mind, because it is my father who did not want to be bothered. I just don't want to make you lie.

Denis xoxoxoxoxoxox

Denis didn't hear from the newspaper reporter after his story was published. Nobody ever contacted him about Jeannine. Corporal Meloche had told him to come back when he was eighteen if he wished to file a formal complaint, but Denis didn't think about it very much. He had nothing more to add. He felt as though he'd already revealed everything he knew.

As for the Boissonneaults, they simply endured. Aunt Berthe had made another round of the mental hospitals and had peered into every room, walked through every dormitory and had not seen any patients who even looked like Jeannine. She didn't know what more she could do.

The Boissonneaults' lack of initiative frustrated Denis. He was no longer frantic, though. Now and again he would hear a song that was popular in 1968 and that would trigger a wave of longing for his mother but it would pass. If Jeannine's own parents weren't going to help, there wasn't much more he felt he could do.

He worked in a body shop owned by an uncle in the summer of 1973, and when school started again in the fall, another uncle found him a new cleaning job at the Lord Elgin Hotel in downtown Ottawa. He started on a Saturday morning, and while he was waiting in the lobby he saw two girls walk by. One of them had brown hair, an eye-catching figure and looked a bit like Sally Field. Denis exchanged glances with her. He discovered an hour later that she was working as a maid on the same floor that he was cleaning. Her name was Line (pronounced Lyn) Lafond and they were soon taking lunch breaks together. She was seeing another boy at the time, and Denis was still dreaming of Gayle, so they became friends and nothing more. By late fall, however, they were dating and Denis had a new job cleaning a bank near his grandmother's house.

Once they began dating, Denis would call Line's house almost every day. Line's father, Ben, a balding, ruddy-cheeked man, ran a scrap yard and car repair shop next to his house along the highway that runs parallel to the Gatineau River about seven miles north of Pointe Gatineau. He had one phone for both his business and his residence. Whenever Denis would call Line, Ben would answer in the shop and have to run over to the house to tell his daughter to take the call. Denis knew the arrangement and always hesitated because he feared that one day Ben would lose his temper and hang up on him. He remembered when his own father had worked in a shop under the house and he could imagine what Ray's response would have been if a friend of one of his kids had called. But Ben was always polite and friendly, and Denis came to admire his patience. Line's mother, Rolande, was a clerk in a Hull department store. Short and pleasant, Rolande was equally welcoming. When Denis and Line dated, Rolande would pick Denis up and drop him off at home as if it was no bother at all. There were five children in the family, three girls and two boys. Denis discovered that the Lafonds were a close family, deeply rooted in the region and in Quebec culture. Ben had heard of Ray and knew his reputation but didn't hold it against Denis.

That Christmas, Denis felt his life was changing. He was about to turn eighteen, he was falling in love with Line, and he felt accepted by the Lafonds. He didn't have to pretend he was some-one else. He had loved Gayle passionately but he had never really let her into his life. He had been too ashamed of his family to reveal to her anything of his past. With the Lafonds he didn't have to hide anything. They lived not ten miles from Denis's old house on Michaud Street and they knew all about the Durands. They had read the story of Jeannine's disappearance. To them Denis was a decent kid whom their daughter cared deeply about. They felt sorry for him. Line, too, was understanding. Denis began telling her stories about his family that he had never before told anyone.

Denis was over at Line's two days before Christmas, just before his eighteenth birthday, when he was called to the phone. It was Ray. He told an astonished Denis that he was living in San Diego and he wanted him to come down for a visit. But a quarrel erupted during the call and Denis hung up. He knew that Ray had seen the newspaper story and wondered if his father knew that Corporal Meloche had told him to come back when he turned eighteen. A few days later Ray called again. Again they quarrelled and Denis hung up. The third time Ray called, he emotionally ambushed Denis.

"You're heartless," he told Denis. "You don't care anything for your brother and sisters."

That did the trick. Denis said he wanted to see the kids and Ray agreed to buy Denis and Line airplane tickets to fly down for a two-week visit. They flew in just before Denis and Ray's birthday. A photograph taken at the time of Denis and Ray blowing out the candles on their cake shows Ray sporting long sideburns, a moustache and Denis with hair over his ears. He was tall and his blond hair had got darker. Another photo taken during that visit shows Denis with Martine sitting on his knee. Martine is laughing and looks remarkably like Denis. With their high foreheads and blonde hair they both resemble their mother.

Denis and Line stayed two weeks and were persuaded by Ray to extend their visit for another week. Denis spent most of his time working with his father at National Paint. Denis remembers Ray was especially nice to him during those three weeks. While Denis worked, Line got to know the kids, and went to the beach with them. Line and Denis also helped the family move to a new house Ray had bought on Greenford Drive on the northern edge of San Diego.

Denis worried about the abuse the kids were enduring at Pat's hands. Anne told Denis that Pat had broken her nose. He hated seeing Anne get up at 6 A.M. to do the cleaning before getting ready for school while Pat slept off the previous night's drunk.

Denis tried to talk to Anne about Jeannine, but Anne refused. She wanted Denis back in the family and didn't want him starting fights with their father.

Throughout the visit, Ray made repeated attempts to convince Denis to stay in San Diego. "One night," Denis remembers, "he brought me to his work. He showed me a Jaguar. He asked if I wanted to work with him and stay. He said he'd sign for the Jaguar and that I'd pay for it." Like his father, Denis has a weakness for cars, and the Jaguar was a beauty. It was a silver 1959 convertible in mint condition. Denis resisted, and in mid-January he and Line flew back to Hull. Line's parents were relieved to see them return. The trip had cemented Denis and Line's relationship and they began thinking of marriage.

Denis went back to his room at his grandmother's and his evening job cleaning the bank. He had cried when he had left his brother and sisters behind in San Diego, and he thought about them constantly. One night, in early March he set out to work suffering from a bad head cold. Along the way he stopped to buy a package of Contac C at a pharmacy. Shivering and sick of winter, he let himself into the bank with the key he had been given when he had got the job. He drew himself a glass of water, intending to battle the cold with the cold medication. He searched all his pockets and discovered that he had lost the package of cold capsules. He hadn't a cent in his pockets to buy another package. He slumped to the floor. Sick and exhausted, with almost no money and few prospects, he began to think about the calls from his father. OK, he remembers thinking, enough. He reached for a phone and called Ray, collect.

"Dad. I've changed my mind. I want to come down."

The next day Frenchy bought a plane ticket for Denis and wired him the money to buy travelling cases for his drums. By mid-March Denis was back in San Diego, working with his father. The plan was that he would earn a stake, return to Hull in June to marry Line and both of them would settle in San Diego.

Denis moved in with his family temporarily, and Ray immediately set out to obtain new identification for Denis. Both he and Denis had copies of Denis's baptismal certificate. Ray took one copy, forged a new birthdate on it, turned Denis's middle initial H into Holben and erased Durand. When he had completed the forgery, he sent Denis down to apply for a driver's licence. The clerk spotted the forgery immediately, and Denis slunk out embarrassed. But Ray was not so easily put off. Ray took the second baptismal certificate and applied himself to it with more attention to detail. When Denis returned a second time, he obtained without question a driver's licence in the name of Denis Holben. Ray supplemented the driver's licence with a Social Security card that he had obtained before Denis's arrival that also bore the name Denis Holben. With the new identification, Denis was given a job in the body shop at National Paint.

Almost as soon as he had settled in Denis regretted his decision. His father hadn't changed and neither had Pat. She was drunk all day long and his father was as hard-hearted as ever. Now that Denis was eighteen he had a new perspective on Ray and Pat. He had lived without them for three years and had forgotten how much he hated their dishonesty and their drinking.

Despite his unease, Denis hung on, attempting to re-establish relations with his brother and sisters. Shortly before he was to be married, he leased an apartment, bought furniture on a layaway plan, sold the Jaguar and made a down payment on a van. As he was preparing to leave for Hull, he told his father that he wanted

Anne to join him so she could attend the wedding. Ray threw a fit and said she wasn't going, period.

"Why?" Denis asked. "Why can't she come? Is it because you've changed your name to Holben? This has something to do with Jeannine, doesn't it?"

Ray looked at him coldly. "I know where Jeannine is. When she is good and ready to see you, I will take you to her."

Denis was dumbfounded. This was the first time his father had ever told him anything other than that Jeannine had returned to Canada. Now, despite his better instincts, he believed Ray. He was elated at the thought that Jeannine was still out there somewhere and that someday he'd get to see her again. So Denis shut up. He didn't want to alienate his father and risk having his only link with Jeannine severed. Denis had been having second doubts about the wisdom of returning to San Diego after the wedding. Now he felt he had to return. He began planning how he would get his father to reveal Jeannine's location. He figured he could probably catch him when he was drunk and ease it out of him. Or maybe, Denis thought, after he had married, Ray might just take him one day to Jeannine.

Back in Hull, the day before the wedding, Line won a five-thousand-dollar lottery prize. They were ecstatic and Denis phoned his father to tell him the good news.

"Great," Ray told him. "That'll give you money for a start down here."

After the wedding Denis and Line flew to San Diego, and Ray greeted them at the airport. He told the happy couple that he had paid off Denis's furniture and car loans to save them the interest charges. He said if Denis gave him three thousand dollars, he'd call it even. Denis pulled out his bankroll and counted out the money.

"Cash," Denis remembers. "Right on the table. July 28, 1974. I said, 'You gonna give me some receipts?' He said, 'I'm waiting for the furniture place to send them.' I said, 'Cool.' I still owed him $300. I had spent the rest on stuff for the apartment and food. He said, 'OK. You can pay me from your weekly pay.' I was making only $125 a week. A month later, at the shop, he said, 'You still owe me $300. I'll make a deal with you. That stereo I bought you for a wedding gift, I paid $300 for it. I bought it on credit. You make the monthly payments and we'll be even.' I agreed and again

I asked him about the furniture receipts but he put it off.

"Then one day I came home and Line said some man had called about the furniture. She didn't speak English very well. So I called the furniture place and this guy told me I was three months behind in my payments. I said, 'That's impossible. My dad paid.' The guy said, 'I'm sorry but he didn't give us any money.' So I called the car company [which had sold him the van] and they told me the same thing."

"So I called my dad. I knew from the tone of his voice that it was true. I called him a fucking son of a bitch. He said, 'Shut up. I'm coming over.' He lived about fifteen miles away. He drove over and he buzzed the apartment. Line didn't want to let him in so I went down. He said, 'Follow me to the shop.' We got there and he said, 'You're a liar. I didn't do that.' I said, 'Look, I talked to these people.' I told him I'd had it and that I had called my father-in-law and was going back to Canada. Ben had agreed to buy our tickets.

And I said, 'Fuck you. On top of that, I'm going to look for Jeannine. You killed her.'

"I was loading my tools into my small tool-box. He grabbed me by the neck. He lifted me by the neck across the tool-box and pinned me against a pillar. He had a hammer in his hand. He was so nervous he had been banging away on a car while we talked. He was in his good clothes."

"I said, 'Go ahead and kill me like you killed Mom.' I said it in French. I saw his eyes. Man, he had lost it. I thought he was gonna hit me."

For a moment Denis thought he was going to die. The world came to a stop. Then, just as quickly as Ray's rage erupted, it dissipated. His hand fell from Denis's throat and he stood there, slumped in defeat.

Ray had jeopardized his relationship with Denis for the sake of three thousand dollars. He just couldn't help himself. Giving Ray a glimpse of money or something he wanted was like giving a shark a smell of blood. It made no difference who had what Ray wanted—his son, his uncle or a vulnerable neighbour—the only thing that mattered was how he was going to get it.

The next morning Denis emptied his bank account of some fifteen hundred dollars and that evening his father arrived to take him and Line to the airport. He knew that Denis had fifteen hundred in the bank, and he asked if Denis had left enough money to pay for his rent, telephone, electricity and van payment. Denis lied and told him he had left the fifteen hundred. Ray immediately suggested that Denis leave him a blank cheque that he could use to cover other costs Denis hadn't considered. So Denis signed a blank cheque, knowing that the account was empty anyway.

A day after their return to Hull, Ray called Denis, sputtering with anger. He had attempted to empty Denis's account of the fifteen hundred dollars and discovered that Denis had got to it first.

"I've got long arms," he told Denis. "I'm gonna make you disappear."

Denis replied that he was going to visit Corporal Meloche the following day. "It was Beech Street in Bellaire, wasn't it, Dad?" he asked.

Ray hung up.

Two weeks later Denis's mother-in-law received a letter, postmarked Tijuana. It was from Ray. In the letter he said that he had been obliged to flee to Mexico because of Denis's delinquent loans. He complained that Denis had cheated him. He ended the letter with a warning: "Denis Boissonneault, when he is not looking behind him, when he is not thinking about it, that'll be the end of him."

Chapter Sixteen

San Diego, California, 1975

Anne was angry with Denis when he and Line packed up and fled California. She felt abandoned again and she was annoyed that Denis wasn't willing to restrain himself and get along with Frenchy. Denis's blow-up with Ray—and Anne knew nothing of the details—made her wonder whether he wanted to be part of the family.

By the time Denis left, Anne had blossomed into a chestnut-haired beauty. She had clear, brown eyes, a sprinkling of freckles across a perfectly formed nose. She was the peacemaker of the family; she soothed bruised feelings and protected the kids from Pat's rages.

After the family moved into the townhouse on Greenford Drive, Anne met and began dating Paul Brady, a boy who lived across the street. Paul was blond and six feet, two inches tall. His mom was a San Diego police officer. Anne began seeing Paul when she was fourteen but she did it on the sly. Frenchy was suspicious of boys who were interested in Anne. For her part Anne was confused by her father's and Pat's contradictory desires to both isolate her and have her out of the way. "They never wanted me to see anyone or have any friends. But they wanted me out of the house until bed-time. At night I used to sneak out of the window to see friends. [Bedtime was still 8 P.M. and it never changed as Anne got older.] I'd take Marc with me so he wouldn't snitch. He was a scared kid, too. Pat was mean to him but not like she was to me and Denis."

Pat, Anne felt, was the bane of her existence. "She would make us do the dishes right after we ate. She would put the water in the sink so hot you couldn't put your hands in it. And I'd say, 'It's hot.' And she'd say, 'It's not hot.' And shove my hands in it. Oh, it'd burn. I remember crying so many times when I did the dishes because it was so damn hot. She was awful."

Unlike Denis, now back in Hull, who couldn't forget Jeannine because he was constantly running into people who knew her or finding himself in places they'd visited together, Anne could put her mother out of her mind for long periods. Everything about her past had been buried, even her name. She had become indistinguishable from other kids in the neighbourhood. Nothing connected her to Hull and her Quebec origins. So when she did stumble across her past, it was like finding herself on a precipice, about to fall.

One day she climbed into the attic of the house on Greenford Drive in search of a pair of pants that she thought Pat might have thrown out. Rummaging through the boxes, she noticed a suitcase in a corner.

"I opened the suitcase and saw pictures of my mom. And I looked at them and I threw them down and zipped it back up and I stood there and I shook and I shook. And I thought, what am I gonna do? What am I gonna do? I was freaking out. It was my mom. I got out of there and I went to my room and then I don't know what made me do it but I went downstairs and I said, 'Pat, I saw her.'"

"Saw who?"

"You know, her."

"What are you talking about?"

"You know. Jeannine."

Anne remembers, "I didn't say, "Mom." I said, "Jeannine." And Pat goes, 'What in the hell were you doing up there, you little bitch?' And she backhanded me. 'Don't you ever go up there nosing around.'" Anne said she never saw the suitcase again.

On weekends the family still took trips together to Butterfield Country. Anne made a friend there and saw her often. But when she was fifteen, the friendship ended abruptly. "My friend came and told me that my dad had grabbed her boobs. I didn't say anything. I just pretended she didn't say anything. We were not friends after that."

Later the same thing happened at home. "I had friends over. We had bunk beds and he'd sneak in the room and I know he was grabbing them. I didn't hear anyone say, 'Stop it.' I don't know if they were asleep or what. But I could see him reaching over them."

Anne herself never said anything, never talked about it. At least at first. She was now helping out at the body shop after school, and one day there, too, a friend of hers who was working with her confided that Frenchy had grabbed her breasts. This time she decided to tell Pat.

"I told Pat that my dad had grabbed my friend's boobs. Pat said, 'Really?' Then the next day Dad comes in with my friend. They confront me. He says, 'So, Anne, you were trying to cause trouble. You said I was molesting your friend.' I said, 'Yeah.' So he turns to my friend and says, 'I just grabbed your boobs, right?' And she says, 'Yeah.' She was really shocked. Pat and my dad just shrugged it off. Like it was no big deal. I was put on restriction for that. No TV, couldn't go out."

Anne's growing anxiety about life at home finally came to a head later that year. She ran off and hid out at Paul's place. She stayed in his room, and even his folks didn't know she was there. In the mornings she could see her father heading off to work. Frenchy phoned all her friends and searched the neighbourhood. Finally, he discovered where she was staying. He thought Paul's parents were in on it so he called Paul's mother's superior at the San Diego police department. He complained that she was harbouring a minor. When Anne found out what her father had done, she gave herself up to the police. The police asked whether she was being abused. She went mute, found herself unable to begin talking about her life. When she was returned to Frenchy's custody, she felt she was re-entering prison.

Some months later, after she had turned sixteen, she and her father had another spat and he told her that if she didn't like it at home, she should move in with her girl-friend Marcie's family. Anne told Marcie, who asked her folks. They agreed and for seven happy months Anne lived with Marcie's parents and her two sisters. She continued to work at her dad's shop after school, so he saw her every day. She made the mistake one day of telling her dad how happy she was. Almost immediately afterwards he forced her to move back in with him, Pat, Marc and Martine. "It just seemed that he didn't want me to be happy," she remembers.

Within a year of Denis's departure, Frenchy became the sole owner of National Paint. He never explained to the family how that came about. All they knew was that the original owner was suddenly gone and Frenchy was in charge. Frenchy hired Daniel Knight, Anne's boy-friend, Paul Brady, and later, when Anne began dating Fred Angelo Jr, he took him on as well. (Fred is the son of Fred Angelo, Sr, who had worked with Frenchy at Guy Hill Cadillac and was astonished to find Frenchy back in town.) There was real camaraderie among the boys in the back. But they all agree that Frenchy was the worst boss imaginable and the turnover of workers was constant. There were two painters, four body men, a half-dozen preppers on staff, as well as a secretary up front. Daniel says the shop was always humming with work. "The monthly income was about eighty to ninety thousand dollars. But there was a large turnover among the staff. There were new faces on the staff all the time because Ray was always jacking them around."

Fred, Jr, who now works at a body shop just north of San Diego, wasn't yet twenty when he joined the staff and he remembers the lunacy of the scene: "There was always some excitement in the shop. Frenchy was either screwing somebody over or there was a problem and he was blowing one of the body men out or putting him in a spot. Sometimes the payroll didn't jive up and we'd get our cheques and there'd be insufficient funds. We'd go to Frenchy and say, 'Hey, can't cash the cheque.' He'd say, 'You don't like it, get the fuck out.' He even told me that a couple of times. And this stuff was minor for him."

Fred, Jr, a lithe, olive-skinned, good-natured wisecracker, dated Anne for several years and got to know Ray both at home and at work. He recalls Frenchy's philosophy of business: everybody gets the same treatment. "Frenchy used to say, 'All they got to do is come in here once and let me get a hold of them and, kaboom.' North Park [the area around the shop] had a lot of old people and he would just fuck them to no end. You'd see them go in there and be surprised they'd get out of there with their pants on. He had no heart. He'd say, 'Fucking old son of a bitch.' That was his favourite saying. 'Fuck the old guy.' He was a pathological cheat. He couldn't get enough of it. Just to screw you on your car was not good enough. He'd want your house, to get into your old lady's pants."

As he started making money, Frenchy made a new set of friends. They became the closest pals he had ever had. The one Frenchy was closest to was Harry "Skip" Dawson, who was blond, pudgy and short. Several times Fred saw him drop into the shop and hand Frenchy an envelope. Frenchy saw Fred looking one day and explained that it was cocaine.

His two other fast friends were Brian Rand, whom Frenchy called Pumpkinhead because of his round face, and Dick Dickson, who was tall, slim, blond and handsome. They were into land development.

Fred remembers Frenchy and Skip, especially, had "open minds." They were game for anything. They were nimble-witted and aggressive. Brian and Dick, he remembers, were more laid-back.

Frenchy, Skip and Brian became inseparable. The clubhouse was the Old Ox in Mission Valley. It was a combination bar/restaurant with a stone fireplace, an oak bar, salvaged brick walls, leaded glass windows and a fast-moving crowd. Frenchy and his buddies became such well-known regulars that someone mounted a group photo of the gang on one of the walls.

They got to know several members of the San Diego Chargers football team who drank at the Old Ox, and Frenchy and the lads shared the conceit that they had enough inside poop on the team to keep their bookie busy. Fred remembers Frenchy and his pals talking about bets they had made and disputing who owed whom two thousand dollars this week. They were often surrounded by well-turned-out women who favoured silk blouses and short skirts. Frenchy was by now driving a navy-blue Lincoln Continental and carried a thick roll of bills in his pocket.

Frenchy and his buddies drank and loaded their noses and chased skirts, and each of them pursued crooked business interests. If they weren't at the Old Ox, laughing, drinking and eating, they were up at Frenchy's place, partying. Anne remembers seeing her father snorting coke with Pat and a couple of his buddies.

Frenchy turned forty during those prosperous years in San Diego. Pointe Gatineau, Jeannine and Denis belonged to the misty, distant past. If entering his forties filled him with anxiety, his successes must have helped calm his nerves. He had become a well-off businessman and was known as a character. He lived in a sun-drenched city on the California coast. He had like-minded pals and a hang-out where they scouted the possibilities for sex and crime. He had everything he had once wanted. And like many men who have everything they want, it wasn't enough. By now, though, Frenchy apparently understood his own appetites well enough to know that none of his accomplishments would endure. It was as if he sensed that one day he'd go over the top. And when that happened, he'd need a refuge.

Martine remembers being at Butterfield Country one weekend when her father looked up into the hills to the north and told her he was going to buy a place up there one day. Early in 1975 Frenchy took a drive into the desert-dry, rattlesnake-infested, sagebrush-covered hills an hour and a half northeast of San Diego and discovered a remote, hilltop development ten miles from the nearest settlement, the hamlet of Aguanga. The land was cheap; he and Brian Rand bought neighbouring twenty-acre plots for seventeen thousand dollars each. They put $141 down and made monthly payments of $141. It was Big Thicket again, only this time the land was in the high desert instead of the forest.

Frenchy called his place the ranch. He put a triple-wide mobile home on the crown of the hill and cleared the cactus, manzanita, chaparral and sage. The soil was a mixture of red clay and decomposed granite.

The ranch was Frenchy's ace in the hole. If he ever needed to lose himself again, that's where he'd do it. The ranch was only sixty miles from the Mexican border and thirty miles from the ocean. From it, Frenchy could see for miles in three directions. He could spot the dust cloud trailing an approaching car while it was still far down in the boulder-strewn valley. It was an hour and a half over back roads to the desert oasis of Palm Springs, and about the same distance, once you made the freeway, to both San Diego and Los Angeles. There was no posted street address for the ranch, and you needed a realtor's map to navigate the maze of dirt trails that ran off the Sage Road into the area.

Bill Parker, a barrel-shaped mailman who lived in the small town of San Jacinto, twenty-five miles north of the ranch, also bought a twenty-acre plot in 1975. His place abutted Frenchy's. He remembers Frenchy and Pat were "real friendly. They were real party people. They said they were from Canada. Said they just up and left and went to Florida. Then they had a body shop in Texas. Then bought one in San Diego. He told me he had been with the Mounties and got shot in the leg. He always carried a pistol in his boot."

Throughout the late 1970s Frenchy and his family frequently spent weekends at the ranch. He sunk a hundred-foot-deep well, put in a pool, brought in power, expanded the mobile home, built a fireplace and a shop and turned the place into a second home. If he ever had to move up there, it was going to be comfortable.

Anne broke up with Paul Brady before she turned sixteen and began seeing Fred Angelo, Jr, after she moved home from Marcie's place. Fred was crazy about her but wary of Frenchy. "He was very protective of her," Fred recalls. "He was worried about guys getting into her pants."

One night, there was a confrontation. "I met Fred at the ice arena," Anne remembers. "My dad found out. He went over there and said he was going to kill Fred. He said I was screwing him but I wasn't. I was a virgin."

Anne met her father at the door to the arena. Fred was still inside but saw Frenchy "pointing at me, saying, 'you son of a bitch.' He was waiting for me to come out. He was going to beat the shit out of me. I didn't know what to do. He was big. So I called my dad and he said, 'I'll be right up.' He drove up in his Cadillac. They looked at each other. Ray. Fred."

After greeting each other—they hadn't crossed paths since Guy Hill—both men took charge of their respective offspring and swore the kids wouldn't have anything to do with each other. That night, Fred, Sr, told his son what he knew about Ray, including the story of how Frenchy had cheated his own uncle. Frenchy scared Fred, Jr, but he couldn't stay away from Anne. "We began seeing each other and fell in love," Fred says. "And little by little I got to know Frenchy."

Fred was working in a hospital kitchen when he began dating Anne. Once Frenchy had accepted Fred's relationship with Anne, Fred was offered a job prepping cars at National Paint. He took the job and learned the trade that he still works at today.

By then Anne had begun working at the shop as well. She prepped cars on weekends. She was paid for the work, but as with all the other employees, Frenchy would occasionally short her pay cheque, too. She fought with Ray, and by the time Anne was in high school, she and her father were constantly at each other. When she finished high school, her father obtained a birth certificate that showed she was eighteen, a year older that her actual age.

"I moved out with Fred and got an apartment. My father was the one who told me I should move out with Fred. A year earlier he was ready to kill Fred and then he's suggesting I move out. I was happy to get out....It was nice to have my own life, to go to the fridge when I wanted, eat when I wanted, knowing somebody was not going to throw my clothes out, something that I really liked."

Her first job was as a parts driver for a Pontiac dealership. It wasn't a great job but she felt she had landed the most coveted gig in the world. She was earning a living and on her own. "I worked, came home, went out with my friends, cooked. I was a very, very clean person. I drove everybody crazy. It was nuts. I would dust and vacuum every single day. I started smoking at sixteen. I would put a cigarette out and go and clean the ashtray." She was obsessive and terribly responsible. "I always held a job, always paid my own way, was never late for work, never called in sick unless I was sick. I was a good employee."

She didn't visit home often but worried a great deal about Marc and Martine. She never forgot birthdays and always bought every-one gifts at Christmas and showered Martine with presents. She continued to see her father, largely because he used her as unpaid help. He did that with everyone. For Frenchy there was no such thing as a casual friendship. Everyone he knew did things for him, including, perhaps even especially, his kids. Years after Anne had moved out he'd still call her and tell her to pick up something he needed and run it over. The same applied to Anne's boy-friends. Paul Brady ended up working for Frenchy both at the shop and in other enterprises. So did Fred, Jr, and he recalls how crazy it made him: "Frenchy was the kind of guy who could manipulate you into doing stuff. He always got that straight with you. If I was going to be a son-in-law, I had to be a robot. He was like, 'If I tell you to do this, you drop that and go do this.' It just got real scary. The family seemed like it was sucking you in and you didn't have a life."

Fred says Anne made it clear to him that Pat wasn't her real mother. She never explained what had happened to her mother and Fred never pressed the matter. He saw Anne and Pat in some real "cat and dog fights." In the last year or so she spent at home, Anne had lost her fear of Pat. Fred said it was clear to him that Pat was "real hooked on Frenchy." But he couldn't understand her relationship with the kids: "Pat would get drunk sometimes and start mouthing off and Anne would retaliate. 'Hey, you are not my mother.' And then Pat would say, 'Frenchy, you get that?' And Frenchy would say, 'I'm not saying a fucking thing. Keep me out of it.' Anne was real tough about that. She could go off like a firecracker. She had a pretty good temper. If Pat crossed her, she'd set her straight. Anne wouldn't take shit from anybody."

The year before Anne moved out, Frenchy had bought a bigger house in the nearby Scripps Ranch subdivision. He had also borrowed money to open a second National Paint shop near his home. He had visions of opening other shops across the city. Daniel Knight, who eventually left to run the first shop, says the new shop was on Dowdy Street in the Mira Mesa area: "It was in a brand-new building. He bought a brand-new paint booth, heated. All state-of-the-art stuff. The overhead was incredible. Everything was financed."

Frenchy could have made a bundle on the operation but by then he had his nose too deep into bags of white powder. He had become a cokehead. "He was a user and he used large amounts," Daniel recalls. "You can pack an awful lot of profit up your nose. That's killed lots and lots of businesses. If you keep it on a personal basis, you can keep it under control. He didn't do that. He had lots of wheeler-dealer friends and he was always trying to impress people. If he found out one of his employees would do it, he'd—every time he came around—crack off lines for everyone." According to many people who knew him then, Frenchy had also started dealing in coke.

Fred says Frenchy was doing so much coke that "I don't think he even had a nose left. The cartilage in his nose was gone. He was on that wacky powder all the time. He always had it."

The cocaine made Frenchy paranoid and seemed to propel him to deeper excesses, seemed to liberate his depraved sexual desires. Fred remembers that Frenchy used to encourage Anne to invite along her friends for weekends at the ranch. Fred was always suspicious of Frenchy's invitations: "Frenchy would attack anything. He'd go after anybody. I wouldn't even bring my parents up there [to the ranch] for fear he'd get drunk and corner my mom."

What Fred didn't know was that at home Frenchy had already crossed into forbidden territory. He had begun visiting Martine's room at night. She never said anything, but she knew the visits, the touching, were wrong. Then, when she was nine, he upped the ante: "Dad used to dress as Santa. I was sitting on his lap. I knew it was wrong. He put his fingers in my vagina. Pat saw. She knew but she couldn't do anything about it."

Later, a friend of Martine's told her that Frenchy had grabbed her as well. Again Martine was too frightened to say anything but she began to avoid having friends for overnight visits or weekend trips to the ranch.

As Frenchy submerged himself deeper and deeper in drugs and sex, Pat got left behind. She tried coke and it made her happy. But she could do without it. She must have seen Frenchy spinning out of control but she remained devoted to him. The further his experiences took him from Pat, the more confined he felt by their relationship. And so he took to batting her around. He had occasionally slapped her in the past. Now, when he went after her, it was with his fists. He'd blacken her eyes, pound her head against the wall, throw her across the room. Sometimes the attacks were unprovoked. Other times Pat would trigger them by verbally attacking him for chasing other women. She called him a roadrunner, and on a number of occasions she threatened to tell the children something she knew about Jeannine. Years later Pat said those threats provoked some of the worst beatings she received from Frenchy. Still, she never left him. She apparently still loved him, still needed him, still wanted him.

Marc and Martine say that things got much worse at home after Anne left. Martine bore the burden of her father's secret sexual interest in her. He also introduced her to drugs. At eleven years old, she remembers him rubbing cocaine on her gums: "I knew it was a drug of some sort. When I got older, he said he'd rather that I do it at home than in the streets where you could never tell what you were getting."

Marc's burden was feeling unwanted. Despite the fact that he was older than Martine, when they moved to the house in Scripps Ranch, Martine got the bigger bedroom. Then she was given her own phone.

"Marc resented it," Martine remembers. "He felt that I was being treated better. I agree. I used to get all these presents, clothes, make-up. Marc got nothing."

By the time he was in his teens, Marc was uncontrollable. He burned with resentment and, like his big brother before him, had a series of fights with his father. He dropped out of school at fifteen, moved out and lived with buddies for a time. He had an affair with a much older woman who had been Frenchy's secretary. He was a scrapper, a fast talker and fast thinker. He'd grown up quick and learned to take care of himself. He continued to do occasional work for his father, and he held jobs in various body shops. Eventually he became an auto body painter. He was good at his work but his personal life was frequently in shambles.

Not long after Marc moved out, Frenchy's time in San Diego came to an end. The bubble burst, the good times were over. Frenchy took a fall but not nearly as hard a fall as his pals did. In some respects it was a repeat of Pointe Gatineau. Frenchy was the only one who didn't wind up eating out of a tin dish and wearing a jailhouse tan.

Financially overextended by the late 1970s, Frenchy could see the writing on the wall. There was no way to avoid bankruptcy so he took advantage of it. According to Fred, Frenchy began "taking things out of the shop and running them up to the ranch. He knew it was going to go down." He had built a cement-block garage at the ranch, and in the garage he hid all the equipment he would need to set up another auto body shop. After Frenchy had made all his preparations, the authorities appeared at the shop on Dowdy Street one day. Fred remembers that "they put locks on the door and all the guys tools, and whatever was left in the shop, that stayed."

Frenchy lost everything in San Diego—his businesses and his home. He packed up the personal effects he had been allowed to keep and moved up to the ranch. Anne and Marc remained behind in San Diego, so it was just the three of them up there—Frenchy, Pat and Martine.

Shortly after Frenchy's move, federal authorities in San Diego began investigating a development project in which more than fifty people had invested a total of almost five hundred thousand dollars. The probe took more than a year, and when it was completed, Frenchy's buddies Brian Rand and Richard "Dick" Dickson were charged with multiple counts of mail fraud. They were found guilty of most of the charges and each pulled two-year prison terms. Neither Anne nor Marc or Martine ever saw the three men again.

At almost the same time that the land fraud trial was getting under way in San Diego, federal agents raided the AA-1 U Store-It warehouse in San Jacinto, the small town near Frenchy's ranch, and seized $11 million in counterfeit bills. The seizure was described as the largest confiscation of phony money ever in California. Three men were arrested in a nearby city in connection with the seizure and a day later a fourth suspect, thirty-three-year-old Harry "Skip" Dawson, was arrested at a cabin near San Diego. Searching the cabin, police found $40,000 in counterfeit twenty-dollar bills.

Before the arrest Frenchy told a number of people that Skip, who visited the ranch several times after Frenchy moved up there, had once arrived with an attaché case full of funny money handcuffed to his wrist. And after his arrest, Anne said, "Skip called me. I don't know if he was out on bail or what. He said, 'All you know about me is that I'm your insurance agent. Tell your dad that.' He said he couldn't talk. I told my dad. I never saw Skip again."

Skip was found guilty and, after the appeals were over, was sentenced to two years in prison.

Chapter Seventeen

Aguanga, Riverside County, California, 1980

Riverside County runs from the Santa Ana Mountains, which rise from the Pacific coastal hills below Los Angeles, two hundred miles east straight into the furnace of the Colorado Desert. Forests of lodge-pole pine crown the cool mountain tops. Down on the desert floor around Palm Springs, in the western portion of the county, Hollywood gentry live like lizards in the heat.

In the eastern quarter of Riverside County, separated from the Pacific by the Santa Anas and the desert by the San Jacinto Mountains, are a series of fertile, boulder-strewn valleys, canyons and mesas. The climate is Mediterranean, the geology fragile. The San Jacinto fault, which joins the San Andreas fault farther north, runs along the base of the San Jacinto Mountains and regularly shakes loose house-sized chunks of granite. In the San Jacinto Valley, one of the largest between the two mountain ranges, oranges ripen in groves planted in fields that have been, for the moment, cleared of the movable rocks.

At the turn of the century, Hemet and San Jacinto, a pair of adjoining cities at the centre of the valley with a combined population of about a hundred thousand, were surrounded by apricot, orange, apple and grapefruit orchards. But by the late 1970s, when Frenchy moved to his ranch, which lies down the Sage Road, a canyon road that runs off the southern edge of the valley, fruit growing was on the decline. The land had become too valuable for orange trees, which still line some streets in Hemet and San Jacinto. Housing and land prices in Los Angeles propelled people over the mountains, and the orchards were rapidly replaced by new subdivisions. Frenchy's ranch was a half-hour drive from Hemet, and suburban sprawl hadn't then and still hasn't now come close to his place, largely because the area is not nearly as hospitable as the valley. In the canyon there were no municipal services, little water, rough roads, almost no level land and soil that couldn't be turned into lawn.

Still, by 1980 there were people buying land around Frenchy. For the most part, they were refugees, people, like Frenchy, who appreciated the forbidding qualities of the territory. They were paranoid Vietnam vets and grizzled prospectors from Nevada and families of hippies and bug-eyed hermits, and most of all, they were entrepreneurs in the booming drug business. Back in the rocky hills off the Sage Road they built cabins and lived in buses and set up crystal amphetamine labs and trans-shipped drugs coming across the Mexican border and hid out. Those who weren't into importing became local producers of some of the highest quality marijuana in the state. For a time in the early 1980s there was so much grass under cultivation that the area became known as Pot Hill. The climate, the altitude and the long growing season were ideal for the cultivation of pot. The only element missing was water, but for enough money a well driller could be paid to keep crunching deep into the granite bedrock until the bit tasted water. For a few years pot growers made fortunes in those hills, and Frenchy made as big as pile as anyone. He did better than most, in fact, because unlike almost everyone around him, he never got busted.

Almost as soon as he had moved, Frenchy subscribed to the pot growers' journal, *High Times,* and began assembling the equipment needed for large-scale pot ranching. His full-time assistant was Martine. For a couple of bucks a week and all the leaf she could smoke, she tended the plants year round.

Frenchy installed fibreglass skylights in a cinder-block shed he had built and laid down a rich bed of soil. Every November he germinated top-quality seeds in the house and put them in small pots under heat lamps and let them grow until January, when he transplanted them in the shed.

"From January to October," Martine says, "I was responsible for watering and caring for the plants. Once they got to six feet high, I'd start cutting the water leaves. They inhibit the growth of the buds. You can smoke them. It's called shake. About July or August we would start paying attention to the buds. Buds can get two feet long if you manicure them right. You want to get a pound of bud off a plant. We had plants over fourteen feet tall in there. It was a full day's work to maintain them."

The shake was Martine's, and before her thirteenth birthday she was smoking pot to take the edge off her days on that hilltop with Frenchy and Pat. She attended a small school, tucked under a stand

of cottonwood trees just down the canyon road. And she was turning into an eye-catching beauty. She had straight, strawberry-blond
hair, blue eyes and her mother's long legs. She had been told that
her father was originally from Quebec but knew nothing about the
place. She believed Pat was her mother, and no one ever told her
otherwise. Anne and Marc wanted to tell her about Jeannine, but
they kept putting it off.

The good times and the bankruptcy in San Diego had emptied
Frenchy's pockets. He figured the pot ranching would put him back
in the money. It did. A well-maintained plant could produce a
pound of top-quality pot, which retailed for up to two thousand
dollars. At times he had up to a hundred plants in the shed, which
was not much larger than a one-car garage. Not all of them produced a pound of bud, and often he wholesaled his crop so his
income from the pot varied widely. He once told his kids that he
was making eighty thousand dollars a year in small bills, all of it
tax-free.

They harvested at the same time every year, around the full
moon in October. "We'd chop the plant off at the bottom and hang
the entire plant upside-down on wires strung across the living
room," Martine says. "It would take three days for them to dry and
cure properly. Then we'd separate the buds from the stalks and
burn the stalks. We'd lay out a big sheet on the table and pick out
any seeds that were in the buds. All the seeds would go into a jar,
and some would be germinated almost immediately. We had a scale
and we'd bag them in pounds."

With each crop he took off, Frenchy became more paranoid and
more security-conscious. After bagging his crop he'd seal it in
forty-five-gallon drums and bury the drums in nearby washes. He
put in fences and locked gates, so many that to get in and out of his
yard he had to unlock and lock three gates. He mounted a security
camera on a pole near the final gate to his yard, and trusted friends
and buyers were instructed to blow their car horns in a prearranged
sequence so he would know to let them in. Within the area, none of
this was unusual. The hillsides around the ranch were dotted with
makeshift houses and tent camps surrounded by fierce dogs and
"No Trespassing" and "Keep Out" signs. Strangers were shouted
off, and nobody, but nobody, who didn't live in the area went for a
casual hike in the hills. Around harvest season, gunfire often ripped

open the silence of the nights. Locals still tell the story of the long-hair who put a bullet into the buttock of a police officer one season. Most of the growers were armed, and down there that didn't mean armed with a rusty old squirrel gun. It meant M-16 assault rifles and nine-millimetre automatic handguns and high-powered hunting rifles with night-vision scopes.

One year Frenchy, who had his own arsenal and frequently carried a holstered handgun on his hip, chased off two pistol-packing, would-be crop thieves who showed up in Hallowe'en masks at the end of October. They confronted a helper of Frenchy's on the property and he shouted for help. Frenchy appeared and spooked them. They commandeered his Cadillac and sped off. Frenchy chased them down the hill in a truck but pulled back when one of the masked men put a bullet through the windshield. They abandoned his Caddy down the road where they had hidden their own car. Frenchy never found out who they were.

Most of Frenchy's crop was sold in San Diego. For a time Marc had a condo and Frenchy paid Marc's phone bill. He did most of his business out of the condo. Marc would haul trunkloads of the crop down to San Diego. Frenchy sold to guys who had worked in his shop, and for a time he even had one of his ex-employees distributing pounds for him.

Within a year or so after the move, Frenchy had made a wide circle of friends around the ranch. He was, as usual, charming and funny, and he threw parties that everyone attended. He often had Bill Parker, the mailman from San Jacinto, and his wife over for barbecues. He showed Daniel and Arlene Knight a twenty-acre plot nearby and convinced them they should buy it and move up to the area, which they did. Everyone knew him as Frenchy Holben. He was a retired RCMP officer and a first-class body man.

During that first year the man he became chummiest with was a rotund, red-faced retiree named Byars B. Clark. B.B., as he was known, and his wife, Frances, who walked with a cane, lived in a trailer along Thomas Road. They were in their sixties and became frequent visitors at Frenchy's. He introduced them to the relaxing pleasures of pot, which eased the arthritic pain in Frances's legs. After an evening at Frenchy's she'd often forget her cane and would have to call for it in the morning. Not long after they met, Frenchy suggested they might want to buy Brian Rand's place next door. Rand needed money and Frenchy offered to co-sign for a loan so B.B. could buy the place. B.B. bit and the Clarks became Frenchy's nearest neighbours. Frenchy soon had B.B. running errands for him.

In October, 1979, Frenchy and Pat invited all the locals they had met and some old friends from San Diego, including a psychiatrist who had lived next to Frenchy, up to the ranch for a party on October 30 to celebrate their twenty-fifth wedding anniversary. For some years they had been celebrating their fictitious marriage on that date but this year was to be special. They told everyone they had been married for two and a half decades. Bill Parker remembers the party was a huge success. They served steak, shrimp and lobster, and partied into the small hours of the morning. What none of the guests knew, what not even the children suspected, was the secret significance of the date of the party. For on that date— October 30th, twenty-five years earlier—Frenchy had married not Pat Holben but Jeannine Boissonneault. For some perverse reason Frenchy had selected the anniversary of his marriage to Jeannine to celebrate his union with Pat. He had made Pat the mother of his four children, and he pretended she was the woman he had married on an afternoon in late fall of 1954.

About a year after they had moved to the ranch, Frenchy and Pat drove their motor home to Florida for a vacation. There they met one of Ray's brothers and his mother, Marie-Anna. During the vacation Marie-Anna gave Frenchy Denis's address and phone number. They hadn't talked or written to each other since the fight in 1974. Marie-Anna told Frenchy that Denis was working in a body shop in Hull and that he and Line now had two daughters, Mélanie, born in 1976, and Geneviève, born earlier that year. Frenchy was a grandfather, twice. The news surprised and apparently touched him. When he returned to the ranch, he called Anne and told her. Not long afterwards, Anne was up at the ranch for the weekend and she and Frenchy decided to call Denis. She rang the number and a voice she recognized as Denis's answered.

"Hi, Denis. It's Anne. Your sister."

That phone call from Anne, always the peacemaker in the family, threw Denis for a loop. He had made a new life for himself and hadn't had any contact with his brother or sisters for more than seven years. After his return to Canada he and Line had moved into the top floor of an old house in Hull, and he had gotten a job in a body shop owned by Serge Dagenais, who had once laboured for Frenchy. Denis worked for Serge for more than six years, and during all that time neither Serge nor his wife Rollande can remember Denis ever talking about his past.

Denis had matured into a tall, serious-minded man who rarely spoke unless spoken to. He played drums in a country and western band on the weekends, didn't smoke, rarely drank and was devoted to Line and his kids. He had become like a son to the Lafonds. He was particularly close to Line's father, Ben, and often used Ben's garage to paint cars for friends at night. He had sad eyes and a generous nature that endeared people to him. Among the men working at the body shop he was a regular joe, well liked and accepted but different. Unlike the rest of the guys, most of whom spoke only French, Denis spoke flawless English. He could curse like a sailor in both languages, but he didn't rough-house with the other guys. The mechanics and body men he worked with favoured tattoos, were often missing teeth and many laboured with a stogy stuck in the corner of their mouths. With his blond hair and sparkling white teeth, Denis looked like a beach bum thrown in with a gang of hard rock miners.

When Denis realized who was calling, he greeted Anne enthusiastically. Anne was fifteen the last time he had seen her, Marc was just a little boy, and Martine was a grade schooler. Now Denis was in his mid-twenties, Anne was living on her own, Marc was working in a paint shop and living in San Diego, and Martine had just become a teenager. Denis and Anne caught up on the past, and he told her about his kids. Then she urged him to come down for a visit.

"Come this summer," she suggested.

"I'd like to," he told her, "But I don't want to see that prick."

"Oh," Anne answered, "Dad's changed so much. He's right here beside me. Why don't you talk to him?" And she passed the phone to Frenchy before Denis could object.

Denis remembers they greeted each other awkwardly. Frenchy told Denis that he was now retired and living at a ranch he had bought. The conversation didn't last long, but Denis thought about it constantly for weeks afterwards. He wanted so badly to see his brother and sisters. Finally he called Anne back and said he and

Line were going to visit California for a couple of weeks in July. He asked her to make reservations for him at a motel near the beach in San Diego. He told her he didn't want to see or visit his dad and asked her to meet him at the airport in Los Angeles. He figured they'd go straight to San Diego and hang out with Marc and Anne and maybe get Martine down for a visit so he could see her, too.

When they flew into Los Angeles airport, Denis and Line didn't see anyone waiting for them so they collected their luggage and were wandering around when Denis thought he saw Pat, shorter than he remembered, not as heavy, wearing glasses and looking confused, and a tall, blonde girl whom he figured might be Martine. Was that really baby Martine? He walked over and greeted them. He hugged Martine and the four of them walked out of the terminal together. And there, standing in front of a Cadillac convertible, was Frenchy himself. He had grown a beard, had permed his now greying hair and he still had a big jellyroll around his waist. They looked at each other. Frenchy appeared nervous and, Denis thought, stoned or something. They shook hands and climbed into the car.

Denis fumed for most of the long ride back to the ranch. Anne, he said to himself, was going to get an earful. He had told her he didn't want to see Frenchy.

Denis had never been in the San Jacinto Valley before and didn't know what to expect. The ranch, Frenchy called it. What was it going to be like, he wondered. They drove through the San Jacinto Valley entered the canyon on the Sage Road, hooked left on Thomas Road and then finally swung off on the dirt trail leading to Frenchy's. It looked like a rocky desert, he thought. Three times Frenchy stopped to unlock gates and lock them again behind him. At the last gate Denis noticed a camera mounted on a post and, about a hundred yards off, a mobile home that had been set on a concrete pad on a hilltop. Stubby shrubs lined the drive and a couple of small buildings sat off on the southern slope of the hill. Everything was dry, brittle, brown.

As soon as Denis and Line had stowed their bags in Martine's bedroom, they put on swimming suits and jumped into the pool. They swam and sipped cold drinks for about an hour before Frenchy pulled Denis aside and took him out for a walk around the property. He showed him his well and two 250-gallon cisterns that he filled by turning on the well pump. Then he showed Denis a half-dozen plants growing beside the house.

"Know what that is?" he asked.

"Looks like marijuana." Denis was taken aback. The old man was now smoking pot? That was new. While he pondered this development, he heard rock music coming from one of the out-buildings.

"What's that music?" he asked.

"Hang on," Frenchy answered and ran into the house. He returned with a key and led Denis to a padlocked door on one of the sheds. The music was coming from inside.

"The music is for my plants," Frenchy told Denis, who was puzzled, until his father swung open the door, and he was hit by a wave of intense, moist heat, the sweet smell of cannabis and the brilliant green colour of the plants. Inside he saw neat rows of pot plants, some of them fourteen feet high. Each had a plastic tube tied to it from which water dripped on the roots. The tubes were attached to a timer, Frenchy explained, and he showed Denis a desk cluttered with bags of nutrients he fed to the plants.

"This is how I make my living," he told Denis. "I do the odd car to fool the government. There're eighty plants in there. I started with a hundred. It's worth eighty to a hundred thousand dollars."

Denis was flabbergasted. His dad had become a drug dealer.

That weekend, Denis and Line met B.B. and Frances, who lived in a trailer right behind Frenchy's house. B.B. drove an old truck and wore coveralls; Denis noticed that Frenchy used him as an errand boy. On Saturday, Anne came up with her friend Marcie. Marc was living with them but hadn't come along because he was working.

"I couldn't wait to see him," Denis remembers. So Sunday night Denis, Line, Anne, Marcie and Martine drove to San Diego. Denis and Line checked into a motel and met Marc at Anne's.

"I wouldn't have recognized him. He was just a little boy when I left," Denis says. Marc was now close to six feet tall, had brown hair and eyes and an engaging smile. They had some tender moments together that week. For the first time in their lives all four children were together without Frenchy looming in the background. Three of them were living independently of him, and

Martine seemed able to deal with Frenchy and Pat. Denis longed to talk to all of them about Jeannine but hesitated. He didn't want to spoil the magic of the visit.

One night Frenchy and Pat drove to San Diego, and they all went out to a bar. They danced and drank. Denis found himself sitting next to Marc at one point. The music was so loud they could barely converse. So when Marc shouted over at him, "How's Mom?" Denis was confused. Maybe he meant Pat. He pointed to her. "She's over there."

Marc looked, then shook his head. "No. Mom. How is she?"

Denis stared at him for a moment. "Come outside with me, Marc."

The two of them walked out. As soon as they hit the cool evening air, Denis turned to Marc.

"What did you mean in there?"

"Well, Frenchy said Mom was living with you in Canada."

Denis went rigid with anger. He calmed himself and patiently recounted for Marc the story of their lives since Houston. He listed all the lies Frenchy had told them about Jeannine; he described his meeting with their Boissonneault grandparents and concluded by telling Marc why he had returned to Canada in 1974.

Now it was Marc who was wild with rage. He had heard his father say so often that Denis was a bit soft in the head that he himself had begun to believe Frenchy. He had never known why Denis had left in 1974. He, too, had had his battles with Frenchy and Pat, and now, hearing Denis's history of the family, hearing the truth about his life, he was ready to kill his father. Marc has a hair-trigger temper and Denis had to grab him and talk him out of marching back into the bar and tackling Frenchy. Denis finally cooled him down and they returned to their table but Marc was sombre all evening.

Denis and Line took Martine back to the ranch the next day, and that afternoon Marc drove up with Marcie. He stomped in, looked at Denis and said "I want to talk to you." They walked outside and Frenchy followed at a distance, trying to eavesdrop on their conversation.

When they were alone, Marc questioned Denis again, made him tell the story in greater detail. In return, Marc told Denis about his relations with Frenchy, how his father made him steal paint supplies for him from the shop Marc worked at, how Frenchy was dealing in pot and coke.

After their talk, Marc left, deeply troubled, and Denis felt a sense of foreboding. Marc, he had discovered, was volatile, and he worried that his brother would do something stupid to Frenchy, whom he clearly hated with a passion. But he was elated, too. Now he had his brother on his side, someone who knew Frenchy and knew that Denis wasn't making up the stories about the abuse and the lies and the pain they had suffered. But Marc didn't know enough to be really helpful. What he needed, Denis thought, was Anne's collaboration. She had memories of Jeannine; she might remember things about their mother's disappearance that he had forgotten.

He and Line left the next day. Back in Canada Denis became obsessed with connecting with Anne. Several weeks before Christmas, he called her in San Diego and invited her to spend Christmas with him. He offered to buy her plane ticket and said he'd cover all her expenses while she was in Canada. Anne was enthusiastic, so enthusiastic that she called her father to tell him the good news. Two days later Frenchy called Denis to tell him that he had decided to return home for Christmas as well.

"Don't worry about the plane tickets," he told a crestfallen Denis. "I'm paying for them." Frenchy said that Marc couldn't make it but that he was coming with Pat, Anne and Martine. Denis insisted that Anne stay with him. Frenchy agreed, explaining that he, Pat and Martine would stay with Marie-Anna.

Soon after, rumours began swirling within the Durand family about a fight Denis was planning to pick with his father. Denis was unaware of the gossip until, a week before Christmas, his grandmother Durand called him at the shop and asked him to drop over after work. He often stopped by to see how she was doing, so the request wasn't unusual. But when he arrived that night he could see she was nervous. "Sit down," she told him, and she set out a bowl of soup for him. As he ate, she told him that she was planning a birthday party for Raymond. They had rented a church hall and all his brothers and sisters were going to be there. She had ordered a plaque as a gift for him on which would be engraved the names and birthdates of his parents as well as those of his siblings. He hadn't been home in years and had done so well for himself in the United States. She was proud of Raymond and hoped Denis was, too.

Then she dropped her bombshell. She had heard, she told Denis, that he was planning to have his father arrested when he returned. Denis stopped and stared at her.

"Who told you that?"

She wouldn't say, then admitted that one of his uncles had passed the word to her. Denis felt wounded. He swore up and down that it wasn't true and demanded that she bring over the uncle who had told her so he could confront him. But his grandmother remained sceptical.

Finally, Denis walked out. When push had come to shove, his grandmother, who had treated him like a son, had sided with Raymond. She knew about Jeannine, knew that Raymond was a thief and a liar and that he had something to do with Jeannine's disappearance, and yet she was throwing a big party for him. And she was accusing Denis of plotting to spoil it all. He was furious. The whole family knew what kind of man Raymond was, but they were treating him like some kind of hero. He despised them for refusing to open their eyes to who and what Raymond was. A big success, Denis thought. A big success as a drug dealer. He wondered if they knew that. And what about Jeannine. They all knew she hadn't been seen since Houston and that Frenchy had lied about what had happened to her. Didn't any of them care?

Somebody within the family apparently told Frenchy of Denis's alleged plot because although Frenchy, Pat, Anne and Martine all flew up from California to Toronto, only Anne caught the connecting flight to Ottawa. The others rented a car in Toronto, Frenchy later told Denis, and drove to Hull.

It was just as well, Denis thought, as he waited for Anne's flight in the Ottawa airport: he wouldn't have to deal with his dad. When Anne finally arrived—her flight had been delayed by a snowstorm—Denis bundled her into his car and within fifteen minutes they were in his cosy upstairs apartment in central Hull. Anne hugged her two nieces and played with them until bedtime. She was tired but Denis wanted to talk. He led her into the kitchen at about 10 P.M. and for the next five hours talked to her about their past.

Anne remembers sitting at that kitchen table and watching Denis bring out a box that contained photos and newspaper clippings. She had never before seen the story that had been published in the

Montreal tabloid, and as he translated it for her, she couldn't believe what she was seeing and hearing.

"Anne, I think Dad killed Mom," she remembers him saying. She remained composed but inside, "I was pissed at him for saying that my father killed my mother. I thought he was making it up. I thought that he wanted to know so badly what had happened that he had made it up. At that point I believed that she [Jeannine] had just gotten remarried and didn't want anything to do with us."

Denis talked and talked but realized that Anne wasn't buying it. She's so goddamned hard-headed, he thought. Why can't she see the truth?

Denis told her that when her grandfather Hermas Boissonneault had succumbed to cancer four years earlier, Denis had gone the church early for the funeral. He scanned all the faces in the crowd, even contrived to pass the collection plate during the mass, all so that he could check the mourners for Jeannine.

"Anne," he told her, tears now streaming down his face, "she wasn't there. If Mom was still alive, she would have been at her own father's funeral."

Later, Denis remembered another story about Hermas that he hadn't told Anne. Hermas had spent the last months of his life on the sofa in the front room of the family home. One night his condition worsened and he was taken to the hospital. He died the next day. After he was taken from the house, Laurette or Réginald had found his wallet on the sofa, opened to a photo of Jeannine. He had been thinking about her, scrutinizing her photo, right to the painful end of his life.

When Denis finally gave up at 3 A.M., he went to bed feeling defeated. Anne fell asleep upset with her brother for keeping alive old hatreds. Why couldn't he just give it up and end the feuding with his father? she wondered. She had taken the initiative to reunite the family and Denis wasn't responding. He wasn't interested in making up. Worse, he had infected Marc with his crazy ideas about murder. After five hours of Denis's pleading and crying and patient explanations, the only point of agreement between the two of them was that Anne would join them for Christmas dinner at the Boissonneaults. She was eager to see her grandmother again.

A couple of days after Anne's arrival, Frenchy drove into town and the warm greetings of his large family. They stayed with

Marie-Anna, and Martine began meeting her father's bewilderingly large family. She could never sort out who was who. She enjoyed all the attention though, and she got to know her grandmother.

Martine had often heard her father say that Denis was crazy, that he had some kind of mental problem, but she wanted to see him and Anne and did get over to Denis's place on a number of occasions. On Christmas Eve she was visiting Denis and decided she wanted to go skating on the Rideau Canal in Ottawa. The surface of the canal, which starts in downtown Ottawa and winds its way through the city, is groomed for skating in the winter. On the night Denis and Martine went out, light snow was falling, the ice reflected the colours of Christmas lights along the banks of the canal, and they found themselves alone.

"Martine was doing little twirls. She was so happy," Denis remembers. "I skated over to her and said, 'Martine, I want to tell you something.' She looked over at me. And then I couldn't do it. I couldn't tell her about Mom. I didn't want to screw her up. She was so happy and so innocent. She had bugged me for hours to take her. There was nobody else on the ice. It was peaceful and I kept saying to myself, What's it gonna change if I do tell her? And so I didn't."

Years later, when asked about that visit to Canada, Martine remembers feeling that people were trying to tell her something that just wouldn't come out. There was the night with Denis and another time at her grandmother Durand's. "It was as if when I was there she wanted to tell me something. She acted like there was something on her mind. I asked her, 'Is something wrong? Something that I've done?' She said, 'No, it's not important now.'"

On Christmas Day, Anne, Denis, Line and the children drove to the Boissonneaults'. Anne remembers Réginald answered the door. She greeted him and he disappeared soon after into the upper recesses of the house. Laurette was elderly and ailing. Although no one knew it then, she was to live only another two years. By 1981, Denis remembers, she spent her days sitting quietly with a far-away look in her eyes. It seemed to Denis that she was constantly thinking of Jeannine. She talked about her and Raymond often but would still stop herself from criticizing her former son-in-law in Denis's presence. "Oh," she'd say, "I shouldn't be saying that, Denis. He's your father." By now Laurette thought that maybe Jeannine had made a new life for herself. For the longest time she had believed that Jeannine had entered a convent. But after years of no news, she had come to believe that Jeannine didn't want anyone to know about her new life. She refused to entertain the possibility that Raymond had committed murder. She remained naïve, hopeful.

In 1971, when Raymond had visited and had left Hermas and Réginald a Vancouver address for Jeannine, Laurette immediately wrote to Jeannine in Vancouver. That letter came back, unopened, stamped "NO SUCH ADDRESS." Yet even after Denis had told her all that he knew, she continued secretly to write to Jeannine in Vancouver. Réginald remembers each time one of her letters would come back, unopened, she'd sit down and draft another, assuming there was some problem with her handwriting or with the way she had printed the address on the envelope. She sent off nine letters and finally gave up after the last one bore a personal note from a postal employee. As far as Réginald can recall, that note said simply, "NO SUCH ADDRESS IN B.C."

Laurette was delighted to see Anne all grown up. She hugged her and told her that Jeannine had loved her very much. After dinner Laurette played the piano, and Anne remembered many of the tunes were pieces that her mother had played. Laurette took out her photo albums and gave Anne several pictures of Jeannine. A number of them had been trimmed with a pair of scissors, Anne noticed. After Laurette had sent her last letter to Vancouver, she had fallen into despair and, in a moment of anger, had cut Raymond out of all the pictures she had in her albums. Now, not a single photo of Raymond was left in her house.

Later that evening Denis suggested they call Marc in California. They reached him at his apartment, and Denis translated for Laurette. Having Anne in her house and hearing Marc made her so happy that Christmas, Denis remembers, she seemed filled with light and joy. Anne left that night "feeling, once again, that I had a grandmother, even if I didn't have a mother. I felt real good."

Although Marie-Anna called Denis to invite him to the birthday party, Denis refused to go. He felt estranged from the old lady and the entire Durand family. Anne declined the invitation as well. She didn't want to see anyone. She doesn't remember why she didn't want to see the Durands. She was still annoyed with Denis but was nonetheless content to hang out with him and his family.

A month after Anne returned to California she was visiting her father and recounted for him what Denis had told her.

"Denis thinks you killed Mom. Isn't that crazy?" she remembers telling him. Frenchy laughed it off but that's not what Anne wanted to hear. Inside, she was terrified that "what Denis had told me was the truth." What she wanted to hear from her father was a rational, believable explanation of what had happened to Jeannine. More than anything else she wanted to be able to call Denis and say something like: Jeannine is living in Armpit, Kentucky. She's married to a coal miner and has four kids and if you want to talk to her, go ahead. She wanted Frenchy to dispel the fears and the doubts and allow her to go on loving him like a father. He was the only parent she had left and she didn't want to lose him, as flawed as he was. But Frenchy did nothing to reassure her that day, didn't offer her even the smallest bone to chew on. That day he made it much harder for her to love him, but she didn't show it. If anything, she became even closer to him than before. It was as if she wanted to get inside his head and tell his story for him. If he couldn't defend himself, perhaps she could do it for him.

That year Frenchy expanded his pot ranch. B.B. Clark, whom Martine remembers as her father's "right-hand man," was made part of the operation. Frenchy still had plants in his shed with the skylight. But now he talked B.B. into putting in a crop on his twenty acres. Two neighbours who knew B.B. say Frenchy told him that with the profits from one crop he could pay off the land. Frenchy set up an irrigation system and put in more than 150 plants. He put a layer of broken glass around the bottom of the plants to keep animals from nibbling on them. All that year B.B. and Frenchy tended them, and by fall they were coming along nicely.

"We normally harvested in October at the full moon," says Martine. "But that fall Dad sent me out to the greenhouse earlier than normal, ahead of schedule. It was premature to take them out. He just said do it. The crop on B.B.'s land, that was his business. But we harvested ours too soon. And [Dad] didn't just chop the plants as you are supposed to. He pulled them out of the ground. We did it together. We pulled out the stalks and raked it like nothing was there before. And we planted regular lawn grass. I didn't ask why."

The crop was brought inside and dried. Within a couple of days it was packaged up and taken somewhere by Frenchy. Then, after the shed crop had been taken away, Martine recalls, "We had a few plants inside the ranch gate beside the house—probably ten plants. I remember Pat was out there pulling the plants up, recklessly, like she had to do it real quick. She pulled up all the plants and stuck them in the bathtub in the house. I didn't know what all that was about. Shortly after that police cruisers raced up to the house along with an unmarked car. All I knew is she put the plants in the bathtub but they searched the whole house and didn't find them. Dad told me later that he had stuck the stuff up in the false ceiling. The cops went through everything—my dresser, the mattresses, the closet. But they didn't check the false ceiling.

"The police had guns on us. They walked dad across the property. Dad seemed cool. They had a helicopter fly ahead while they were searching the land."

When the police didn't find anything on Frenchy's property, they turned their attention to B.B.'s place. They apparently had search warrants for both properties. In B.B.'s house they discovered a scale that Martine says belonged to Ray, and then, fanning out behind his place, they found the plantation.

Arlene Knight was at her place next door to B.B.'s that day. "I saw B.B. get into the cop car with his wife screaming and hollering, saying it was all Frenchy's fault. She told the cops that it was all Frenchy's stuff," Arlene recalls.

B.B. was charged with cultivation of marijuana and released on bail. Arlene says that he had a heart attack shortly afterward and lost the land. Frenchy said he now owned the property. Others say he also got B.B.'s car and trailer. B.B. was eventually found guilty and, because of his age, was put on probation. About a month after the bust, Martine saw B.B. talking to her father: "It sounded to me, from what I could hear, that he felt bad and that Dad had done him a wrong turn. He did something bad to him. At that point Dad was trying to get out of the situation, saying, 'You knew what you were doing while you were doing it.' But this is an old man. I mean, it's enough to grow pot on his land but to let B.B. take the whole rap for it? That's not right."

It has never been clear how the bust came about. Frenchy said later that he spotted a surveillance aircraft several days before the bust and knew the police wouldn't be far behind. Local investigators say they were then using surveillance aircraft with infrared cameras to search for plantations. But they say when a plantation was spotted, they moved quickly. They say they wouldn't have waited for three days. Whatever the case, Frenchy knew the police were coming and made sure he was clean.

Some months after the bust, a quitclaim deed to the property was filed with the Riverside County recorder's office. In the quitclaim deed, "Beyers B. Clark and Frances M. Clark" transferred to "Ray D. Holben and Patricia D. Holben" their interest in the twenty-acre plot that they had purchased from the Rands. On other legal forms that B.B. signed, his name appears as "Byars B. Clark." But on this one he signed his name "Byers B. Clark." In the absence of an expert analysis of the signature on the document it would be unfair to suggest that it was forged. Still, it is odd that B.B. would have misspelled his own name.

B.B. moved from California shortly after his arrest, and according to people who knew him, both he and his wife have since died. After they left, Frenchy began looking for new tenants. It didn't take him long to locate renters, a couple, Rick and Jenny, and their little girl. According to Arlene and Daniel Knight, Rick and Jenny leased the property from Frenchy, put in a pot crop with his knowledge and assistance and intended to make a large land payment to Frenchy from their profits. But things took an unpleasant turn when Jenny did a little legal research and discovered that Ray didn't own clear title to the land. She also heard the story of Frenchy and B.B.

"Rick was a pretty spooky person," Daniel remembers. "He was a big guy, real sinister-looking. He'd been down the road. He could paint pictures for your mind."

After Rick tumbled to Frenchy's reputation, he began to make Frenchy nervous. "One night Rick put on a gorilla mask," Daniel recalls. "Frenchy was having a party. Rick looked over the fence [at Frenchy's], then went to another place and looked over the fence. Then he took a small rattlesnake and let it loose inside Frenchy's compound. When people saw the rattlesnake, he rose and let them see him, too, in his gorilla mask. That just freaked everyone."

That fall, when the crop was ripe for harvesting, the police arrived at the house en masse. "There were so many of them it really frightened [their little girl]. She went running to the house, hysterical. Rick went out the back door. The cops never found him," says Daniel.

They found the crop out back and arrested Jenny, who was pregnant and almost due. Daniel recalls, "I walked over by the gate and Jenny said, 'What about my baby?' That's when we went over and offered to take care of her little girl. We saw Jenny a few days later." She was out on bail.

While she was out on bail, Jenny, who had apparently at one time worked with a private investigator, obtained a copy of what is known as an affiant's declaration. It had been prepared by a Riverside County deputy sheriff, Joseph M. De Armond, Jr, who was at the time attached to a county police narcotics task force. Apparently, the declaration was filed with the courts in support of a police request for a search warrant of Rick and Jenny's property. In the declaration, De Armond stated that he had met in a public restaurant at 11:20 A.M. on September 28 with a "citizen informant" named Raymond Hoben:

Raymond Hoben said that he had picked a sample of marijuana he found growing on some property he owns that he is currently renting to Rick and Jenny. Mr Hoben told your affiant that he is currently allowing his tenants to use water from his well because the well on the rented property has run dry....Mr Hoben said that he took the liberty to check the well located on the property and discovered that an additional water line ran down the property in the form of a black plastic hose to the area of some sage and brush. Mr Hoben told your affiant that when he checked the area he saw 50–60 marijuana plants growing under the brush....Your affiant has no reason to believe that Mr Hoben would give false information and your affiant believes that Mr Hoben acted as a concerned citizen.

Jenny was found guilty and sent to prison, but she left the declaration with people she knew. Within short order, copies of it were posted on bulletin boards, at the post office and in restaurants throughout the area around Frenchy's ranch. Frenchy was now known as a snitch and began to receive death threats.

Frenchy never put another crop in his shed after the incident with Rick and Jenny. That fall he rented the place to Scott Hall, a brother of Scott's and one of his buddies. Scott was a 185-pound, six-foot, blond-haired Californian who looked as though he had just stepped off a surfboard. He had grown up on a ranch within sight of the coast between San Diego and Los Angeles and, at eighteen, got a job working for a company that built ultra-light gliders. The company had transferred him to Temecula, a small town near Frenchy's ranch, and he heard a guy named Frenchy had a place to rent. Scott moved into the trailer within sight of Frenchy's place, saw Martine in the yard one day and fell in love. He began dating Martine and hanging out with Frenchy.

"[Frenchy] was a sneaky fucker, very secretive," Scott recalls. "And he told us all this shit—he said he was a master brewer and that he had been a cop. He was a pro bullshitter. He was good, too, at manipulating people. But he was intelligent, too. And I liked him, liked being around him. He was quick and he'd make everybody laugh. We had a blast with him. There were good times, lots of good times."

Scott moved out that fall but he continued to date Martine and hang out at the ranch. After Scott's departure Frenchy decided to make some improvements to the double-wide trailer that first B.B. and then Rick and Jenny had lived in. So one night there was a fire in the trailer that scorched the walls. Daniel remembers walking over after the fire to look at the place: "It was pretty obvious that someone had splashed something around inside and lit it. It wasn't enough to burn it down. A flash fire and that was it."

With no crop in the shed, Frenchy expanded his body shop operation at the ranch. He had all the equipment and a small garage, and he began taking on more jobs. He taught Martine the trade, and the two of them were soon repairing and painting several vehicles a week. Frenchy was also regularly buying cars at auctions and repairing them for resale.

Some years earlier, while Anne and Fred Angelo, Jr were still dating, Fred remembers Frenchy acquired a small caterpillar that he used around the property: "There was a little road out the back of the property to a spot [where] he always hung out for some weird reason [and] where we weren't supposed to go. He'd always be down there with a dozer. He was like a dog with a bone down there always digging up or moving stuff. He'd tell us, 'Hey, don't you be messing around down there.' He loved that dozer and we'd say, 'What are you digging?' And he'd say, 'Trash.' He drove that dozer all over those hills."

Anne broke up with Fred when they began fighting. He hit her a couple of times and she decided to end it. Fred admits he was rough with Anne and says part of what was making him crazy was Frenchy. They never saw each other again. Anne moved in with a couple of girl-friends and began dating other guys. She was happy that her father had left San Diego: "I really felt free. I thought that he couldn't bother me any more. I used to hear things from people, things like 'Your dad ripped me off.' or 'Your dad shorted my pay cheque.' I thought I wouldn't hear any more of that."

But she was lonely. She wasn't close to Marc. He had married and had a child. He'd found a steady job and was doing well for himself. So, with increasing frequency, Anne found she was spending weekends at the ranch. She often brought friends along, and they would spend the days in the pool at the ranch and the nights in clubs and bars down in the valley. They frequented joints in Temecula, Winchester, Hemet and San Jacinto. All were within a half-hour drive of the ranch. Many of the places featured western music and dancing. Often her father would join her for an evening out.

Brenda Nares, a friend of Anne's from San Diego, said that for more than a year, "every Friday night we'd drive up to the ranch and spend the weekend. We'd go out with her dad. He was a pretty wild guy, sly. He did a lot of coke. Mostly he left Pat at home. But sometimes she'd come along and get pretty sloshed."

Brenda said Anne and her father were good friends. She said Anne once told her that Pat wasn't her real mother. Asked where her real mom was, Brenda recalls Anne said: "She just left us." Once Brenda knew that much, Anne told her never to mention it in front of Martine. "She doesn't know Pat isn't her mom and we don't want her to ever know because it would hurt her."

Frenchy was still dealing coke and was still jacked up on the white crystals himself. He was also chasing skirts. He had affairs with a couple of women he had met on his evenings out. Relations between the Frenchy and Pat were growing steadily worse. In the early years of their relationship Pat had held her own. She was never an equal partner and he rarely took her into his confidence when he was planning a scam, but they partied and drank together. She ran the home and he made the money. After they moved to the ranch, they took annual trips to Hawaii, often went on extended travels around North America in their motor home and got into the habit of visiting Las Vegas to gamble. When they weren't on the road, they ate in local restaurants a couple of times a week. At the ranch, they frequently threw big parties. Martine says there'd be weekends when twenty to thirty people would sleep over: "Drugs would be flowing freely. He'd buy all the booze. Everybody brought their own sleeping-bags. The next morning he'd cook eggs, sausages, biscuits—the whole nine yards."

The more he was around young people, friends of his kids, the more he began to put down Pat. He'd tell her she was ugly, stupid and fat. She began to live in his shadow. He wasn't ready yet to leave her but the time was coming.

One day in late 1983 or early 1984, Martine was in the shop at the ranch painting a car with Marc. Both of them had become skilled painters. They worked for a couple of hours, finished well before noon and sat down together to have a smoke.

"Pat was drunk," Martine remembers. "She came out and started getting on me for smoking cigarettes. She came up to me and slapped me in the face. I grabbed her by her lapels to nail her. But I didn't. I said, 'Mom, go back in the house.' I couldn't slug her. She left and I said, 'She's not acting like Mom.'"

Marc was squatting in a corner and he stared up at her with a strange look in his eye.

"She's not your real mom, Martine," he said quietly. "Dad killed your real mom."

Martine was speechless with confusion. "I believed him. I finished my work. Dad came home and he knew something was wrong. He called me into the house and said, 'Whatever Marc told you isn't true.' I said, 'She's not my mom.' He said, 'But you understand that I'm your real dad?' I knew then, when he said that, that it was true, that Pat wasn't my mom."

While Martine stood there, thinking her life had been a lie, she saw her father walk out of the house with a .22 rifle. He was drunk and he was after Marc: "He was going to shoot Marc. Marc lunged for Dad, had his hands on Dad's neck. Then Marc grabbed the gun and smashed it and splinters [from the stock] sprayed all over the car we had just painted. I jumped on Marc's back."

Somehow, Martine remembers, she managed to separate the two

of them. Marc left, and Frenchy retreated to the house. Once the threat of violence between her brother and father had been dealt with, Martine fell into a funk that lasted weeks. She was angry with Frenchy and Pat, even angrier with Denis, Anne and Marc. She called Denis and Anne.

"Why didn't you tell me?" she wailed at them over the phone. They were embarrassed. Nothing they said made her feel any better. She didn't know whom to love or trust. She couldn't very well abandon the woman who had been her mother—not a great mother but the only one she had known—but wondered at the same time how she could ever look Pat in the eye again, knowing that she had lied to her all of her life. And she wondered who her real mother had been. Who was Jeannine? Did she have grandparents and relatives somewhere that she didn't know about?

And what about Frenchy? Had he killed her mom? She thought about her father and his contempt for others. "If he wanted something real bad and you were in the way, that'd be it, you'd be in the graveyard."

She remembered things he had said and how often he had threatened to kill people. "He'd say, 'Well, if this guy is not going to do this my way, I'm going to kill the son of a bitch.' People say things like that. They don't mean it. You don't take it literally." But maybe, she began to wonder, "maybe he did mean it literally. There was a guy named Bill See. He hated that S.O.B. so bad he was going to kill him. Customers, he'd say, 'If he's not gonna pay, I'll kill him.'"

Revenge, she knew, was "a big thing" with Frenchy. "He'd say, 'This guy thinks he's gonna fuck me over. Well, I'm gonna fuck him over so bad he'll never see the light of day.' He will step all over somebody just to get where he wants to get."

Scott Hall remembers how upset Martine was, how the news "knocked her for a loop. I'd always felt there were secrets. After Marc told her, she kept wondering who her real mom was and where she was. It was really painful for her and she couldn't deal with it."

And so a couple of months after Marc's revelation Martine left home and moved in with Scott. She was sixteen. She visited the ranch and maintained contact with Frenchy and Pat, but she couldn't go on living there.

Scott says by then he wanted no more to do with Frenchy. "I had to deal with Martine. What bothered her most was who her real mom was and where she was. And what the hell happened. Over and over and over. Nightmares, the whole shot. Martine's been through hell."

When Scott eventually heard Denis's stories, he said, "You put it all together and I would tell her that her dad had killed her mom. I didn't doubt it." What Scott couldn't figure was why Anne hadn't drawn the same conclusion, why she remained close to her father. "They were tight. They were on the phone constantly."

Did Martine and Anne ever talk about it? "It's weird," Scott says. "They might have but it's like they didn't want to talk about it. It was like everybody knew but didn't know, and knew that if they confronted the situation, it would just explode and everybody would be against each other. So they kept it under the table and when they got together they wanted to talk about it but they knew if they did, it would just fuck everything up."

Scott says in the first year or so after Martine moved out, they'd visit the ranch, but every time Martine would end up deeply disturbed. His solution was to keep her away from the place for months at a time. They lived together for more than a year and then married. Thinking back on it now, he says he didn't realize what he was getting into.

After Martine moved out, Frenchy embarked on a series of changes in his life. His San Diego bankruptcy was far behind him, and according to Martine, he had made enough money dealing pot and coke to bankroll a new business. He decided it would be in Temecula. At the time, Temecula's biggest business was a western leather-goods company. Its main street was made up of wooden, false-front western buildings that housed curio and antique shops, western-wear stores and boutiques. But new subdivisions were being laid out and shopping malls were being planned, and within a couple of years Temecula's population would explode.

In Temecula, Frenchy had met Rick and Sharon Dial, who owned their own auto repair shop. He did some body work for the Dials for free, and they struck up a business relationship. Together they leased a building on Front Street in Temecula and divided the building in half. One side was Dial Automotive, the other Frenchy's Body Shop. Martine was his first employee.

"The money to [set up Frenchy's] came from pot," Martine believes. "When I was working there, the turnover was incredible. It was Dad, me and another guy. Then he hired a painter. He was right on Front Street. Prime location. From that point on he was making money hand over fist."

Frenchy called Marc in San Diego and told him he'd lease an apartment for him in Temecula and give him a good job in the shop. Marc was unsure. He had finally freed himself from Frenchy. He was now twenty-two, had a house and a job he liked. He called Anne and she told him not to do it. Marc then called Denis in Hull, and Denis pleaded with him to stay in San Diego. But Frenchy upped the offer and Marc made the move.

Anne was by then seeing a man who lived in Hemet. She decided she'd move to Hemet to be closer to him. Frenchy was delighted. Anne was going to be living nearby, he had a new business and two of his kids working for him. He put Pat in the front office as his secretary and the money was rolling in. He was still loading his nose and dealing coke. The business would permit him to launder his drug profits.

Chapter Eighteen

Aguanga, California, 1985

Frenchy's Body Shop grew as rapidly as Temecula itself. The prime location and the fact that Frenchy advertised widely, just as he had done in San Diego, brought in a steady stream of customers. Not long after he opened he had six body men on staff, two painters, three preppers and several other casual hands. Again, though, there was a continuing and rapid turnover of staff.

It was the same old drill. He was cheating customers, cheating his employees and dealing dope. Many ex-employees and customers say Frenchy often had a noseful of coke, and several saw him with pound-sized bags of pot in the office.

An ex-employee says he'd occasionally go out for lunch with Frenchy: "He'd stop, put a spoon in a bag and snort up. And he was connected. He knew some big-time dealers."

Customers' complaints were handled by Frenchy with his usual tact. "When angry customers used to come in, he'd say, 'Get out of here or I'll call the police,'" says a former handyman Frenchy employed.

Neither Martine nor Marc lasted long in his employ. Martine got a better job, and Marc, within a couple of months of his move from San Diego, had a blow-up with Frenchy and stalked out. He claimed Frenchy owed him money. Years later he said that Frenchy frequently withheld his pay and told him he'd get his money if he made drug deliveries for him. From that point on, Marc and his father were bitter enemies. Marc moved to Hemet and, by the summer of 1985, had broken up with his wife. He had, by then, two children.

That summer Denis, Line and their kids returned to California for a visit. Denis had done well since his last trip. He and Line had moved into a house next to her folks' place in Chelsea, just up the highway from Pointe Gatineau, and Denis had his own body shop. His father-in-law, Ben Lafond, had opened a new scrap yard, towing service and repair shop on a piece of land he had acquired two minutes up the road from his house. He invited Denis to set up a shop in the yard, which Denis did. He called his place Collision Chelsea, and signs and business cards bore the slogan: "We Take the Dents Out of Accidents."

Denis had two employees and the business provided him with a decent living. He and Line and the kids spent their weekends on a piece of lakefront property her father had given them next to his cottage at Lac Serpent, deep in the Gatineau Hills. Denis was building a cottage on the lot, and as it emerged from the foundations he had a tremendous sense of having found his place in the world. He had his own family and was part of the Lafond family. He still played drums on the weekends but he didn't push it. He wasn't a driven or a gregarious man. He didn't have close friends aside from Line, and he was comfortable with himself.

Laurette Boissonneault died in 1983. Again Denis arrived at the church early on the day of the funeral and checked the faces of every mourner. His heart sank when he realized that Jeannine wasn't among the crowd. He saw Jeannine's cousin, Michel Béland, whom he knew was an RCMP officer, but didn't get a chance to chat with him. He wanted to but kept thinking that he had no new information about Jeannine to offer Michel or anyone else.

The more rooted he felt, the more preoccupied he became with answering the question that had hung over his life for so long now. At some level the trips to California were part of what was now a quest for the truth about Jeannine.

Denis and Line and the kids drove to California that summer. When they arrived, they discovered his grandmother, Marie-Anna Durand, was visiting her well-to-do son, Frenchy. Denis and Line stayed in B.B.'s old trailer at the ranch. The day after they arrived Marie-Anna beckoned Denis into the kitchen of Frenchy's house for a talk. She made him feel guilty by telling him that she had to travel to California to visit him. He hadn't seen her since their quarrel before the party she'd thrown for Ray in Hull. Then the real reason for the chat emerged. She'd heard from Frenchy that Denis was going to take Marc back to Hull with him. That much was true. Denis and Marc and talked, and Denis had urged him to move to Canada. Marc was intrigued and agreed. Denis had obtained a copy of Marc's birth certificate to ensure he'd have no problem crossing the border. Marc had then apparently told Frenchy, taunted him with the news that he was moving to Hull. Frenchy, in turn, had asked his mother to persuade Denis to abandon the plan.

"Denis, I don't want you to take Marc back with you," Marie-Anna told him. "Your father says he's trouble. He said Marc will only mess up your life for you in Canada."

Denis was incensed by his grandmother's meddling, by her assumption that she could tell him what to do.

"I'm sorry, Grandma," he told her. "But if Marc wants to come back, that's fine with me." And he walked out of the kitchen.

Denis spent a week working with Frenchy in the new body shop. He made an effort to be civil to Pat. He took the kids to Disneyland and visited San Diego.

He enjoyed the visit but was unable to accomplish a goal he had set for himself. He wanted all four of them—him, Anne, Marc and Martine—to get Frenchy alone somewhere and put the question to him: where's Jeannine? But he discovered that Marc wanted to kill Frenchy, Anne didn't want to hurt the old man's feelings, and Martine was lost. She was drinking heavily and bouncing from home to home, from job to job. Denis did talk to Marc on several occasions but found his brother unstable and unpredictable. Then Marc changed his mind about moving back to Canada; he told Denis that he didn't think it was a good idea. Marc was also angry with Anne. He felt she was protecting Frenchy. Anne, for her part, felt Marc was trying to make trouble. When Denis's vacation was up and he left for Canada, he felt a vague, inchoate sense that everything he needed was out there but that he hadn't been able to order it into something meaningful. Something—not the truth, but an element needed for him to discover it—was within his grasp; he felt that. What was needed? he wondered on the ride home. Were there clues he had overlooked? Should he have tried himself to take on Frenchy again? He doubted that. He had discovered that there was a unspoken line that couldn't be crossed with Frenchy. He could actually tolerate his father as long as Jeannine's name was never mentioned. He knew it, Frenchy knew it, his brother and sisters knew it. Denis and Marc were the only ones willing to cross that line. Marc did it but he did it for the same reason he would have enjoyed poking Frenchy with a sharp stick. He nurtured a visceral hatred of his father and he took pleasure in getting under Frenchy's tough, perpetually tanned skin. But Denis was long past the point where he could derive enjoyment from antagonizing his father. He'd cross the line if it served a purpose. Otherwise he preferred to be watchful. One day Frenchy would slip, and Denis would find what he was looking for.

By the time Frenchy had set up the body shop in Temecula he had completely isolated himself at the ranch. All the friends he had made, all the neighbours who had been over for parties now despised him. He knew he had enemies and grew so wary of them that when he drove into his yard at night he'd make Pat get out of the car first and enter the house. He'd received death threats and took them seriously. Scott had been with him in a truck one day when a young guy had fired a shotgun at them. Arlene Knight, whom he suspected of conspiring against him, says a couple of guys once sprayed Frenchy's house with gunfire. And another man who lived near Frenchy and was suffering from cancer told several people that the last thing he planned to do when the end was near was to put a bullet in Frenchy's head and do everyone a favour. When the time came, he was too weak and he died unfulfilled.

Arlene Knight has bright, brown eyes, long, silky dark-brown hair and an intimidating, prescient understanding of human nature. She says she knew Frenchy was evil long before her husband, Daniel, recognized it. By 1985 she had begun watching him at night from her place. She'd see him out in the yard, burying things: "He had hiding places all over the ranch. He'd put the stuff down, then cover it with a layer of glass so animals wouldn't dig it up and then cover it with dirt."

Frenchy apparently sensed he was being watched and came to fear and loathe Arlene.

"One day Frenchy thought I wasn't home," she remembers. "He came over. He had a key to our house. I was inside. I saw him coming and I hid in the washroom. I stood right in there and waited for him to come in. I had my Betsy-Lou, a .357 magnum. [He came in] and I put it to his head. I said, 'I'm going to kill you. If you don't get out of here right now, I'm going to kill you.' And he backed up. I knocked him off the porch. He had cocaine in his shirt, which fell out. And I know he was going to plant it [in my house]. Why else would he be carrying it?"

About the same time Pat came over and confided to Arlene that she had begun to fear Frenchy and that he had asked her to keep an eye on Arlene. They became friends—for a time Arlene was Pat's only friend—and as Arlene got to know her she came to see how obsessive Ray was about cleanliness and how absolutely he controlled Pat. Frenchy wanted everything spotless, and Pat worked like a maid cleaning and cleaning. "The place was so spick and span that she was regularly cleaning the runners on the sliding doors," Arlene says.

At Arlene's suggestion, she and Pat began searching the house for Frenchy's hiding places. "We started searching. In the closet she had beautiful clothes but she never wore them. Fur coats. The closet [in the master bedroom] looked normal. There was a shoe hook and you grabbed onto that and it opened up the whole floor. A hidden doorway. His trailer looked like it was on a cement pad. But it wasn't. It was higher." Daniel recalls that there was a raised foundation under the house but that Frenchy had graded the soil all around it so that it looked like the house was resting on a pad.

In the space under the closet, Arlene says they found "six bags of coke. Pat discovered it with me. She hadn't known about it."

At about the same time Frenchy had heart pains one night and spent a week in the hospital. It's not clear whether it was a heart attack or just a warning signal, but his physician told him to take off some weight and get more exercise. He began walking every morning and then running. He lost a great deal of weight in a short time and came to enjoy the physical discipline of keeping fit. He had a pair of Doberman pinschers by then, and when he ran it was with one or both of the dogs and a pistol. He said the pistol was for snakes. As his physical condition improved, he decided to indulge his vanity, and he had a surgical tummy tuck and the bags around his eyes removed. He also got a new haircut and had it and his beard trimmed regularly. The changes made him look distinguished. He was fifty years old, and his hair and beard were greying. He began wearing sunglasses and telling people he was a film star and that he had a house in Hollywood.

The cosmetic changes made him acutely aware of the most aggravating bit of ugliness left in his life: Pat. He complained to Anne that he was sick of being married to a drunk. Pat showed up at the shop one day with a big, black eye. She told one of the guys that she had stumbled off the porch at home and hit her head. But people who knew her suspected that Frenchy was smacking her around.

One of the people Frenchy met after he opened his shop was a woman in her early fifties with a trim figure, a deeply lined face, a tentative manner and joyous smile. She asked that her name not be used so I'll call her Jane. She had a teenage daughter who was still living with her whom I'll call Janet. Jane met Frenchy one day at Rick Dial's shop.

"He was always happy go lucky, joking and kidding," she says. "He was fun. He had a Christmas party at the shop and a lot of us went. It was nice. There was a big gang there. Pat was there. They were always together. Then they had barbecues up at the house. They had a nice big swimming pool. I went up with others. Well, then, he asked me to go out and he surprised me. I just looked at him. It surprised me. A week or two later he asked again. I said no. 'Why?' he asked. Because he was married, I said. He said, 'She's not my wife. She is a lady I went up to Canada to get and brought back to Texas to take care of my children after my wife vanished.' He told me two different stories. He told me his wife ran off with another guy and left him with four kids. He knew Pat because he used to work with her in Canada at an auto place. Then another time he told me that his wife had a mental breakdown and he had to institutionalize her. He told me it was so terribly expensive to keep her in this real nice place. At the time I remembered the other story and I thought: Well, maybe he was embarrassed about his wife. And so it sounded better to the neighbours to say she had run off with another guy. I just left it at that."

Frenchy confused Jane and he pressed his advantage. "He said he felt sorry for her [Pat]. She had been so good to the kids. So he said, 'I just kept her. But we are not married. Ask her.' Then he said his name was Durand and he took her name. I mean, the stories he told. I'm embarrassed that I could have been so stupid. Well, anyway, he told me the reason he took her name was that he was with the Mounties and he was on a case where he caught one of the bad guys but there were still others out there and it was dangerous to remain in Canada. And they paid his expenses to move him and his family to Texas. When he left he couldn't even tell his own mother. Then he had to find some way to make a living. He worked for an auto body guy and the family that owned it they loved him so much they wanted to give it to him when they retired.

"Well, I'm from Minnesota. My grandmother always had a calendar of a Mountie on his horse. So romantic. How exciting his life was, I thought. He couldn't communicate with his family up there. He just vanished. It was really hush-hush. Big secret. That story never changed. But the story of his wife had two versions."

Frenchy poured on the charm and Jane finally succumbed to his attentions. "We started dating. Then he wanted to get married. Pat stayed up there at the house for some time while we were dating. He said he didn't know what to do with her because she never worked. And he felt guilty about moving her out. Then he decided to do it. He asked me what I thought. He said she had helped with the business. And I said she had raised his kids. He didn't want her to get part of the business. So he had a guy go up and appraise the house and then he said he was going to give her half of whatever it was worth. I thought he did. [He later said he had given Pat $100,000]. Then he rented an apartment for her in Hemet. Anne was with us. We went to a nice area and he paid the first and last month's rent and said she can take care of it from all the money I'm giving her."

After eighteen years with Frenchy, after following him all over the continent, after working as his unpaid maid, cook and baby-sitter, Pat was given the heave ho. Years later she said she still loved Frenchy when he threw her out and was hurt and surprised. She had kept his secrets, suffered his infidelities, taken his beatings. She had also drunk his liquor, snorted his coke, gambled his money and vacationed with him in Hawaii, Florida and other spots all across the continent.

Frenchy bought her a used car and, for a time, gave her seven hundred dollars a month. He also told her they would split up the property, that she would get title to Rand's twenty acres and the trailer on it. In turn, she would sign over to him clear title to their own twenty acres and the house on it. He had improved it considerably. A second storey had been added to the house and the pool had been enclosed.

On December 4, 1985, two quitclaim deeds were filed on the adjoining properties. The deeds show Frenchy relinquished all claims on the Rand property and transferred it to Pat's name. And she did the reverse with the property they had lived on together. Another quitclaim deed filed two years later shows Pat transferred the Rand property back to Frenchy. And a year after that, the property was sold. Pat later told a woman who searched the title to the property that she never received a cent from Frenchy for it or from the sale and has no recollection of giving it back to Frenchy.

When Frenchy moved Pat into her own apartment, she was fifty-two years old, a serious alcoholic and well travelled but not at all worldly and, as Martine once pointed out, "dumber than a flat rock." She had no employable skills, few friends, little education and no legal status in the United States. She was hiding some dark secret about her past. She was now at fate's mercy. Frenchy was no longer there to pay her way. Forced to rely on her own resources, she responded with spunk and cunning. Although she may not have been any great thinker, she managed very quickly to make a new life for herself.

During the years at the ranch, Pat had got to know a hairdresser in Hemet. Liquor may have been the basis of the friendship because they were both known as drinkers. They began hanging out together. The hairdresser knew a single man in his fifties named Bert Matheis, who owned his own house and was a general handyman/entrepreneur about town. Bert, a talkative, lonely, cat-lover who seemed to know everyone in Hemet and spent his days driving around repairing things and swapping goods, was at home one night when the phone rang.

"It was this gal [the hairdresser]," he recalls. "She said 'I'm going to bring somebody over.' She brings Pat. Pat had been her client—hair and nails—for what I guessed to be seven or eight years. Anyway, they came over. She said Pat's husband had just thrown her out and set her up in an apartment. She said Pat's husband used to beat the hell out of her. She was a heavy drinker."

Bert says that the hairdresser stayed for only about twenty-five minutes and then said, "I gotta go home. Let me take your car home, Pat." And she left Pat with Bert: "I liked Pat. She told me she was going through a divorce. She had her apartment, and before too long I said, 'It's kind of stupid to keep paying rent.' She was over all the time. I told her she might as well stay with me."

Not long after Pat moved in, they married. "Pat's not a pretty face," Bert now says. "But she was one of the kindest persons I'd met. She rescued two baby kittens from next door. We raised them. She used to tell me how mean Ray was, how he was dealing drugs.

She was just scared to death of him."

Anne was elated by Frenchy's decision to give Pat the toss. She had never forgiven Pat for the beatings and for the housework she had made her do. She didn't wish any injury on her but she didn't want her in the family either. She was now closer than ever to her father, talked to him daily and knew he was excited about the woman he was seeing, Jane. She didn't think he should feel saddled with a woman who had caused her and her brothers and sister such misery. Still, given Anne's nature, despite her feelings, she continued to call Pat and gave her gifts on her birthday and at Christmas. They were now both living in Hemet, and Anne kept in touch.

Denis reacted differently. Frenchy and Pat's split jolted him. He had always assumed that Pat knew something about what had happened to Jeannine. Now, though, he was no longer certain. If Pat knew something, he figured, his father wouldn't have thrown her out. Wouldn't he be worried that she might talk? He no longer knew what to think. He began to doubt all his long-held assumptions. He stewed all that winter and decided to return to California in the summer to assess the situation.

With Pat out of the way, Frenchy redoubled his efforts with Jane. He wanted to marry her. "He was charming," she says. "But I had been single for many years and I kept putting it off. I said, 'Let's wait till Thanksgiving.' Then I said, 'Wait till Christmas.' I had my own place. My daughter was living with me."

Part of her uncertainty stemmed from a visit that she had received from Marc one night. "He came over and he said, 'I'm going to tell you something. My dad never has anyone around him that he can't use in some way. I think you should know this before you get involved.' I didn't know what to make of it. It didn't make sense. Marc said he felt sorry for Pat. He said his dad controlled all the money and that Pat didn't have any money. I thought Marc was telling me this because he felt sorry for Pat."

Jane had misgivings after Marc's visit. But then she learned that he and Frenchy had been at odds for some time and she wondered if Marc's remarks were his way of getting back at his father.

As Christmas approached, Jane and Frenchy made plans to spend a month in Hawaii. Frenchy suggested they marry in Vegas before they went over. But Jane held off and finally offered a compromise.

They would marry in Hawaii. They flew over just after Christmas and Jane remembers that Frenchy was carrying at least twenty thousand dollars in cash. "He carried a lot of money on him. I used to think it was ridiculous."

They spent their days on the beach. All Frenchy wanted to do was tan and eat, she remembers. The wedding was held on a chartered boat off the island of Maui on December 30, Frenchy's fiftieth birthday. Photos of the occasion show them both tanned, wearing leis and feeding each other wedding cake. There was a prime rib dinner on board. Jane's cousin and his wife, who live in Hawaii, were there as witnesses.

Within two days of the wedding Jane felt that everything had changed and she began to fear that she had made a mistake: "You know how you get a gut feeling that something's not right? That's what it was like. I'm not the world's greatest swimmer. He knew that. One day he wanted me to swim way out. I said no. He all but dragged me into the water. He wanted me to come with him. I said no. It was a long way out. Then he became very nasty."

Back in California, Jane and her daughter moved to the ranch and quickly learned more about Frenchy's family. Jane had met Anne before and knew that Frenchy called her every day and often invited her to join them in restaurants on the weekends. She thought they were unusually close, given that he was so distant with his other kids. Frenchy told her that Denis lived with his grandmother in Quebec and that Martine wasn't welcome at the ranch because she had stolen something from him. Marc did show up at the ranch once. He may have been working for Frenchy again at the time. He'd work for him for a few months, then Frenchy would fire him and rehire him again months later. The night that Marc showed up, Jane says, "We were in the den at the bar. Marc and Ray were talking and I walked up. Marc was standing there and he reached in his billfold and took out a picture and laid it on the counter. A little picture. The expression on Frenchy's face was like daylight to dark. A cloud came over him. He never said anything. He went ahead with whatever he was doing behind the bar. Then he left to go into the kitchen. I glanced at the picture. It was a woman. Then Marc says, 'It's my mother.' I said, 'Oh.' That's all I said to him. In the meantime, I was thinking: Why would that upset him so much? Because the kid had a picture?"

Not long after they moved to the ranch, Frenchy rattled Jane with a series of demands: "When we got married I had a black Camaro that my son had bought me. Frenchy wanted me to put it in his name. I said, 'Why?' He said, 'For good faith.' Then he wanted to know if I had any money in the bank. I wasn't very truthful. I felt he was seeking control. He wanted me to work in the office [at Frenchy's]. I wanted to stay at my job. He got me to work there. Never paid me one dime."

Not long after, Frenchy had another suggestion that made her shudder. "He said, 'You know I've never gone with a woman who didn't have large breasts.' Well, I'm just as comfortable as can be with myself. He said, 'Why don't you get a boob job?' And I said, 'I've worked in the medical field and I've heard some real horror stories. I just don't want to do something like that.'"

Jane says for the longest time she couldn't quite figure Frenchy out. He often surprised her, and one of the things that surprised her the most was seeing him break down, twice. "One night he had a couple of the guys from the shop," she says. "He had taken them up to the ranch to hoe weeds on the property. It was cold. He was supposed to be up there at a certain time to pick them up. We were driving up and he said, 'I don't want you to think that I treat every-body like dogs.' Then he started crying. I mean he cried—like you really boo-hoo over something. Sobs. And then another time it was a Sunday morning. I had some Windex and I was doing the kitchen windows, and he went out to do the outside. He had taken the screen off and we were talking through the window and he said, 'I used to help Pat do the windows all the time.' And he said it again. 'I don't want you to think that I treated everybody like a dog.' And then he started crying. Sobbing. Like somebody died or something. I told Anne about this. And Anne said, 'My dad. He never cries.'"

Jane thought about the crying for a long time and what struck her most was the thought that he wasn't crying for someone else. He was crying for himself. He felt misunderstood. He felt so sorry for himself that he had moved himself to tears.

Jane saw Frenchy snorting coke a few times but he was discreet. What troubled her more was the discovery that he was interested in making money, drinking and not much else. "He didn't watch much TV. He listened to music once in a while—Willie Nelson. He hardly ever rented videos. We never went to a movie. He didn't read books, magazines or newspapers. He could drink a lot though. He told me that he and Pat, when they would leave Temecula at night, would stop at the liquor store on their way out of town. He liked rum and Coke. He'd get a fifth and she'd get one. By the time he got home [in twenty to twenty-five minutes], it would be gone. He could really put it away."

And every night, as soon as he walked in, Jane remembers, he'd take out his wad of cash and count it. "He'd go to the bar and take it out and count it. He said he carried cash because sometimes guys would come in broke and they'd need money and he'd buy their car for a song."

Jane saw Frenchy burying cars just down the hill from the house and began to wonder what that was all about. She saw a Mercedes parked down the hill without a dent in it. Then it disappeared and she wondered if he had buried that.

Then Frenchy began taking off, sometimes overnight. "He'd say he had to go to San Diego for a part. He'd take off on a Saturday and be gone till Sunday."

One night they went out to dinner. Frenchy was driving a black sports car. "Just as we started, we saw a police car coming towards us. Frenchy said tighten your seat belt. The cop got right behind us and Frenchy hit the gas. Frenchy lost the cop, pulled into a side-road and killed the lights. The cop went racing by. I was scared to death. I said, 'Why?' He said, 'Well, he was after us.' I said, 'We weren't doing anything.' He said, 'Oh, you'll never understand.' He was terrified of the police."

At the body shop Jane began to notice how Frenchy cut corners. She saw insurance appraisers come in to do estimates on damaged cars. "Ray would leave a hundred-dollar bill on the desk. He'd never hand it to the guy. The guy would come in and I guess he would increase the damage estimate. Then he would sit there at that other desk, and when he left, that hundred would be gone. Ray always just laid it there."

Another man who worked with Frenchy said for the hundred-dollar bribe, the appraiser would allow Frenchy to turn a seven-hundred-dollar repair bill into a fifteen-hundred-dollar bill.

But the final straw for Jane was an incident that occurred one night at the ranch. "He and my daughter were watching TV. I was just kind of standing there and got interested in what they were watching on TV while the dinner was cooking. He turned to her and said something in French. [Jane's daughter had studied French.] Just by the expression on her face I knew that it was something she sure didn't like. Then he said it again. At that, she got up and left the room and went into her bedroom. So the next day I was taking her to school and I asked her to tell me what he said. She said he'd asked her to go to bed with him. That really was the end. Of course, he said she was lying. I told him what I thought of him. My kids come first."

Jane told Frenchy she'd move out as soon as she arranged for a place and a new job. In the meantime, they slept apart. Janet says that shortly after, "Frenchy came home drunk. I don't know where Mom was. He came into my room. He had a .38. He got me out of bed, twisted my arm behind me. He was angry because my mom had confronted him. He had the .38 pointed in my ribs. I thought he was going to break my arm. He said I was a liar. Told me to get out. I walked out of the house down to the neighbour's place. In my nightgown. I called my brother and he came and got me."

But by then Frenchy had someone else in his life. Some weeks before he had advertised in the paper for a secretary. One of the women who answered the ad was a shapely forty-year-old with coal-black hair, china-white skin and painted, geisha-girl lips. Her name was Gloria Ann Seicher. She was from Leduc, Alberta, but had married a man in Hawaii and had moved to Temecula with him. They had a house just out of town with orange trees around it, and her husband was an engineer. She took the job, and within a matter of weeks, she and Frenchy were seeing each other. They fell madly in love; she left her husband, and within two months of Jane's departure, they were living together at the ranch.

That summer, when Denis arrived in Hemet with Line and the girls after a long drive from Hull, Frenchy was in Alberta with Gloria visiting her family. Denis picked up the key to Frenchy's house from Anne and was relaxing at the place when Frenchy and Gloria arrived two days later. Marc had told Denis that Gloria was a bitch, that she listened in on his phone calls, but Denis and Line thought she was pleasant enough. While Denis was there he gave Gloria a ride into town one day. She had a doctor's appointment. She told him that she had had her breasts enlarged because Frenchy wanted her to. But she was having trouble with the enlargements and was upset with Frenchy for making her do it. Denis couldn't believe she'd agreed to the operation.

Denis and Line had decided they were going to stay in California for only two weeks. They wanted to see more of the country. So after a couple of increasingly tense weeks, Denis told his father one night that they were leaving.

"How are you going back?" Frenchy asked.

"I want to go back through Texas," Denis replied. "I want to see Big Thicket and Houston again."

Denis saw that he had struck a nerve. Frenchy was upset and nervous and attempted to talk him out of it.

"What are you going to do that for? It'll be hot," he told Denis.

Over the next two days, as they prepared to depart, Frenchy kept at Denis, attempting to persuade him to take another route back. He began giving Denis tools for his shop, and soon the trunk was almost full. Denis, in turn, became increasingly suspicious. What was bugging the old man?

Finally they drove off, crossed Arizona, New Mexico and entered Texas. He remembered driving the other way, to California, in the last week of 1969. By the time they got to Houston, his mind was racing. All the memories that haunted him had begun here. With some difficulty he found the house on Beech Street and videotaped it from the car. There, between the garage and the house was the door he remembered his father had come in with the two suitcases. Denis remembered returning again and again to the corner on his bike, waiting for Jeannine to come home. In the back seat, Denis's daughters couldn't figure out what was wrong with him. He seemed on the edge of tears. Line was patient. She had lived with this story for almost as long as he had.

They drove out to Big Thicket on the Liberty Freeway. He found the cottage. It had been abandoned. He remembered building it, lying in the tent waiting for Pat to come after him, the letter from his football coach, sitting in the library studying the maps. His grief, he discovered, was just as acute now as it had been then. Years had passed, and still he was pursued by the same demons. He'd lived with the uncertainty for so long that he couldn't believe it hadn't driven him mad. All he wanted was to know what had happened. He'd made his way back to Hull and he'd reclaimed everything that his father had abandoned: his language, his culture, his community. He'd rebuilt the identity that his father had jettisoned. He'd made a life for himself. He had a happy marriage, kids, a house, a cottage, a business. He was as psychologically rooted in his world as it is possible for a man to be. He took great pleasure in the feeling that he belonged. He had a place in the world where he was known and welcomed. Yet he was still unable to take quiet pride in his accomplishments because of an unanswered question that hung over him like the sword of Damocles.

From the moment he had entered Texas, Denis had mused about the possibility of talking to the police. "I'll ask them if they ever found a body that they couldn't identify," he told Line. "I'll explain what happened," he reasoned, "and surely someone will help." Line offered encouragement. But by their final day he still hadn't worked up the nerve to do it. He was plagued by uncertainty, inhibited by his lifelong shyness. What if I go in there and they show me a picture of Jeannine, dead? he asked himself. What would I do? I'd turn around, drive back to California and kill the son of a bitch, he thought. Should I ruin my own life and everything I have just to get back at him? Denis debated with himself right up until the moment they pulled out of town and headed north to Quebec, following the route that seventeen years earlier he had traced with his finger on a map in the library of Hardin School.

Jeannine (right) and girlfriend
Rollande Guenette in the early 1950s.

Jeannine & Ray's wedding day, left to right: Donat Durand,
Maria-Anna Durand, Ray Durand, Jeannine Boissonneault Durand,
Laurette Boissonneault and Hermas Boissonneault.
The little girl in the front row is one of Ray's sisters.

Denis, Martine and Anne in
December 1967, only weeks before
their mother's disappearance.

Denis and Marc in
Houston, 1967

The rented house in Fort Lauderdale, 1967.

Ray Durand, Pat Holben
and Robert Durand in
San Diego, 1970.

The house on Beech Street that the
family lived in at the time of Jeannine's
disappearance. Photo taken in 1992.

Pat and Ray at a party in Quebec City, 1971.

Denis and his girlfriend Line Lafond (now his wife) in Hull, Quebec, 1973.

Denis Durand and Laurette Boissonneault (Jeannine's mother) in 1972.

Ray and Denis in San Diego, 1974 with the Jaguar that Ray promised to buy him if he moved from Hull to California.

Martine, Pat, Marc, Anne, Denis and Ray at
Anne's apartment in San Diego, 1981.

Aerial shot of the ranch taken in 1991 by Riverside County DA investigator
Jean Nadeau. Area in box is the site where Nadeau hired a Caterpillar to dig.
About 35 vehicles were uncovered.

Ray and Gloria Durand
on their wedding day, 1986.

Ray Durand at the ranch, 1986.

Denis Durand at the unmarked grave beside Liberty Freeway in
Houston where corpse 68-500 was buried until it was identified
as Jeannine Durand in 1991.

Left to right: St Sgt Michel Béland, Lt Robert Madeira of the Texas
Rangers, Denis Durand, Lt Mike Talton of the Harris County homicide
unit, Lt François Cloutier of the Gatineau police, Hull, 1991.

François Roy

Riverside County District Attorney's investigator Jean Nadeau. Hull, 1991.

Denis Durand, his daughter Geneviève, and Anne Hallberg in Hull, 1991.

François Roy

Funeral services for Jeannine. Far left, Réginald Boissonneault; St Sgt Michel Béland; in front from left to right, Phil Hallberg, Anne Hallberg, Line Durand, Geneviève Durand. Hull, 1991.

Anne and Phil Hallberg
in San Jacinto, 1992.

Ray's lawyer
Jack Zimmermann.

Le Droit

Le Droit

Ray and Gloria sit in the courtroom.

Chapter Nineteen

San Jacinto, California, 1986

Once during her mercifully brief marriage to Frenchy, Jane discovered that Anne had said something hurtful about a man Jane knew. During a telephone conversation not long after, Jane confronted Anne and called her on the remark she had made.

"Lots of people think I'm not a very good person," Anne had replied. "But I'm getting better all the time."

Jane was struck by the optimism and the forthrightness of that remark. Seven years later she remembered it and mused about what it had meant. She hadn't much liked Anne; she thought she was Frenchy's confidante and his defender. After the marriage had ended, Jane wondered what it was between Frenchy and Anne that allowed them to be so close. Anne, she thought, must be well aware of her father's nature. He needed to control people. Did he control Anne, too? Still, Anne's remark betrayed a self-awareness that seemed at odds with her devotion to her father.

Anne had always been a good daughter, and Frenchy had rewarded her for it. She had never betrayed him as the other children had. He often paid for weekend excursions and parties with her, and he bought her gifts. She knew about his drug dealing, knew about his groping of her friends, knew that he was a thief and a liar. Frenchy was at ease with her because Anne had always protected him with her silence, her denials. She had once broken the silence by telling Pat that Frenchy had grabbed her girl-friend's breasts. But she never did that again. There were other incidents with other girl-friends. She dealt with them by pretending they hadn't happened.

Frenchy played Anne like a fiddle. He could play Marc and Martine as well but they weren't as useful to him, Martine because she drank too much, and Marc because he was consumed with anger and hatred. Anne, though, was as good as her word. Frenchy traded on her loyalty to family and her desperate need to be liked. At first he had simply used her to run errands.

"He would order me around. I wasn't living with him anymore

and he would still order me around," Anne remembers. "He'd want me to pick up parts or paint for him or just come and help him in the shop. That's just what he did. You just did it. But whenever he gave me money, I always paid him back."

Then, when Frenchy began thinking of leaving Pat, he turned to Anne for advice and comfort. "He could talk to me about anything," Anne says. "He'd sell dope to my friends and he'd go out with me and one of my girl-friends. Everybody liked him. He loved to party. I think I just wanted some kind of family and he was it. He was all I had. I wasn't close to Denis. I wasn't close to Marc. I'd see Martine once in a while. So he was it. When you sit there and see all your friends with a mom and a dad, well, all I had was a dad."

Frenchy had never been capable of relationships of equality. Everyone he met he either corrupted or simply destroyed. He hadn't destroyed Anne; there was something indomitable in her character that defied him. But he had drawn her and the other children into the moral *demi-monde* that he inhabited simply by exposing them to his lies, his cruelty and his selfishness. In addition, there were the parties. Anne had a front-row seat for most of them, saw her dad at his most demented, crazed with liquor and drugs, and she heard plenty of complaints from women on whom her dad had preyed. Anne wasn't a silent observer at the parties, which were always an education and sometimes an initiation. But she was never able to abandon herself completely to the moment in the way that her father or Marc and Martine could. An inner moral compass that Marc and Martine didn't seem to have kept her pointed towards something deeper in her nature. During those years she may have been bobbing on stormy seas but she never lost her sense of direction. Even at the most chaotic, bustin'-through-to-the-crack-of-dawn parties she was always elsewhere in her mind. She still felt she was living someone else's life. What she couldn't figure was, who was living her life? When would she connect with Anne Durand, who had long ago been buried under the identity of Anne Holben?

Anne had a fragile sense of self-worth and thought of herself as not very smart. She wanted, needed, people to like her. She had a number of boy-friends, after Fred Angelo, Jr, several of whom were abusive. But she was never so emotionally crippled that she wasn't able to walk out on a man when he raised his hand against her. Part of the complications with the men in her life had to do with her father. Frenchy would quickly ferret out their vulnerabilities, and within short order they'd be retailing pot or coke for him or, if they weren't criminally inclined, contracting to do work for him that he'd later cheat them on. Frenchy made Anne's boy-friends realize that he'd be part of any equation with Anne. For some of them, Fred Angelo in particular, that was a daunting proposition.

Anne must have given off the same signals. Her boy-friends saw pretty quickly that she protected Frenchy. She knew enough about his drug dealing and his avarice that she must have seemed like an accomplice. Anne didn't think of it in those terms. She respected loyalty. And she was a loyal daughter. That meant she was a good person. At least it should have made her feel that she was. Can you be a good person and protect someone who isn't?

By 1986 Anne had become a full-time employee of San Jacinto city government. It wasn't then and isn't now a large bureaucracy. The city has a population of about eighteen thousand and a police force of twenty-three. It is a small town of *faux*-adobe houses and tidy streets that spill down the flanks of the San Jacinto Mountains. To the south, San Jacinto merges with its neighbour, Hemet, whose population is close to a hundred thousand.

Anne had got her first job with the city, whose offices are in a store-front on the eight-block-long Main Street, in 1985. She had been dating a man whose sister helped her get a job as a temp in the water department. Her new job brought her into day-to-day contact with a whole new world. She had always worked in car dealerships and body shops and hung out with rowdies. Now, she was working with secretaries, clerks, white-collar managers and, for the first time in her life, cops. She had already met, through a friend, the chief of police, and she began meeting the officers who worked under him. The police station was only a couple of blocks from her office, and the cops were in often on city business. It wasn't so much the class thing that struck her, although they were mostly solidly middle class. It was their engagement in the community. They played on softball teams, helped out with the heart fund drives, sat on school boards, took their kids to soccer and piano lessons, visited their elderly grandparents and did all sorts of other things that didn't just slake their thirsts or fatten their wallets.

"I had never known people like that before," she recalls. "It felt good to know law-abiding citizens. It felt good to be clean. I felt like I had come from a trashy background."

Anne was then in her late twenties. People called her cute, and she paid a great deal of attention to her clothes and make-up. She tended to think that if people liked her it was for her appearance. Since she was deeply suspicious of men and their motives, she found it awkward at first to enter into friendships and collegial working relationships with people who liked her for her alertness, her wry humour, her diligence and her intelligence. She had fits of anxiety about learning to work on a computer but she did learn and that bolstered her self-confidence. Then, when her boss heard that she was entertaining a job offer from a local hospital, he hired her on full-time in the water department. A year later she was transferred to accounts payable. The full-time job and the transfer made her much more aware of how others viewed her and that, too, buttressed her self-image. She was proud of her accomplishments and the fact that she had earned the respect and trust of her employers and colleagues.

Inside, though, she was a quivering mess. Her anxieties manifested themselves in her obsessive behaviour. Her apartment was spotless, and she was fretful to the point of neurosis. The more accepted she found herself at work, the more anxious she became. She was straddling two worlds, polar opposite ones at that. On weekends, now that she didn't have a boy-friend, she'd be up at the ranch or out with her father. And he was everything that the people at work weren't. He was psychopathically selfish, always lived outside the social framework of the communities he inhabited, considered charity work something for saps and suckers—she remembered how he used to pocket the UNICEF money she collected at Hallowe'en—and devoted all of his still considerable energies to feeding his appetites and adding to the roll in his pocket. The gap between his world and that of her new friends and colleagues was the size of the Grand Canyon.

She coped by living three lives. There was Anne, Frenchy's daughter; Anne, the diligent city employee; and finally Anne at home by herself. Everybody knew a different Anne. She felt fragmented and had the sense that she was hanging on by her fingertips, that everything was about to slip from her grasp. When she was growing up, Denis and Marc had called her "the captain" because of her tendency to assert leadership at any and every opening, regardless of how sliver-thin that opening might have been. That was her response to a life that was completely out of her control. It was her survival mechanism. While others might have plunged into a life of self-destruction or complete submissiveness, Anne had always responded by pouncing on the slenderest of opportunities to take charge. In each of her separate lives she could be fierce. But there wasn't much depth to her fierceness; her anxieties and lack of self-confidence fuelled her assertiveness but couldn't sustain it.

Frenchy, now with his new wife Gloria by his side, was doing gang-busters business at his shop in Temecula. Temecula's rapid growth was bringing in waves of new customers who hadn't lived in the area long enough to have heard about Frenchy. Those who had been through the place once knew his prices were high, the customer was never right, and if you left anything in your car when you dropped it off, you could kiss it goodbye. Suppliers had also learned to keep a close eye on Frenchy. One of his dodges was to snag both copies of invoices from delivery boys. A kid would come by with a load of paint and somehow Frenchy would end up with the kid's only copies of the invoice for the delivery. When the paint supplier mailed him a payment-due notice, he'd simply deny that he'd ever received the paint.

As if running the shop weren't enough to keep him occupied, Frenchy continued to deal drugs. With each month his reputation spread. Ex-employees, customers and his kids all saw or knew he was a dealer. Yet the local police never tumbled to him. But his reputation was widening and in San Jacinto, a half-hour north, Anne was terrified that her new friends would learn that her father was trafficking in narcotics.

The next time Frenchy did encounter the police it had nothing to do with narcotics. It was because of Marc, who had driven to the ranch one night in a rage. Frenchy owed him money and he wanted it. It isn't clear what transpired that night. Marc says Frenchy fired a shotgun at him and tried to kill him. He also says he busted down Frenchy's gate with his car. Marc filed a complaint with the police but so did Frenchy, who said that Marc had threatened to kill Gloria. The upshot of the incident was that Marc was ordered to pay for the damage to the gate.

Marc, by his own account, had now become a police informer. He had got himself in a scrape related to drinking and was sentenced to a work furlong, a form of community service. During his furlong he met a number of the officers on the San Jacinto police force, and he began feeding them tips on dealers in town. He says he was eventually going to lead them up the ladder to Frenchy and Frenchy's connections.

One of the closest friends Marc made was San Jacinto police detective Mike Sherbondy. Marc says he was working with Mike and his colleagues setting up busts. For a time Marc worked as a bouncer in a western bar and dance hall that Frenchy frequented. He said that he made regular reports to Sherbondy about who was selling in the bar, who was connected. Marc claims that his information led to a series of busts, each one taking the police closer to Frenchy. But sources in the San Jacinto police department say Marc's information, with few exceptions, was mostly of dubious value and they eventually stopped using him.

Nonetheless, Marc's activities around town made Anne extremely uncomfortable. One day she was at work when Mike Sherbondy or one of his colleagues walked in to handle some paper work and spotted Anne. "He walked over and blurted this stuff out in front of all the girls. He started talking about the fact that my dad had killed my mom and the fact that I was working illegally and that dad was dealing drugs."

Anne, mortified, maintained her cool and blew him off with a dismissive wave. "Oh, gosh, you'd believe anything Marc tells you," she said.

For Marc, the incident provided another example of how Anne protected Frenchy. For Anne, it was another spear that Marc had driven into her heart. They were no longer on speaking terms.

Anne says she never told Frenchy about the incident but Frenchy by then certainly knew that Marc was a snitch. (Marc insists that he was a paid informant and not a snitch, who is someone who trades off information in return for a lesser charge or sentence.) The closest Marc ever came to implicating Frenchy was when he informed on an employee of Frenchy's who drew a jail sentence on a drug charge. Each encounter tightened the murderous tension between Frenchy and Marc. It seemed to everyone who knew them that they were headed for a showdown.

When Anne first met Gloria, she thought Frenchy had made a mistake in marrying her. Anne had thought she was a gold-digger. Gloria knew how to spend money. They were often in Las Vegas for weekends, where they'd drop five thousand dollars in a night of gambling. They made several trips to Alberta and eventually bought a lakeside home that they talked about turning into a bed and breakfast. They bought two pieces of property near Temecula for investment purposes. Gloria was always heavily made up and dressed for uptown life.

Despite her apprehensions, Anne came around to the view that Gloria really loved her father. She was astonished by her discovery. She dined with them frequently, visited them at the ranch and generally kept in touch. Maybe she hoped that he was changing, that Gloria was steering him towards a more conventional life. Since he had a legitimate business that was booming, Anne had reason to believe that Frenchy was closing off his old pursuits.

One of the spots Anne and her friends favoured was a country and western club in Hemet called the Embers. Anne was there one night with her group when she spotted a guy throwing meaningful glances at her. It was just before Christmas, 1986, and she was with a group of men and women her age. The guy, who was with another crowd, had raven-black hair combed straight back, a moustache, a dark complexion and an easy-going shuffle. When he smiled, his face lit up like the desert sky. His name was Phil Hallberg, and for months they exchanged glances whenever they saw each other in the Embers. Finally, in February, 1987, they connected.

"He'd see me with friends from work and he thought one of them was my boy-friend. He was very shy," Anne remembers. "He kept eyeing me. Finally he asked me to dance. He didn't even look at me. Just looked at the floor the whole time. Said thank you. He was polite. Then one night a mutual friend named Darrel knew that Phil really liked me and that I liked Phil so he set it up for us. It was near Valentine's Day. We had dinner and went out dancing, and they played 'Looking for Love in All the Wrong Places.' And that's the first time he ever kissed me."

Anne was twenty-eight years old and Phil was thirty-four. He was a welder and steel construction contractor and had been married but was now divorced. His two children then lived with their mother. He had grown up across the valley in an adobe farmhouse. His father, Donald Hallberg, is a farmer, and his mother, Sally, is a tiny, warm woman with kind, bright eyes. Phil has an older brother, Bob, who served in Vietnam, and three sisters, Nancy, Becky and Anita. They are close, affectionate and deeply religious but non-sectarian. Although they were by no means poor, they lived without electricity until the early 1970s, and at family gatherings they tell and retell stories of how they almost set the house on fire with a kerosene lamp and of doing homework by the glow of the lamp.

All the Hallberg children still live in the area and gather for family meals at Thanksgiving, Christmas and on other holidays. They are respectful of each other and supportive. When they met Anne, they all made an effort to make her feel like part of their remarkable, close family.

Not long after Anne and Phil began dating, Anne called him to invite him to brunch with her father and Gloria. "We met at the Acapulco restaurant," Phil recalls. "Frenchy seemed really flashy. All kinds of gold on. Two or three chains around his neck. Gold on his fingers. Gold watch. Gold bands. Driving a black Mercedes. Gloria seemed like a classy gal. Real good-looking. I thought, What's going on here? We had a nice brunch. He paid. He was a big tipper. The bigger the crowd, the louder the noise, the bigger the tip he left. He had a big money clip with a coin on the side. Always had a big wad clipped in there. I thought he was rich. Anne told me he had a body shop. Anne seemed close to Frenchy. Some weeks she and Gloria got along better than others. They got along almost like sisters. Gloria is a month older than me."

The following weekend the four of them got together at the ranch, says Phil: "For a while we spent almost every other weekend together. That first weekend at the ranch, I thought it was real family life. We took the chain-saw and cut wood for the fireplace. Got the barbecue ready, cleaned the pool. We talked. He wasn't drinking heavily. He had a little pickup and we drove around. Didn't go see anybody but he pointed out his neighbours' places."

Over the next year and a half, the four of them spent a great deal of time together. Frenchy paid for three trips to Las Vegas and three trips to Palm Springs. "Most of the time in Las Vegas, he paid. I tried to pay but it'd be a fight. They'd go up on a Wednesday, get a room and we'd come up on Friday. He'd spend in four days, maybe, ten to thirteen thousand dollars. Gloria would say, 'I just lost another five thousand on the slots.' She'd drop five thousand dollars over a couple of days. Frenchy had a safe in the car, in the trunk, with a burglar alarm. It was bolted and welded in the trunk. He'd keep his cash and jewellery in there. Gloria would have fifty to sixty thousand dollars' worth of jewellery in there. She liked jewellery. I don't think she was trying to take Frenchy but she'd say, 'Oh, that's a beautiful ring. But I don't want it.' So you knew the next time we saw her she'd have it. He'd buy it."

Phil has a gentle and trusting nature. He isn't much of a drinker and has never experimented with drugs. He says he snuck a ciga- rette or two when he was growing up but that's pretty much the extent of his rebelliousness. They don't grow them much straighter than Phil in southern California. He accepts the world in all its strangeness and lives by his own standards. So, despite the improb- ability of it, Phil came to like Frenchy a great deal. He thought he was outrageous but generous to a fault. Frenchy and Gloria were still snorting coke but Anne made it clear to them that Phil wasn't a user and neither was she so they should be discreet. While Phil may have suspected that Frenchy walked the thin line between the legal and illegal, he never saw Frenchy cooking openly crooked deals.

On the other hand, he saw things that astounded him. One night, he recalls, he was up at the ranch when a contact of Frenchy's walked in. "The guy was high. He owed Frenchy twenty thousand dollars but he actually paid him twenty-eight thousand in cash. Frenchy and I counted it after he left, and it was eight thousand over [what Frenchy had been expecting]. It was all in hundreds, made up in bundles with big paper clips." Phil figured the money was made illegally but that the payment to Frenchy was for a legiti- mate business deal.

By sheer force of habit, Frenchy felt compelled, apparently, to test Phil's good nature. He hired Phil to erect a steel-frame shed for an outdoor shop at his place in Temecula. In return he promised to paint a vehicle for Phil, which he did, but the paint job was so shoddy it faded quickly and came nowhere near compensating Phil for the steel-beam work that he had done at the shop. Anne was livid but Phil took it in stride. He figured that somewhere down the road he'd get Frenchy to do some body work or another paint job for him and it would all even out.

Phil also met Martine and Marc and heard about Denis. Anne told Phil that she had been raised by Pat and that she didn't know what had happened to her mother. She didn't elaborate, and Phil figured if there were more to it, she'd tell him in her own good time.

At the same time, Anne was becoming part of the Hallberg family. She attended a number of family gatherings and couldn't believe how decent they all were to each other. There was no quarrelling; one of the kids always said grace before the meal, and Phil seemed genuinely close to his father and his mother. Anne developed a particular fondness for Phil's mother, Sally, who always had a moment to call if she knew Anne was ill or needed help. Anne had spent a lifetime guarding her feelings. Now she found herself immersed in a family whose members were open and affectionate. With her work and her connections to the most wholesome family she had ever known she felt she was being reborn. She didn't think she deserved the happiness the Hallbergs seemed to take for granted. She felt unclean. They had accepted her for who she was and didn't inquire into her background.

Anne and Phil started dating in February, and by late fall of that year they had decided to marry. They were in love, and Anne couldn't recall having felt such trust for a man before. Phil was supportive; he wasn't driven around the bend by her fretfulness, and he had accepted her dad. The wedding was set for January, 1988.

The wedding was Anne's opportunity to knit together at least some of the strands of her life. She invited Denis and Line from Hull, worried about Frenchy and Gloria meeting the Hallbergs and included her closest friends from work in the plans for the reception. Frenchy picked up a portion of the bill, and both he and Anne decided they didn't want Marc at the celebrations.

Anne was a nervous wreck by the time the wedding day rolled around. All the Hallbergs, Martine and Scott, Denis and Line, and Frenchy and Gloria were there. A video shot at the reception shows a small hall, a country and western band and folks milling about dancing and chatting. Marc showed up that night and Denis invited him in. Marc waltzed over to Frenchy and shook his hand. He extended the same greeting to Gloria but she snubbed him. Frenchy and Gloria left shortly afterward. Anne was relieved when it was over. There hadn't been any ugly incidents.

Phil and Anne spent ten days in Hawaii on their honeymoon. When they returned, they moved into a small house Phil owned. By the end of the year, though, they had bought themselves a house in a new subdivision of San Jacinto. Phil had a shop nearby and the projects that he bid on were all within the valley.

For the first six months after the wedding they continued to see Frenchy and Gloria often. But by that summer, the intimacy between the two couples had faded. They began going their separate ways. Anne and Phil had their own friends, and Anne had begun thinking of having kids. She wanted a family that she imagined would be as happy and as loving as the Hallbergs. "I felt secure that my husband wasn't going to leave me. I knew he loved me very much. I felt loved. I knew his family and that did it too. They are such loving people. I thought: why couldn't we have a family like this? Why can't all of us get along like this?"

The more Anne wanted children of her own, the more she felt the need to sort out everything in her life. She had become Anne Hallberg when she married, so jettisoning the Holben name was no longer an issue. But she was still, after all these years, not living legally in the United States. She had never obtained U.S. citizenship and was, in fact, working illegally.

"I called my dad and said, 'Look, I want to get my status. This is crazy. You always sat there and told me it was OK for me to work here. It isn't.' He had got me a Social Security number a long time before. But I knew it wasn't legal. So I told him, 'I work for government. I've got to do something about this.' He said, 'Well, I'll get an attorney.' I said, 'Either you get one or I will.' I think that's what scared him. I said, 'I'm going to have to tell them what happened from the very beginning.' I think that's why he went and got an attorney. He would never have. Then Tex [Tex Ritter, the lawyer Frenchy hired] called me at home and said, 'Your dad called me to get your papers. It's going to cost you a thousand dollars.' And I thought, 'Oh, great. It's going to cost me. My dad brings me out here illegally.' I was so mad. But I wanted to get it over with. So I set a date for a meeting in Tex's office."

On the afternoon of the appointment, Anne and Phil arrived in their own car and met Frenchy and Gloria at Ritter's office. They all took seats in the lawyer's office and Ritter pulled out a number of official forms and began asking questions about her birth date, names and so on. Then, pen poised over the form, he asked, "Where's your mom?"

Anne was silent for a moment. Whenever she had been asked that question in the past, she had answered that Pat was her mother. Now, Pat was out of the scene. It never occurred to Anne to tell Ritter that Pat was her mother. There was no more reason to lie. She'd always assumed that they had been obliged to call Pat mom because she was responsible for them and it would have hurt her feelings to say otherwise. But that was no longer the case. Anne hesitated because she genuinely didn't know what to say. She had no idea what had happened to her mother. The story that her father had finally made her believe was that Jeannine had left and didn't love her. So her moment of silence echoed through the room. Then, just as she was about to say, "I don't know," Frenchy jumped in and snapped off an explanation.

"I divorced her."

Ritter made a note. "Where?"

"In Canada," Frenchy replied.

The conversation flowed on, and the moment passed. But Anne sat there quietly, listening and thinking. Divorced her in Canada? When? Where? This was a brand-new story. It threw out of whack all the mental images Anne had created of her mother since child-hood. She had this sense of Jeannine striding out of the house, heedless of the cries of her kids, whom she didn't love. That sense of Jeannine had resided within her imagination for a long time. But it had never been connected to any of the real memories that she did have of her mother. She remembered driving in the car with Jeannine to visit an aunt who was a nun and who let her draw on a blackboard with chalk, of snuggling in her mom's lap, of the piano at night. All those memories now floated, like bubbles, to the sur-face of her consciousness. And she began to imagine, for the first time in years, the outlines of the mother who had slipped sound-lessly out of her life more than twenty years earlier.

On the drive home from Ritter's office, Anne sat frozen in time. "I was shocked. In a state of shock. A million things were going through my mind. Mom tried to kill me. No, she left us. She didn't love us. Why did he say that to Grandma on the phone that time? And then I thought: Maybe what Denis said is true. For the first time in my life."

That night in bed Anne began talking to Phil about her feelings and her suspicions. For the first time she told Phil the bits and pieces of what she knew about Jeannine's disappearance.

And then she said, "You know what? Maybe he killed her." Phil was astounded. He couldn't believe that Anne could even think such a thing about Frenchy.

"Oh, Anne. You always make up these stories. Where do you get them from?"

Hearing Phil's incredulity, Anne quickly reversed herself. Maybe Denis is lying, she thought. But why would he say those things?

"I knew something was wrong. I couldn't understand it. And I said to Phil, 'You don't think he killed her?' And he said, 'No. No way. No way, Anne. Your dad's a nice guy.'"

A month later Ritter arranged to meet them in Los Angeles in the offices of the Department of Immigration.

"Phil and I went down," Anne recalls. "We went over my file with Ritter. We were in a big office waiting to see an immigration officer, waiting to get my green card. So Tex said, 'So your dad says you got your name Holben from your grandmother, your father's mother, some Indian tribe.' And I just said, 'Yeah, I guess so.' That was a totally new one on me. I thought it was funny. In the immigration office [an official] asked me if I'd ever been in trouble, if we'd ever been deported. I said no. I didn't know that we had. I told them my name was Anne Marie Durand. But that I use Holben. They didn't ask why."

Anne got her green card, and she and Phil didn't talk about her mother again. She knew that Phil put up with her flightiness and fretfulness and she was reluctant to keep circling the issue and risk exasperating him. All the questions were still on the horizon of her consciousness but they weren't pressing in on her. At least she didn't think they were.

But at work whenever her mind would wander she'd think of Jeannine and her father. He'd always been there during the bad times and the good times. She couldn't make the leap of imagination that would have permitted her to think of her dad, the man who had taken her on vacations, made her friends laugh, shared meals with her, watched movies, driven her to the beach, as a killer.

When Anne had transferred to accounts payable, she had met a woman named Mary Anne Smith who worked in payroll. Their desks were close, but initially they didn't like each other. Mary Anne is a petite, olive-skinned Filipina. She's pretty, talkative and engaging. Once they got over their mutual dislike they became bosom buddies. As they drew closer, Mary Anne told Anne about herself and her husband, who has since died. Mary Anne's husband had been adopted as a child and in adulthood had embarked on a lengthy search for his mother. He eventually found her and, in the process, learned much about himself. Anne responded to Mary Anne's intimacies by telling her about her mother. She had never before told anyone the story in such detail.

Mary Anne remembers Anne first telling her "that she hated her mom for leaving her." Later, though, their friendship shook loose other stories. "She told me that her mom gave her a big doll. She said her mom was like an angel. She said her mom was close to Denis and that before leaving Canada her mom told Denis, 'We don't know where we are going.'"

Mary Anne was deeply moved by what she saw as a great tragedy at the core of Anne's life. Some days, Mary Anne remembers, Anne thought she should just forget the whole thing, let it go. But Mary Anne kept at her, turning over and over again what was known and attempting to piece it together in a way that made sense. She thought about it and asked herself what would make a man murder his wife. "So I asked Anne. 'Does your dad drink?' Does he have financial problems?'"

To Anne those questions must have been the equivalent of asking: Does Mick Jagger sing? Although the two women didn't plot a course of action for Anne to pursue, the talks helped Anne. Unburdening herself to someone who cared made her feel less alone and helped erase the residue of the feeling that she had been responsible for the family's breakup. It also made Anne realize there were a lot of sad feelings buried deep in her subconscious. The one piece of advice Mary Anne gave her that Anne often thought about was that somehow Anne had to honour her mother and the memories she had left her with.

Anne's thoughts about her mother often took her back to Pat, who had played the role of mother in her life. She still harboured deep, bitter feelings about Pat, but none of those feelings prevented her from seeing Pat, who lived nearby. "I honestly felt sorry for her. I took her flowers on Mother's Day. I called her from time to time," she says.

Pat's marriage to Bert lasted for two years. He says he asked her to leave because of her drinking. She moved out, they divorced amicably, and by 1989 Pat was living in a small town a half-hour north of San Jacinto. She had met a new man, moved into his trailer home with him and got a job slinging hash in a run-down roadside bar. She seemed happy and devoted to her new husband. Their trailer home was crowded but neat and well kept. Their life together appeared to be based on mutual respect. Those that saw her after the move say she appeared to have finally found a measure of peace in her life.

After her visit to Tex Ritter's office Anne remembered a call she had received from Pat after Frenchy had thrown her out. Pat hadn't yet met Bert, and she was crying. Anne had been happy that her father had finally left Pat and, at the time, didn't want to hear from a woman she considered a vicious old drunk. When her tears subsided enough for her to talk, Pat had told Anne: "You know I could get your dad in a lot of trouble."

"What are you talking about?" Anne had demanded.

"You know," Pat had responded before clamming up again. Anne had hung up and hadn't given the conversation much thought. But after the incident in Ritter's office she remembered it and wondered if she should call Pat now and ask her to spill what she knew. She decided she would but kept putting it off.

At Anne's wedding in January, 1988, Gloria had asked Denis and Line what they had planned for Christmas that year. They hadn't any plans so Gloria suggested they join her and Frenchy in Florida. She offered to take them to Disneyworld, to pay for a couple of days of treats at the park for Denis's girls, Mélanie and Geneviève. That summer, as Anne was mulling over her memories, Gloria called Denis and repeated the offer, and by that fall they had all agreed on the timing and the place.

They met in southern Florida, and the vacation was a bust. Gloria was on edge and kept nattering about driving down to the Keys. Ray, who was drinking, was his usual offensive self. Denis remembers sitting in a lawn chair listening to the old man going on and on, telling stories about his past. As Frenchy rambled on Denis would say to himself: That's a lie, that's a lie, that's a lie, that might be true, that's a lie, that is not quite true....He was amazed by how consistently Frenchy invented new roles for himself, rearranged old incidents. The old man is an even bigger liar than I remember him, Denis thought.

During the vacation both Frenchy and Gloria harped on how unhappy they were with the house at the ranch. It was too far from Temecula, they complained. They had added a second storey and they moaned that they hated climbing the stairs. Frenchy regretted he had ever spent so much money on the place.

The two couples finally parted company in Fort Lauderdale. Frenchy had agreed to take Gloria down to the Keys, and Denis and Line bid them good riddance.

Ray and Gloria arrived back at the ranch sometime around 6 P.M. on January 7, 1989. It was a clear, cold, starry night with no wind. According to Frenchy's account of the evening, they decided to unpack the motor home in the morning. They went inside and he attempted to start the furnace. He says he was unsuccessful and lit a fire in the fireplace instead. They watched TV for a bit, then went upstairs to bed. At 9:15 they awoke to the sounds and smell of fire. Frenchy says he walked downstairs, saw the place ablaze and headed back to the bedroom. He grabbed Gloria and they escaped by way of the veranda off the upstairs bedroom and scrambled to the house of their nearest neighbours, a young couple who had purchased B.B. Clark's old place. By the time the first of nine pieces of fire equipment arrived, the place was engulfed in flames. The house, which he had begun building in 1975, burned to the ground. Neighbours who he had cheated and threatened and lied to and sued watched from the darkness beyond the glow of the flames. Frenchy's life at the ranch had drawn to a spectacular close.

Chapter Twenty

San Jacinto, California, 1989

Frenchy's insurance company, Allstate, paid him a total of $286,000 for losses related to the fire. Allstate agent Dave Noble, who had been insuring vehicles and property for Frenchy since 1983, says he remembers Frenchy was "so easy to get along with. He never griped." The claim was settled quickly and without any dispute about Frenchy's account of how the fire had started.

While Allstate may have had no suspicions about the fire, others did. Martine and Scott heard about the fire and drove up for a look. They examined the rubble and found the bedsprings to what had once been Martine's bed. What they didn't find struck them both as curious. Frenchy had, says Scott, maybe twenty thousand dollars' worth of weight-training and exercise equipment. "It would have to get real hot to melt those weights," says Martine. "So why is it that the springs from my old bed were there but the weights were gone?"

Neighbours and family members also say that Frenchy kept long water hoses easily accessible around the yard in case of fire. Yet in the fire report prepared by an official with the California Department of Forestry, which maintains the fire station closest to the ranch, the husband of the neighbour who called in the fire reported that he "tried to assist in controlling the fire with a garden hose from Frenchy's storage tank but the hose was ten feet too short. The fire was in the large family room when he saw it and he stated it was small enough to put out with the garden hose if it would have reached."

Another neighbour remembers a distraught Gloria saying that Frenchy was being audited by the tax department and that they had brought all their files up to the ranch and now they had burned. When Jane heard about the fire, she recalled that Frenchy had once told her that if he ever decided to get rid of the place he'd just burn it down. And Denis and Anne say after the fire they saw Frenchy with possessions that they had assumed would have been lost in the blaze. Despite the children's suspicions, there is, of course, no direct evidence that proves Frenchy started the fire.

The fire touched off a busy year for Frenchy. As had happened so many times before, his activities were catching up to him.

In July, Frenchy began seeking a buyer for the body shop. He placed ads in a number of papers and was called by Carl and Glenna Bowers of Yuma, Arizona. They met in Temecula, and Frenchy showed them his books. He said the business grossed one million dollars a year and that his annual net profit was $250,000 plus about $150,000 per year in free advertising and trades for goods and services with local merchants. The Bowerses bought the business for $295,000, took over the shop and by October had paid Frenchy a total of $178,832. By then, they had had operating losses of $27,000 in August and $29,000 in September, had learned that the paint and auto parts that Frenchy said he owned were actually on consignment, had been told by Frenchy's landlord that they would have to negotiate a new lease and couldn't, as Frenchy had advised them, pay him rent and let him keep the lease, and had discovered that owners of several of the vehicles that were in for repair had paid Frenchy deposits which he had kept. They filed a lawsuit alleging that Frenchy retook possession of the business in October, threw them out and kept their $178,832. In their suit they demanded their money back, plus interest, plus damages.

By the time the Bowerses had filed their suit, however, Frenchy had sold the business again. This time the buyer was Sharad Mogul of nearby Murrieta and the agreed upon price was a more modest $180,000. By Christmas, however, Mogul had discovered that the Bowerses were suing, and he wanted out of the deal. Soon after Frenchy again retook possession of the property. Mogul filed a lawsuit, demanding the return of property Frenchy had seized from him, plus legal fees, costs of the suit and "exemplary and punitive damages."

At about the same time that Frenchy had begun seeking a buyer for his business, Anne visited her doctor for a routine Pap smear test. The results were troublesome. Further tests were scheduled. "I told Phil and I said, 'I hope I don't have cancer.' And he said, 'There you go again. You always think something is wrong with you.' So anyway, I called up Gloria at the shop. I said, 'Gosh, I got a bad Pap smear. I hope I don't have cancer.'"

With Anne still on the line, Gloria turned to Frenchy and related to him the news about the test and Anne's fears about cancer.

Frenchy's response was loud enough for Anne to hear: "That's what happened to her mother."

Once again Frenchy had thrown Anne into a spin. "I hung up the phone—Phil was in the living room and I was in the bedroom—and I sat there, thinking. Cancer. My mom died of cancer? How could she have died of cancer? How could he know if he divorced her? Now I couldn't get rid of the questions. I thought about it a whole lot, more than I ever had. I started reviewing what I knew. I started thinking of my childhood with Pat. I tried to put it aside because I felt sorry for her. But things started coming back: how she used to beat me, how hateful she was, how my mom was just gone one day, and how I had to call Pat mom. Things like that. I felt hurt, betrayed. I told Phil about the call. He said, 'Maybe you heard wrong.' And I said again, 'Do you think he killed her?' He said no."

Emotionally it was a rough summer and fall. Anne was prepared to have a baby, to cuddle a newborn in the first house that she could call home. She had decorated it the way she wanted. It was all soft colours and frills and laces and plaques on the fridge and walls with poems about happy homes and happy hearts. It was sparkling clean and everything was always neatly in place, the dishes always done. The house spoke of Anne's search for an oasis of harmony and order.

Anne and Phil had begun trying to have a baby but Anne's doctor had conducted a battery of tests and, after studying the results, told her that even if she did manage to conceive, the pregnancy would be high risk. That shook her and she began to doubt that she'd ever have a child. She drove herself to distraction worrying. In her mind, it seemed that there was an abyss separating her from the family she felt she was destined to have. Somehow, she'd have to cross the abyss. Part of it, she believed, was that she'd have to relax and let her body prepare itself for the rigours of pregnancy and childbirth. But there was more to it than that. She'd created a harmonious environment in her home. Now, she needed emotional harmony. She needed to feel confident that she was capable of being a good mother. Most of all, though, she kept thinking about Mary Anne's remark: you've got to honour the memory of your mother. The longer she thought about it, the more she chewed it over with Mary Anne, the more she came to believe that somewhere deep inside her mother was speaking to her. The desire to have a child had awakened maternal feelings, and those feelings beckoned forth memories of Jeannine's caresses, her soft, quiet voice, her music and her smile. After an absence of more than two decades, Jeannine had returned to Anne's life.

Marc was still living near Anne, and she had heard that something was brewing. The story finally broke late that year. Marc's work as an informant came to an abrupt end when his contact, Mike Sherbondy, was charged with corruption. Sherbondy, who served as best man at Marc's second wedding, was convicted and sent to jail. Investigators had linked Sherbondy to the theft of a valuable gun collection. After his buddy's bust, Marc says, "I became just like the old man. I was cold. I had bad business dealings. I'd fuck over anybody. I hit bottom." He had made plenty of enemies by then and had to watch his back. After he bottomed out, Marc, with the help of his new wife, Carole, slowly pulled back from the brink. He was a skilled painter and got a steady job. Carole told Anne and Denis that Marc had found religion. Those who knew him locally and had been exposed to his treachery were doubtful.

Meanwhile, Martine, who was now twenty-one, had moved with Scott to San Marcos, forty minutes south, near the coast. She had become an alcoholic, had been in two life-threatening accidents and her marriage was on the rocks. Scott, who still sees her and likes her, says he'd about had it with her infidelities, her disappearances, which sometimes lasted three days, and her drinking. Anne helped out when she could, lending Martine money and buying her a truck. But Martine seemed so lost, so completely without the resources or the will to chase even the most modest dream. She occasionally worked in body shops and she was good at her work, but none of her jobs lasted, and those who loved her—Scott, his family, Anne—wondered how or if they could ever help her when she seemed so unwilling to help herself.

Shortly after Christmas, 1990, Anne came to a decision that was to change her life. After brooding for months about her mother's fate and her father's lies she decided to gather her courage and plunge back into the past. She still wanted a baby and she felt her mother's presence more acutely than ever.

"One night," she recalls, "I got home from work, made dinner and was sitting there and I said, 'I'm going to phone Denis.' I just

wanted to ask him about all the stories he knew about Mom. I
dialled. 'Hello.' I said, 'Denis. You know what? Something is
wrong. And I think it is time we find out what happened to Mom. I
didn't tell him about Tex Ritter or the Pap smear. I just said, 'It's
time.'"

"I remember him saying, 'It's about time, Anne.' He couldn't
believe it."

Three thousand miles across the continent, Denis felt a wave of
relief.

"Why?" he wanted to know, "Why now, Anne, after all this
time?"

But Anne couldn't put into words what had moved her. "It's just
time, Denis." As she said that, Anne flashed back to 1981, sitting
in Denis's kitchen, listening to him pleading with her to believe
him, seeing him cry. "I remember I was so pissed off with him. I
remember getting on that plane and thinking, That dumb S.O.B.
All he wants to do is cause trouble in the family. Saying Dad killed
Mom."

For Denis, Anne's call seemed to end a long loneliness. He was
happy that Anne was on his side but he wasn't convinced that her
change of heart was going to lead them to the discovery of
Jeannine's fate. Frenchy, he thought, was never going to tell us the
truth.

Anne's first suggestion was that she call Frenchy and just ask
him. "I said that I'd never tried to do anything and let's see what he
would do. Maybe he would tell me," Anne remembers.

But Denis told her that it would never work. "Frenchy's just
going to lie to you, Anne."

So they mulled it over on the phone and then Denis had an idea.
"Listen, Anne, let's tell him that there's an investigation going on
in Hull, started by someone on the Boissonneault side. That the
cops have been around to see me at the shop and that he should call
me as soon as possible."

Anne was willing to give it a try. So she hung up, called the
ranch and then the shop and learned that her father was on vacation
somewhere. She thought that he was still paying alimony to Pat
and thought she might know where to reach him. So she called Pat
and told her she was looking for her dad. She said that an investigator had begun looking into Jeannine's disappearance, had talked

to Denis and that Denis wanted Frenchy to call him. Then she asked Pat to tell her what she knew.

"I said, 'If you don't tell me I'm going to give the investigator your address and you are going to have to tell him. But if you tell me, I won't give him your address or phone number.' So she said, 'Well, don't get me involved.' I just said, 'Tell me what happened and I won't get you involved.' And she was silent for a while and then she said, 'Well, it's a family matter. You need to talk it over with your dad.' So I said, 'OK.' I was ticked. I was so pissed off I wanted to go over there and wring her neck. I knew she knew. I told her, 'Pat, I know you know.' She says, 'It's a family matter.' I knew she was lying. If she didn't know, she would have said, 'I don't know. I have no idea.' Instead, she said, 'It's a family matter.' I said, 'Fine.' And I hung up."

But Anne wasn't finished with Pat. She simmered for a bit and called her back. "I said, 'I'm gonna have to tell them where you are at.' She said, 'Don't get me involved. I'll get hold of your dad.' So I said, 'OK.' I was mad but there was nothing I could do. I was frustrated. Phil was sitting on the couch listening. He said, 'Why are you doing this?' I said, 'I know she knows something.' He said, 'Maybe she doesn't.'"

The next day Denis was called to the phone in his shop. It was his father. He was terse.

"What's going on?"

"Some investigators were here asking about Jeannine. I called Anne. She's all upset, crying," Denis told him.

Ray cut him off. "Tell them if they want any fucking answers, they can call me at the shop. You have my fucking numbers." And he slammed down the phone.

Denis immediately called Anne and told her about the call from Frenchy, which he figured had lasted less than a minute.

"I told him you were upset. He's going to call you, Anne."

Sure enough, Frenchy called Anne that evening. Again, he was terse.

"What's going on?"

"I said, 'Well, they are looking for Mom.' I was scared to tell him because this was the very first time I had ever confronted him in all these years. I said, 'Dad, what happened? Did she just leave?'"

Fed that opening, that out, by the daughter who still considered him her father, who at once loved, pitied and feared him, Frenchy gave it back to her.

"Yes. She just left."

"What am I going to do when they ask me questions?"

"I'm not hard to find. I'm at the shop. Send them to me."

When the call ended, Anne wanted to kick herself. "I thought, Why didn't I just ask him if he killed her instead of asking, 'Did she leave?' I thought, 'Here goes another lie.' I thought he would give me some kind of explanation, like, 'Anne, she left one night. Didn't love you guys.' or 'One night we got in a fight.' Anything. Anything."

Anne called Denis after her chat with Frenchy.

"Anne, we are never going to find out," Denis told her in despair.

"Denis, I don't want to die never knowing."

"We'll never know. He's never going to tell us the truth."

After they had made their move, Frenchy cut off all contact with Anne and Denis. For the first time in her life, Anne had no idea where her father was.

"I never saw my dad after that phone call. I tried the shop. A week later. I called Gil [Frenchy's shop manager]. He said he would have Frenchy contact me. He never did. I called the ranch. The phone had been disconnected. I thought there was something fishy. I thought he was on the run. I thought I had done it [scared Frenchy in to fleeing]."

In fact, Frenchy was still in the area, although he was rarely at the shop. He was beset with legal and tax difficulties and was still trying to untangle himself from his business.

In early spring Martine finally split with Scott, and Anne called Denis to plead with him to help her. Denis phoned Martine, bought her a plane ticket to Hull and told her she could stay with him and work at his shop. But she had to start helping herself. The deal was that as long as she stayed off the bottle she was welcome. With the support of Denis, Line and their girls, Martine did make an effort to reclaim her life. She worked happily for some months, and the future looked promising. That summer Anne and Phil flew up for a visit and they all spent time together at the cottage. Denis and Phil went fishing and became friends. Denis had met most of Anne's former boy-friends and thought Phil was the best of the bunch by a long shot. Denis took Phil on a tour of Hull, one day, showing him where Jeannine had been born and raised, where they had lived. Denis talked about her disappearance, and for the first time Phil began to get a clearer picture of the outlines of their lives. He still couldn't believe, though, that Frenchy was a murderer.

At the cottage, Anne and Denis talked about what their next move should be. Denis thought he could try the Quebec provincial police again but he didn't think he had anything new to add. And he wondered whether they would simply tell him that it was out of their jurisdiction. Anne suggested they write to the TV program "Unsolved Mysteries." Since Denis wasn't opposed to the idea, she decided to send them a letter when she got home. Other than that, they were at a loss. And to complicate matters, they had no idea where Frenchy had gotten to.

Anne came away from the holiday with a clearer sense of who her big brother was and who he had become. They were both by now deeply fond of each other. Like many siblings, they had reached an age when the quarrels of childhood fade into insignificance next to the durability of the blood connection.

Less than a week after Anne left, Denis discovered that his father had been in Hull while he was with Anne at the cottage. From two of Frenchy's brothers he learned that Frenchy and Gloria had cruised through in their motor home, visited several of his brothers, then left without ever calling his son and two daughters who were vacationing not twenty miles away. That's interesting, Denis thought. He's scared.

By fall, Martine had fallen off the wagon several times and Denis warned her he would throw her out if it happened again. When it did, he put her on a plane to California. She needed help but he had no idea how to assist her.

When Anne returned to San Jacinto she wrote to "Unsolved Mysteries" and then decided, on the spur of the moment, that she wasn't just going to sit and wait for a reply. One day at work she looked up Lieutenant Dennis Warner of the San Jacinto police, whom she had met six years earlier. Tall and gaunt, Warner had been with the San Diego police department before moving to San Jacinto. When she told him her story, he agreed that it warranted some further investigation. "She wasn't a fruitcake or anything," he says. "It didn't sound like the [Boissonneault] family had followed it up. Then the story of Jeannine being locked up didn't make sense. I really thought that something had happened to her. The other stories just didn't sound good. Why hadn't she made contact? I'm sure she would have tried over the years."

Anne told Warner that they had lived in Bellaire, a small municipality within the metro Houston area, so Warner dug up the number for the police in Bellaire and spoke to a lieutenant in investigations. "Basically," Warner says, "I asked him if he had anything on a Jeannine Durand. He called me back. All he did was run a records check on the name and birth date I had given him. Also the gas and electric company. No record of a Jeannine Durand. He called me back the next day. When he said they didn't have anything, couldn't find anything, I thought that maybe she had moved somewhere else."

Warner told Anne that he had turned up zero. He had made an effort but it sounded more like a gesture than an investigation. And the Bellaire lieutenant had likely done nothing more than sit down at his computer terminal, pump in Jeannine's name and birth date, and watch to see if anything from a parking ticket to a noise complaint to a larceny conviction came up. When nothing did, he checked to see whether she had ever had an account with the electric and gas companies. It probably took him no more than a half-hour, and it confirmed nothing more than the fact that a woman named Jeannine Durand, born October 29, 1933, had never been in contact with the Texas police and had never paid a gas bill in Houston. It was precious little but it allowed both the Bellaire lieutenant and Warner to say they had made an effort.

Anne was grateful that Warner had at least made some calls. But now she was back at square one, waiting on the remote possibility that "Unsolved Mysteries" would kick in and answer the question that wouldn't stop itching.

That fall while Anne thought about her mother, worried about having a baby and fretted about Martine, another problem surfaced that eclipsed, for a time, all of her other worries. At work one day Mary Anne had brought her an invoice that looked "weird." Checking, she found others.

The transactions were linked to her boss. At first she and Mary Anne were puzzled. They discussed it, and when they had explored all the possibilities and they confronted what they feared was the truth, that the transactions appeared to be illegal and fraudulent, they became scared. Who were they to tell? That depended on who was involved. Was there more than one person? How could they know? They didn't want to have to deal with it but they couldn't just wish their knowledge away. It was Anne who suggested they have a talk with the police chief, Joe Kozma. She planned to show him the invoice and ask him not to say anything.

In retrospect, it seemed a faint hope that the chief would be able to keep their secret. Kozma, who has since left the city, met with them, looked at the invoice, heard them out, and told them he had no choice, that he'd have to hand the matter over to district attorney Grover Trask.

The Riverside County district attorney's headquarters are in the city of Riverside, twenty-five minutes northwest of San Jacinto. Kozma's information was relayed through all the proper channels, and sometime in early December an investigator was assigned to the case.

District attorney's investigators have all the powers and authority of police detectives. They generally take on cases once an arrest has been made. Their work is to complete the investigation, help assistant district attorneys prepare cases and initiate investigations in cases of illegality involving police departments within the county. At the time, the Riverside County DA's office also had a special prosecutions unit, which devoted part of its energies to political corruption probes. One of the investigators in the unit was a muscular, forty-eight-year-old with shaggy grey-white hair and a Fu Manchu moustache named Jean Nadeau. The San Jacinto assignment was tossed on the desk in his small cubicle one morning. He looked over the material. From what he could see the case was about a high city official who was suspected of embezzling funds.

Jean Nadeau had spent twenty-three years with various police forces in southern California. He'd started off as a patrolman with the city of Orange, transferred to narcotics, made detective and then got hired on with the Orange County DA. There he worked narcotics, fraud, fugitive detail and narcotics again. In the mid-1980s, seeking work in a smaller urban environment, he applied for a job with the Riverside DA's office and was hired. When the San Jacinto case was handed to him, he had been there about three years.

By the time Nadeau began working on the case, the official involved had left the city's employ. Nadeau contacted Anne's new boss to request permission to interview her. He was given the green light, and on December 19 he hopped into his police-radio-equipped car, and twenty-five minutes later was driving into San Jacinto. Nadeau, who favours blue blazers, grey slacks and striped ties and wears a nine-millimetre automatic high enough on his hip so that his jacket conceals it, found Anne at her desk in the small work area she shares with Mary Anne.

"The office she was in was very small and there was no privacy," Nadeau recalls. "So I said, 'Do you want to sit in my car. Or we could drive up to the park.' I wanted to tape the interview. She didn't want to, didn't trust me. I realized that right away. I said, 'OK. Whatever you wish.' She arranged to have her boss's office."

Nadeau liked Anne from the start. "She was very honest. She had seen something that she didn't approve of and reported it to the chief of police. She was also very shy. I don't think she trusted men."

They talked and he outlined what he'd need, how he would have to reconstruct a paper trail. Anne was in charge of the files and she knew what was accessible, what wasn't. And so from that first meeting it became clear to both of them that they'd be in frequent contact for the next few months. When the meeting ended and Nadeau was preparing to leave, he pulled out a business card and handed it to Anne with a line he'd used before.

"Don't laugh now. My first name may be spelled like a girl's but I'm not a girl. It's a French-Canadian name."

Anne stared at him for a moment. "Oh. I'm French-Canadian too," she finally replied.

They compared notes. Nadeau told her he had been born and raised on a farm in southern Manitoba. Anne replied that she was from Quebec and that Hallberg was her married name. By the time Nadeau left, Anne felt a bond had been established. She liked this cop with the easy manner who knew how to listen, could take a joke, had a rumbling laugh and shared an ethnic identity with her. She didn't meet many French-Canadians, even fewer who had blended so completely into the life here. Nadeau had said he still spoke French but you couldn't tell from his English that he wasn't a native of California.

Nadeau felt the same. He was tickled by Anne's straight-faced, wry humour and pleased that she was so helpful. He needed her trust and felt that he'd won it during the encounter. "I liked her because she had class, had morals."

Over the next month Nadeau was often in the office in San Jacinto or on the phone with Anne. At first she didn't tell him much about herself. "She was very private. I knew she was married. One day we were talking, and I asked her what her maiden name was. She said, 'Well, I go by Holben but it should be Durand.' And I thought: 'Well, a second marriage.' Durand was French. Holben not. It came out a little bit at a time. She told me she was born in Quebec and lived there until she was six years old. I asked her if her mother and father spoke French. She said yes, but that she hadn't seen her mother in a very long time. Over twenty years. I didn't pay much attention. I thought: Divorce or something."

Meeting Anne had evidently touched a chord in Nadeau as well. He had come a long way since his departure from Canada in 1964. Born and raised on a dairy farm at La Broquerie in southeastern Manitoba, Nadeau was the fourth youngest of fourteen children. He dropped out of high school in grade ten, drove a gravel truck, pounded nails on a construction crew and worked in a lab assaying gold from northern mines. The day he turned eighteen he marched to the RCMP recruiting office in Winnipeg and promptly failed the entrance exam. "I had a real chip on my shoulder," he remembers. "I hadn't graduated from high school. I spoke English poorly and didn't speak French very well because I'd gone to school in English. I felt like a flop." He became a draughtsman's apprentice in Winnipeg in his early twenties. He hated the draughtsman's job and had always wanted to be a policeman.

In early 1964 he quit his job to travel in the United States for a couple of years. He applied for and received his immigration papers, drifted out to the west coast and headed south. He arrived in California in the fall of 1964. He was twenty-five. He had to register for military service because he'd immigrated. America was plunging deeper and deeper into Vietnam and Nadeau was drafted almost immediately. He'd been in the United States for about two months.

He spent two years in the service, most of it as a combat engineering instructor in Texas and Missouri. When he got out he returned to California, finished his high school, went on to complete a Bachelor of Arts in criminal justice and found a job with the police department in the city of Orange. He married, had a son and, by the time he met Anne, had divorced his first wife, married a second time and had seven-year-old twins. He had had a long and distinguished career as a peace officer and less and less contact, each passing year, with the huge family and the country he had left behind. He still spoke French but it was getting rustier all the time. Like all immigrants he'd left part of his heart back in the country of his birth and could wax nostalgic about home. He was a career cop and could separate his feelings from his work but meeting Anne evidently touched something in him. She, too, was a transplanted French-Canadian. Unlike him, though, she hadn't made the choice to leave the cradle of French culture in North America. Her parents had made the decision for her. In some ways, Anne was like Nadeau's eldest son, now in his early twenties. Canada was a foreign country to him, just as it was to Anne.

Frenchy and Gloria disappeared from California some time near the end of 1991. The shop was now in Gil's hands. The story around Temecula was that Frenchy had made Gil, Frenchy's shop manager, an offer that he couldn't refuse. Up on pot hill, the ranch had a for sale sign on it. The house was empty.

In late January Anne got a call at home one night from Frenchy. "He wouldn't tell me where he was at, wouldn't give me a phone number. He even told me that he knew he hadn't been a good father. He said that he and Gloria were through because she didn't want him to talk to us kids."

The more Anne worked with Nadeau, the more she came to appreciate how his mind worked. She was impressed. Talking with Mary Anne one day, she wondered out loud whether she should tell him about her mother and ask if he could help. Mary Anne was enthusiastic. That night she called Denis and told him she had met a detective. A French-Canadian. "Go ahead," Denis told her. "See if he can help."

It was March before she worked up the nerve. Nadeau recalls she phoned him at work and asked: "You police officers have ways of finding people, don't you?"

"Sure, we do it all the time."

"How hard would it be to find somebody who's been missing for twenty-three years?"

Nadeau chuckled. "Depends who's missing?"

"My mom," Anne answered. She told him that there was a lot that she didn't remember, but that she'd get Denis to write it all down.

She phoned Denis and told him to write down everything he remembered. She'd do the same, and between the two of them, they could assemble a reasonably accurate portrait of their life before and after Jeannine's disappearance. But Denis kept putting it off. Finally, one weekend in April, he was at the cottage by himself, and he sat down and wrote out three pages of names, dates, places. He mailed his account to Anne, who cleaned up some of the grammar, typed it along with her own account, then called Nadeau again.

"She asked if the next time I came to town she could take me to lunch," Nadeau recalls. "And ask me something personal. I said OK. Next Wednesday. I thought she had something else about some other person in the city. I wasn't thinking about her mom.

"We went to a Mexican restaurant. Then she kind of shocked me because she gave me about six typewritten pages. She said the top three had been written by her brother Denis, who lived in Hull. And the other three were written by her. And then there was information that she said they had sent to "Unsolved Mysteries" in hopes of finding her mom. That's when I realized she was talking about her mother."

Once Anne handed over the material, she sat, seized with anxiety. "He browsed through it. Didn't really read the papers. He was pissing me off. I thought, Well, is he gonna do something? Just tell me. He said, 'Well, I'll see what I can do.' And I thought, Are you gonna do something or not?"

But Nadeau was interested and impressed with the precision of Denis's memory. He asked a few questions.

"I started reading the material as she was talking to me. It was lengthy. I was willing to try but I didn't think I could do anything. I really didn't. The thing is, I told Anne, if your mother did leave and run away, that's not against the law. We are not going to find any record of that. If, however, something bad happened, she was killed perhaps, then I have to find a dead body.

"I asked her what she thought. She said she did not want to believe that her father had killed her mother but she had to agree that it was a possibility. One of the things that really came to the fore was: which would be the worse hurt: knowing that your mother abandoned you because she didn't love you, or knowing that she had been killed? I think she wanted to know where her mother was more than anything else. And that if she were dead, she could accept that. But she would have a great deal of trouble accepting that she did not love her and just ran off."

After lunch Nadeau dropped Anne off and drove back to his own office, musing about the story all the way to Riverside. "In the office I sat and read the whole thing again [and] brainstormed it with one of the other investigators. My first thought was that if the lady is dead and buried and has never been found, nothing would ever be done about it."

Since Jeannine Boissonneault Durand had never been seen or heard from again, it seemed to Nadeau that he had to begin by looking for a body. Nadeau talked to his superior and told him what he had. "I told him it was interesting and that I wasn't sure what sort of chance I had. I also acknowledged that it wouldn't be my case, that if there was a murder it probably had happened in Houston. I said I would like to make a lot of phone calls and that I was willing to do it on my own time. He said to go ahead but not to forget that I had a lot of other cases."

When he had the clearance, he went back to his cubicle and set to work. "I took a map of Texas and located the names of the places that Anne and Denis mentioned. Bellaire. Big Thicket. And using a cross-reference I looked up those towns and what counties they were in and if they had law enforcement or had a county sheriff. Then I wrote down the places I was going to call. [First] I called the Bellaire police department. I explained very briefly what I was interested in and what I wanted. She recommended that I call the Texas Rangers. She gave me a phone number and said I should ask for Captain Robert Prince. She said, 'He's been around a long time in the Houston area.' So I called Prince. Told him what I had. I was very surprised that a captain would be all that interested in a twenty-three-year-old case. But he took the information and said he'd get back to me. He called me the next day and said, 'On the surface I don't have anything. But call the medical examiner and talk to a guy named Cecil Wingo.' So I called Wingo and told him what I had."

Cecil Wingo looks out on the chaotic, violent city of Houston from a corner office in a new, red brick and glass, six-storey building called the Joseph A. Jachimczyk Forensic Center of Harris County. Approaching the building, the first thing that strikes visitors is the Latin inscription above the doors at the front entrance: *"Hic locus est ubi mortui docent et uvant vivantes memento mor"* (This is the place where the dead teach and help the living).

Within the medical examiner's office, Wingo, who has brilliant white hair, the muscular forearms of a logger, sad eyes and a gentle, deliberate manner of speech, is in charge of a twelve-person investigations unit. He's in his early sixties, has a doctorate in public administration and is both a licenced psychologist and a veteran police officer. He's erudite, thoughtful and sensitive to the suffering of the living.

Texas law requires the medical examiner's office to determine the cause and manner of any death that occurs within twenty-four hours of admission to a hospital, or at any time after admission if trauma is involved, as well as all deaths at any location within the county that are the result of trauma—accidents, suicides and homicides. Wingo's investigators are generally first on the scene when a death is reported. They record the place, time and cause of death, and they attempt to establish the identity of the deceased. If the cause of death is not readily apparent, an autopsy is scheduled.

In a normal year, the investigations unit handles almost ten thousand cases, which means they examine ten thousand bodies and pin down where and when death occurred, how it occurred and exactly who it was that passed on from this world. The latter question is one that they don't always manage to resolve. Of the almost ten thousand corpses they see in a year, about three hundred are found without identification. And of those, Wingo says that in recent years about eighteen to twenty are never identified, despite the best efforts of his investigators. Many of the bodies, he says, are simply too decomposed to yield any clues. And in 1979, he says, the number of unidentifieds rose sharply, a fact that he attributes that to the escalation of the wars in Central America. Houston's proximity to the Gulf and to Mexico means a fair number of illegal immigrants enter the city every year. When they die, they are sometimes without family to claim them or their families avoid identifying them for fear of being discovered by immigration authorities and deported.

Several years before Nadeau called him, Wingo had asked one of his investigators, Pat Banks, to pull together a rapid-reference index to all the bodies found in Harris County and never identified. Banks worked up a form on which the pertinent data for each case could be listed. For each unidentified body, the form lists the year, month and day the body was found, the autopsy number and the race, sex and age of the deceased. The forms were put into a black, three-ring binder and separated by dividers with tabs that note the year. Banks' reference book goes all the way back to 1959.

Nadeau told Wingo that Jeannine had disappeared sometime after January 1, 1968. Denis remembered she was there for his birthday on December 30. Nadeau also told Wingo that Jeannine was thirty-six at the time, that she was white, and that she'd had four kids.

After talking to Nadeau, Wingo told Banks the information he had been given. She opened the binder, flipped to the tab marked 1968 and noted there were six bodies found that year that had never been identified. Four were foetuses, another was an adult woman whose body was found in September and the sixth was a thirty-five to forty-year-old white woman whose body had been found on February 11, 1968. Pat noted the autopsy number—68-500—and walked into an adjoining office to a bank of tan filing cabinets where the autopsy reports for the unidentified bodies are kept. She found 68-500 and extracted it. A yellow envelope the size of a legal notepad, it bulged with the autopsy report, morgue photos, investigator's notes and related material. In all likelihood it hadn't been opened since 1968. She brought the file and the black binder to Wingo. On the outside corner of the file envelope, Wingo read that the dead woman was white, thirty-five to forty, had brown hair, and had been murdered by a blow to the head.

By the time he had finished examining the file and the black binder, Wingo was convinced they were on to something. "We had come up with this, and only this, case in February, 1968."

He also recognized the names of two of the police officers who had been on the scene the night that the body had been found. Robert Madeira had been with Fort Bend County and had been the first cop to see the body. Wingo knew that he had gone on to become a Texas Ranger and was now based in Houston. The second name was that of Johnny Klevenhagen, the detective who had driven Gilbert Pavliska back to the station and had questioned him. Klevenhagen was now sheriff of Harris County.

As soon as Wingo completed his examination of the file, he rang Nadeau in Riverside. "I told him about the case, told him the woman had been murdered. I told him we needed more information but that everything fit so far."

Nadeau was electrified by the call. "Cecil was reading from the file over the phone. He said this is what I have. February 11, 1968. We found a white female, wrapped in a bedspread, thrown in a dump, just outside of Houston, right near Bellaire. And the lady was white, in her thirties. She had been there a while so the body was not in perfect condition. Advanced stages of decomposition. And then he told me that the lady had a tag on her skirt that was from an outlet in Canada. It existed only in Canada."

Part Three

+—※❦❦※—+

The Investigation and the Trial, 1991–1993

Write down the vision,
inscribe it on tables so it can be easily read,
since this is a vision for an appointed time;
it will not fail but will be fulfilled in due time.
If it delays, wait for it,
for it will come and will not be deferred.

Habakkuk 2, 605–600 B.C.
The Old Testament

Chapter Twenty-One

+-※※-+

Riverside, California, 1991

The last thing in the world that Jean Nadeau expected was that it would be so easy. A half-dozen phone calls across the country and someone in the Harris County medical examiner's office managed to pluck from a vast stack of paperwork the autopsy records of a body that resembled Anne's missing mother. For twenty-three years that file had gathered dust in a cabinet. It contained notes and photos of every little bit of information that it had been possible to glean from the swollen, discoloured corpse found by Gilbert Pavliska in the gathering dusk on February 11, 1968. It contained everything but a name. All those years the file had been safeguarded by the medical examiner's office. They could even track down the number of the plot where the body had been buried.

By the time Wingo had finished reading to him from the file, Nadeau was convinced that the body was that of Jeannine Boissonneault Durand. Nadeau had asked about the possibility of using the dental work to make a positive identification. Wingo said that wasn't possible; the lady in question had full dentures, upper and lower, with no markings on them. She also had a small scar below the navel, brown hair, stood five feet, seven inches tall, and weighed about 144 pounds. The autopsy report noted the eyes "appeared brown." Wingo also said there were morgue photos and that a family member should look at them as well. Nadeau said he'd check with Anne and her brother Denis and obtain from them a more precise description of Jeannine.

Nadeau said he was so excited the morning he talked to Wingo, so sure in his gut that this was Jeannine's body, that he couldn't restrain himself. He called Anne immediately. She was at work.

"I could hardly talk. I said, 'Anne, are you sitting down?' She said, 'No, I'm in a hurry. But what have you got?' I said, 'Are you sure you don't want to sit down?' She said, 'Well, go ahead.' I said, 'Anne, I think I found your mom.' And she practically went hysterical. Phone went dead for a few seconds. And she started to scream. And I knew she was in a big office with lots of people. I said, 'I'm not 100 percent sure yet. But it sure looks good.' She started to cry. I said she was dead, murdered, that there would probably be a murder investigation. I didn't tell her how it happened."

Nadeau asked Anne to get Denis to call him, then eased off the phone. Anne was in no condition to talk, and he immediately regretted that he had chosen to tell her over the phone. "I was so excited that I couldn't wait. If I had told her personally, it might have made it a little easier than doing it on the phone. I guess I just couldn't wait. I was thinking that it was so far removed that it didn't dawn on me that it would hurt her a lot."

But Anne was hurt, dizzy with fear and panic. It wasn't just an abstract, historical inquiry for her. It had a direct link to her current life. For if her mother had been murdered all those years ago, that meant the prime suspect in the killing was her own father. Once again she felt that she was going to be the one responsible for driving another parent from her life.

"I told Jean I couldn't talk," she recalls. "I ran to the bathroom. Mary Anne was closest to me. She was the only one who saw me crying. I locked myself in the bathroom. I heard knocking. 'Anne, let me in.' I said no. She said, 'It's your mom, isn't it?' I said yes. I let her in and she just hugged me. 'It's going to be OK,' she said. I couldn't really talk. I was shaking."

Mary Anne said she had "been praying that they would find her mother alive. But when I saw her crying, I knew that she was dead. I went into the bathroom and cried with her."

Anne composed herself enough to tell her boss that she had to leave work for the day, that something terrible had happened. She drove home and sat and looked at the phone, then slowly picked up the receiver and dialled Denis at his shop in Chelsea. As she dialled she thought about her brother's insistence, from age twelve until now, that Jeannine had been taken from them by their father's hand. She remembered how he had been abandoned at fifteen, how he had remade his life, organized it around the hole at the centre of his being, how he had grown to be such a decent man in spite of it all, perhaps because of it all. It was all too much. By the time she heard Denis's voice on the other end of the line she was crying again.

"They found Mom, Denis. She was murdered."

Standing in his small shop, his employees working on a car nearby, the compressor throbbing in the background, Denis felt his world drop out from beneath his feet. Yet he sounded strangely calm on the phone. Anne was so distraught that he reacted by trying to sooth her feelings.

"Anne, it's over. Don't cry. We know now." Anne recalls that "he was so calm it freaked me out. How could he be so calm? I thought, Why isn't he crying?"

Denis was, as he later put it, "devastated. I couldn't work. I couldn't think. I felt like jumping in my car and driving straight to Houston."

His finger shaking so badly he could barely dial, Denis called Nadeau. He had never spoken to him before and didn't know what to expect. Nadeau greeted him warmly and told Denis he needed a more detailed description of his mother to assist the Houston medical examiner's office in making a positive identification of the body. He asked if Jeannine had worn dentures.

"Yes," Denis replied, thinking of the nights he'd asked his mother to bring him a glass of water so he could make her laugh when he knew her dentures were out.

"Upper or lower,' Nadeau asked.

"Both."

Wingo asked whether she had a scar below her navel. Denis said he wasn't sure but that he knew his mother had had some sort of operation in Florida after Martine's birth, an operation to prevent her from having more children. He also estimated her weight and height and both of his estimates were close to the description of the body. He said she had blonde/brown hair and that her eyes were blue. That was a discrepancy, Nadeau thought, but otherwise everything else fit.

After talking to Denis, Nadeau passed on the new information to Wingo, who told him that the homicide unit of the Harris County sheriff's department had been advised.

Nadeau says he didn't get a lot of sleep that night, worrying about Anne. He called her in the morning to see if she was all right and to apologize for the manner in which he had broken the news to her. He told her that he would be speaking to the homicide unit and said they would be in touch with her.

After calling Denis, Anne had called Phil at work. That night they talked. Again, Anne asked Phil, who had once served jury duty, whether he thought Frenchy had killed Jeannine. Phil thought about all the stories he had heard about Pat's viciousness and he couldn't figure what sort of evidence could be assembled to convict Frenchy.

Back in Chelsea that night, Denis told Line and the kids and then called his cousin, Staff Sergeant Michel Béland, who was now stationed with the RCMP in Ottawa and was in charge of the traffic patrol units in the national capital region. Michel offered his support to Denis, and they agreed they would have to tell Réginald, the only surviving family member, but Michel suggested they wait until the identity of the body had been confirmed. Denis told Michel that he had passed his name on to Nadeau and that there might be information he could provide that would be needed in the investigation.

Throughout it all, one thought kept burning in Denis's mind: the son of a bitch killed her. He found he couldn't sit still, couldn't relax, couldn't concentrate on what he was doing. He paced and filled the house with his nervous energy.

The next day Denis called Wingo in Houston. Wingo told him that he should write him a letter stating the reasons that he believed that the body they had found was that of Jeannine and have it signed by all four children. That night Denis drove to Béland's house and together they prepared the letter Wingo had asked for. They pointed out that, like the body found in the dump, Jeannine had full dentures, was in her mid-thirties, about the same height. By now Denis knew she had had a tubal ligation and that it had left a scar below the navel. They noted that the body was found thirty minutes from where they had lived and that the skirt found on the dead woman had come from Canada.

Soon after, Béland called Wingo and introduced himself, said that he was Jeannine's cousin and was willing to help identify her if it was necessary. Wingo thought it was a good idea to have a professional police officer look at the morgue photos. He told Béland he would send four photos up to him. He asked Béland to examine the photos and, if he was able to conclude without any doubt that the photos were those of his cousin, to draft a statement to that effect and mail it to him. Béland agreed and wondered just how grisly the photos were going to be. Wingo had told him that the body had been in the dump for about ten days before it was discovered so he assumed it would be badly decomposed.

In Houston, Detective Mike Talton was sitting at his desk on April 18, clearing up odds and ends. It was a Thursday morning. A promotion to lieutenant was in the works. A trim, fit, thirty-four-year-old, Talton had spent eight years with the Marine Corps before joining the sheriff's department. Now in his twelfth year with the department, he had spent the last seven working homicide and was about to be promoted out. He wasn't expecting another case. That morning his superior had crooked his finger at him and said, "You look like a man who's got time on his hands." He had dropped a 1968 case file on Talton's desk.

An hour later Talton received a call from Jean Nadeau in Riverside. "I wanted to work with him," Nadeau recalls. "I wanted them to know that I was willing to help but I didn't want to step on any toes and mess up their investigation."

After they chatted, Nadeau said he'd keep in touch. He said he had found out where Pat was living and was making some discreet inquiries into Frenchy's life.

Later that morning, Talton dropped in on the property room and asked the sergeant on duty for the evidence from the investigation that had been undertaken in 1968. But the sheriff's department had moved several times since 1968, and everything related to the case, Talton was told, had been misplaced or tossed out. That meant that the ring, dentures, fingerprints, clothing, rope, bedspread and towel had disappeared. Talton then checked with the photo lab and got another piece of bad news: the department had no crime scene photos from crimes that had been committed before 1975.

Talton says he didn't consider the loss of the evidence to be critical. Still, it was a setback.

A short time later Talton was called to the phone again, this time by Lieutenant Robert Madeira of the Texas Rangers. Based in Houston, Madeira is what's known as a Concrete Ranger. Most of the ninety-odd Texas Rangers work in rural areas, providing police expertise to small-town police departments. Madeira is one of the few involved in big-city crime. The Rangers have been around as a police force since the 1800s. They are now a unit within the larger Texas Department of Public Safety, which Madeira joined in 1968, two months after he and colleague Buster Dennis of the Fort Bend

County sheriff's department had Gilbert Pavliska show them where he had discovered the "two blue feet" sticking out of a wrapped bedspread in the Barker Reservoir.

Madeira is a trim, erect man in his late forties with twinkling eyes, a ready smile and a sense of humour. He wears a large gold Ranger ring with a star at its centre, western-cut suits, cowboy boots, a cowboy hat and is utterly devoted to the mystique and legend of the Rangers. The Rangers are the official state police of Texas and as such responsible for investigations that involve out-of-state travel. Cecil Wingo had contacted Madeira's superior and told him that Madeira had been on the site the night the body had been found and that the investigation was being reopened. The following day Madeira was told to call Harris County homicide and work with them on the case.

Madeira and Talton discussed the case on the phone. It was understood that it was to be a Harris County case but that they would work it together. Talton remembers that Madeira told him he was on the scene the night the body was found, that it was cold and windy and that he had never forgotten the sight of the wrapped corpse.

On Tuesday of the following week Talton met Wingo and obtained from him the autopsy report, the morgue photos and Michel Béland's statement. He and Madeira discussed them and began their investigation in Houston. They visited Sam Montgomery Oldsmobile and drew a blank: no one there remembered Ray Holben. They checked with the Bellaire police department and learned that no one had ever filed a missing persons report on Jeannine Boissonneault Durand. As far as they were concerned, Raymond Durand was their prime suspect. As Talton later put it: "If the police back then had identified the body, they'd have locked onto him [Ray] like an ol' bloodhound."

While Talton and Madeira were sifting through Ray's past in Houston, Jean Nadeau was making his own discoveries in Riverside County. The weird thing was that at every turn he kept running into other investigations that he had been involved in. He visited the ranch and remembered having been in the area busting a meth lab. And then, when Nadeau met Frenchy's son Marc, he learned that Mike Sherbondy had been best man at Marc's wedding. Nadeau had worked the Sherbondy case and had helped put the crooked cop behind bars on seven felony counts.

Up at the ranch Nadeau saw a for sale sign and noted the name of the real estate agent. A day or so later he popped in on the agent in Temecula and asked whether he could get in touch with the owner. The realtor said he'd contact Frenchy and invited Nadeau to leave his card. Later that week Nadeau was in his office early one morning when the receptionist signalled that he had a call.

"I answered," Nadeau recalls, "and here was this voice saying, 'This here's Frenchy Durand. I hear you want to talk to me.' I almost fell off my chair. I told him I was interested in his property and was there an address I could write to him at? He said he was travelling and that he'd be in California in a couple of weeks and that he'd call me when he got here."

The sound of Frenchy's voice stuck in Nadeau's memory. Frenchy, he said later, spoke in a sort of drawl, still had a French accent, and he slurred all his words so that they ran together like a sentence without punctuation. By now, Nadeau had developed a professional interest in Frenchy's twisted character. Marc, in particular, had told him some pretty hair-raising stories about Ray Holben a.k.a. Ray Durand. He told Nadeau about the drug dealing and said that when he worked for his dad, Frenchy would sometimes withhold his pay to force him to make drug deliveries. Marc talked about the dodges Frenchy used on customers in the shop and the enemies he had made over the years. Nadeau didn't believe everything Marc told him. Still, he got a clearer picture of Frenchy's home life from Marc. And although Marc didn't have any direct evidence of what Frenchy might have done to Jeannine, he was certainly convinced that his father had killed his mother.

Since Nadeau was worried about overstepping his authority and interfering in the Harris County case, he took care not to approach anyone he thought was still close to Frenchy or Pat. He discovered that Pat had married Bert Matheis, lived with him for a couple of years and then had moved out. He figured it would be safe to approach Matheis because the marriage had ended on a sour note and Pat no longer lived in San Jacinto. "So I told Talton that I had found her [Pat's] ex and that they were no longer together. And it didn't appear that they were close at all. In other words he could not burn us to her. And Talton told me to go ahead and talk to him."

So on the morning of April 24 Nadeau found Bert Matheis doing repair work on a rental house he owns in Hemet. Matheis is a short, energetic man in his fifties with greying hair, a square jaw and an impatient manner. His yard was filled with tools and half-completed carpentry projects and his house was dusty and clearly the home of a bachelor. Nadeau soon had Matheis talking his ear off. It was an investigation into Durand, he told Matheis. Nadeau asked a few questions and let Matheis run on.

Matheis told Nadeau about how fearful of Frenchy Pat was, how she had met him at a Ford car dealership in Ottawa, how he was "so crooked. He was a thief's thief." Pat told him, Matheis said later in an interview, that Ray used to beat hell out of her. Matheis described Pat as uneducated but an avid reader, a kind woman who once rescued a pair of kittens but who, when she was drinking, "could be the meanest, rottenest son of a bitch there was."

Matheis told Nadeau that during the first year he lived with Pat the story of her life with Ray dribbled out slowly. Then one night about a year after they married, when Pat was drinking and feeling melancholy and sorry for herself, she started talking: "She said [she and Ray] were never married," Matheis told Nadeau. "She said 'I'm just worthless. Here I am fifty years old. Never been married. I'm just nothing.' I said, 'That's not true. Why do I care if you were married or not? He's out of your life. That doesn't make any difference to me. I like you like you are.'"

"And then she said, 'He killed his first wife.' She said, 'He got away with it.' This was in Houston. Pat said she moved in and took care of the kids. Martine was only six months old."

"I said, 'What are you talking about?' She said he just took her out and dumped her body in a dump. She never said whether he killed her and took her body out there, or killed her there. I said, 'Why didn't you leave him?' She said she had no place to go, had never had a job, that she was still an alien. And she just felt, you know, the lesser of evils....They had a place to live, food, booze, cars, travel."

Matheis's story set Nadeau's pulse racing. Here was the key to unlocking the puzzle. "There were only two people in California who knew that Jeannine's body had been found in a dump in Houston—Anne and I. Nobody knew if Pat had anything to do with it. But this story fit with what we knew. So I immediately called Texas and they got really excited."

In an interview some months later Matheis said he was shocked more by the fact that Pat continued to live with Frenchy after the murder than that he had killed Jeannine. He says he's seen enough of the world to understand how marital conflict can turn violent. And, he says, since Frenchy had gotten away with it for twenty-three years, there was no reason for Matheis to think that Frenchy could ever be brought to justice for it. So Matheis didn't tell anybody what Pat had confided to him until a police officer asked him.

Nadeau later told Anne about Bert Matheis's revelations, and she, in turn, passed the story on to Denis. Both of them were stunned and furious. If Bert's story was true, and there was no reason to think it wasn't, that meant Pat had known all along that their father had killed Jeannine. She had known since 1968 that she was living, drinking and sleeping with a murderer. What chains had tied her to Frenchy? How could she have looked him in the eyes, shared a bed with him? they wondered. By then, Denis no longer had any doubt that his father was a killer. Anne was still willing to give Frenchy the benefit of the doubt, though. She thought it might have been a quarrel that had gotten out of hand.

After discussing it with Line, Denis flew to California with the letter he and Michel had drafted. He and Anne would get Marc and Martine to sign it and then he'd mail it to Houston. He didn't have any plans beyond that. He figured he'd at least meet Nadeau, spend a couple of days with Anne, then fly back. He still had no idea where Frenchy was living or what he was doing. But he figured that one day soon Frenchy was going to get the surprise of his life.

Denis flew to Ontario, a small city an hour from Los Angeles, and Anne met him at the airport. They drove back to San Jacinto together, feeling like co-conspirators. They had been talking on the phone almost every day since the discovery of Jeannine's body and their respective phone bills were running into the thousands of dollars. Their friendship was deepening, and as they both probed their memories for bits of information that Nadeau and the Texas investigators might be able to use, they both, for the first time, discovered what they had separately gone through. They had never before discussed with such frankness the feelings they'd had, the pain they carried and how wounded they'd both been by their experiences. When they talked about Pat, they shared identical feelings and often identical memories. They both despised her for what she had done to them as children. Neither could remember anything other than Pat being drunk or smelling of liquor and beating them or trying to set them against each other. She had been so hateful that the memory of her malevolence still stung all those years later. When Anne and Denis discussed what Bert had told Nadeau, both drew the same conclusion: Pat probably had knowledge of the murder.

If Anne and Denis focused almost exclusively on Pat's behaviour, it was partly due to the fact that they still didn't agree on what should happen to their father. Denis hated him more acutely now than ever. But Anne was still ambivalent. She had loved her father all her life, had defended him and protected him and now felt sorry for him in a way that Denis couldn't begin to understand. Anne didn't want to have to get up in a courtroom and face him. She imagined him, sitting there, grey and gaunt with the pain of her betrayal. She knew it wasn't right for him to have killed Jeannine—if he had done so. But he was still her father. How could she wish to see him in jail at his age? she wondered. And why wasn't Denis troubled by the same concerns? she kept asking herself.

The day after Denis's arrival they went looking for Marc. He wasn't home, but while looking for him they ended up at a flea market. There Denis met a painter who specialized in reproductions of photos. Denis had one small photo of his mother and decided on the spot to have a large oil painting made from it. He struck a deal with the painter—it wasn't going to be an outstanding work of art but he hoped it would at least bear some likeness to Jeannine—and arranged to pick it up the following week.

They found Marc later that day and, sitting in his living-room, recounted for him all that had happened. Marc exploded when he learned of the discovery of what everybody now agreed was Jeannine's body.

"She was murdered," Denis told him.

"Frenchy," said Marc without the slightest doubt in his voice.

Marc signed the statement Denis proffered, and shortly after they left him alone with his grief and anger. They returned to Marc's that night for dinner and traded stories about Frenchy and their mother. It was a grim evening.

Martine was more difficult to track down. No one seemed to
know where she was staying or working. They eventually gave up,
and Denis decided that, rather than mail the statement to Wingo,
he'd fly to Houston and deliver it by hand. He also hoped that he'd
be able to find the grave and have Jeannine's remains shipped back
to Canada for reburial.

The next day was Sunday, and Denis got on a flight that would
put him down in Houston just about nightfall. He brought a thriller
along to read on the plane but he couldn't focus on the story and
eventually gave it up. For almost the entire flight he sat thinking,
running his whole life through his mind. As the plane came in for a
landing he suffered an attack of self-doubt. Perhaps he shouldn't
have come. How would he bear up? How would he be able to stand
the thoughts that were flooding back into his memory? He wanted
Line to be here but he was just as glad that he was alone. He could
grieve in solitude.

The next morning Denis raced over to the medical examiner's
office, asked the receptionist for Cecil Wingo and within a couple
of minutes was seated with Wingo in his office.

"Now that I have seen you," Wingo told him, "there is no doubt
in my mind that these pictures are of your mom."

In an interview later Wingo said that he had "studied the case so
much, looking for identifiers. When Denis came to my office, I
knew exactly who he was. There was a great similarity."

Denis was astonished. Did he really look that much like his
mother? he wondered.

Pointing to an envelope on his desk, Wingo asked, "After
twenty-three years, do you think you can look at these?"

Denis didn't hesitate. He didn't think he'd ever be able to sleep
through the night again if he looked at pictures of his mother in a
morgue. "I'd rather not. But I could look at pictures of the clothing."

The photos of the clothing were startling enough. A black bra,
white panties, a yellow and green striped top, a green skirt. He
didn't recognize any of them but he remembered that his mother
never wore pants. He remembered tagging along with her when she
bought the foldover suitcase in Ottawa for the trip to Fort
Lauderdale. So my dresses and skirts won't get creased, she had
explained. If they had showed me a picture of pants, then I'd have
wondered, Denis thought to himself.

Another photo showed the bedspread and the rope. As soon as he saw it, Denis said, "Chenille. We had bedspreads like that at home. Chenille bedspreads." He couldn't say they had had a bedspread exactly like that but he knew the fabric, knew the name for it.

After examining the photos of the clothing, he began to worry that he hadn't been helpful at all and that the whole matter would be dropped for lack of evidence. He asked Wingo if an investigation was under way. Wingo assured him that there was and said that Mike Talton, a homicide detective with the Harris County sheriff's department, was in charge. He offered to call Talton to let him know that Denis was in town but when he called, he couldn't reach him.

When Wingo hung up the phone, Denis said, "If I have one worry it's that if I see my father, I don't know what will happen."

Wingo looked at him with sad eyes. "Don't worry. God will take care of things," he told Denis.

Wingo said he'd try Talton again later. In the meantime he offered Denis a seat at a desk in the investigators' office. He gave Denis the number of a woman named Sue, who, he said, was in charge of records at the Harris County Cemetery. Denis called and explained what he was looking for. Sue said she'd dig up the information. "Call me back this afternoon," she told him.

After making the call, Denis sat there, examining a large map of the county on the wall and listening to the investigator next to him answer the phone, which never stopped ringing.

After lunch Denis made his way over to the sheriff's department and asked the first person he met for Mike Talton.

"Talton?" the guy shouted and received a "yeah" from behind a partition. He motioned to Denis to walk over.

Denis found the detective on the phone in a tiny cubicle. Talton gave Denis a hard, direct look. Denis put on his desk a copy of the letter he, Anne and Marc had signed. It was in the RCMP envelope that Michel had given him the night they drafted it. Talton noted the RCMP logo, hung up the phone and continued to look at Denis.

"My name is Denis Durand," Denis began.

Talton stood up. "Before we get started," Denis remembers him saying, "I'd like to extend my sympathies." He stuck out his hand and Denis shook it, at once grateful and moved by Talton's thoughtful remark,

Denis asked what was happening with the investigation.

"Stupid as it sounds," he remembers Talton said, "I'm waiting to get money to go out to California. I've got to get approval. But let me tell you something. The people involved in the investigation back in 1968 are top guns around here now. They want to find out what happened. We are going to go to California."

Talton found a secretary and arranged for her to take Denis's deposition. When they finished, Denis called Sue, the woman at the records office of Harris County Cemetery. She told him his mother was buried in Section C, Row I, Gravesite 5. She gave him the address for the cemetery and told him the gates closed at 4 P.M. It was 3:15 and he said he wasn't sure he'd make it in time. Sue said she'd speak to Kenny, the caretaker, and would leave a stick in the ground so he'd find the right grave.

Denis was in such an upbeat mood after his talk with Talton that when he said goodbye and walked out the front door of the sheriff's department he took a picture of the place.

"I jumped in the air and shouted I was so happy. I figured I'd show that picture to people and they'd finally believe me, what I had been saying for so long."

He raced over to the cemetery and parked outside the gates. He walked down a long drive bordered with shrubs and lilacs and trees and well-tended lawns. It looked peaceful and strangely comforting but something was nagging at him. He looked off to his left as he walked and saw how close it was to the highway, a highway he realized he had travelled many times. It was the old Liberty Freeway that ran out to Big Thicket, the road they had driven down every weekend from late winter, 1968, to the summer of that year when they finally moved out to Big Thicket. It was the road that his father had driven every day to and from work for more than a year. It was the road that they had driven with building supplies for the cabin they had built, he and his father, in the woods.

The cemetery itself was nothing more than rolling lawns with no visible headstones. Each little field was bordered with pines. He approached a workshed and a middle-aged black man emerged and asked, "You the Canadian guy?"

Denis nodded, returning his smile.

"Looking for your mom, huh?"

Denis nodded again, feeling a tightness in his chest.

"What happened?" Kenny asked.

"My dad murdered her."

"Thought he was safe after all these years, huh?"

You got that right, Denis thought.

Kenny led him over to Section C and pointed to the stick that had been planted in the ground. Denis walked over. He saw a long, narrow band of concrete running along what he figured would be the top of the graves. At regular intervals a tiny two-inch square metal plaque was embedded in the concrete. Most of them were blank but on the grave that had been marked with the stick someone had scratched in the initials GB. They got it wrong, he thought. It should be JB. He rose and then knelt at the foot of his mother's grave, his sunglasses hiding the tears that began welling up.

"I finally found you," he whispered to himself, to his mother's memory. "I'm not going to leave you here," he promised, the tears now rolling down his cheeks. "I'm going to bring you back to Canada."

Looking up from the grave, again he stared at the ribbon of asphalt and the cars zipping by. He wondered what his dad was doing. I wish he could see me now, Denis thought, right here. He remembered the twelve-year-old boy who had been in the back seat of the big Oldsmobile, surrounded by hammers and saws and food for the weekend and his timid little sister and his little brother with the brush-cut and his little sister with the blonde curls. He remembered how he just wanted to protect them. He remembered the fear that knotted his stomach and the bottles of whisky that were always on the front seat between his dad and Pat. He remembered asking about his mom, who all the time was lying right here in this grave, and being told she didn't love him and to shut his fucking mouth. The wave of pain that swept across him was so intense that he wondered whether he'd be able to get up and walk back to the car. He wanted someone to be here with him but he also wanted to be alone with this pain, these feelings that he had carried all of his life. He wanted just to sit there and suffer in silence, to let all the hurt flow out of him. And he wanted everyone to know that he had never, ever given up, that he had taken every emotional and physical hit his father and Pat had aimed at him and he had survived it all and it hadn't destroyed him. And that in the end he had not just survived but had triumphed by discovering the only truth that mattered. He had found out what had happened to his mother. My dad can be damned, he thought. It doesn't matter what his explanations are. She's dead and he killed her and I know and soon everybody else is going to know.

He looked down at the grave again. I'm the first person to come here who knows her, he thought. He looked at the stick, pulled it out and wrote on it, JEANNINE BOISSONNEAULT. BORN OCTOBER 29, 1933. DIED FEBRUARY, 1968.

Kenny walked over.

"Your mom's at rest now. She's at peace here."

"But it's not where she belongs."

Denis left the cemetery and drove aimlessly for a time. Then he discovered he was heading towards Bellaire. He was so tangled inside that he didn't know what he was feeling. He found Beech Street and found the house they had lived in when Jeannine disappeared. He sat in the car, staring at the little house, the big oak in the front yard. Down the street was the Bellaire water tower and the Maud W. Gordon Elementary School where he had learned to speak English. He remembered his father had told him he was going to go to a French school and he remembered his shock when he discovered nobody spoke French in Maud W. Gordon Elementary.

He remembered joining Scouts and the new bikes Pat had bought them all and how much he liked her then. Aunt Pat.

He drove again, looking for Holly Street but couldn't find the house he was looking for, couldn't find Jack's place either.

Finally he was so worn out he pulled into a motel, arranged for a room and locked himself in. He called Anne in California, Line in Quebec, told them what had happened, that he had found Jeannine's grave. But he couldn't talk and rang off and sat in silence. That night he couldn't sleep. He paced, he tried to watch TV, and he felt consumed by his memories. He dozed and had a nightmare in which his dad appeared, grinning. He woke and cursed and wished he could get Frenchy and force him to come to the cemetery with him.

The next morning he called a funeral home and explained he wanted to have his mother's remains dug up and shipped to Canada. They told him to come down and he spent the morning learning how complicated it was going to be. They needed an amended death certificate and permission to disinter the remains and all sorts of other papers. But they were helpful and said they'd handle all the details. So he signed some papers and left them some money and then found a flower shop. He ordered a huge arrangement, told them he wanted all sorts of flowers in it and told them he'd be back for it after lunch. He had a hurried meal and rushed back, picked up the flowers and drove to the cemetery.

Kenny greeted him and followed him to the grave. He placed the arrangement on the grave and took some pictures. Then Kenny persuaded him to give him the camera so he could take a picture of Denis with the flowers and the grave. Denis resisted but gave in and was happy he did so. Everybody wanted copies when he told them about it.

Denis left the cemetery and pulled up at the airport with only minutes to spare. He dropped off his car and raced to his departure gate. All the way to California his mood was sombre. Anne and Phil met him at the airport, and he told them what had happened in Houston.

The following morning Anne told him they were going to have lunch with Jean Nadeau. They decided to buy him a gift. They bought a wristwatch and had engraved on the back, "EVERY MINUTE WE THANK YOU." They drove to Riverside, parked in front of the DA's office and there was Nadeau coming out. Anne called to him and he walked over, saw Denis and began speaking French to him. They had never met before.

"You have no idea what you have done for us," Denis told him. "I'll never be able to repay you."

They bought him lunch and gave him the watch. Nadeau had tears in his eyes when he opened the gift. The case had moved him in a way that he hadn't expected. He felt involved in their lives now. He said later that he had agreed to help because of his friendship with Anne, a friendship that had been initiated by the "integrity she had shown in refusing to keep silent about what her boss was doing." To be fair, he also said that the case was an interesting challenge. As he learned about Frenchy, he developed a deep contempt for what he had done to the children. After the body had been identified, he saw what his efforts had meant to the two children who remembered their mother.

After lunch Nadeau asked if they wanted to see where Pat was living. They drove to the little town she had moved to after her split with Bert Matheis. They cruised into the trailer park and Nadeau pointed out Pat's place. At that very moment they saw the door open and Martine step out. They ducked down in the car so she wouldn't see them. She still hadn't been told about the body. They hadn't been able to find her and neither of them had thought to check with Pat. It was just as well, they thought. Nadeau didn't want Pat to suspect anything when they picked her up. Both Denis and Anne felt terrible that Martine hadn't yet learned about the discovery of the body and they talked about it all the way back to Nadeau's office. He took them up to his cubicle, sat down and the phone rang. It was Talton. He had received approval for the trip and was flying to California with Madeira the following week. He asked Nadeau to arrange for a polygraph for Pat and a video camera so her statement could be taped.

Denis returned to Chelsea later that week. From then on he and Anne talked on the phone daily, sometimes hourly. They couldn't stop calling each other.

Talton and Madeira flew in on Tuesday, May 14. They spent the day going over the details of the case with Nadeau, who told them what he knew about Frenchy, about the drug dealing and his relations with the children. He said he had run a driver's licence check on Frenchy and had discovered that he had surrendered his California driver's licence in South Carolina, presumably for a South Carolina licence. He took Madeira and Talton up to the ranch and told them about the people he had interviewed. They were eager to talk to Pat but they wanted to make sure everything was in place before they picked her up.

The following morning all three of them interviewed Bert Matheis, who repeated his story about Pat being drunk and melancholy one night and telling him that Frenchy killed his first wife and left her body in a dump. When they finished, they had lunch, then drove to the trailer park in San Bernadino County where Pat was living with her latest husband. "We were all on pins and needles," says Nadeau, "because we had no idea what to expect. I had everything set up in the office—a video—and we set off."

They pulled up, Talton says, knocked on the door and found nobody was at home. "So we got a coffee, came back, parked and ten minutes later they [Pat and her husband] drove up."

They let Pat and her husband enter the house, then the three detectives walked up and knocked on the door. When Pat answered, Nadeau showed his badge and told her that he was with the Riverside DA's office and that the two gentlemen with him were with law enforcement in Texas. He said they wanted to talk to her.

Talton says he told Pat "that we are here to talk about the disappearance of Jeannine Durand. Her first words were, 'I don't know anything more than the kids do.'

"We didn't give her a choice. We said, 'We'd like you to come with us.' She didn't even ask if she had to come with us. She just said, 'Let me get my purse.'"

Pat told her husband that three detectives wanted to talk to her and, Nadeau remembers, "he followed us in his car."

Pat sat in the back seat of Nadeau's car. "She had a very passive face," Nadeau says. "We didn't know what to make of her. She did ask once or twice what it was all about. And we said we'd rather wait till we got to the office.

"Our office is on the second floor. Her husband stayed on the first floor, in the lobby. We took her to the second floor. No cuffs. We made her aware of the fact that she didn't have to come with us, that she could refuse to talk to us and all that."

They sat her in a chair in a private room, had the video camera on her and began asking questions. Talton remembers she looked meek: "I was looking at a woman almost sixty—no way I could gauge what she was like in her thirties. I've worked a lot of killings. One in particular, I tracked down an outlaw biker in his mid-fifties. He was so wore out and broken down he could barely climb stairs. But thirty years earlier he'd have just as soon killed you as looked at you. Real hell bent for leather. With Pat, from the stories the kids told we got a vision of her and Ray. But looking at her she just seemed old, wore out, broke down."

Nadeau says they sat around her and Talton and Madeira took the lead in the questioning: "We started asking her about Ray. Frenchy. She know Ray? Yeah. She used to live with him? Yeah. Did Ray ever say anything about killing his wife? No. For a long, long time, maybe an hour, an hour and a half, she didn't say anything. I was pretty sure we weren't going to get anything out of her. And she would throw us off. They [Talton and Madeira] did most of the talking. I would just kind of look at her. And she'd look away from them and throw us off completely by looking at me and saying, 'Where do I know you from?' I had never met her in my life. And then she'd say, 'I think I played shuffleboard with you.' I don't know if that was planned. But it worked. It would throw us off."

Talton says it was frustrating: "We'd go back and forth. It was clear she wasn't going to tell us anything. [Finally] I told her, 'OK, we'll just get you to make a statement and then you can take the polygraph.' Just as we were going to get up I said, 'Wait, Pat, you're just going to waste our time. You're going to fail that polygraph. What you've told us is a lie. You know that. Why don't you go ahead and take a big old deep breath and tell us?'"

At that point Nadeau, who was born and raised a Catholic, jumped in. "I said, 'Pat, do you know what confession is? Wouldn't it be nice to confess something and then have a clean slate?' And then Talton threw in, 'Frank [Pat's husband] sure looks like a nice guy. Don't you think Frank has the right to have you level with us? And come clean?' And we worked on that aspect of it. And finally, she said, 'OK. I'll tell you.' And she turned just like that."

Nadeau said even after the break occurred it was still "very, very difficult for her to start. Of course, we had to prod her, to ask her questions. We asked her to start from the beginning, with her contact with him for the first time. She said they had worked together. They started dating. She didn't know he was married. One day he said he wanted to go to the U.S. and asked if she wanted to go with him and she said yes. They left, a kind of happy-go-lucky thing, and went to Florida. After a period of time he finally told her he was married. In the meantime, she said, she had fallen in love with him and was in bad straits because she had no education, no job, no money and she was stuck thousands of miles from home and so she went along with him. He had his family come down and then sent them back. And then they went to Texas together and she said she got close to the family."

On the night in question she said he asked her if she would come and stay with the kids. The kids knew her well. They called her Aunt Pat. And he asked her if she would baby-sit the kids because Jeannine had to go back to Canada because her mother was seriously ill. And she did. Said she got there that night and Jeannine was dressed well, had suitcases packed, and she and Ray were talking. No screaming, no yelling. She didn't know what they were saying because they were speaking French and she doesn't speak French. Then they left. She said she assumed he was taking her to the airport. And he didn't come back that night.

"In the morning the kids got up and she told them about their mom, and sometime that day she took them to her apartment because her apartment building had a pool. And they went swimming and then they went back to his house. He finally showed up later in the afternoon. She said everything was pretty normal. She assumed that Jeannine had gone back to Canada. And she said within a few days they moved to another house not far from there. And it was there, one night, about ten days from the day Jeannine had left, that they were watching the TV news and the police came on the air asking for assistance in identifying this lady whose body had been found. Thrown in a trash dump. And he supposedly says to Pat, 'They found Jeannine.' And she says, 'I thought you told me she was in Canada.' He says, 'She's right there in the dump where I put her.' And then he says something like, 'If you open your mouth, the same will happen to you.' And she says that's the first she knew that he had killed her."

In the videotape of her statement Pat looks calm and co-operative. She said she asked Ray why he killed Jeannine. Pat says he told her, "She had cancer. She was going to die anyway."

It was an electric moment, Nadeau recalls, watching this frightened, elderly woman tell for the first time in her life a secret about a murder. He wondered who she really was and what had shaped her character. Nadeau noticed that she had been very careful not to incriminate herself. She may have been frightened and not very worldly but she had cunning enough to ensure that she herself couldn't be snared by her own admissions.

After the first run-through the three investigators took her back over the story and she expanded on and clarified certain points. She said it was late January of 1968 when Ray called her to come over and that he had called from a pay phone. She said that at the house Jeannine told her in broken English that she was returning to Canada to take care of her sick mother. Pat said after Jeannine's murder they stayed in Houston for part of the year and then had to leave because Ray had written some bad cheques and the authorities were after him. She said Ray was always chasing after other women and that she called him "a road runner." She said seven times she threatened to tell the kids about the murder, and when she did, Ray would say, "Go ahead, if you're tired of living."

Chapter Twenty-Two

Brockville, Ontario, 1950

When Denis and Anne were growing up, they believed that Pat was the personification of evil. All they knew of her was what they had experienced. They judged her on that basis alone. She set a standard by which they measured others. Pat was unadulterated wickedness. No one else—with the single exception, in Denis's mind, of Ray himself—approached that degree of purity of malevolent purpose.

But they knew her as children, and their assessment of the woman who was, for so many years, their stepmother was harsh and uncompromising. Like any parent she had a good deal of control over their lives, and they judged her on the manner in which she exercised that power. Their views of her weren't tempered by an understanding of where she came from, what she had endured as a child or the position Ray had put her in. She never explained herself, never talked about her past and seemed always to be guarding secrets about herself. During the questioning by Nadeau, Talton and Madeira, Pat gave up one of the great secrets of her life. But there were others. All three investigators were curious about her formative experiences and about what kept her in Frenchy's household. However, for the purposes of the investigation, they had what they needed. Her statement linked Frenchy to the murder and they believed it was credible.

"After it was over," Nadeau remembers, "we looked at one another and agreed it made sense. Between us we had sixty or seventy years of experience and we all felt it made sense."

They worried about how she would hold up under defence questioning but they felt that she had told the truth. Indeed, the story did make sense given what they and the children knew about Ray. But her story also raised deeper questions about who she was. Why was she so reluctant to talk about what had happened? What had attracted her to Ray? What had kept her in his house for eighteen years after Jeannine's murder? Why had she been so rough on the kids? What terror or hurt was locked in her heart?

Pat was never able to tell the children, whom she had so often claimed were her own, about her childhood. She refused all requests to be interviewed. But interviews with her far-flung siblings and people who knew her, as well as some patient digging through court files and old newspapers, revealed the outlines of her life story. Nothing about her past in any way excuses her treatment of the four children she became responsible for so suddenly in February, 1968. But her past does help explain something of why she acted the way she did.

Patricia Dorothy Holben was born in October, 1933—the same month and year in which Jeannine Boissonneault was born—in the tiny mining town of Hayley Station about an hour up the valley from Ottawa. She had a brother a year older and three younger sisters. Her father was a British immigrant and her mother was a local girl who had trained as a nurse at the Civic Hospital in Ottawa. When World War II broke out, her father enlisted and went overseas. The family was by then living in Kemptville, a small town south of Ottawa, and life quickly fell apart for them.

Pat's brother, Harold, says after "Dad went away Mom was drinking wine by the case and doing a lot of other things she shouldn't have. I used to go out to Beckett's Landing and work as a caddy. One night it was late and I was hitch-hiking home, stuck out my thumb, a car stopped and it was the social worker from Brockville. Two weeks later we were all in the care of the Children's Aid Society."

The Children's Aid Society in Brockville, on the St Lawrence River directly south of Ottawa, was founded in 1894 by local churches and members of local "well-known families," says Stephen Heder, in a short monograph he wrote on the history of the society. The society provided a shelter for children from broken families as well as for those who had abusive parents. The society arranged for the children to be taken in by foster parents, many of whom were farm couples in the area. Harold remembers the shelter was in a "big white house on a hill," likely a rambling Victorian mansion called Fairknowe, which had been built in 1860 and was used as a home for orphans until the 1930s. The director of the Children's Aid Society when the Holben kids arrived was Claude Winters, a local notable who had been on the board of the society as early as 1917.

Harold remembers all four of his sisters were placed in foster homes soon after their arrival at the shelter. He was separated from them and placed on a farm. Pat and two of her younger sisters spent four years with an elderly couple. The baby of the family, Lily Mae, was placed with another family. Pat was about eight or nine at the time, and she and her two sisters remained with the same family until she was about twelve.

Laura, Pat's sister, who was two or three years old when they arrived at the farm, remembers their foster father "was nice but the old lady was an old crone, a real winner. She whipped us. She used to take us behind the house, strip us naked and use a switch on us. She used a razor strop on Pat once. She'd pinch our ears so hard it would break the skin."

For four years they endured the abuse until someone at the Children's Aid Society discovered how they were being treated and had the girls taken back into the shelter. Pat was almost a teenager by then. At the shelter, Laura remembers the matron "was a real battleaxe. If you didn't eat your breakfast, you ate it at dinner, and if you didn't eat it then, you ate it for supper."

Within short order, Pat's two sisters were placed with new foster families. Meanwhile, the baby, Lily Mae, was moved several times and Harold remained on the same farm. "We all ended up with families except Pat," says Laura.

Harold says his father came to see him once after the war ended and later sent him a new "CCM Ranger bicycle." But he never made an effort to reunite his family. He eventually drifted out to Victoria, British Columbia, married again and had another family.

Laura says she was finally placed with a supportive family with whom she remained until her late teens. Harold ran off at fourteen years old. Several years later he lied about his age and enlisted in the Canadian army. When the Korean War broke out, he shipped out of Tacoma, Washington, with one of the first contingents of Canadian troops thrown into the conflict.

By then Pat was working as a maid and still living in the Children's Aid Society shelter in Brockville. Laura never went to high school and her recollection is that Pat didn't make it to high school either. Her siblings say Pat had the roughest time. Asked about her character, they say she kept to herself, never confided in anyone and, perhaps most significantly, never defended herself, never stood up for herself. "Pat never had courage. She was not the kind to talk about anything. She carried everything on her back instead of letting go," says one of her siblings.

Harold was in Korea only a few months before he was wounded and evacuated to a hospital in Seoul. From there he was shipped to another hospital with American troops and the Canadian government lost track of him. "It was a year before my records and pay caught up with me," in the American troop hospital, he says. In the meantime, back home, he was listed as missing in action. Pat, apparently, took that to mean that he was dead.

By now she was seventeen and working as a maid in a large apartment house owned by Claude Winters, the then elderly director of the Children's Aid Society. At 10:44 A.M. on April 18, 1951, fire broke out in one of the rented flats. When the fire department arrived, the local newspaper reported, the firemen found that the apartment had been "ransacked. A pile of clothes, apparently taken from a dresser drawer, was found burning on a bedroom floor." A mattress had been set aflame in another room. According to a front-page story that afternoon in the paper, *The Recorder and Times,* the police chief was called in to investigate the "peculiar circumstances surrounding the fire." Within a matter of hours Young was able to announce to the press that he had arrested seventeen-year-old Patricia Holben in connection with the fire and had charged her with arson. He said that the girl was being held in the county jail.

The following day Pat appeared in court without a lawyer and was ordered held in custody until her trial on April 23. On the day of her trial she was ushered, "clad in a brown garbadine suit," into a courtroom filled to capacity, *The Recorder and Times* reported. Again she appeared without a lawyer.

She was charged with four counts of arson and immediately pleaded guilty. One of the charges was for the fire in the apartment owned by Winters and the other three counts were for fires she apparently had set in the woodshed at the home of Mr and Mrs Colin Brundige, where she had been employed as a maid. All three fires caused nothing more than minor damage, Mrs Brundige testified, and all three had been set the same day.

According to the police, while in custody Pat gave a statement to them in which she admitted that she had deliberately set the fires.

"She told of noticing Mrs Ross [the renter of the apartment that had been set aflame] leave the apartment and of her decision to enter and set fire to furnishings," the newspaper reported.

"After this act had been accomplished the young girl returned downstairs and considered waxing floors. She said she had taken a key to the Ross apartment from a table drawer containing keys to all apartments in the building. Later the key was replaced in the drawer after other women in the house reported the fire. "Miss Holben, in her statement, said she had set the fires so that she would be able to change her employment. She no longer wanted to work for Mr Winters and thought this was a good way of getting away," the newspaper reported.

Called to the stand, Winters testified that Pat was never held back from seeking other employment. To the contrary, he said, she was encouraged to do so.

The trial judge also heard that Pat had been visited in jail by her mother, Dorothy Mae Holben, who testified that she had learned little from her daughter. The newspaper reported that Pat refused to elaborate on her story, that she reportedly said on several occasions that she had nothing to say. "I am guilty. I set the fires. I have nothing to say" was all she was willing to tell the court.

Two weeks later Pat was sentenced to two years in Kingston's Prison for Women, Canada's only federal women's prison. When she appeared for sentencing, she had, for the first time, a lawyer by her side. He urged that she be released on a suspended sentence. But Magistrate Gordon Jermyn said he couldn't contemplate a suspended sentence.

"It is impossible to get a hint as to why she set fire to these buildings and in her present condition she is a menace," he said before pronouncing the sentence. He added, in a remark that seemed to contradict what he had just said, that the "girl has an idea she is one of the underprivileged of society and her way to change this is to draw attention to herself by setting fire to buildings. She is capable of appreciating what might happen."

And so at the tender age of seventeen, Pat was shipped downriver to the outskirts of Kingston, which sits on the St. Lawrence River halfway between Montreal and Toronto, to serve time in a federal prison with hardened felons from every corner of the country.

The Prison for Women, a pale limestone complex, was built in 1928. It is surrounded by high concrete walls and sits in the shadow of the notorious Gothic fortress, Kingston Penitentiary, which houses some of Canada's most dangerous male convicts. P for W, as the women's penitentiary is known, held about 120 women the year Pat was brought in. She and another woman who was not much older were the only prisoners admitted for arson that year. The other woman, who had been in for arson before, drew a five-year sentence. They served time with murderers, thieves, brawlers and, of all things, a group of Dukhobor women who were in for public nudity. (A splinter group of Russian dissenters from the Orthodox Church, many Dukhobors immigrated to Canada, and a number of them eventually settled in British Columbia. They were pacifists, and in the 1940s and 1950s some of them took to protesting in the nude against provincial government's school policies.)

By the time Harold made it back to Canada, Pat had been released from prison and was in the Brockville area. When he saw Pat, she told him that she had set the fires because "she was angry that I had been killed in Korea. She blamed the Children's Aid Society for the fact that I had run away."

From then until she showed up in Ottawa and found at job at the café next to Campbell Motors, where Ray was working, Pat was involved with a number of men. Harold remembers a Polish man whom she helped to become a legal immigrant and a motorcycle mechanic that he knew.

In 1965 Pat Holben showed up in the Ottawa city directory for the first time. Her occupation is listed as waitress, Ellis Tea Room, and her address is given as Apartment 23, 333 Metcalf. Apartment 24 was occupied by Albert Dudley, described as a technician at the Department of National Defence. The following year, 1966, they are both listed as the occupants of Apartment 22, and Pat is described as Mrs Pat Dudley. Her occupation was switchboard operator, Campbell Motors. It was while working there that she met a fast-talking painter named Ray who always had a roll of cash in his pocket, drove a brand-new, top-of-the-line Buick and talked her into chasing the good life in Florida.

By then she was a chunky woman in her early thirties who frequently changed her hair colour. She told dirty jokes and laughed often and loudly. Men sought her company. She appeared to be independent and content. In fact, she had endured a great deal of abuse and hadn't caught any breaks in her hard life. Why didn't Pat have the wherewithal to walk out on Ray after Houston? Someone who has known Pat for years and doesn't want to be named replied: "Pat's life was never anything more than pain and abuse so why would she have had any expectation that things could be better if she left?"

Chapter Twenty-Three

+—✦✦—+

Houston, Texas, 1992: Part I—The Case

The day after their session with Pat, Talton, Madeira and Nadeau interviewed Marc, then tracked down Martine, who was no longer living with Pat. She still hadn't been told about the discovery of her mother's body, and they were the ones to break the news to her. Again she was the last to know and the least able to cope. She was still drinking heavily and living out of a suitcase. Denis and Anne talked to her afterwards, and she was understandably upset and angry that she hadn't been told.

Neither Marc nor Martine were able to add anything to the investigation. They had been too young when their mother disappeared to remember anything of her or of the circumstances surrounding her disappearance. They did confirm, however, the fact that their father had told them many different stories about Jeannine. And they offered more detail on their father's character and the extent of his criminal activities.

The two Texas investigators flew back to Houston on May 17. Nadeau had told them that Frenchy had surrendered his California driver's licence in South Carolina. They called colleagues there, and a computer check revealed that Frenchy had obtained a state driver's licence on March 14, 1991, and that Gloria had obtained hers on January 15. The home address listed on their licences showed they were living in Myrtle Beach, a coastal resort town surrounded by dozens of golf courses. Many of the tourists who converge on Myrtle Beach every winter are Canadians. Now Talton and Madeira knew where Frenchy was. Since they assumed he still didn't know anything about the investigation, they weren't particularly worried that they wouldn't be able to find him if the Harris County district attorney accepted their evidence and agreed to file charges.

To check out Pat's story the two investigators visited local television stations seeking a copy of the newscast she said she and Frenchy had been watching the night he confessed to her that he had murdered Jeannine. But none of the stations kept video files going that far back.

Talton wrote out a report of their trip to California, and he and Madeira decided it was time to talk to someone in the DA's office about the case. He ended up in the office of Ted Wilson, an assistant district attorney who is chief of the organized crime division in the special crimes bureau.

Tall, thin and bespectacled with greying hair, Wilson is in his late forties and exudes an air of bemused confidence. He favours button-down shirts, silk ties, loafers and cotton twill suits. He was born in Ann Arbor but moved to Texas at age seven. In February, 1968, when Jeannine was murdered, Wilson was in the armed forces at Fort Knox, Kentucky, attending tank school. He made lieutenant and later served in Vietnam. From Vietnam he went straight into law school, worked as a court clerk while still in school and joined the district attorney's office on graduation. When Madeira called him, he had been with the DA's office for eighteen years. He headed a unit that targeted major, repeat offenders and worked at getting them off the streets.

Wilson says he talked to Talton and Madeira, examined what they had and got interested in the case. It looked like a challenge. It was going to be the oldest murder ever tried in Harris County. Wilson agreed that Talton and Madeira should make a trip to Canada, and he suggested a number of questions they should answer while there.

The two investigators had been in frequent contact with Denis and RCMP Staff Sergeant Michel Béland. At Madeira's request, Denis rounded up and sent the investigators photos of the family in Houston. Denis and Michel Béland also attempted to track down, without success, the dentist who had made Jeannine's dentures. They called on Jeannine's reclusive brother, Réginald, to ask if he had, in any of the many boxes stacked in his small apartment, a lock of Jeannine's hair. Apparently Madeira and Talton thought if a hair sample could be obtained and matched, through genetic testing, with the remains of corpse 68-500, it would enable them to prove conclusively that the body was that of Jeannine Boissonneault. But Réginald said he hadn't kept a lock of his sister's hair. When he spoke to Réginald, Denis simply told him that police in Texas were finally investigating Jeannine's disappearance. It wasn't until Madeira phoned and told Denis and Michel Béland that he and his colleague were planning to visit

Ottawa that they decided to break the news to Réginald.

One night shortly before Madeira and Talton's arrival, Denis and Michel made their way to Réginald's apartment, sat down with him and told him that Jeannine's body had been found and that she had been murdered. Once he had absorbed and fully understood that Jeannine was dead, the first thing he asked was: "And where is Raymond Durand?"

After the death of his parents, Réginald had moved into an apartment by himself. His life hadn't changed much over the years. Since he was now obliged to do his own shopping, he got out a little more. But the only person he saw with any regularity was his aunt Berthe, his mother's sister who had left her religious order and was now living a couple of blocks from Réginald's apartment. Réginald had put on weight and was balding. He was still a passionate fan of baseball, played his collection of classical music records and enjoyed his own company. Denis and Michel warned him that two investigators from Texas were coming to Hull and that they might want to talk to him. He was nervous and insisted they come to his apartment. He assumed that he would talk to them and he'd never see them again. It never occurred to him that he might actually be asked to travel to Houston and testify at a murder trial. After all, he hadn't left his neighbourhood in his entire adult life; he hadn't crossed the Ottawa River since his childhood, and the only real trip he had ever taken was a half-hour train ride north of Hull to see a waterfall. He inhabited a tiny but familiar world and made every effort to minimize his contact with other people. He couldn't imagine anyone imposing on him, obliging him to step completely outside his little universe.

When they were planning their trip, Talton and Madeira assumed they'd just fly to Ottawa, conduct their interviews and return to Houston a day later. It was Michel Béland who told them they'd be entering a foreign country and should therefore follow established procedure. So they contacted Interpol, the international police organization, which in turn put them in touch with Lieutenant François Cloutier of the Gatineau police. He was assigned to help with translations and assist them in assembling the evidence they hoped to gather. Michel received permission from his superiors to assist them as well. So, on Monday, June 3, when Talton and Madeira flew in to Ottawa, both Cloutier and

Béland were there to meet them.

That evening Talton and Madeira interviewed Robert and
Claudette Durand, Raymond's uncle and aunt, and statements were
taken from them separately. Robert told of flying to Fort
Lauderdale for the christening of Martine and of Raymond splitting
his time between Pat's place and the house he had rented for
Jeannine and the kids. He described how Ray had cut short their
visit, telling them he had to leave and putting them on a plane for
Ottawa.

He described how Ray had talked him into moving to San Diego
several years later and how he cheated him out of his money and
made off with his car and credit cards. He said that Ray told him
that Jeannine was in a mental hospital. And he described the conversation about bodies he had had with Ray. He said Ray, who
knew he had worked as an embalmer, asked him how long it would
take for a body to decompose, and how a body could be identified.
Asked if he was willing to testify in court, Robert reluctantly
agreed that he would if necessary. He was about to submit to major
heart surgery and wasn't keen to endure the strain of being cross-
examined. However, everyone assured him that he wouldn't be on
the stand long.

The following morning the four cops worked together ferreting
out other information Wilson had requested. The Texans asked
Cloutier to search Gatineau police records to determine whether
Raymond Durand had ever filed a missing persons report on
Jeannine. He hadn't. Cloutier then introduced them to Lieutenant
Roch Menard of the Hull police, and he conducted a similar search
of Hull police records. Again, there was no sign that Ray had ever
reported Jeannine missing.

The two Texas policemen were also given a grand tour of the
region. Michel showed them where Jeannine and Ray had been
born and raised and other places the family had lived.

The night of Madeira and Talton's arrival, Denis called Réginald
and told him the investigators wanted to speak to him the following
day. Réginald said he couldn't meet them because he had an
appointment at a government office to renew the paperwork for the
subsidy he receives for his apartment. Denis said he'd drive him
down to the office and they would be back in plenty of time for the
1 P.M. interview. Réginald refused to meet with the investigators at

the Hull police station. So, after discussing it with Talton and Madeira, they arranged to interview Réginald at his apartment.

Before Denis arrived the next morning to pick up Réginald he remembered something his great-aunt Berthe had recently told him. She said that when Jeannine and Réginald's father, Hermas, died he left money for Jeannine in his will. The money was from a life insurance policy and he had split it among his wife, Réginald and Jeannine. He had gone to his grave hoping that Jeannine was alive and thinking that she'd need the money one day. So when Denis and Réginald got into his car, Denis asked Réginald if he knew about the money. "Sure," Réginald said, pulling out his worn, bulging wallet, which was bound with an elastic band, and extracting from it a bank-book. The bank-book was for an account in Jeannine's name and it held about five thousand dollars. Réginald told Denis that he didn't know what to do with the money and so he had just ignored calls over the years from the bank asking for instructions. With Réginald's assistance, Denis and his siblings eventually got access to the money, and Denis proposed that they use it to have Jeannine's remains shipped to Hull for reburial.

When Denis pulled up at the government office, Réginald turned to him and said, "This will take five to eight minutes." Denis looked at him quizzically, but, sure enough, exactly five minutes later Réginald was out, his business completed. He had timed it in previous years, Denis thought, struck once again by his uncle's eccentric character.

That afternoon, with Cloutier translating, Madeira and Talton questioned Réginald in his crowded apartment about the period surrounding Jeannine's disappearance. They discovered that he had a nimble mind and that he could often understand their questions before they had been translated. He clearly understood a fair bit of English but didn't speak it.

Réginald told the investigators about the six calls Jeannine had made to her family in 1967 between Christmas and New Year's Day. He said they had never heard from her again and that his mother hadn't been ill in January or February of 1968. He said between February, 1968, and the end of 1970, Raymond Durand had called them every few months to say they were all doing fine and that Jeannine couldn't come to the phone because she was out. The family was suspicious and worried but had no means of contacting

Jeannine. Then, he said, in early 1971 Raymond had driven up to their house one day. A surprised Hermas had invited him in for a visit. Inside, Raymond had told them that Jeannine and the children were in Vancouver and he gave them a phone number and an address for her. He assured them they were all doing well and, after a short visit, he left. Réginald said when his mother returned and learned what had happened, she was furious. She assumed that Raymond had waited until she was out of the house to visit because he didn't want to submit to her questioning. Nonetheless, Réginald said, his mother called the Vancouver number and discovered it was out of service. Then, he said, she wrote to Jeannine at the Vancouver address. Nine letters she wrote, he said, and all nine came back unopened.

That night the four cops and Denis had dinner together and Talton told Denis that they had obtained what they needed from Réginald. The assumption was that Réginald would testify at the trial. But Denis and Michel Béland weren't so sure. They knew that it would take a superhuman effort on Réginald's part to make the journey. They knew he was obstinate and that it would take some persuading to convince him that his testimony was essential. They figured the only thing they had going for them was the fact that Réginald was angry about what had happened to Jeannine. Livid, in fact.

When Talton and Madeira returned to Houston, they met with Wilson and the three men reviewed the case. Wilson says that at the time he knew about Réginald, whom they all took to calling Reggy, and that he considered his testimony vital. But, he says, "I didn't know what Reggy was." Wilson says that the evidence Madeira and Talton had assembled convinced him "that we had sufficient material to present to a grand jury." They decided that Madeira and Talton would fly to Myrtle Beach, and, at the same time, Wilson would present the case to the grand jury and ask for a sealed indictment. The sealed indictment would ensure the press wouldn't know about the story before the arrest could be made.

On June 27, Wilson presented the case to the grand jury, obtained the indictment for a charge of murder with malice afore-thought and immediately faxed it to Talton and Madeira. Accompanied by a local officer as well as an officer with the South Carolina State Police, the two Texans piled into a patrol car and drove across town to Frenchy's Foreign and Domestic Auto Repair, Ray's latest business venture.

"We rolled up," Talton recalls, "and Robert and I were both wearing black western-cut suits with black ties and white hats. We had saved them just for that, for the effect. He [Frenchy] was in shorts and a blue golf shirt wrenching on an old Mercedes. We figured the only possible alibi he could have had was that they'd had a fight and she packed and he dropped her off at the airport. I wanted to see what he would say. I used her [Jeannine's] maiden name, said we were investigating her disappearance. Wanted to talk to him. He said, 'Yeah. OK.' Read him his Miranda rights. We sat down. He said, 'We used to be married, had kids.' He was like a Dobermann who, even when he's lying down curled up, you know has twenty thousand things running through his head. He was calm on the outside but you could tell the wheels were clicking. He said, 'She just got up and left one day. Last I heard, she was living in Canada with her mother.'

"That took the wind out of our sails, when he didn't cop to the story about the suitcases. Then we showed him morgue photos of Jeannine. He said, 'What's this?' We said, 'That's Jeannine. Found in a field.' He said, 'What's this got to do with me?' At that point we arrested him, cuffed him and took him to Myrtle Beach police department.

"At the station I said to Ray, 'Hey, look, you get into court and the only thing the prosecutor is concerned about is getting a conviction and the only thing the defence is concerned about is avoiding a conviction. Nobody is going to give a rat's ass about the truth. Your contention is that she just left. We can disprove that. Do you want to start over and just tell us what happened.' He looked us right in the eye and said, 'I want to talk to my attorney.' And that was that.

"Gloria came down. I feel sorry for her. She was a blithering wreck. She wanted to believe it was all the fault of his dirty, rotten kids."

Later, at a press conference in Houston, Harris County sheriff Johnny Klevenhagen told reporters that, when arrested, Durand also said, "This case is twenty-three years old. If you think you can make it stick, go ahead and try. You'll never convict me."

Frenchy spent the night in jail in Myrtle Beach and the next morning he boarded a commercial flight to Houston with Madeira sitting next to him and Talton behind.

"Ray didn't say a word on the plane. I even let Robert sit next to him on the off chance that he'd say something to Robert, who is closer to his age. He didn't say anything."

Talton had left a car at the airport in Houston and they retrieved it and drove to the county jail, on the edge of the downtown area. As they approached the jail they saw the press was swarming around the entrance. Evidently, Sheriff Klevenhagen had let the media know about the case and Frenchy's arrest. Wilson says the two investigators called him from their car and told him about the press mob. He suggested they meet him at the Harris County courthouse on San Jacinto Street. Wilson called a judge, arranged for a hearing and had Frenchy in the courtroom before the press found out.

"Frenchy comes into court," Wilson recalls. "He's handcuffed and he's got this look on, like, this is bullshit. He doesn't have a marked sense of concern. The judge had asked me before the hearing what the penalty range was, back then [1968], for murder with malice aforethought. I said, 'Two years to life, or death.' Frenchy comes in and the judge tells him the penalty range is life or death and Frenchy's jaw dropped."

(Although the penalty in Texas in 1968 for murder with malice aforethought did include the death sentence, a U.S. Supreme Court ruling in the 1970s overturned the penalty provisions of the law. That meant Frenchy could not have been given a death sentence.)

After the brief hearing, Frenchy was ordered held in custody.

That night the local TV newscasts ran stories on Frenchy, and Klevenhagen was interviewed on all of them. He praised the investigators and said that the arrest showed "that we do not close any murder case." There were shots of Frenchy in handcuffs being led into the county jail. He looked grim.

In San Jacinto, Frenchy's arrest only heightened Anne's anxiety about the trial. She felt sorry for her father and wondered how he was faring on his first night in jail. She also worked herself into a nervous state worrying about how she would be able to testify.

In Hull, as soon as Madeira phoned and advised him of Frenchy's arrest, Denis got on the phone to Frenchy's eight brothers and two sisters. He told them he needed to meet with them the following day, that he had some important news to pass on.

Arrangements were made for the family to gather at the home of Frenchy's brother Gerry, who had changed his name from Albert. Most of them showed up. Denis arrived carrying a large, flat cardboard box under his arm. They gathered in one room, Denis stood up and slowly pulled from its box the oil painting he had commissioned of his mother.

"I want to talk about her," he said. "Jeannine. My mother. You all know that I have been looking for her most of my life. She's been found. She was murdered. In 1968. And yesterday your brother, my father, was arrested in South Carolina for her murder."

It wasn't what they were expecting to hear and they were clearly shocked. Many of them hadn't seen Ray in years. The gathering didn't last long; everybody, including Denis, left soon after.

Frenchy spent the night in the overcrowded jail, sleeping on the floor. He went about barefoot because there weren't enough thongs for all the inmates. He suffered, he said later, and was desperate to get out. On the charge sheet made out when he was booked into the jail, Frenchy reported that he was fifty-four years old, weighed 180 pounds and stood five feet, eight inches tall. He gave his income as five hundred dollars a week and said he was the assistant manager at Frenchy's. He said his supervisor was his wife, Gloria. He said he had completed grade six and had neither an alcohol nor a drug problem. He said he had $104 on hand, no money in his chequing account and no money in his saving account and that his car was a 1984 Honda. He appeared to be close to broke, but within days he had engaged one of Houston's best-known criminal lawyers, Jack Zimmermann. And shortly after he was released on a thirty-five-thousand-dollar bond.

When Nadeau heard that Frenchy had made bail, he was dismayed. He believed that Frenchy was a "flight risk" and that there was a good chance he would not show up for his trial, which had been set for the spring of 1992. So he began probing deeper into Frenchy's past in California. If he could gather evidence of crimes Frenchy had committed in California, he could have him arrested and extradited to California, where he would likely be kept in custody. He decided to focus on the cars that many people had told him Frenchy had buried behind his shop. Martine showed him where she believed he had buried a Cadillac that was in "cherry condition." He consulted auto theft experts, obtained a search warrant, hired a caterpillar and descended on the ranch one morning to excavate Frenchy's burial grounds. With him were several auto theft experts from the state police and insurance agencies.

A video made of the dig shows that it went on all through the day. In all, they uncovered the flattened, dirt-clogged remains of an estimated thirty-five cars, including the Eldorado Cadillac and a Mercedes, as well as several barrels oozing chemical wastes. Nadeau said he was told that the barrels contained wastes from the body shop.

Nadeau ran a check on the plates recovered from the Mercedes and discovered the registered owner was an elderly lady who lived in southern California. He talked to her and she said she had sold it to her former hairdresser, an Iranian immigrant who had developed a drug habit, lost his business and had apparently died of an overdose. How Frenchy came to be in possession of the car and why he had buried it remained a mystery. Checks on other vehicles and parts found in the dig didn't turn up much more. The Cadillac, for example, had never been reported stolen. Why had it been buried? Nadeau figured it was some sort of insurance scam but it soon became apparent that uncovering the scam wasn't going to be an easy task. It would take a good deal of time and more resources than he had available. The auto insurance company investigators were interested but said that the cost of conducting the investigation wasn't worth it. So eventually Nadeau let it go. The Texans seemed confident that they were going to be able to convict Frenchy and that he would show up for his trial. Why, they asked, would Frenchy have bothered to hire such a crackerjack lawyer, who had a private investigator digging up material for the defence, if he was planning on fleeing?

After he was sprung on bail, Frenchy returned to Gloria in Myrtle Beach. Whatever he had told her about his past, she was standing by him. According to two of Frenchy's brothers, the murder charge deeply depressed him. The story they tell—and one of them visited him in Myrtle Beach—is that shortly after his return Frenchy locked himself in his shop, papered over the windows and refused to come out. One account has it that in a rage he smashed equipment and flung tools around the shop. Another account has Frenchy simply wandering around in the twilight inside the cinder-block building. It was Gloria, apparently, who came up with a way to pull him out of it. She found a Christian preacher who visited Frenchy with her. After several days, the three of them emerged together. Later, Gloria confided that she and Frenchy had found God, that they had been born again.

With his new-found faith, Frenchy settled in to assisting his attorneys—Jack Zimmermann and his partner, Jim Lavine—prepare his defence. One of the first things he did was travel to California with Gene Boyd, the private investigator Zimmermann had engaged. Among the people they wanted to talk to, no one was perhaps as important to them as Frenchy's youngest child, Martine. Frenchy was going to have two of his children testify against him. At least one for the defence would have been helpful.

Martine says her father contacted her in August and asked her to meet with him at his old shop, Frenchy's. Months before his arrest he had called her from Myrtle Beach: "Scott and I were sitting around watching TV in our trailer and he called and said he had moved to South Carolina and that he planned to come down and give me the ranch. He said to meet him on the weekend, Saturday, and pick up the key and all that. So we went up there and, needless to say, he wasn't there. I was real fucking pissed. Because he had explained it to me that I was the only one who liked the place up there. I lived there the longest, I enjoyed it. He had [a new] shop already built—the big one—with a lift and a compressor. I could start my own business, my own body shop. I thought it was great."

When Frenchy called again in August and said he was in California, Martine knew he had been charged and was out on bail. She met him at his old shop. "Dad came in and said, 'I didn't do it,'" she recalls.

They chatted briefly. Again, he told her he was going to give her the ranch. He made arrangements to meet her the following day, and, she says, "he explained that I'd have to pay the property tax and all that."

Then Frenchy left Martine alone with the private investigator Gene Boyd. They talked for about an hour, she says, and at the end Boyd asked her if she thought Frenchy had killed Jeannine.

"I said, 'Yeah.' So shortly after that the interview ended."

The following day, Martine showed up for the meeting her father had arranged with her and discovered he had left town. "I thought, 'You are a total dweeb.'"

After she learned of her mother's fate, Martine, like the other children, was haunted for the longest time by visions of how the murder had occurred. "The way I see it happening is a big fight," she says of her attempts to reconstruct the events in her imagination. "I see a baseball bat. I see a side of a road in a dump area and him driving up in his car, getting out, him getting her out, forcing her down to the dump site and beating her. Till she died."

But why? What puzzled and continues to puzzle Talton, Madeira, Wilson, Nadeau, Denis and Anne was why he had to kill Jeannine. Why not just send her back to Canada? Asked the same question, Martine had a ready answer, an answer that hung on something in Frenchy's character that his own daughter had seen and lived with: "Dad has to have it all. He could have had an affair with Pat. But he wanted the kids and Pat. He wanted it all."

Call it Frenchy's greed. If Martine's intuition is right, then Frenchy killed Jeannine for no other reason than that it was the most convenient thing to do. No mess about divorce, no fuss about having to fly her back to Canada, no worries about Jeannine revealing his whereabouts to his enemies or to people to whom he owed money back home.

Martine again: "He's a really evil, evil man, and he will do anything that he can to better himself. He's done it. Not only is he evil and conniving, but he's intelligent."

Frenchy and Boyd, this time in the company of Zimmermann, also travelled to Canada. They spoke to his brothers and sisters, attempted to obtain a copy of Jeannine's driver's licence, interviewed Robert Durand and also attempted to talk to Denis. Zimmermann and Boyd showed up on Denis's doorstep, denied that Frenchy had accompanied them to Canada, and asked if he would speak to them. Denis refused, saying that he would be available for questioning in court. Just as Zimmermann was leaving, Denis offered the lawyer a piece of advice: "Make sure you get paid in advance for your work."

A couple of days later, a distant relative called Denis, breathless, with the news that he had seen Raymond in Ottawa's Byward Market. Denis grabbed a video camera, jumped into his car and sped off to the market, in downtown Ottawa. He cruised the streets and within minutes spotted his father. He parked, aimed the camera and captured on videotape his father, now an accused murderer out on bail, meandering down the street. Frenchy saw Denis and walked towards the car.

"What's this for?" he asked Denis.

"See you in court," Denis answered before driving off.

If Denis was feeling particularly bloody-minded that day he had good reason. He had finally managed to have his mother's remains disinterred, cremated and shipped to Canada. He had placed a death notice in the local newspaper and arranged for a proper funeral, which was held a week before Zimmermann's visit.

Anne and Phil flew up for the funeral along with Jean Nadeau and his wife. Denis and his in-laws were there, as were Réginald and Michel Béland and his family. Several of Ray's siblings showed up. So did a few old school friends of Jeannine's. After the church service the mourners went to the Notre Dame Cemetery in Hull. Denis had arranged for Jeannine's remains to be buried next to her parents.

Anne's husband, Phil, remembers the day was misty and grey. But as the priest was saying a last prayer over the grave, Anne remembers the sky suddenly opened up. She felt a lot of turmoil standing there at the gravesite. She had thought often about what had happened and had come to the conclusion that her mother had been prodding her all along. "This may sound weird but I felt my mom was pushing me to find out. Because I had never wanted to know. I didn't want to be the one to find out. When Denis was telling me stuff, I didn't want to hear. That's why I never wanted to do anything."

While Anne was grappling with her feelings, a childhood friend of Jeannine's stepped forward and placed a yellow rose on the urn in which Jeannine's ashes had been placed. Anne said the sun came out then, and standing there in the sunshine with Phil, she felt she had been blessed.

Two days later she learned that she was pregnant, that she had been pregnant while she was at the gravesite. After all the medical difficulties she had had, after doubting that she would ever be able to have a baby, it felt to her that her mother had once again intervened in her life. Now she felt confident that she would bring this baby to term, that she would and could do it, that her mother's memory had been honoured and that she could now make her own life, have her own family, be a mother herself.

Chapter Twenty-Four

Houston, Texas, 1992: Part 2—The Witnesses

The trial, for Michel Béland and Denis, actually began in Hull. They had shouldered responsibility for getting Réginald Boissonneault to Houston and for getting him to testify. That proved to be every bit as difficult and delicate a task as they had always assumed it would be. As Wilson mapped out how he would present the case to the jury, it became clear to him, and then to Denis and Michel, that Réginald's testimony would be vital. He was the only living member of Jeannine's family, the only person who could give evidence about Raymond Durand's brazen and duplicitous attempts to keep Jeannine's family off balance by maintaining the fiction that they were still together. But how to get Réginald from Hull to Houston and then up on the stand? Here was a man who considered a trip to the corner grocery store an epic journey and who, in his whole life, had never before conversed with a room full of people. Réginald is so socially maladroit that people sometimes mistakenly believe he's a dim bulb. In fact, he is anything but.

When Denis and Michel broke the news to Réginald that he was needed in Houston, he was incredulous. "No, no," he had replied, "if they need me they can come up here." He had seen it often enough on television. A witness would be dying and the court would assemble around his bed and testimony would be taken. They would have to do that in his case, he told Denis and Michel. He was too sick to go. Michel patiently explained to Réginald that that only happened in exceptional circumstances, that the court officers and jury weren't going to fly to Ottawa, take a bus across the river and gather in his, Réginald's, apartment so that he could answer a few questions. He would have to go. There was no alternative. Réginald had the greatest respect for Michel, whom he remembered as a little boy visiting him in his room to talk baseball. Now, Réginald knew, he was a staff sergeant in the RCMP and had been with the force all of his working life. Michel knew what he was talking about. If he said the court wouldn't come to Hull, then he had to believe Michel. But Réginald wasn't willing to throw in the towel yet.

Réginald's second line of defence was that he couldn't fly. So Denis and Michel said, "Fine. We'll drive." Again Réginald balked. He couldn't get in a car and sit there for a two- or three-day drive. Absolutely couldn't do it. No car.

So then someone came up with the idea of taking the train. "We'll all take the train together," they told Réginald, who by now had begun to appreciate that these guys were serious, that no amount of dodging or equivocation was going to make them give up. And so he gave in, agreed to take a three-day train trip to Houston. Now they weren't sure. Had Réginald said yes to get them off his back? Would he change his mind at the last minute? And, equally important, what would happen if and when they got him down there? Would he actually be able to get up on the stand and not choke on his own words?

In the months leading up to the trial, Denis and Michel lived on pins and needles. They took to dropping in on Réginald to see how he was doing. They phoned each other to compare notes and reassure themselves that they were going to be able to pull this off. In the process, they got to know each other and to know Réginald himself. They reawakened the bonds of family and altered their views of this now-elderly man who had locked himself away from the world.

Originally the trial had been set for spring. As the date approached, Michel told Denis that they should show Réginald the morgue photos of Jeannine before their departure. He was going to have to look at them in court anyway, and it would be better for everyone involved if Réginald saw them now. Nobody wanted a surprise in court.

One night in early spring they arrived at Réginald's apartment together, sat down with him, and Michel produced the grisly morgue photos of Jeannine's face. There were also a couple of shots taken by a medical examiner's investigator of the site where the body had been found. When Michel had received them in the mail, he had looked at them and been able to conclude without a doubt in his mind that they were photos of his cousin. They weren't easy pictures to look at. The person in the coloured photos was not just dead but ravaged. Part of one cheek had been eaten away by animals. The skin was grey and bloated; the wound at the top of the skull was shockingly long and wide. In one of the pictures, part of the skin on the scalp had been peeled back.

Michel didn't know what to expect when he showed them to Réginald. But Réginald simply looked at them carefully and said, "Yes, it is Jeannine." He didn't show much emotion but then he never had shown emotion about anything. They knew, though, that he was still deeply angry about Jeannine's murder. He told them often that Raymond Durand—he always called his former brother-in-law by his full name—would have to be punished for what he had done.

Denis, too, saw the pictures for the first time and surprised himself by actually being able to look at them without fainting. It wasn't the way he wanted to remember his mother and he hadn't wanted to ever look at the pictures. But curiosity and the fact that he would be shown them in court prompted him to change his mind. The photos were a shock, and they haunted him, as he feared they would. And they tightened the cinch on his anger, made his rage just a little bit more visible.

As spring approached, Anne bloomed in pregnancy. Her condition was monitored closely. She realized her baby was going to be born very near the trial date. She called Wilson and advised him. At the same time, Robert Durand was admitted to hospital for his long-awaited heart surgery. With one witness about to give birth and another about to undergo a heart bypass, Wilson felt he had no choice but to ask for a delay. He applied to the court for a new trial date and Frenchy's trial was rescheduled to August 17, 1992.

Wilson wanted all his witnesses in Houston several days before the trial so he could meet them, brief them about what to expect and go over their testimony. Michel, Denis and Réginald agreed they would leave on August 10. They'd take the bus from Ottawa to Montreal, board the train there, travel south to Philadelphia, east to Chicago and then south all the way to Houston. The trip would take a total of four days.

The morning they left, Denis, wearing jeans, a sports shirt and his dark sunglasses, stuffed his suitcase, a leather bag and a carrying case for his cowboy boots in the trunk of my car. I had offered to drive him and Réginald to the bus station.

I had, by chance, happened to be in Houston when Frenchy was charged. I had seen him on the evening news and wondered what evidence would be presented to convict a man on a twenty-three-year-old murder. Then, in the morning paper, I learned that Frenchy was a native of Hull, which is next door to my home in Ottawa. I made a number of calls, talked to the Houston *Chronicle*'s court reporter, John Makeig, and decided to pursue the story for a magazine. On my return to Ottawa I contacted Michel Béland who, in turn, led me to Denis.

Denis had been avoiding reporters, and when we met, he refused to discuss the details of the case until after the trial. But when I said I wanted to begin by retracing his father's history, he told me that his father had been a businessman in Pointe Gatineau and that he had a large family in Hull. Throughout the winter of 1991/92 I dug through archives and court files, interviewed former cops and a judge, found Ray's old pals and gradually pulled together the narrative of Ray's early life. My research intrigued Denis, who didn't know much about his father's early business activities, and we began to meet regularly to discuss what I had learned. He came to trust me and offered tidbits of information that helped fill in some gaps. By the time the trial was about to get under way, I had done eight months of research and knew a great deal about Raymond Durand and had drawn my own conclusions about whether he was guilty or not. Denis had agreed to speak with me about his evidence after the trial and I began planning to write a book.

After Denis had loaded his luggage into the car, we drove over to Réginald's and found him tossing a bag of garbage into the dumpster in the parking lot in front of his apartment. He was trying to appear calm and was all dressed for the trip. He had on a new pair of sneakers, navy-blue polyester trousers and a cream polyester shirt. His trousers were held up by suspenders whose frayed fastenings were secured with string. For extra support, he wore a leather belt. On his head he had a blue, canvas hat. He is missing several front teeth and probably tipped the scales at two hundred pounds. He stowed in the trunk a thin, nylon suit bag, a black leather satchel and a plastic bag containing an extra pair of shoes. On his wrist he wore a watch and two elastic bands. The elastic bands were a bit of a mystery but neither Denis nor I could bring ourselves to ask about them.

We crossed the river, something Réginald hadn't done in forty years, and minutes later, pulled into the bus station parking lot. It was clear from the way Réginald looked around that he had never been there before.

Michel Béland, also in jeans, sneakers and a sports shirt, arrived fifteen minutes later. He had been so certain that Réginald was going to skip out that he had told his colleagues that he would be back in the afternoon.

I bought Réginald a French-language newspaper and he was exceedingly grateful. I suggested we could attend an Astros game in Houston. His eyes lit up but he didn't say anything.

I saw them off on the bus at noon. Over the next four days Réginald fussed and fretted. He later called the trip a "*voyage de tristesse*," (a journey of sadness), and said he was too preoccupied with the trial to read or to do anything other than think about the events surrounding his sister's murder.

In Houston they were booked into a small motel near the airport. They were soon joined at the motel by Robert Durand, who had flown in with Lieutenant François Cloutier of Gatineau police and Lieutenant Roch Menard of Hull police. Anne, her robust new baby, Justin, her sister-in-law, Nancy, and Jean Nadeau arrived from California. All of them except Réginald dined together and relaxed around the pool. Réginald spent almost all his time in his room. Anne showed him her baby and actually managed to get him to hold his nephew.

They all met Ted Wilson and his boss, Bill Taylor, who was to assist Wilson in prosecuting the case. Taylor, a compact, intense and intimidatingly aggressive man in his fifties, had also been in the service but had been spared the experience of Vietnam by former president Richard Nixon's decision to steadily reduce the size of the American forces engaged in the war. Taylor is a native of Texas. He spent a year in private practice after law school before joining the district attorney's office. He now heads the special crimes unit and supervises the work of twenty-five lawyers and fifteen investigators. While Wilson seemed laconic and easy-going, Taylor struck the witnesses as jumpy and cutting. No one doubted Wilson's or Taylor's competence or experience. They both held senior positions within the huge district attorney's office, which has well over a hundred assistant district attorneys on staff.

By that Sunday, August 16, everyone was in town, had been

briefed and had visited the district attorney's office on Fannin
Street in downtown Houston. The trial was to begin the following
day but Wilson told them that the first day would probably be taken
up with jury selection. He warned them not to discuss their testimony with each other after they had appeared and to be ready for
Frenchy's lawyer, who was a skilled attorney.

There are twenty-two state district courts in Harris County that
handle felonies, and on the day Frenchy's trial began there were a
half-dozen other murder trials under way. A couple of weeks
before, two death sentences had been handed down on the same
day. In 1968 there had been 305 homicides committed in Harris
county; by 1991 the annual homicide rate was running at between
700 and 800 a year.

The district attorney's office is a fearfully busy place. In 1968,
the office filed 252 murder cases. By 1991 the workload had
increased along with the murder rate and the DA's office prosecuted
378 murder cases and 60 capital murder cases. Texas law now
makes a distinction between murder, which includes premeditated
murder, and capital murder, which is murder committed in the
course of undertaking another felony. Kill a guy while robbing a
gas station and that's capital murder, for which the maximum sentence is death. Plan the killing of your wife and that's just murder,
punishable by a maximum of a life sentence. If you kill your wife,
however, in order to collect on an insurance policy, and the state
can prove that, then the charge would be capital murder, the
penalty death.

Raymond "Frenchy" Durand was tried in district court 248 on the
fifth-floor courtroom of the Harris County Criminal Courts building
on San Jacinto Street in downtown Houston. A well-worn, seven-
storey stone building, it sits kitty-corner from the DA's office, a
block from one of the county jails and on the edge of a district
where winos sleep in doorways, whole blocks are boarded up, and
homeless men sit hunched in weed-infested lots. At the main doors
to the courthouse, a constantly smiling, blond-haired man in his forties stands and courteously opens the door for all visitors. He's been
there for several years, voluntarily manning the doors seven days a
week. He isn't paid for the work and is the subject of much speculation and curiosity. Inside, everyone entering the courthouse is

obliged by a team of bored security guards to empty their pockets and march through a metal detector. Throughout the day gangs of up to ten accused, chained together and wearing thongs and county jail coveralls, are marched down the street from a nearby jail. They are led into the courthouse and lodged in holding cells at the back of the courtrooms on each floor. One day during the Durand trial, a man who had just been sentenced to fifty years in jail somehow managed to free himself from the chains that linked him to a group of other prisoners, sprinted down a stairwell and escaped.

On the fifth floor, to the right of the elevators with green doors, is a marble-faced wall with FREEDOM, TOLERANCE AND JUSTICE UNDER LAW written on it in polished silver lettering. To the left is the courtroom presided over by Judge Woody Densen, a broad-faced man with a deep voice, thick black eyebrows and a receding hairline.

Densen was to be Durand's trial judge. His court contains five rows of benches, each of which sits ten comfortably, twelve chairs on a platform a step above the courtroom floor, a computer screen and telephone for the court orderly, a clerk's desk right next to the judge's bench and a couple of tables for the prosecutors and defence attorneys. Every morning before the Durand trial began, Densen would spend a half-hour or so dealing with other cases before his court.

Frenchy arrived for his trial wearing a charcoal-grey suit, silk tie, white shirt and black patent-leather shoes. His grey/white hair was carefully coiffed, his beard trimmed and he was deeply tanned. He could have been called handsome except for his jutting lower jaw and a tendency to sit with his mouth open. He appeared unable to breathe through his cocaine-ravaged nose. He looked tense but in control. He was accompanied by Gloria, who looked glamorous in a tan suit and paisley silk blouse. Her hair was coal black, her eyes deep blue. Leading the way for Frenchy were his attorneys, Jack Zimmermann and Jim Lavine, both of whom were in dark suits and cowboy boots. Zimmermann was wearing his trademark white stetson.

Zimmermann is a decorated, former U.S. Marine Corps officer who served two tours of duty in Vietnam and remains a colonel in the Marine Corps reserve. He grew up in San Antonio, graduated from the U.S. Naval Academy in 1964 and spent fourteen years on active duty with the Marines. He attended law school on the GI Bill and later worked as a lawyer for the Marines and was appointed a military judge in 1978.

Several years later he joined the Houston law firm of Racehorse Haynes, a legendary local criminal lawyer. By the time Zimmermann was hired by Durand, he had moved on and formed his own firm with Lavine.

Zimmermann has close-cropped hair, big ears, a small, pursed mouth, a high, phlegmy voice and wears large, square spectacles. He seems charged with a nervous energy that keeps him twisting his Naval Academy ring or plucking at his lower lip.

His partner, Jim Lavine, is from Ohio. He worked as an assistant state's attorney in Illinois from 1975 to 1980, then as an assistant district attorney in Harris County from 1980 to 1985. He and Zimmermann met while working the opposite sides of a case and have been practising together since 1985. Lavine is calmer than Zimmermann and often has a look of wry scepticism on his face. He comes across as a thinker. He's dark-haired and medium-sized. His hair is black and blow-dried and he's got a winning smile.

When Zimmermann arrived, he was evidently pleased to see that there was press interest in the case. Asked by a photographer engaged by the French-language Ottawa/Hull paper *Le Droit* to pose for a shot, Zimmermann obliged like a pro. Lining up with Lavine, he asked whether he should be walking or talking as the photographer took his shots. It was clear that he understood that newspapers prefer action as opposed to still, grip-and-grin shots. Zimmermann also agreed to get Frenchy and Gloria out of the courtroom and stage a shot of them all coming out of the elevator together. Frenchy didn't look pleased but went through the motions of striding towards the courtroom from the elevator while the photographer walked backwards, his camera's motor drive whirring.

Densen got the trial under way at 1:30 that afternoon. Gloria sat in a front row bench with members of Zimmermann's staff, Frenchy sat between his two lawyers facing the jury box and Wilson and Taylor set up across from them, facing the judge. Wilson looked casual. In a navy-blue blazer, blue Oxford shirt, burgundy silk tie, pressed tan cotton trousers and loafers. Taylor appeared more formal. He wore loafers and a dark-blue suit that he never unbuttoned.

Zimmermann immediately went on the attack. He moved to deny the introduction of the photo identification of the body, arguing that Wingo had sent only one set of pictures to Michel Béland and had asked him to say whether or not it was Jeannine. He argued that by failing to send Béland a group of pictures of different decomposing bodies and asking him to choose which, if any, was Jeannine, Wingo had prejudiced the identification. Densen denied the motion. Zimmermann then asked the court to instruct the prosecutors to caution their witnesses not to engage in "theatrical outbursts, speculation, conjecture, fabrication and injection of inadmissible and untrue testimony." Zimmermann said the case was highly emotional and hotly contested and he urged the judge to prohibit "emotional outbursts" and any references to the "alleged funeral of Jeannine Durand." Densen looked faintly amused and told Zimmermann that he couldn't prevent someone from being emotional.

The reference to the "alleged funeral of Jeannine Durand" suggested the outlines of Zimmermann's defence. It appeared that he was going to contest the identification of the body. The prosecutors and the witnesses had wondered how Zimmermann planned to explain all Frenchy's stories and the various bits of circumstantial evidence. They couldn't imagine Zimmermann putting Frenchy on the stand. That would expose him to questioning about his past. So, they wondered, how would the defence attorney construct a response to the charge? Zimmermann's motion offered a peek at the answer. He was going to deny that 68-500 was the body of Jeannine Durand.

Then Zimmermann, who spoke quickly but softly and kept darting from his seat to the judge's bench depositing his paperwork, introduced his boldest motion. He asked the judge to rule on whether a common-law marriage existed between Frenchy and Pat Holben. According to the state's theory, Zimmermann argued, "approximately two weeks before February 11, 1968, Jeannine Durand died at the hands of the Defendant. Their marriage was accordingly terminated." Immediately afterward, Frenchy and Pat began living together and continued to do so until 1985. If Densen agreed and ruled that they were legally husband and wife, then, Zimmermann reasoned, Pat Holben should not be allowed to testify at Frenchy's trial. He cited a 1968 Texas law which specified that "both spouses and ex-spouses were prohibited from testifying, over objection, as to any communication made while the marriage existed."

To the layman, it seemed like a hell of twisted argument. Basically, what Zimmermann was saying is that if, as the state contended, Frenchy killed his wife so Pat could move in with him, then Pat shouldn't be allowed to testify because she was now his wife. Asked about it later, Lavine pointed out that they were responding to the prosecution's theory and that they were working in the realm of abstract legal principle. Still, it didn't sit easy in the imagination. What if Frenchy managed to beat the murder rap by this legal manoeuvre? It would be a win by any means and it would certainly demonstrate to all those interested that Zimmermann was indeed a wily advocate well worth the reportedly large fees he charges. But it brought to mind a line that writer Martha Gellhorn once offered in an essay on the workings of the courts in St Louis: "Nobody talks of justice, a condition not to be obtained here."

Densen remained impassive throughout Zimmermann's presentation, concluding that he would rule on the motions at an appropriate point during the trial.

At 2 P.M. fifty prospective jurors, including a grandmother accompanied by her thirteen-year-old granddaughter, who had been milling about in the hallway for hours, were ushered into the courtroom. They were seated according to numbers that had been assigned beforehand. The first person on the right-hand side of the front row was number one and the last person on the left-hand side of the back row was number fifty. The numbers corresponded to a list that included each prospective juror's name, address, telephone number, occupation and marital status. Thus it was possible, with the list in hand, to put a name and occupation to every face.

Densen asked Frenchy to stand and face the crowd. He told them that the defendant, Raymond Durand, had been charged with the felony offence of murder, the indictment having been brought down by a grand jury. He explained that the state has the burden of proof. While he spoke, Frenchy kept looking at Gloria and appeared unable to focus on the faces of the jurors.

Once Densen had completed his introduction, both sides set to work determining who might be hostile to their arguments and who might be receptive. Both the prosecution and the defence had the right to identify ten people that they didn't want on the jury. The jury would be composed of the first twelve people on the list who had not been rejected by either side. All four lawyers had in their hands a copy of the list. Each side worked as a team. Wilson began, and while he asked questions designed to probe for deeply held convictions, Taylor stood off to the side, noting responses and scribbling remarks next to the names.

"Anyone opposed to the idea of a life sentence?" Wilson asked. One hand went up and Taylor spotted it and made a note.

This crime, Wilson went on, happened twenty-four years ago. "You're going to see some similarities in what people say but not everyone is going to remember the same thing." He asked if anyone had ever been a victim of crime and he asked each person to respond. The responses were astonishing and reflected the character of life in a big American city. Number one said his car had been broken into; number two said his wife had been accosted in the street; four and five said they had been burglarized; six said his ex's half-brother had been murdered; ten, eleven, twelve and fourteen said they'd had stuff stolen from them; eighteen said her daughter had been mugged; twenty-four said a family member had been raped and their car stolen; twenty-six said her father had been murdered; twenty-seven and twenty-nine said they'd had possessions stolen; thirty-two said a brother had been robbed by armed men; thirty-four said he'd lost four cars to theft. Many of the remainder reported thefts. All in all, it was an impressive list of crimes that these fifty, randomly chosen citizens had been exposed to. If Wilson and Taylor were looking for people who took a dim view of crime, virtually everyone in this crowd seemed likely to share that attitude.

Lavine had taken careful note as well of the responses to Wilson's questions, and now, as Zimmermann rose to put questions of his own, Lavine moved off to the side, just out of the line of vision of most of the jurors, to better observe their responses. Again, Zimmermann revealed great tactical skill. He told the group that he was a Marine Corps colonel in the reserves and asked if anyone would hold that against him. When no one said they would, he asked Frenchy—and he consistently called his client Frenchy while Wilson had referred to him as Raymond Durand—to stand. Then he asked the jurors whether there was anything about his appearance that would prevent them from considering his case with an open mind. Again, there was no response.

Now he moved to more specific questions. Anyone ever study law? Anyone have a relative with the police? One woman said her husband was a police officer, and several others said they had relatives on various forces. Anybody ever serve on a grand jury? Again, a few people raised their hands.

Then he moved to families. Zimmermann talked about how often families are torn apart by divorce and custody battles. Anyone know of families torn apart by these things? Anybody know a person who felt rejected by his or her father? Who hates a parent?

Anybody have a problem with Frenchy not being an American? Zimmermann suddenly asked. Anybody have relatives in Canada?

Then, just as suddenly, he veered back to families. Anybody know a woman who just walked out on her husband? Can you envision a situation where a woman would leave her children with their dad? A woman scorned—everybody understand that term? How many of you have seen *Fatal Attraction* (a popular Hollywood film, released several years ago, about a jealous mistress who attempts to destroy her lover's marriage)? Hands went up. Or *Presumed Innocent* (Another popular film, this one based on a Scott Turow thriller, featuring murder and a vengeful woman)? Many had seen it, too.

Then Zimmermann moved to an area that, upon reflection later, proved to be his most effective stroke. It also revealed why he had chosen to refer to his client as Frenchy.

"Now," he began, "we talked about if a person starts off presumed innocent, the burden of proof is on the state. Can you see why the system says that a person has a right to remain silent? Because the burden is on the state.

"Mr Wilson gave you some reasons. He told you that usually or many times it's the lawyers who—remember, because of the status of the evidence—[recommend] that the client not take the stand. The judge gave you some other reasons.

"Let me ask you if maybe you might think about the question, why would a person not testify in his own criminal trial? Can you think of a reason that comes to your mind as to why a person might not do that?"

"Anxiety," said one of the jurors. Lavine noted his number.

"Mr Lang says anxiety," Zimmermann reflected. "And that could be a reason why a person would elect not to testify if he didn't have to, right?"

"OK, ma'am," Zimmermann said, turning to another juror. "Can you think of another reason why a person might elect not to testify in a criminal trial? The judge gave an example. Perhaps a person has a speech impediment or stutters and would be afraid that someone would think he was guilty because he couldn't speak as quickly as, say, the lawyers are questioning him. Could you imagine that?"

Another juror: "I could imagine that."

Turning to a yet another juror, Zimmermann asked again: "Could you envision that?"

"Yes."

"And that even though he knows there are some people who say, I want to hear your side, he might elect not to because he was afraid that stuttering might be interpreted, as the judge said, for guilt. Do you see that?"

"Yes."

"Can you think of another reason, ma'am?"

"I suppose," a juror suddenly spoke up, "maybe there is something else in the past or something, you know, where the other side would have a chance to attack them."

"Like if somebody had a criminal record," Zimmermann asked.

"Yes."

"We don't have that situation," Zimmermann said hastily, "but can you think of another?"

"That's the only one I can think of right now—something else in the past that was unrelated that they could bring up."

"How about a language difficulty?" Zimmermann asked, circling finally on the point he wished to impress on the jurors. "Someone that might not speak English as well as Mr Taylor or Mr Wilson and they could be innocent as driven snow, but could be worried about how to understand every word that was asked....Have you ever talked to somebody that didn't fully understand English or had a really heavy accent and you couldn't understand him or her?"

"Right," another member of the panel announced. Again, Lavine quickly noted his number.

"Would that be something you might consider in judging

whether this person were to take the stand?" Zimmermann asked.

"Sure," came a voice from the group. "I had college professors I couldn't understand sometimes."

That remark drew scattered laughs.

"Several of you said that perhaps, maybe, something that happened twenty-four years ago might be hard to remember. Do you think, knowing that when you take the stand that you can be questioned in detail about matters that happened twenty-four years ago, and you might not remember everything, and you are concerned that that might be mistaken for guilt because you don't remember something and that would be a factor?"

By now Zimmermann had accomplished what he had set out to do. His client was a French-speaking Canadian, and the crime had occurred a long time ago. The law says a defendant's refusal to take the stand can't be held against him. Common sense says, why the hell not? What Zimmermann was doing—and doing effectively—was planting in the minds of the prospective jurors sound and believable reasons for Frenchy's silence. From here on in, Zimmermann hoped that every time he mentioned his client's name—Frenchy—the jurors would be reminded of the fact that he was not a native English speaker. Here then was going to be the second element in Zimmermann's defence strategy. He was going to clear away all the circumstantial evidence, throw a shower of doubts upon the twenty-four-year-old memories that the prosecution witnesses were going to recount, and suggest that Jeannine had simply left. And there was no way in the world he was going to let Raymond Durand get on the stand and be asked to explain all the stories he had told about what had happened to Jeannine.

He had done a masterful job. Now Densen asked if anyone felt they should be excused. An elderly man approached the bench and told the judge that he'd have a hard time convicting a man on the basis of twenty-four-year-old memories. Densen spoke with him and he resumed his seat. A burly fellow admitted that he had a relative doing life in prison and that he couldn't possibly consider such a sentence.

The jurors were then ushered out of the courtroom, the two legal teams discussed what they had learned, then both sides submitted their lists of the people they wanted excluded. Those who made it on the jury included the wife of the police officer, the pretty, young college student, a mail carrier, three secretaries, a geologist, a bookkeeper, a computer expert, an ex-nun and a couple of house-wives. It wasn't clear whether either side had gotten what it wanted. Both sides appeared pleased. Zimmermann had set the stage for his defence. Wilson presumably wanted a jury of victims.

There was, however, one surprise for Zimmermann, who had mapped out his strategy so carefully. Raymond Durand was going to be tried for the murder of his wife by a jury composed of nine women and only three men.

Chapter Twenty-Five

Houston, Texas, 1992: Part 3—The Trial

"Sooner or later we all have to answer for our deeds," Ted Wilson told the jurors the following morning in his opening address. "The crime that brings us here today is the crime of murder."

His remarks, delivered with the pacing and emphasis of a stage actor, plunged the courtroom into attentive silence. Over the next half-hour Wilson outlined his case. The jurors had been told when the indictment was read out that the charge Raymond Durand was facing was murder with malice aforethought. They were told, in language peculiar to the courts, and perhaps more specifically, the language of Texas courts, that malice aforethought means "the doing of a wrongful act intentionally," and "a condition of the mind which shows a heart regardless of social duty and fatally bent on mischief." What Wilson was going to try to prove was that Durand had killed Jeannine, had killed her not in a fit of rage but deliberately. Wilson explained that all of the physical evidence had been lost but that there was sufficient circumstantial evidence to prove that Durand was guilty of the charge. He revealed the essence of what each witness would testify to and he told the jurors that the evidence would lead them to conclude that Raymond Durand had killed his wife.

When Wilson finished his address, Densen called a ten-minute break and the jurors retired to the jury chamber.

When the jury was seated again, Zimmermann rose, walked over to the jury and, without warning, flashed at them a photo he had been concealing in the palm of his hand. Holding it in front of their faces now, he strode swiftly along the length of the jury box and began speaking, clearly and rapidly.

The prosecution identified the body on the basis of this photo, he said. It was the morgue shot of corpse 68-500, and the horror of that photo was reflected in the faces of the jurors as they each caught a glimpse of it. "Our evidence will show this is not Jeannine Durand" was all Zimmermann managed to get out before Wilson realized what was happening and jumped to his feet to object. The photo hadn't yet been entered into evidence, Wilson told the judge, insisting that Zimmermann be instructed to put it down. Zimmermann stopped, turned and, while continuing to hold the picture in full view of the jury, challenged the objection. By the time it was clear that he had angered Densen, the entire jury had had a good look at it and Zimmermann put the photo back on his desk.

"The identification," Zimmermann continued, "was made by two people who had not seen Jeannine in a quarter of a century. One of them was twelve years old when he last saw her." The features in the picture, he said, are unrecognizable. The body is decomposing.

"So why the prosecution?" Zimmermann asked. You will hear, he told them, that Frenchy had a romantic involvement with Jeannine and Pat and that that arrangement existed in Canada, Florida and Texas. Jeannine, he said, had left her husband once in Canada, once in Florida and once in Texas. "After she left home in 1968, Pat, who had been with Ray in Florida and Texas, moved in. Pat and Ray lived as husband and wife for eighteen years. You are going to hear that in 1985/86, Frenchy left Pat. Rejected her." A couple of years later Frenchy married Gloria. The testimony of the witnesses, Zimmermann said, is the story of a family torn apart.

"You're going to hear about the children hating their father. About Frenchy's uncle hating Frenchy. About stories told by one child to another, stories told and retold so many times that they became reality." You are also, he said, going to hear the testimony of a woman scorned and seeking revenge. "We don't know where Jeannine is. Don't know whether she is alive or dead."

By the time Zimmermann resumed his seat he had managed to establish in the minds of all those who had listened to him and watched his earnest and seemingly heartfelt performance a plausible alternative view of the events that Wilson had outlined. Now two narrative lines had been established, two completely different interpretations of Jeannine's sudden disappearance and Ray's subsequent behaviour. Nobody had ever assumed it was going to be a cakewalk for the prosecution. Now it became clear just how high the hurdles were that Wilson and Taylor were going to have to clear.

The parade of prosecution witnesses began. Sheriff Johnny Klevenhagen, a burly, smiling, fleshy-faced man with white hair combed straight back, described the scene the night the body was discovered, identified several photos of the site that had been taken by a medical examiner's investigator and said that the clothing, bedcover, rope, ring and a set of false teeth had been turned over to his department by the medical examiner after the autopsy. He said his officials had conducted an exhaustive search for the artefacts after the investigation had been reopened in 1991 and that they couldn't find any of them. He explained that since 1968 there have been five different areas where seized property is stored and that the department itself had moved once: "At the last move, several million pieces of property were in those rooms."

Klevenhagen was cross-examined by Lavine, who began by asking about the condition of the body. Klevenhagen said it was not "terribly decomposed." So Lavine read from the autopsy report: "Extreme state of decomposition. Slippage of body tissue. You did not look at the body?"

"I did not move it."

Again, Lavine read from the report: "Parts of the left side of the face and jaw area were missing."

"I did not view the body in the face."

Finally, Lavine asked if the woman had been wearing an overcoat or topcoat.

"I have no knowledge of a coat."

After a break for lunch, Cecil Wingo was sworn in. Wingo explained that, among other things, he was responsible for the medical examiner's records. He described how, after Jean Nadeau's call, he had requested the autopsy of corpse 68-500. He said he made a presumptive identification based on information given to him by Nadeau about Jeannine's hair colour, height, weight, dentures and scar below the navel. After Béland identified the pictures, Wingo said his office had concluded that 68-500 was indeed the body of Jeannine Durand.

Zimmermann conducted the cross-examination.

"In your business, have you ever made a false identification?"

"I can't remember a false identification."

"Have relatives ever made an identification that is false?"

"I've experienced it twice in my years."

"Even parents can't identify children sometimes?"

"Yes."

"Any dental comparison made in this case?"

"There was nothing to compare to."

"Were there dentures?"

"The autopsy showed no teeth."

"Were the false teeth kept?"

"I don't even know whether they were part of the body."

"Fingerprints were taken?"

"Yes, but I don't know where they are. There were no prints on file."

After Wingo was excused, Lieutenant Robert Madeira was called. He strode into the courtroom in boots and his western-cut suit. On the stand, he described, briefly, when he had become involved in the investigation, the fact that he had been the first police officer on the site the night the body was found in 1968 and who he and Talton had interviewed. He said that when he had arrested Frenchy, he found a Social Security card in his pocket in the name of Raymond D. Holben.

The next witness, Michel Béland, was called and Zimmermann objected, arguing that the fact that Béland had been sent only one set of photos invited him simply to endorse a conclusion the medical examiner's office had already drawn regarding the identity of corpse 68-500. The jury was sent out, Béland examined and cross-examined and asked several questions by Densen himself. At the end of it Densen ruled that the jury should hear Béland.

So the following morning, Béland, wearing coat and tie, re-entered the courtroom and was sworn in. The Houston *Chronicle*'s court reporter, John Makeig, had described Béland, in the morning paper as a "lantern-jawed Mountie." Béland was puzzled by the expression until the reporter for *Le Droit,* Denis Gratton, explained to him that it meant he had a jaw like former Canadian prime minister Brian Mulroney.

Béland did indeed look like a Mountie of legend, like the original Dudley Do-right. Tall, with wavy black hair, he was composed and unflappable on the stand. He answered precisely what he knew. If he wasn't certain, he said so. He came across as terribly decent and honest, a man of great moral fibre—which was exactly why Wilson wanted him on the stand. Wilson knew that the jurors would, in all likelihood, have been exposed to the myths propagated by Hollywood of the Royal Canadian Mounted Police. They always got their man, they were incorruptible, imbued with the British, upper-class sense of what constitutes fair play and gentlemanly behaviour. Béland fit the bill. If Wilson could have managed it, he would have had Béland march into the courtroom in his scarlet tunic. But he was pleased enough that physically Béland didn't disappoint. Wilson knew perfectly well that the morgue photos showed a faced so ravaged that many of the jurors would wonder how anybody could identify it. To cement his argument that 68-500 was Jeannine Durand he needed a witness whose credibility would be unimpeachable, someone who knew Jeannine, was not so intimately involved in the case that they could be accused of allowing their emotions to dictate their testimony, and who could be definitive on the stand.

Wilson began by having Béland recite his credentials. He said he had been with the Mounties for twenty-nine years, that he had worked in narcotics, had taught at the Canadian Police College and that he was now in charge of the traffic unit in and around Ottawa, Canada's capital city. Asked how he knew Jeannine, Béland replied that they were cousins, their mothers were sisters, that like Jeannine he had been born and raised in the Ottawa/Hull area and that he saw her at her home and at the home of their grandparents. He said she was nine or ten years older than he was, and his memories of Jeannine were mostly of her as an adult.

Béland said his father was a milkman and his route included Jeannine and Ray's house on Michaud Street in Pointe Gatineau. He said that after he joined the RCMP he'd often return home for the weekends and would sometimes help his father on his route. He said he last saw Jeannine on August 7, 1965, the date of his own wedding.

Béland described how he had been contacted by Denis and how he had talked to Wingo and offered his help. "I said if you have pictures, send them to me. I might be able to identify them."

At that point, Wilson produced the morgue photo that Zimmermann had shown to the jury, had it entered into the court record as prosecution exhibit 1, and showed it to Béland.

"That's my cousin, Jeannine Durand," Béland replied without hesitation.

"Are you sure?"

"Yes, I'm sure," Béland said, adding that he had last seen

Jeannine a little over two years before the morgue photo had been taken.

Asked if he had understood the implication of identifying the photo as Jeannine, he said he realized at the time that likely it meant he would be asked to testify and that, for that reason, "I had to be sure. I was sure without a doubt."

Thus far in the trial, Frenchy had remained impassive, sitting between his lawyers, occasionally scribbling notes to them, occasionally throwing glances at Gloria. She was poised, devoted, apparently certain of her husband's innocence. For the most part, the jurors had been attentive. The ex-nun bowed her head from time to time and closed her eyes, giving the impression that she was dozing off. The young student, too, looked as if she was having a hard time keeping her attention from wandering. She kept peering off into the mostly empty benches.

By the time Wilson had completed his questioning of Béland, he had managed to underline for the jurors the fact that the witness was a respected career police officer, a professional who not only knew the deceased well but presumably had the essential skills of all police officers: trained and acute powers of observation and the ability to describe and report in precise, detailed language.

To challenge Béland's testimony, the defence raised doubts about how well he knew Jeannine, and questioned whether he had the skills to make an accurate identification. To accomplish the first, Lavine asked Béland to repeat when he last saw Jeannine.

At my wedding in 1965, he replied. And no, he further admitted, he hadn't had much of an opportunity to talk to her that day. He'd been busy, he acknowledged. It was, after all, his wedding.

Was she wearing glasses? Lavine asked, out of the blue.

"I don't remember Jeannine wearing glasses."

Did she wear glasses?

"I don't remember if she wore glasses."

Lavine had scored two quick points and he pressed his advantage.

"Did you visit the Boissonneault home?"

"Yes."

"Did they visit you?"

"Very little."

Again, suddenly, "Do you know whether Réginald ever worked?"

But before Béland had a chance to reply, the prosecution objected and the question was disallowed. The question seemed so out of place in the scheme of Lavine's questioning that it could only have been calculated to serve some as yet hidden purpose. The very fact that he had asked the question meant that he knew the answer. Réginald had never worked. Why would he want the jury to know that? Granted, the question had been disallowed. Still, Lavine had managed to signal to the jury both that the question of whether Réginald had ever worked was a relevant issue, and that the prosecution didn't want Béland to answer.

Now Lavine embarked on a line of questioning on which Béland was at a distinct disadvantage. Describing, accurately, a person's face is a surprisingly difficult task. It demands a specific vocabulary. It is one thing to say a person has a prominent nose. It is quite another to say a person has a an aquiline profile or a Jimmy Durante schnozzle. The latter expressions are much more evocative but how often does one employ such phrases? Furthermore, many people have noses that don't have distinguishing features, that can be described only as regular-looking. And, finally, to add to Béland's disadvantage, his first language is French. He is fluently bilingual but there is no doubt that had he been asked the same questions in French, he would have been able to call upon a much richer vocabulary for his responses.

For openers, Lavine asked Béland to describe Jeannine.

"Jeannine was heavy-set, had light-brown hair. Weighed about 130 pounds."

"What colour were her eyes?"

"I don't know the colour of her eyes."

How tall was she?

"About five feet, six inches."

Asked to give more detail, Béland responded, "I can't describe anything else about her."

"Do you remember a birthmark on her forehead?"

"Personally, I don't recall seeing one."

"Can you give this jury any other description of her face?"

"No, but just looking at the picture I know it is her face."

Lavine produced two photos, had them labelled as defence exhibits, then showed them to Béland. Béland picked out Jeannine in both photos and Lavine pointed out that her hair appeared to be too dark to be called blonde and that she was wearing glasses.

Then Lavine queried Béland on his professional credentials. Béland acknowledged that he had never taken a course in fingerprint identification.

"You have no formal training in identification, then?"

"No, sir."

"Is this the only decomposed body you have been asked to identify?"

"Yes."

"In your training, did you either learn or have training in interviewing techniques?"

Béland said he had. So Lavine asked, "In interviewing, you don't suggest answers."

"Yes, sir."

Or implant, even accidentally, a response.

"Yes, sir."

Lavine established the manner in which Béland had come into contact with Wingo and then asked: "Cecil Wingo didn't send you a number of photos of partially decomposed bodies and ask you to pick out Jeannine?"

"No."

"Do you know whether Jeannine had large or small breasts?"

"No, sir. I recall only that she was heavy-set, a bit tall for a woman, and her face."

Is it fair to say that had you looked at this photo, without it being in the context of the search for Jeannine Durand, that you would not have been able to identify it?

"No. If I had been shown it, I would have said, 'I know this person. Let me think.'"

Pressed again to admit that he would not have been able to identify the photo had it not been in the context of the investigation, Béland disagreed. He said that it would have taken him longer but that ultimately he would have been able to say it was Jeannine.

Lavine asked how he had presented the photo to Réginald.

"I showed Réginald the photo. I said it was Jeannine."

"You did not show it to him and ask him if it was his sister?"

"No."

And Denis, Lavine asked, "You identified the photo and told him you had identified it as Jeannine?"

"Yes."

When Lavine finished, Wilson rose to pose several additional questions. He asked Béland why he had never launched an investigation into Jeannine's disappearance.

Jeannine's parents were introverts, he said, who didn't confide in anyone. Béland said that if his aunt had asked, he would have made some inquiries. But she didn't and he respected her privacy. He said he also thought, after 1972, that the Quebec police were pursuing the matter after Denis talked to them.

Wilson showed him the photos that the defence had introduced and Béland said he hadn't seen them before. He was able to identify Jeannine in the photos.

After Béland completed his testimony, Densen called a ten-minute break. Béland made his way out into the hallway and found himself, at one point, standing near Frenchy, who said, in French and loud enough for him to hear and to know that the remark was meant for him, "He's a puke."

Dr Robert Bucklin, a stooped, white-haired pathologist with a Vandyke beard, had been assistant medical examiner in Harris County in 1968 and had performed the autopsy on corpse 68-500. He had left Harris County at the end of 1968, studied law, had set up the medical examiner's office in Galveston and was now working as an independent consultant on forensic matters. Wilson called him to give evidence on the autopsy he had performed. On the stand, Bucklin said that over the course of his career he had performed about twenty-five thousand autopsies and that, in 1968, when he worked at the Harris County medical examiner's office, he was performing an average of fifty to seventy-five autopsies a month. Wilson showed him a copy of his report on corpse 68-500. Bucklin said he had no memory of "this autopsy independent of the file."

Bucklin's testimony raised the most contentious issues debated during the trial. By the time both sides made their closing statements, the state, which began by emphasizing Bucklin's vast experience, would be arguing that he had made a mistake and the defence would be insisting that his professionalism and accuracy was unassailable. It was a bizarre reversal, the state challenging its own witness and the defence defending a supposedly hostile witness.

Asked about his autopsy report, Bucklin read out to the court the essentials. The body measured, from crown to heel, five feet, seven inches, weighed 144 pounds, had no teeth but full dentures, was wearing a wedding ring and had a three-inch scar on the abdomen. He described how six ribs had been fractured in front and back. He discussed the skull fracture in the left, frontal bone that radiated to the base of the skull.

"Rather extensive force was involved in producing that injury," he said while declining to speculate on what type of weapon was used. He said the force of the blow was comparable to a person hitting a windshield in a car accident. However, there was no evidence to suggest it was an auto accident, he emphasized.

Asked if the head wound was produced by several blows, he said: "One blow would have done it. The fracture was continuous."

He said the rib and head injuries had occurred in the same general time frame and that he believed that death had been caused by the head injury.

Bucklin was the witness for whom Zimmermann was best prepared. Zimmermann had met with him before the trial, had dug up learned papers Bucklin had written, had examined the autopsy report and had sent his private investigator across the country chasing down material he was going to use in cross-examination. If Zimmermann were going to argue successfully that 68-500 was not Jeannine Durand, then his cross-examination of Bucklin was the point at which he would have to make his most telling mark.

Zimmermann invited Bucklin to agree that, when he began the autopsy, he would have been careful to look for identifying marks. Bucklin concurred and added that he had written learned papers on the subject of identifying bodies in autopsies. Zimmermann pulled out a copy of an article Bucklin had written and quoted from it: "Eye colour must be identified, hair,...fingerprints are best evidence of identification."

Bucklin said he had noted the hair and eye colour but added that sometimes decomposition can affect eye colour. Weight, too, will be changed, he said.

Asked to comment on the recorded weight, 144 pounds, Bucklin said, "Chances are that she would have weighed more than 144 pounds than less."

Asked about eye colour in the autopsy report, Bucklin told Zimmermann that "the words I used were that the eyes appeared brown."

Then Zimmermann turned to the scar below the navel and asked whether it was a "surgical scar or an injury scar?"

Bucklin said he couldn't be positive. "A laceration and a [surgical] cut are identical but not a trauma-type injury." He said it could have been a surgical scar or a laceration.

They discussed the state of decomposition of the body and Zimmermann asked Bucklin if he agreed that it would be difficult to recognize the woman because of the condition of the body.

"That depends on how well the person knew the [dead] individual....If a person knew this individual in life and knew the appearance of the features—the nose, the shape of the face—that person might have a far better ability to make an identification than someone like myself."

Dissatisfied with the response, Zimmermann had Bucklin recite, while Zimmermann held the morgue photo before the jury, a description of the condition of the face.

"There are signs of animal activity about the lower lip....The lids are closed....There is tissue gas formation in the face and part of the chest...missing portion of the left cheek, eyes are swollen, cheeks swollen, skin slippage, hair that was peeled back during the autopsy, nose flattened, discolouring of the face."

By now many members of the jury looked distinctly queasy. Zimmermann had made his point.

Asked about the organs, Bucklin said he had taken out the internal organs and examined them. He said he found one kidney was abnormal and, most controversial of all, Bucklin said the ovaries and Fallopian tubes were normal.

Zimmermann turned and pulled out a large colour graphic that he had had an artist prepare. It showed all the essentials of the female reproductive system—the ovary, the uterus and, most prominently, the Fallopian tubes.

Then he produced another surprise: Jeannine Durand's medical records of her last known stay in hospital. Obtained from a hospital in Fort Lauderdale, they were the records of her hospitalization from June 16 to 20, 1967, for the birth of her last child, Martine. Those records showed Jeannine was thirty-three years old, five feet, three inches tall, weighed 186 pounds before delivery, wore contact lenses and full dentures, didn't speak English well and "had a bilateral tubal ligation without complications" the day after she gave birth.

Reading from the report, Zimmermann showed on his chart how Jeannine's surgeon had removed 1.8 centimetres from one tube and 2.7 centimetres from the other. All four tube ends would then have been tied off with catgut, which would have dissolved in a matter of weeks.

"To return to your autopsy report," Zimmermann asked Bucklin. "You found the Fallopian tubes to be present and normal. Had there been a [cut] you would have seen it?"

"I would have expected to have seen it. If nothing had changed positions."

"You were looking for abnormalities and changes. You would have seen any type of tubal ligation?"

"All I can say is that they looked normal to me."

"You had to reach in and pull them out. You found them to be 'present and normal.'"

"That's right....The normal reparative process [of the body] would be to try and repair it. If that had happened, it could have been missed."

Bucklin explained that, in addition to the reparative tendencies of the body, the surgeon "would not have left a 2.4 centimetre gap." He would have drawn together the cut and tied ends, Bucklin said.

Not entirely satisfied by Bucklin's comments, Zimmermann nonetheless decided to quit while he was ahead. He had gotten Bucklin to say that the tubes looked normal and that he would have expected to have seen evidence of the ligation. Now he turned to the other discrepancies between the hospital records and the autopsy. The hospital records showed a woman four inches shorter and forty pounds heavier than 68-500. In addition, other testimony showed Jeannine had blue eyes and blonde hair and the autopsy showed a woman with eyes that "appeared brown" and hair that was described as dark brown. He asked Bucklin to comment, to repudiate the identification, but Bucklin was cautious, reserved.

"I did not make the identification."

Finally Zimmermann produced a hefty and authoritative reference work entitled *Medicolegal Investigation of Death; Guidelines for the Application of Pathology to Crime Investigation,* and read:

The least reliable methods of identification include personal recognition by relatives or friends and the comparative examination of clothing and personal effects. Personal recognition of a person is based upon recall from experience as well as upon a rapid comparative analysis of physical characteristics. Examination of unidentified remains by possible relatives or friends is often a highly emotional experience, and failure to achieve an identification under such circumstances is not uncommon; it is also possible for an erroneous identification to be made.

(What Zimmermann didn't cite was a footnote on the same page, which revealed that in Detroit the medical examiner's office had begun inviting relatives to view bodies via black and white, closed circuit television. Doing so, they found, diminished the emotional impact of the moment and, interestingly enough, "increased the accuracy [of identifications] considerably.")

When Zimmermann completed his discourse on the identification of bodies, Wilson rose to repair some of the damage the defence attorney had inflicted on his case. Examining the hospital records, he asked Bucklin to comment on the fact that Jeannine's weight was recorded as 186 before giving birth, and 181 immediately after she had given birth to a six pound, eleven ounce baby.

"I questioned it when I first saw it," Bucklin replied.

Wilson then noted that both the person who had been hospitalized in Florida and the corpse had full dentures. He noted the presence of contact lenses in Florida and Bucklin said he hadn't found contacts on the corpse. But, he said, a hit on the head could cause the contacts to come out.

What about the scar? Wilson asked: "Would that be the type of scar one would normally find in someone who had had a tubal?"

"Yes."

"Is there anything in your report that would show a reason for the scar?"

"No."

After a tubal, Wilson asked, does the surgeon try to place the tube ends together?

The gap would be closed, Bucklin replied, "so no other viscera would be caught in it."

What about the healing process?

Healing is the body's natural reaction to injury, Bucklin replied, and when tissue is removed, fibrous scar tissue appears.

"That sort of process, does that make it easier or more difficult for a pathologist" to see evidence of a tubal?

"It would tend to obliterate the process as time goes on. All I'm saying is they looked normal."

Wilson turned back to the hospital records again and, with Bucklin agreeing, pointed out that both Jeannine and the corpse had had their tonsils and adenoids removed.

Finally he had Bucklin agree that there were no major discrepancies between the description of the woman in the hospital records and the corpse.

Zimmermann immediately shot to his feet to recross-examine.

"Many people have their tonsils out?"

"It's common."

"And one of the big differences [between the medical records and the corpse] is the height, five feet, three inches. That's four inches shorter than the body autopsied?"

"Yes."

Jeannine didn't "lose four inches in height as a result of child-birth," he asked, his voice dripping with sarcasm.

The next morning, Wilson's first witness was Nadeau. He looked completely at ease when he entered the courtroom. Wearing a grey suit, blue shirt and red and grey paisley tie, he described how he had met Anne in the course of an investigation into political corruption and how he had ended up calling Wingo. Under cross-examination, Lavine suggested to him that Wingo had identified Jeannine based on information that he, Nadeau, had provided.

"I believe what I gave them helped," Nadeau deadpanned.

After Nadeau, Wilson brought up in quick succession Lieutenant François Cloutier and Lieutenant Roch Menard, both of whom simply confirmed that Ray had not filed a missing persons report with them in 1968.

That afternoon Anne was scheduled to appear. As she waited in the hallway to be called, she began shaking with fear. Her baby, whom she was still breast-feeding, was back at the motel with her sister-in-law. She was worried that she'd be on the stand long past his feeding time. But, more than anything else, she was worried about sitting a few feet from her father and talking about their life. Just as she seemed about to lose her composure, Nadeau took her by the shoulders and said, "Anne, you gave birth. You can do anything."

That remark seemed to buck her up. It was 3:35 before Anne was finally brought in. She wore a flowered summer dress, had light make-up on, her long brown hair tied back and was carrying a hanky in her hand. She looked nervous and distressed, and many members of the jury appeared to feel sympathy for her. She walked past the defence table without looking at her father. For the first time since the trial began, Frenchy looked uncomfortable.

Taylor conducted the examination. He wanted the jurors to identify with her, to feel something of her suffering.

Taylor patiently led Anne through her early life—the house on Michaud Street, the move to Florida, the fact that Aunt Pat was in Florida with them, returning to Grandmother's house, then Bellaire, and Aunt Pat again. In a soft hesitant voice she said the last time she remembered seeing her mother was in that house in Bellaire. She said she remembered the organ her mom got for Christmas and that suddenly, sometime after Christmas, she was gone.

She said she was told that her mom was in Canada, taking care of her grandmother. Then the family moved to another house and that, while they were living there, her dad shouted at Denis in the car one day, "Your mother's not coming back and that's that."

With Taylor's prodding, Anne told about moving to Big Thicket, San Diego and Victoria. In Victoria, one day she heard her father talking on the phone to Madame Boissonneault.

"He said Jeannine and us kids were just up the street and we were going to come over."

"And that surprised you?"

"Yes, because Pat was there. I was probably ten or eleven years old....We were told not to talk about our mother. Pat was our mother and that was that."

Anne told about the move to Ottawa and then back to San Diego and asking her father why Denis wasn't coming. "He said he [Denis] caused a lot of trouble and he didn't love us."

She talked about moving out at seventeen and about the visit to Tex Ritter's office and about the telephone conversation in which she heard her father say that Jeannine had died of cancer. "I had never heard that before. Never heard before that my mother had died....He once told me she had pushed me out in front of a car. He said she was in a mental institution and then in jail."

By now Anne had calmed down. Taylor had taken her through all the material he needed. What remained was one final dramatic gesture intended to wring as much emotion as possible out of her appearance. Taylor walked over to the witness box and showed Anne a photo of the Boissonneault family. Anne identified everyone in it. He put it down, walked back to the prosecution table and picked up another photo. The tension mounted as he crossed the floor and placed a second photo in front of Anne.

"Who is that?"

Anne looked down and burst into sobs that tore at the hearts of everyone in the courtroom. By the time she managed to get out the words, "That's my mother," several jurors were crying and, surprisingly, so was Gloria. Frenchy just sat there, looking away.

"Your witness," Taylor said as Anne attempted to dry her eyes and compose herself.

Zimmermann had the sense to ask for a ten-minute recess. He needed to cross-examine Anne but he knew that she had the sympathy of the jury and that they likely wouldn't take kindly to him if he hammered away at her on the stand.

He began by getting Anne to tell what kind of mother Pat had been.

"Did Pat treat the children differently?"

"Yes. Martine never knew that Pat wasn't her mother. With us kids, she was very mean. She would treat us differently from Martine....She was just hateful."

"Martine was really Pat's child?"

"Yes."

Anne told how Pat had broken her nose and how it was Pat who told her that Jeannine wasn't coming back.

Memories fade, don't they? Zimmermann asked Anne. He asked if she was really certain that it was her father who said Jeannine had pushed her in front of a car.

"Yes."

"Isn't it true that the reason Denis stayed in Hull was that Pat refused to have him any longer?"

Anne wouldn't agree to that but she did say that Denis and Pat didn't get along.

Asked about the phone call she had overheard in Victoria, Anne insisted she remembered it exactly and she said the reason she remembered it was that "it scared me. I was scared because Pat was there and my mother wasn't. I was scared because we weren't supposed to talk about my mother."

Now Zimmermann attempted to suggest that Anne had been led into suspecting her father.

"This is really Denis's project?"

"It was until 1991."

"For many, many years?"

"Yes."

Anne admitted that Denis had fought with Frenchy often and that, after the family returned to Ottawa, Denis suspected that their dad had killed Jeannine. "Denis kept saying my father had killed her. Any time he talked to me he'd say that and I'd get mad at him."

Zimmermann showed Anne a statement she had made in which she said she suspected Pat. He asked her to explain it. "I thought Pat might have known what happened."

"Think Pat Holben killed your mom?"

"I don't know."

"You don't know?"

"I wasn't there."

"You really don't have a clear picture of your mother leaving?"

"No....I remember what she looked like, her hair, how she liked to wear it."

"In your statement you say that you believe that Pat planned this out?"

"I believed that Pat knew what had happened."

Zimmermann asked Anne about her relationship with her father, showed her a colour photo of her and her father laughing together, and suggested that they had been close.

"Well, he was drunk a lot so I can't say I had a relationship with him."

"Didn't he try to help you get a green card?"

"He got the attorney. I paid for it."

"But your dad tried to help. He hooked you up with an immigration lawyer?"

"Yes."

By now Zimmermann was pushing it, badgering Anne to the point that he was at risk of alienating the jurors. He took her through her stories again about the conversation in Tex Ritter's office and the phone conversation about the Pap smear. In both instances, he tried to get her to admit that she had misremembered or misinterpreted the remarks that had been made. But she clung to her story, and seeing she was adamant, he let go. Before he sat down, though, he attempted to turn the tables on Taylor.

"I am not going to show you exhibit 1 [the morgue photo]. But isn't it true that you were told you were going to be shown that photo? Have you been shown that photo before?"

"Yes."

"By whom?"

"By those two men," Anne replied, pointing at Taylor and Wilson. Now Taylor rose.

"Did your mother love you?"

"Yes."

"Mistreat you?"

"No."

"Care for you?"

"Yes."

"Who told you to call Pat mother?"

"My father."

Some time after she testified, Anne talked to me about the experience. She wondered how her father had felt, listening to her. "I just wanted to find out the truth," she said, "to find out what happened and why. I looked at my father sitting there, drowning, and I just wanted to help him. So he'll know we still love him. He's my father. I have bad memories and good memories. It's so hard....He's going to jail and I'm going to have to live with it for the rest of my life—that I put him there—because I'm the one who initiated the search for my mom. I had to know whether he just told us those stories to protect us, that my mom really did leave, that maybe she didn't love us and he didn't want to tell us that."

She paused for a moment, caught her breath, lost herself in the mists of her past. "What I honestly believe is that my dad did it. They got in a fight and he hit her. She fell and hit her head. And he thought, my God, I'm in a different country. If I turn myself in, I'll be in trouble.

"I know he did it but I blame me. I keep blaming myself. I don't want to see Dad go to jail. I want it to be something else."

Like her brothers and sister, Anne had her own sense of how Jeannine died. All four children had felt a powerful need to envision the way in which the murder had happened. But the narratives they imagined for themselves conformed more to their own psychological needs than to the known facts. In Anne's case, she needed to think of it as a fight that had gotten out of hand. The fact that Jeannine had died from one murderous blow, a blow that had fractured her whole skull, hadn't managed to persuade her that it wasn't a fight in which Jeannine died after hitting her head when she fell. Denis's story about seeing Ray return with the suitcases, and Pat's story about Ray and Jeannine leaving together so she could catch a flight to Canada, weren't stories that Anne could integrate into her mental picture of the events. She just couldn't—for all the best of reasons—allow herself to believe that her father was a ruthless murderer who had deliberately extinguished Jeannine's life.

On Friday morning, the fifth day of the trial, Wilson called in Robert Durand, a thin, frail and wrinkled man with a thick moustache, slicked-back dark hair and glasses. He hadn't quite recovered from his heart surgery and he looked nervous. Robert speaks some English, but he didn't feel that he had sufficient command of the language to testify in English. He had asked for a translator, and the court had engaged the services of a middle-aged, smiling Vietnamese man named Giam T. Pham, who had presumably learned the language in his native country. Several people attempted to point out to Wilson that it was not likely that Pham was going to be familiar with Quebec French, but no one took the concerns seriously enough to quiz Pham on his knowledge of Quebec French and he was sworn in along with Robert.

Via the translator, Wilson took Robert through his story of flying to Fort Lauderdale to serve as godparents to Martine. He said it was clear to him then that Pat was Ray's mistress. He described how he came to move his family to San Diego and how Ray got him a job at Guy Hill Cadillac.

Robert had apparently insisted that he not be questioned on how Ray had cheated him in San Diego—he said he was here to talk about Ray's case and not how he had been duped by his nephew. Wilson probably believed that Zimmermann would have to tread carefully as well. Zimmermann would not want Robert to paint his client as a thief but he would want to undermine Robert's credibility by getting him to admit that he still nurtured a hatred for Raymond.

Robert told Wilson and the jurors that he had worked for a funeral home in the 1940s and 1950s and that one day in San Diego he had been in his Cadillac with Ray when his nephew had asked him how long it would take for a body to decompose.

"I said, 'It depends on where it is.'"

Then, he said, Ray asked him how a corpse would be identified.

"I said, 'By marks on the body, by the teeth, by scars, tattoos.' Ray asked how long they would keep a corpse. I said, 'It could be kept a long time, depending on soil conditions.'"

By now *Le Droit* reporter Denis Gratton and I had begun groaning in disbelief. The translation was not just bad, it was dangerously incompetent. Pham had translated the French word *cicatrice,* meaning scars, as "skeletons." Robert was often able to understand the question better than Pham was able to translate it and, on several occasions, Robert had supplied Pham with the appropriate English word for testimony that the translator was attempting to render in English. Wilson either hadn't heard us or was too close to finishing to interrupt. He concluded with two questions.

"Did Ray ever volunteer what happened [to Jeannine]?" he asked.

"Before I went to San Diego. On the phone Ray said Jeannine threw herself in front of the car with the baby in her arms. He said she became hysterical, sick and needed psychiatric care in a hospital."

Finally, Wilson put the morgue photo in front of Robert and asked him if he recognized the person in it.

"Yes. It is Jeannine Boissonneault."

Robert's evidence seemed a pretty modest contribution to the prosecution's theory. It would have been easy enough to suggest that that conversation about decomposing bodies could have been in the context of something Ray had seen on television or that it could have been a discussion Ray had with Robert about his old job at the funeral home. Nonetheless, Zimmermann threw all his weight into his cross-examination of Robert. He was aggressive and relentless. And he began by asking why Robert was refusing to testify in English since he had once spoken to him in English in Canada. Zimmermann hinted that Robert had something to hide.

Robert, badly served by his incompetent translator, said his English wasn't good enough and that he wanted to be exact.

Within a few minutes of beginning his cross-examination, Zimmermann was frustrated, too, by the translation. Since he had by now heard the groans coming from the two Canadian reporters, a recess was called. Zimmermann and Wilson walked over and asked Gratton and me whether Pham was "even in the ballpark." We shook our heads and they retreated to confer with the judge. Densen listened, turned to Gratton and me and said that one of us would be sworn in to translate. Neither of us wanted to shoulder the task, but I prevailed by promising to take notes. Gratton, who worried about how he was going to explain it to his editor when he filed his story that evening, was led to the front of the courtroom, sworn in and promised a fee for his work. When Zimmermann resumed his cross-examination, Gratton's translation proved to be competent enough that the defence attorney attacked Robert's credibility with renewed energy.

Zimmermann attempted to get Robert to agree that Jeannine had left Ray before, that she knew about Ray's relationship with Pat, that Pat was so close to the family and Jeannine so distant from her kids that it was Pat who held Martine at the christening.

Robert said Jeannine didn't know about the relationship between Ray and Pat and that he had never heard of Jeannine's leaving Ray and that, in Quebec Catholic culture, a mother never holds the baby at the christening.

Now, Zimmermann led Robert into the period in San Diego. He asked about the falling out he had had with Ray in San Diego.

"We didn't have time to have a falling out because he left."

But you had a serious disagreement? Zimmermann asked.

"We didn't have a disagreement."

"And you never spoke to Frenchy again?"

"I never had the occasion. He never called me."

"You never saw him or called him in twenty-three years?"

"Yes."

"You still hold a grudge?"

"If I had to do something for revenge, I had twenty-three years to do it in."

"This is an opportunity [for revenge]?"

"I don't consider this a chance. If you think this is vengeance, that is not the case."

"You sold all your property in 1970 and took your family and moved to San Diego to work with Frenchy. It was a dream to live and work there and within a month and a half, your dream was crushed?"

"Absolutely."

"And you blame Frenchy?"

"I blame myself for going there. I hurt myself and I take responsibility for it."

"In your view, here you were a stranger in a new country and he left you stranded?"

"I worked myself out of it."

"You don't want to see a lot of good things happen to Frenchy, do you?"

"It's not for me to say."

"That conversation about the corpse never happened?"

"Yes, that conversation took place and there were other things that were said."

By now the jury was probably eager to hear the story of what happened to Robert in San Diego. Zimmermann had skilfully managed to limit Robert's testimony to the fact that he was upset with Ray, that he felt Ray had done him a dirty. But the story about what had transpired never emerged. All the jurors knew was that Robert had never spoken to Frenchy again. Could his testimony, therefore, be accepted as detached and truthful? That's what Zimmermann wanted them to ask themselves and that's undoubtedly what they were asking.

When Robert was dismissed, Densen recessed the trial for the weekend. Since the jurors had not been sequestered, they returned home. Robert and Lieutenants Cloutier and Menard flew back to Ottawa. Anne, her sister-in-law Nancy, baby Justin and Nadeau caught a flight back to California. Anne said she was happy to be going home but that she wouldn't get any rest until the trial had ended.

By then the group at the motel had been whittled down to Michel Béland, Réginald and Denis. That weekend, Denis revisited his old school and discovered that Zimmermann's private investigator had been there before him seeking his school records.

Pat Holben had been put up at a separate motel and had spent the first week of the trial alone. Wilson and his colleagues worried that she might begin drinking so they detailed a staff member to keep an eye on her. Denis and Anne had seen her once, in passing, coming out of Wilson's office. They hadn't spoken; now that they knew that Pat had known all along what had happened to Jeannine, they disliked her more than ever.

On Monday, at 2:55, Pat entered the courtroom. A withered and addled woman, she looked much older than her years. Although she wasn't yet sixty, she looked like a confused grandmother. She was short and plump but her red and blue paisley summer dress gave the impression that she paid some attention to her appearance. Her red pumps matched her dress, and she carried a white leather purse which she placed on the prosecutor's desk as she walked by. Lipstick gave some colour to her wrinkled and pasty face. She squinted behind her spectacles and, during questioning, appeared to be concentrating intently. Initially, many observers thought she was hard of hearing and had to concentrate to catch what was being said. Others quickly concluded that she was simply not very bright.

That morning Zimmermann had once again presented his argument that Pat should not be allowed to testify because she was Frenchy's common-law wife and that their communication during their marriage was privileged. As Lavine later put it, the prosecution shouldn't be allowed to have it both ways. Either Jeannine was dead and Ray and Pat were husband and wife, or she was alive and they weren't husband and wife. Pat had been called in to testify in *voir dire* (before Judge Densen alone). At the end of it Densen agreed with the prosecutors that she could testify. Zimmermann fought hard on this point. When he lost, he was upset and it was clear that if Frenchy were convicted, an appeal might well be based on this issue.

It was Wilson who examined Pat. By now his persona had revealed itself during the proceedings. Whereas Zimmermann was brilliant but often annoying and insincere, Lavine self-conscious and absorbed by his own cleverness, and Taylor testy, Wilson was perky and genial. Wilson was a lawyer whose personality did a fair bit of his work for him with juries. Unlike the other three attorneys, Wilson avoided dark blue suits and the relentless combativeness that seemed to accompany that uniform.

Under Wilson's patient guidance, Pat recounted how she had met

Ray at Campbell Motors in Ottawa, how she wasn't aware of his marriage until they were settled in Fort Lauderdale, and how when Ray brought Jeannine and the kids to Florida, she had been introduced to them as the wife of his boss. She told the story of Ray's decision to send Jeannine and the kids back to Canada "because they couldn't speak French," and of how she had driven with him to Texas and settled in an apartment in Bellaire. She said he found work in a body shop and she helped him, sanding and painting cars. Asked how she felt when Ray told her he was going to bring Jeannine and the children to Texas, she said, "Well, the family came first. What could a person say or do?"

Asked why she didn't just pack and leave, she said she "didn't have any money. I was working for Mr Durand."

Pat said that again, in Houston, she was introduced as Ray's boss's wife and she remembered buying Jeannine an organ at Christmas. Sometime after Christmas, she said, Ray called and asked her to come over. When she got there, Jeannine, with Ray interpreting, "asked me if I could look after the children," and said that "her mother was ill and she was going to go and take care of her. It was afternoon, late afternoon," Pat remembered. They all had dinner together, the children were put to bed and then Ray and Jeannine left the house, apparently headed to the airport. Jeannine, she said, had a suitcase with her.

By next morning Ray hadn't returned. Pat said she made breakfast, fed the baby and then spent the day at her apartment with the kids. Ray, she said, showed up at the apartment that afternoon.

From that point on, Pat said, she lived with the family. They immediately got a bigger apartment and then, several weeks later, moved into another house. Then, several weeks after that, they were watching television one night and the news came on.

"Where were the children?" Wilson asked.

"They were in bed."

"Can you tell the members of the jury what it was…in the news broadcast that caught your attention?"

"They said that a body had been found and they were showing clothing, if anyone could identify the clothing."

"Did they state the sex of the body?"

"Female."

"Do you recall if they gave a location?"

"Yes, they did. They said they found a body in a dump."

"Did Raymond Durand say anything to you?"

"He said, 'They found her.' I said, 'Found who?' He said, 'Jeannine.' And I said, 'I thought she was in Canada.' He said, 'She's there,' and that if I said anything about it to anyone that's where I would be, too."

"Did you ask Raymond why he did it?"

"He said she was going to die anyway, that she had cancer."

"Were you shocked?"

"Of course."

Asked why she didn't leave, Pat said simply, "I was looking after the children."

This testimony was the nub of what Wilson wanted. Now he hurried Pat through the rest of it. She described their continent-wide journey from Houston to Big Thicket, San Diego, Victoria, Ottawa and then back to San Diego. She described leaving Denis behind in Ottawa. She said from San Diego she and Ray had bought the ranch in Riverside County and then had finally split up in 1986.

The final question Wilson asked was about Jeannine's height.

"Was she taller than you?"

"Yes, she was."

"Was she as tall as Raymond Durand?"

"I believe she was."

Zimmermann rose, introduced himself to Pat and put her on the defensive from the moment he asked his first question. He asked if she had been able to have children in 1968 and she said no.

He invited her to admit that she had met Jeannine in Canada and that she had given Jeannine all her winter clothes when she and Ray had left for Florida. Pat denied knowing Jeannine in Canada and said she had given Ray her winter clothes to sell or to give to his sisters.

Zimmermann asked his questions rapidly and aggressively and initially Pat was able to keep up.

"Well, did you know her [Jeannine] in Florida?"

"Yes, I did."

"You were over at her house all the time, weren't you?"

"No, not all the time, no."

"Well, at least once a day, right?"

"No, sir."

"Did you not baby-sit those children all the time, Mrs Holben?"

"Not all the time, no."

"After that baby was born, were you not over there every day?"

"No, I was not over there every day."

"Who held Martine at the christening?"

"I did."

"You thought of Martine as your child, didn't you, ma'am?"

"I don't understand that question."

"Let me ask it again. You thought of Martine as your own child, didn't you, ma'am?"

"No, sir. I knew she was not my child."

The rapid-fire questions kept coming.

"Martine thought you were her mother, didn't she?"

"Yes, she did."

"And you encouraged her to believe that?"

"Yes, I did."

"For sixteen years after her birth, correct?"

"That's right."

"And you told everybody she was your child, your daughter?"

"That's right."

"And you considered her your daughter, didn't you?"

"Of course."

"You didn't feel the same about Denis, did you?"

"No."

"And you didn't feel the same about Anne?"

"No."

"And you didn't feel the same about Marc?"

"No."

"You treated them differently than you did Martine, didn't you?"

"She was a baby when I got her."

Zimmermann was relentless. He had now opened up her life, exposed some of the ugly, hard truths about her feelings for the kids she had helped raise. But Pat still had reserves of strength, strength that appeared to be drawn from a fierce instinct for survival. Zimmermann may have opened up doors to her past but she'd taken some hard knocks in her life. If there was one thing she could take, it was punishment. It wasn't clear if Zimmermann understood that he'd never shame her into submission or throw her off balance by hurting her feelings. Her only real weakness was her limited intelligence, a condition possibly induced by a lifetime of drinking.

And so she stood up to his aggressive questioning, refusing to admit that she was the one who didn't want Denis in the house, denying that she ever told Anne that Jeannine had pushed her in front of a car and repudiating the suggestion that Jeannine had planned to leave her kids in Florida. But the longer he went on, the more complex his questions became, the more confused she became.

"I noticed that on some of the questions that were asked of you by Mr Wilson you said, at the end of the answer, that you're not sure, some dozen times or so. Do you recall that?"

"That's right."

"Because it was a long time ago, right?"

"That is right."

"And it's hard to remember those things, correct?"

"Correct."

"Anybody would have a hard time remembering something that happened say ten or fifteen years ago, correct?"

"Right."

"And when you get back beyond that—the twenty-five, twenty-four, twenty-five year—it is even more difficult to remember what happened, isn't it?"

"That is correct."

Having led her to acknowledge the fallibility of memory, Zimmermann took her back to the most critical portion of her testimony. He got Pat to admit that Jeannine spoke broken English and that they had been able to communicate. Then he suggested that Frenchy had flown from Houston to Ottawa to pick up Jeannine and the children. Pat denied it at first, but the second time he suggested it, she said, "He may have. I don't remember." He tried to get her to admit that she had picked them up at the airport but she held firm on that one and insisted she hadn't. So he tried another tack, suggesting she had gone to the airport with Jeannine to pick up her ticket and that Jeannine had told her, a week before Ray called and asked her to come over, that she had made a reservation for a flight back to Ottawa. But again Pat denied both suggestions. Then suddenly he asked about when she and Frenchy split up and suggested that it was Frenchy who had left her and not she him.

"That is correct."

"You still loved him, didn't you?"

"Yes."

"Do you still love him now?"

"No."

Zimmermann asked Pat if she had ever gone to the police before Nadeau, Talton and Madeira showed up on her doorstep. She said no and so he asked why she had talked to them after having concealed the truth about Jeannine's death for more than twenty years.

"Because they asked me. That's why I answered their questions."

"Because they asked you?"

"Yes."

He got her to admit that she hadn't gone to the police after she had seen the news story in 1968, that she had never talked to the RCMP. The cross-examination went on for the remainder of the afternoon, went on until Densen noticed the clock and stopped the proceedings for the day.

Pat must have been exhausted and confused, but the following day she was back on the stand and Zimmermann was ready to pound away at her again. He took her through the statement she had made to Madeira, to the part where she had said that she and Jeannine became good friends in Houston. If that was the case, he said, then "you were able to communicate with her even though she spoke broken English; am I right?"

"Yes."

So, he suggested, when Ray called and she went to the house, it was Jeannine who "talked to you in broken English and asked you to take care of her children." Pat agreed with that and he immediately jumped on her, asking when she had suddenly remembered that Frenchy had been interpreting. She said she was confused so he rephrased the question and again she agreed that Jeannine had talked to her herself.

"Did you just think it would make it clearer if you said Frenchy interpreted or why did you testify that way yesterday?"

"Because what I didn't understand, he would tell me what she was trying to say to me."

But Zimmermann referred to the statement she had made to the police and pointed out that it made no reference to Frenchy's interpreting. Thinking he had cornered her, he asked, "Now, after she

[Jeannine] asked you that [to take care of her children], did she, in your presence, call home and say, 'I'm coming home on such and such a flight, pick me up at the airport.' Did you hear her say that on the phone?"

"They didn't have a phone at the home, I don't believe."

"I thought you had indicated that Frenchy had called you before?"

"From a pay phone."

"From a pay phone? How did you know it was a pay phone?"

"Well, it could have been a neighbour. I'm not sure."

Zimmermann was taken aback. He had made repeated attempts to get Pat to acknowledge that Jeannine was unhappy in Houston, that she had left Frenchy before, that she knew Frenchy was sleeping with Pat, that she had made her own travel arrangements—made a plane reservation, bought a ticket or phoned home about her arrival time. He evidently intended to argue that Jeannine had simply decided to leave Frenchy and that if something had happened to her after she had walked out, he couldn't be held responsible. But the only point he ever got Pat to agree to was that Jeannine had told her, when she, Pat, had arrived at the house after being summoned by Frenchy, that her mother was sick and wanted her to return to care for her.

So he moved on to Frenchy's return the next day. No, she agreed, she hadn't seen him come in with a suitcase.

"He looked like he always did?"

"Yes."

"No torn clothes?"

"No."

"No blood spots on his shoes, right?"

"No."

"Or on his pants or shirt?"

"No."

"Did you see any blood spots in his car?"

"No."

"And there was no blood on the bumper of his car or anything like that, was there?"

"No."

And then he got her to admit that she had immediately moved into an apartment with Frenchy and the kids and then, several weeks later, into another house.

"Now help me," he asked Pat, "and tell the jury why you moved into another house instead of just moving into Jeannine's house?"

"No, I can't tell you why."

"What were you thinking at that time?"

"I had no control over that."

"Well, but you see, didn't you think at the time, didn't you tell the prosecutor that you thought that Jeannine had just gone temporarily to take care of her mother?"

"Yes."

"Well, why would you need to change to a bigger apartment on what seems like perhaps a permanent-type basis if she was just going to be gone temporarily?"

"I have no idea."

So, he continued, they all moved and the children saw Frenchy and Pat sleeping together, and all that began the day after Frenchy came back from the airport.

"Didn't you think it would be exceedingly odd [for Jeannine] to come back to the two-bedroom apartment and find the children there with y'all? Did that cross your mind?"

"No."

"Well, how were you going to explain it to Jeannine, why you were sleeping with her husband and had her children over at your place instead of baby-sitting them in her house? What was your explanation going to be?"

"I didn't think about it."

"I mean, she did ask you to baby-sit them, to take care of them while she was gone, right?"

"That is right."

"Or did she give them to you?"

"No, she didn't."

"Did she say, 'These are your kids. I'm not coming back?'"

"No."

Zimmermann had worked himself into a state of mocking incredulity and he lashed out at Pat.

"You knew she wasn't coming back because she had told you she had had it with this arrangement with you and Frenchy and she wasn't putting up with it any more and she was leaving. Now, she told you that when she left for the airport, didn't she?"

"No, she did not," Pat shot back.

By now Zimmermann had raised troubling doubts about Pat's story, about her account of the events surrounding Jeannine's departure. None of it seemed reasonable, especially to people who knew nothing more about Frenchy than what had been presented at the trial. And the doubts weren't about Frenchy. One could understand why he would have wanted to move. Say, Jeannine had quarrelled with him and left. Maybe he had moved because he didn't want her to come back and make a grab for the kids. But what about Pat? Why would she have gone along with it if she believed that Jeannine would be back in a couple of weeks?

Zimmermann had done some very sharp work. But he wasn't finished yet. He wanted to know more about the newscast. He took Pat through her own testimony, got her to agree that she hadn't left Frenchy in Florida when he told her about his wife and kids because she didn't have any money. And she testified she hadn't left after the newscast because, again, she didn't have any money and she had to care for the kids. He got her to agree that it was all a long time ago and that maybe she didn't remember exactly what had been said and that she wasn't clear on whether Frenchy had threatened her. By now she was confused and he pounced.

"Because that conversation never really did happen, did it, Pat? The conversation at the so-called newscast, that never really happened, did it?"

To his own astonishment, she replied, "It could have."

"It could have?"

"Yes."

"But it didn't for sure, did it?"

"I am not positive."

By now the groans from the prosecutor's table were almost audible.

"You cannot say under oath to this jury that Frenchy Durand made those comments you testified to the jury about yesterday? You cannot say that for sure under oath, can you?"

"No."

"It's what you think may have happened, correct?"

"That is correct."

"And you were in California when you gave that statement and these police officers show up at your door; and, of course, that was a little bit frightening, wasn't it?"

"Yes."

Some of the life seemed to have gone out of Pat. Wilson and Taylor looked shell-shocked. Their case appeared to be unravelling. Their star witness was no longer sure about anything.

Zimmermann kept at it. He pointed out to Pat that she hadn't left Frenchy in Victoria when she was at her own father's house, and that she hadn't left him in Ottawa. "You can't say you didn't have money then because you were right back where you were that you previously held a job that paid money, right?"

"Yes."

And she hadn't left, Zimmermann said, because she wasn't sure Frenchy had done anything wrong.

"I don't know if he did or he didn't."

Now he moved in to deliver the *coup de grâce*: "Because you don't know whether that conversation really happened or not. You're not sure, you're not positive."

"That's right."

"Because you're not the kind of person that would have gone to bed that very night after the newscast with someone who you thought killed his wife, would you?"

"No," she replied in a small, tight voice.

It was all uphill for Wilson when he rose to attempt to salvage what he could of Pat's testimony. She was weary now, sitting there with her mouth open, listening intently and often asking Wilson to repeat his questions. If nothing else, he had to get her to reconfirm her story of the conversation following the newscast. He started off slowly, patiently, speaking clearly and posing simple questions. Her first response wasn't hopeful, though.

"What do you remember him saying when the newscast came on?" Wilson asked.

"Not too much because we had been drinking."

If that unexpected admission floored him, Wilson didn't betray it. He went on but was repeatedly interrupted by objections from Zimmermann. Zimmermann was up and down like a jack-in-the-box. He had scored and wasn't about to let his victory slip from his grasp. It was painful to watch. Pat was now so muddled that Wilson had constantly to repeat his questions, and every time he did, Zimmermann would argue that he was leading his witness. But finally the questions and answers began to click.

"Do you remember the news broadcast coming on?"

"Yes."

"When the news broadcast came on, I want you to tell the jury now what you remember the defendant saying to you first? What did he say first when the story came on?"

"He said, 'They found her.'"

"Okay. Did you say anything to him then?"

"I said, 'Who?'"

"And what did he say?"

"Jeannine."

"And what did you say?"

"I said, 'I thought she was in Canada.'"

"What did he say?"

"No, she isn't."

"Did you say anything then or did he say anything further?"

Zimmermann jumped in again with an objection, and then two more. It seemed to take forever before Pat was given an opportunity to respond. It felt as if Frenchy's fate was hanging in balance and that his future would be decided by what Pat would say next.

"What else was said in front of the television other than what you just testified to to the jury that you remember, Pat?"

"If you say anything about this you will end up where she is."

"Now I want you to look at the jury. My question to you now, ma'am, is did that conversation that you just testified to again before this jury, did that conversation take place back then?"

"Yes, it did."

Wilson looked like a man who had just saved a drowning child. Now he needed to make sure the jury understood what he had just done. He assured Pat that he understood that after all this time he hardly expected that she would be able to recall the exact words that Frenchy had used. But, he said, "if you don't remember the exact words just do you remember generally what was said by the defendant?

"Not the exact words."

"I understand that and the jury understands that but generally speaking is that what was discussed?"

"Yes."

"Are you sure about that?"

"Yes."

Now it was Zimmermann's turn to try to preserve what he had won. He went at Pat for a brief recross-examination.

"Because of the passage of time you really don't remember for sure what was said. Am I right?"

"That is correct."

"You also told this jury that you are not even sure that that conversation really happened that way. Isn't that true?"

"Not word for word, no."

"Whatever it is that happened after that newscast, you slept with Frenchy that night, didn't you?"

"Yes."

When Pat finally left the witness stand that afternoon, it was anybody's guess what the jury would conclude from her testimony. They might simply decide none of it was reliable, that she had contradicted herself so many times that she couldn't be trusted on any point. And, in fact, large parts of her story didn't make sense. Why hadn't she left? Why had they moved the day after? Had she really slept with a murderer all those years?

Wilson's best hope was that the jury would recognize that she had been confused on the stand. As for Zimmermann, his hope was that the jury would have begun to suspect that none of Pat's testimony was true and that if anyone had a motive for killing Jeannine, it was Pat herself. He had left a trail of hints littered throughout his cross-examination: Pat couldn't have children; she had considered Martine her own child; she loved Ray but had been forced to share him, and finally, the moment Jeannine had disappeared, Pat had moved in and had become the mother of the four children. It was a just plausible enough scenario to create the reasonable doubt Frenchy needed for an acquittal.

Chapter Twenty-Six

Houston, Texas, 1992: Part 4—The Defense

Réginald sat on a bench in the courthouse hallway all morning, intimidated by the busy activity of the place. Denis was beside him, headphones on, country music thumping on his Walkman, and a magazine open in his lap. Denis was nervous. He couldn't concentrate and was lost in a sea of his own worries. But he had spent enough time by now with his uncle to know that keeping Réginald company didn't mean he had to constantly stir up conversation.

Denis assumed that Zimmermann would try to hang the whole thing on him, argue that the charge against Frenchy was all his doing and that he had, after a lifetime of effort, dragged everyone else along for the ride. He figured the defence attorney would badger him about how much he hated Frenchy.

What made Denis even more tense was the fact that Ray's brother Gerry and Gerry's wife, Louise, were sitting down the hall. They had been there since the outset of the trial; they weren't allowed into the courtroom because they were expected to testify. Denis wasn't particularly fond of Uncle Gerry and he wasn't about to sit around gabbing with him when he knew Gerry was going to get up on the stand and help save Ray's skin. He figured if Gerry walked over, he'd tell him to fuck off.

Michel Béland had accompanied Réginald and Denis downtown that morning but had decided to remain behind in Wilson's office. He was worried that Zimmermann would think he was coaching Réginald if he spent the day in the hallway with him. Béland was anxious about how Réginald would handle it all.

He needn't have worried. Réginald, in baggy tan trousers, a chocolate-brown double-breasted sports coat, a white shirt and a thin leather tie, made an effort all morning to look relaxed, as if he did this sort of thing all the time. He had combed the little hair remaining on his head, brushed his bad teeth and actually swaggered when he walked. His gestures were exaggerated, studied. But he was holding up.

Finally, at 2 P.M., he was called into the courtroom and sworn in.

He plunked himself down in the witness-box and folded his arms over his large belly. One of the things several jurors later said they noticed immediately was his high forehead. It is exactly the same shape as the forehead of the woman in the morgue photo.

Gratton was called to translate for Réginald, and he stood beside the witness. He had to be quick though, because Réginald had a tendency to answer before Gratton could translate the question. Gratton would still be asking the question, when Réginald would tell him the answer in French. Several times Réginald had to be told to slow down and wait until the question had been asked. It was apparent from the start of his testimony that this man was no imbecile. For several days before his testimony, both Zimmermann and Lavine had hinted to reporters that Réginald was going to be a surprise for everyone. It appeared that Ray had suggested to them that Réginald was a half-wit.

Taylor conducted the examination of Réginald and got him to recite the outlines of his life story—born in Hull, mother died in 1983, father died in the fall of 1979, and his only sister, Jeannine, had married in 1954. He recounted Jeannine's move to Florida, her return, the summer months she and the children spent with them and her departure by taxi for the airport in Montreal. He said that over Christmas, 1967, Jeannine had called home six times and that the last call was on January 1. He said they never saw or heard from her again.

Réginald told about Ray's visit to his house in 1970, how Ray had said that Jeannine and the children were in Vancouver. Réginald said Ray gave them an address and several phone numbers and that his mother rang the numbers when she returned home.

"They were false numbers," Réginald said, without expression.

Réginald said his mother wrote nine letters to the Vancouver address and that all of them were returned unopened.

Then Taylor asked Réginald how tall Jeannine was.

"Five feet, seven inches," he replied.

"And your mother?"

"Five feet, seven and three-quarter inches."

"You recall your sister comparing height with your mom?"

"Yes, my mother was a bit taller."

Asked about Jeannine's hair and eye colour, Réginald said she had blue eyes and light-brown hair but had dyed it at some point.

Taylor then handed Réginald the morgue photo and several jurors held their breaths while he looked at it for a moment.

"It's my sister, Jeannine," he replied without a trace of emotion.

As Lavine opened his cross-examination, the question that Zimmermann had put to Béland earlier in the trial came to mind. He'd asked Béland if Réginald had ever worked. That question and the knowing glances and rolling eyeballs Zimmermann and Lavine had been giving reporters whenever Réginald's name had come up suggested that the defence strategy for this witness was going to be to portray him as either retarded or as a dangerous nutbar whom the family had kept hidden in the attic. But when Réginald revealed himself in the prosecution's examination to be anything but a moron, it appeared that the nutbar option was on. And, sure enough, that's where Lavine's subtle questioning headed.

Lavine began by suggesting to Réginald that he didn't like Raymond Durand.

"Well, yes, because of the false numbers and things like that," Réginald answered through Gratton.

Lavine got Réginald to admit that Jeannine had likely known in Canada that Ray was chasing other women. Then Lavine began working towards the set-up. He suggested that the house had been very crowded when Jeannine and the children had been there and Réginald agreed. He asked about how Réginald had identified the photo and asked whether Michel Béland had told him it was a picture of his sister before he looked at it. Réginald insisted that Béland had just asked if he recognized the person in the photo. Then Lavine zeroed in on Réginald himself.

"What do you do for a living?"

"I have small interests but it is none of your business," Réginald, who was obviously taken aback, replied defensively.

Prodded again on the same subject by Lavine, Réginald became agitated. "I don't think this has anything to do with this case....I've always been sick. It's very hard for me to come here. I'm not in very good health. I get sick during the night—throw up—can hardly sleep."

Asked if he took medication, Réginald said yes. Asked what, he said Aspirin.

There's something about your past that you don't want to discuss, Lavine suggested.

"I've never done anything wrong," Réginald protested. "I don't know what he is trying to say."

That was all Lavine needed and he let up. He concluded by asking Réginald several questions about Jeannine's eye and hair colour and then announced he had completed his cross-examination. Réginald looked greatly relieved when he stepped down, and he forgot to swagger when he hurried out of the courtroom.

After a short break, Denis was called and, more than twenty years after he had first begun telling people that his father was lying about what had happened to Jeannine, he entered a courtroom to give his story under oath. He had been waiting for an opportunity such as this for most of his life. After his mother had been reburied, he said that just the fact that he now knew where she was and what had happened to her had both confirmed his sense of self and allowed him to reclaim his childhood with her. Finding her had been like throwing a lifeline over the dark years, years when he had lived with what Tennyson called "confusion worse than death," to his childhood when he had always had her companionship and love to sustain him in moments of sadness, grief or shame. He had said that what mattered to him was knowing about his mother and not what Texas was going to do with Frenchy. He insisted that he had what he had always wanted, which was the security of knowing that his mother hadn't walked out on him and his sisters and brother, of knowing that she hadn't just abandoned them, that, indeed, as he remembered, she had loved them fiercely, protectively and unconditionally.

Now, when Denis walked into the courtroom, wearing a dark-blue suit, his thinning blonde hair combed back, his eyes betrayed him. After he was sworn in and sat down, he gave Frenchy a look of undiluted hatred, his blue eyes flat and hard. His eyes said what he had denied. The fact was that he despised Frenchy for what he believed he had done to Jeannine. The look he gave his father— and it was a look that did not escape either the jurors or the attorneys or anybody else in the courtroom—said: Burn in hell. He looked as though he was ready to leap from his seat, wrap his hands around his father's wrinkled, fat neck and squeeze the life out of him. Those watching began to wonder if his hatred would undermine his testimony, lead jurors to question his credibility. As it turned out, Taylor's deft questioning allowed Denis to pour his feelings into his testimony and what came out was a powerful, damning indictment of Ray's casually brutal treatment of his wife and children.

Denis told the jury about his early childhood, about life on Michaud Street, of how his father had gone bankrupt in 1966 and moved them to Bernier Street. He said he began delivering newspapers and giving his earnings to his mother because his father had gone to Florida and left them with no money. He described the move to Florida and his introduction to Pat, whom his father described as his boss's wife.

He said his father had sent them back to Hull because there was no French school for them. He said they lived with the Boissonneaults until one night, at the end of summer, they had taken a cab to Dorval airport in Montreal.

"Plane tickets were there for us. For Houston. My father met us at the airport in Houston. He took us to a house on Beech Street. I didn't speak much English."

Denis said he remembered that when they were driving in from the airport his father had told his mother, "Jeannine, you won't believe this. I was driving to Louisiana to find a French school and who do I meet but Pat and her husband." Denis said Ray told Jeannine that he had decided to follow them to Houston and work in their body shop.

He told the court about Pat winking at his dad while his mom prepared Christmas dinner that year, about riding by Pat's apartment on his bike and seeing his dad's car in the driveway. And he recalled the time in Florida, when his mother had been in the hospital having Martine and Pat was baby-sitting and his dad was supposedly sleeping on the sofa.

"I'd get up to take a leak and Dad wouldn't be on the couch. I never told Mom."

He described his mother as "a nice, quiet, shy person. She loved us very much. She was big. I knew my mom was tall but don't recall how tall. She had false teeth, upper and lower."

He said one morning he got up, found Pat at the kitchen table and was told that his mother had gone back to Hull to take care of her sick mother. He said he never saw her again. His last memory of her, that he said he could date, was his birthday, December 30, 1967.

"My mom had baked a cake. Dad's birthday is on the same day. Dad didn't show up. Mom was mad."

He said he was at the house the day after his mother had supposedly left for Canada. He saw his father come in and he always remembered that Ray had been carrying two suitcases, one of which was the suitcase that he remembered Jeannine buying in Ottawa so her dresses wouldn't crease. He said his father told him that Jeannine would be back in two weeks and he kept repeating that until one day "we were in the car, driving by the Astrodome. I was in the back seat [and asked him about Jeannine]. I started crying. He went to slap me and said, 'Shut your fucking mouth and don't bug me about that.' He said she didn't love me and that I was to call Pat mom."

By now Denis had the jurors' rapt attention. Not only was his testimony detailed and compelling, but he, too, like his uncle Réginald, had the high forehead that several jurors had noted in the morgue photo. At the defence table, Ray couldn't look at Denis. He appeared uncomfortable in the extreme. Every now and again Denis would shoot him another contemptuous glance.

Denis recounted the move to Big Thicket and how unhappy he was. Staring at his dad, he said he would often cry and tell Ray and Pat that they didn't love him. He said Ray and Pat both called him "a big baby, a big dummy."

He said at school they still went by the name Durand. But elsewhere they were Holbens. He described the move to San Diego, then Victoria and finally Ottawa. He described the day he snuck out of the house, found the phone number for Hermas Boissonneault, and called up his grandparents. He talked about visiting them and coming home that night to find his father waiting for him, furious at him for having visited the Boissonneaults. He said his father promised to buy him a set of drums if he agreed not to go back there.

He said his father left him with his grandmother Durand and disappeared with Pat and the other kids, and it was several years before he found out where they had gone. He described his visit with the journalist to the police and how his grandparents refused to sign a complaint so the police would take him seriously. He said the police had told him to come back on his eighteenth birthday and that three weeks before that birthday, his dad had called, told him he was living in San Diego and invited him down. He described the fight he had with his dad after he had moved to San Diego and was about to return to Canada to get married. He had wanted Anne to come along but Ray refused to let her go. They had quarrelled, Jeannine's name had come up and he said Ray told him: "I know where Jeannine is. When she is good and ready to see you, I will take you."

Finally, Denis talked about returning to Canada and of not seeing his father for years. He told the jurors about Anne's decision in 1990 to help him search for Jeannine. He described the events leading up to Anne's lunch with Nadeau, which launched the investigation.

Then, as he had done three times before, Taylor placed the morgue photo in front of the witness.

"My mom," Denis said, fighting to hold back the tears.

Now Denis braced himself for a grilling by the defence. Lavine stood and, to the astonishment of everyone in the courtroom, announced, "No questions."

Reporters swarmed around Zimmermann and Lavine after Densen recessed the jury for the day. Asked why they hadn't cross-examined, Zimmermann tried to appear magnanimous.

"You have to look at him as a potential victim of circumstance," he said expansively. "He has lost [his mother]. Why prolong his pain. Denis is a very sympathetic young man."

Lavine justified the decision by insisting that Denis hadn't said anything "that hurt Frenchy's case....He's angry. He gave an historical account."

Both lawyers said Denis had made certain assumptions but had otherwise said nothing damaging in his testimony. They sounded hopeful and certain that they had done the right thing.

Ray had remained composed throughout most of the trial. Seeing Anne and Denis had been unnerving for him but he hadn't broken down or shown anything more than nervousness.

Wilson had originally planned to make Denis his last witness. But he had become concerned about Dr Bucklin's testimony in cross-examination. Bucklin had said he "would have expected to have seen" signs of a tubal ligation during the autopsy and that he "didn't think" he could have missed it. Wilson was also concerned about the discrepancy in eye and hair colour. Jeannine had blue eyes and blonde hair while the corpse had eyes that "appeared brown" and dark brown hair. The height discrepancy he felt he had dealt with. The hospital records showed Jeannine as five feet, three inches, but every witness had said she was taller and Réginald had been precise, had said she was five feet, seven inches, the same height as the corpse. So Wilson called in his heavy gun, Dr Joseph Jachimczyk, chief medical examiner for Harris County.

Jachimczyk has been chief medical examiner since 1960, and was Bucklin's boss in 1968. A short, white-haired, veteran forensic pathologist, Jachimczyk entered the court wearing white shoes, a blue suit and a bow-tie. He was sworn in and in a booming, power-ful voice said he was not only a graduate of Harvard's department of legal medicine but also had a degree in law from Boston College and a degree in theology.

Jachimczyk said he had recently reviewed Bucklin's notes of the autopsy. Wilson asked him if the Fallopian tubes could appear normal after a tubal ligation. With the permission of the judge, Jachimczyk walked over to a blackboard, took up a piece of chalk, drew a sketch and described how the tubes are tied off at two places, a cut made between the ties and the two ends pulled together. He said the surgeon doesn't leave a gap between the two ends because the gap would be a potential source of infection.

"When healing occurs," he said, "it may look normal to the naked eye, or at best it might look like a small dimple."

Wilson showed Jachimczyk Jeannine's medical records and asked if there were anything in them that would lead him to change his mind about the identification of 68-500. He said there wasn't. Asked about the eye colour, Jachimczyk said Bucklin had not said that the eyes were brown but that they appeared to be brown. He said the eye colour itself does not change but the appearance of the eyes change: "Whites of the eyes have blood vessels. In the presence of decomposition, the haemoglobin in the eye breaks down and forms a dark pigment. Light colour becomes a dark colour."

Asked if hair colour changes in a decomposing body, Jachimczyk said, again, the colour itself does not change. "But appearance does. It also looks much darker. Light hair looks dark. If you wash the hair it will turn the original colour."

Wilson was careful not to invite Jachimczyk to criticize the work of his former colleague so he phrased his next question with delicacy.

In fairness to Bucklin, he said, are there difficulties when performing an autopsy on a decomposing body?

It is more difficult, said Jachimczyk. "It's not Chanel # 5, that's for sure."

Asked by Wilson if he might change his mind about the identification of 68-500 if he was told that Jeannine had a birthmark on her forehead, Jachimczyk said no, that it wouldn't make any difference. He had explained earlier that decomposing skin looks darker and presumably could obscure a birthmark.

Zimmermann cross-examined Jachimczyk and insisted that if Bucklin had suspected the eyes were not brown, he would have made a notation to that effect. But Jachimczyk said he accepted what Bucklin had recorded, which was not that the eyes were brown but that they appeared brown. The two men went back and forth, Zimmermann pointing out the difference in hair colour, the difference in height noted in the hospital records, the difference in weight, and Jachimczyk patiently explained away the inconsistencies, assuring the attorney that he was certain his staff had not made an error in identifying 68-500 as Jeannine Durand.

Zimmermann finally gave up and Wilson announced he had completed the presentation of his case, which had taken seven and a half days. Densen allowed the jury to recess. As soon as they had filed out, Zimmermann moved for an instructed verdict for an acquittal. He argued that the evidence was insufficient "to support a verdict of guilty as it does not establish guilt beyond a reasonable doubt." Densen denied the motion, and at 2:20 that afternoon Zimmermann began presenting his defence.

Zimmermann's first witness was a gynaecologist, Dr Gerry Marcontell, who described in detail the surgical procedures involved in a tubal ligation. He described Jeannine's tubal as the standard "Pomeroy procedure."

"An incision is made below the navel," he said, "a section of the Fallopian tube is brought out, ligated, tied with catgut."

Asked what would happen to the tube ends after surgery, Marcontell said "they retract [from each other] corresponding to the amount of tube taken out."

How long would it take for them to retract? Zimmermann asked.

"I can't tell with certainty how long it would take. The sutures dissolve in twenty-one days. The retraction process begins after that."

Asked if the surgeon pulls the ends together to prevent anything from getting between them, Marcontell contradicted Jachimczyk and said no. And, finally, asked if the ligation would be visible eight months after surgery, Marcontell said, "It would definitely be detectable."

Wilson cross-examined and made short work of Marcontell. He asked the gynaecologist how much he was being paid to appear for the defence and Marcontell said, "Two hundred and fifty dollars an hour."

"How many autopsies have you done?"

"None."

"Have you ever heard of Dr Jachimczyk?"

"I believe he lectured in our class in medical school."

"Ever smelled a decomposing body?"

"No."

"You are not here to grade the papers of the medical examiner?"

"No, sir."

"Do you respect Dr Jachimczyk?"

"Yes."

"When a surgeon has finished [the tubal] these two ends are placed back together as close as possible?"

"They are so close the blood supply is cut off."

"Leaving them touching?"

"Yes."

"Over time they move apart?"

"Yes."

The jury had by now heard a great deal about Ray, his life and his family. The jurors knew Ray had brothers and sisters and they must have wondered whether any of them were going to appear and speak for him. Zimmermann's second witness answered those expectations.

The witness was Hubert Labelle, a pompous, long-nosed fire-fighter who was dressed with all the flair of a car salesman and was married to Ray's sister Mireille. Having Labelle testify turned out to be the biggest mistake the defence was to make.

Labelle said he was the deputy fire chief in Gloucester, a small city in the Ottawa area. He said he met Jeannine about a year before she left for Texas and that he had viewed plenty of bodies horribly disfigured by fire. When shown the morgue photo, he was definitive.

"Sir," he said in the petty, officious tone he used throughout his testimony, "I cannot identify this picture."

Now Labelle was asked for a short discourse on language, specifically, on the differences between Quebec French and the French spoken in France.

"We call it [Quebec French] a slang French. It's a French that over the years has been used by Canadian people which is very, very different from Parisian French. We tend to group the syllables together instead of pronouncing them right, the proper way."

So, he was asked, it would be immediately possible to tell if a person speaking French was from Quebec or France?

"Oh, yes, most definitely."

Lavine conducted the examination of Labelle, and in his questioning he appeared to be toiling at the margins of the rules of evidence. He created the impression that Labelle was in possession of vital information but that he couldn't fully reveal it because of the arcane rules of law.

He asked Labelle about a visit he and his wife had made to San Diego in 1973. Labelle said they stayed with Ray, and that one morning after taking a shower in Ray's bedroom he was towelling off and he noticed an envelope on a dresser. He testified that he picked it up and was examining it when Ray walked in.

Given that the defence could not place the envelope in evidence, Labelle was prohibited from telling the jury what he learned from the envelope. Lavine knew that the prosecution would object, as Taylor did, and prevent Labelle from describing the contents the envelope that he said he had seen. Still, Lavine persisted. He wished to have Labelle testify to what Ray then said to him. Taylor objected, and the jury was sent out while they debated the point.

In front of the judge alone, Lavine had Labelle reveal what he wished his witness to tell the jury.

"I picked the envelope up off that little desk that was in his room. I proceeded to look at it. Ray walked into the room and he said, 'This is personal.' I said, 'I'm sorry, Ray. I didn't mean anything.' So, he took the envelope away from me and he put it in his pocket and walked out."

When Labelle had finished, Lavine said, "That's what we would offer, your honour."

Densen ruled that Labelle could not testify to what Ray had said because that constituted hearsay. The jury was brought back in, and Lavine went on.

The entire exchange was puzzling. What was its purpose? If all they had intended to do was to get Labelle to testify that Ray grabbed the envelope and said, "This is personal," then it seemed a bewilderingly narrow objective. On the other hand, if Lavine and Zimmermann were being frank, then it appeared that the only goal they had in mind was to hint to the jury that Labelle had seen something on that envelope, something about Jeannine, that revealed her whereabouts or the fact that she was still alive. Did they really believe that such a ploy would add another gram of doubt to the acquittal side of the scale? In the end, it was just confusing.

Lavine's next question added to the suspicion that he was using Labelle to plant the idea that Jeannine was alive. He asked Labelle whether he had ever made any attempt to find Jeannine.

Again Labelle replied in his officious tone, "I most certainly did."

In June, 1976, Labelle said he had dialled directory assistance for the Houston area. When the operator answered, he said, he asked for Bellaire in the Houston area. Another operator came on and he asked for the number for Jeannine Durand. The operator rang a number for him. He said he passed the phone to his wife, Mireille, but kept his ear close to the phone so he could hear the conversation. Again, the rules of evidence prohibited him from recounting the ensuing conversation between Mireille and the person who answered. But he was allowed to say that the person who answered was female and spoke French, "the French that we currently speak in the Hull-Ottawa area."

Asked what he and his wife did after they hung up, Labelle said, "We both looked at each other for possibly a minute or so pretty shocked. We just kept looking."

Lavine asked a series of questions about the conversation and about whether he thought they had spoken to Jeannine Durand. Taylor objected to every one of them and they were all disallowed.

Labelle was allowed to say that he and Mireille told Ray's mother about the call, but he wasn't permitted to say what her reaction was. The only clarification he was allowed to make was that after the call, they stopped looking for Jeannine.

By now the jury had perked up. They saw the prosecution trying desperately to limit what Labelle could recount of the phone call, a phone call that been made to the Bellaire address of a Quebec-French-speaking woman apparently named Jeannine Durand. And the phone call had been made in 1976, eight years after she had allegedly been killed and left in a dump. Had Labelle really located Jeannine? If so, why was the prosecution doing everything to prevent Labelle from talking about what had happened? And where was Mireille? Why hadn't she been called to testify instead of her husband?

But there was more. Now Lavine produced photocopies of single pages from the Houston telephone directories for the years 1971 to 1976. He showed them to Labelle and got him to tell the jury that, indeed, there was a listing for Jeannine Durand on Bellaire Boulevard in 1971, 1972, 1973 and 1974. In 1975, the listing had changed to an address on Gessner Street. And finally, he got Labelle to note for the jury that in the directory published in December, 1976, Jeannine Durand was no longer listed.

"And the date of your phone call to Bellaire, Texas?" Lavine asked Labelle.

"June, 1976."

Lavine offered no comment on the dates but clearly the implication was that Jeannine had fled after the phone call.

Now, suddenly, the entire case that the prosecution had put together seemed to be teetering. The odds of finding another woman with the same name, speaking the same manner of French, living in the same part of the city, and turning up a few years after Jeannine's disappearance seemed impossibly long. Labelle's testimony had, for the first time, created not just a reasonable doubt about the identity of 68-500, but a convincing doubt. There was no way the jury was going to be able to convict Ray Durand for the murder of Jeannine Durand given Labelle's testimony and those telephone directory listings.

Taylor cross-examined but didn't make an awful lot of headway. He did get Labelle to tell the jurors that in the phone listings the

woman's name was spelled Janine, not Jeannine. And he got
Labelle to admit that he had met Jeannine no more than six times.
Still, Labelle said, he could remember her hair and eye colour and
weight—about 135 pounds. He said he last saw her in the spring of
1967. Taylor asked if he could remember whether she had been
pregnant at the time. Labelle said he couldn't remember. So, Taylor
said, you can't say whether she was pregnant, "but you can estimate her weight?"

"Yes, I suppose so."

As a parting shot, Taylor pointed out that Jeannine was six
months pregnant at the time Labelle said he had last seen her.

When Taylor finished with Labelle, Zimmermann called in
Frenchy's brother Gerry. Short, balding, and wearing rose-tinted
glasses, Gerry testified that he worked for his older brother for
three years in the early 1960s. He said he had lunch with Ray's
family three times a week during those years and got to know
Jeannine well. He said she wore contact lenses, had blue eyes and
blonde hair and didn't have full dentures. He said she was only
missing two or three upper teeth. Shown the morgue photo, he said,
"No. I'm pretty sure that's not her."

Under cross-examination, Wilson got Gerry to say that he didn't
see Jeannine much in the final three years she lived in Canada and
that he had no idea whether she had full dentures by 1967.

Now Zimmermann wheeled out another expert witness, Dr Paul
Radelat, the former chief of pathology at the U.S. Naval Academy
and now a private pathologist in Houston. Zimmermann intended
to use him to refute Jachimczyk's testimony.

Radelat testified that hair and eye colour do not change after
death. And he said that he had performed autopsies on women who
had had tubal ligations and had found that the procedure "leaves a
fairly characteristic result." He said he had never seen a case where
the cut ends remained joined together. "The whole idea is to separate the ends as far away as possible," he said.

Zimmermann had asked Radelat to review Bucklin's autopsy
notes and now he asked his witness to render a professional opinion of Bucklin's work. Radelat said it appeared that Bucklin had
been thorough. Asked again if the tubes would appear normal,
Radelat assured the jury that "they would not."

When Wilson cross-examined Radelat, he first established that, while Radelat was a pathologist, he was not a forensic pathologist and was rarely called upon to identify bodies. Radelat also acknowledged that he was not a gynaecologist.

Wilson asked about eye and hair colour, and Radelat agreed that the appearance of both would change. Radelat told Wilson that he believed that the tube ends would retract within a matter of months. So Wilson turned to other remarks Bucklin had made in his autopsy report. Wilson asked about scars Bucklin had noted on the cervix. Radelat replied they could have been caused during childbirth, that it was reasonable to assume that the woman had had children. Then Wilson returned to the tubes, suggesting that immediately after the tubal, the ends are together and that they retract some time after. Radelat agreed.

Wilson pointed out that Bucklin, Jachimczyk and a third pathologist had examined five hundred bodies in the first six weeks of 1968.

"That's a lot of autopsies. They were doing a lot of work," he suggested to Radelat.

"It does imply they had a lot of customers," he agreed.

When the jurors were dismissed for the day, they had some troubling questions to mull over about the prosecution's case. Zimmermann had created a genuine doubt about the validity of the identification, a doubt that had nothing to do with the endless debate about retracting tubes. The damage had been done by Labelle's testimony. Jurors and observers still wondered why Labelle had testified and not his wife. But even with that question hanging in the air, the story of the phone call plus the phone listings seemed persuasive.

Wilson, on the other hand, didn't seem to have any doubt about the validity of Labelle's testimony. Before Labelle had even finished recounting his story, Wilson had asked a member of his staff to see if he could track down the Janine Durand who had been listed in the telephone book in the early 1970s. To the astonishment of everyone in the prosecutor's office, the staffer located her within a couple of hours and contacted her on her car phone, driving home from work. It turned out she was a sixty-one-year-old immigrant from France who had moved to the United States shortly before Jeannine had disappeared. It appeared that Zimmermann hadn't bothered to check if she was still around.

When Wilson's colleague explained to Janine about the trial, she readily agreed to appear the following day. Wilson talked to her later and she said she would be in his office the first thing the following morning. That night someone from Zimmermann's staff called her at home and discovered that she had already been contacted by the district attorney's office. Spurred by that knowledge, Zimmermann and Lavine apparently began plotting damage control. Having her appear was going to blow Labelle out of the water and damage their credibility.

The following morning, Wilson and his wife drove to the train station to see Réginald, Denis and Michel Béland off. They had been in Houston for almost three weeks and had decided they couldn't prolong their stay. Wilson told them about Labelle's testimony and about locating Janine Durand and promised the three men that he was going to have a great day with the defence team.

When Zimmermann and Lavine walked into court that morning, they had apparently worked out an opening position and two fallback plans. They weren't very sturdy plans, but then they didn't have much to work with. They had skated out on thin ice and were trying to make the best of it. The first plan was to get Labelle back up on the stand. They asked for and received permission to have Labelle take the stand again in *voir dire*. They wanted to clarify, Lavine said, what they had hoped he would testify to the day before and have Densen rule on whether he would permit the testimony. So in front of only the judge and the spectators, Labelle was sworn in again and asked to recount the conversation that had taken place between his wife and the woman he had called in Bellaire.

"She [Mireille] said, 'Hello, Jeannine. This is your sister-in-law Mireille, Ray's sister.'"

"Did the woman respond?"

"There was a pause for a few seconds and the lady responded, 'I do not have a sister-in-law named Mireille and I don't have a husband named Ray.'"

Labelle said Mireille then apologized and hung up.

"I said to Mireille, 'What do you think?' She said, 'It's got to be her.' I said, 'Why?' She said, 'Well, hell, what's the chance of a woman speaking French, the kind of French that I understand, all the way from Houston?' I said, 'You're right.'"

Labelle said he and his wife then told Ray's mother that they had spoken to Jeannine. The old lady, he said, was delighted with the news.

Taylor then questioned Labelle. He asked Labelle again whether the woman his wife spoke to had a French-Canadian accent and Labelle said she did. Then Taylor asked whether Labelle believed that the woman he had talked to was the woman listed in the phone directory. But Labelle responded that he hadn't said that at all, that he'd only said that he had called long-distance information.

At that point procedural wrangling broke out. Labelle was asked to step out of the court, and Lavine revealed why they wanted to be able to present to the jury Labelle's account of the conversation. He explained, in what seemed like serpentine logic, that the defence simply wanted to show that, although it had been alleged that Ray had told many different stories over the years about Jeannine's whereabouts, in fact the defendant was not the source of all the stories, that here was a case where a brother-in-law had, rightly or wrongly, believed he had talked to Jeannine and that he had spread the story through the family.

But Densen wasn't buying it and suggested that what would clarify the issue was not further testimony from Labelle, but testimony from the woman listed in the phone book.

"Did anyone try to find her?" Densen asked the lawyers. "Did the state try to find her, this Janine Durand? Did the defence try to find her?"

Seeing that he was up against it, Lavine admitted to Densen that he had talked to Janine Durand after Wilson's office had reached her. But he asked again to be allowed to "put Mr Labelle back on the stand to testify and clean up this conversation that the jury has the mistaken belief that he talked to Jeannine Boissonneault Durand, and that's not what we offered it for, and if they are then allowed to insert a rebuttal, put a woman on the stand by the name of Janine Durand who had those telephone records in 1974 or whenever it was, that they will then be attacking the defendant over the shoulders of the defence counsel."

By now Lavine didn't appear to be making a great deal of sense, and Densen announced he was "going to deny your offer of this testimony before the jury."

Defeated, Lavine bolted to his first fall-back position. He put to Densen a motion to suppress, demanding that the court "not allow the state to call Janine Durand to the witness stand in rebuttal."

Densen was quick with a response: "I'm going to deny that, counsel, because you are the one who brought up the issue of a conversation with a person....You brought the witness forward and the implication to the jury is very clear that you're implying that this was the deceased in this case, Jeannine Durand, and now you're saying, well, the state has no right to rebut that."

Hammered a second time, Lavine made a last desperate bid to wipe the egg off his face. He told Densen that he was issuing an "instanter subpoena for Janine Durand." The final fall-back position was to try to convince the jury that it was the defence and not the prosecution that had found Janine Durand and that she was their witness. The prosecutors said they had no objection so Densen granted the subpoena and the jury was called in. Densen had ruled that Labelle could not recount the content of the telephone conversation but Lavine apparently believed he could still repair some of the damage by bringing Labelle back. So he called him in and got Labelle to testify that he had gone to see Ray's mother, Marie-Anna Durand, after the phone call and told her what had happened. Then he showed Labelle the phone listings again and asked him whether he had attempted to tell the jury the day before that the person listed in the records was the same person his wife had talked to on the phone.

"Of course not, no," Labelle replied, to the mystification of the jurors.

"You don't know if this is the same person you talked to or not?"

"No."

"Do you recall if you gave the operator the spelling of the first name?"

"Only the last name."

By now the jurors were probably thoroughly baffled. The day before they had been led to believe that Labelle had called the woman listed in the phone book. Now he was distancing himself from that electrifying testimony.

To add to their confusion, shortly afterwards Judge Densen announced: "Call witness Janine Durand." All twelve jurors looked expectant, some looked astonished, and all of them stared when the courtroom door opened and a little old lady with grey hair, wearing glasses and white trousers, walked in and took the stand. Was this the long-lost Jeannine?

Lavine questioned her. In a deep, hearty voice she told the court that she was from France. The jurors relaxed; the dead woman hadn't suddenly come to life. What was even more interesting was that the moment Janine Durand opened her mouth and uttered her first word it became abundantly clear that she was not from Quebec. Even speaking English, she was unmistakably from France.

Lavine didn't have many questions. He simply got her to confirm that she was the woman listed in the phone book.

Taylor rose to cross-examine and inflict some damage on the reputation of the defence team. He asked whether it would be possible to distinguish between the French spoken in France and the French spoken in Quebec.

"Absolutely," she replied.

"So if somebody were to have called you, they couldn't have mistaken you for someone from Quebec?"

"Absolutely."

"When did you first know about coming to court?"

"Last night."

"Who called you?"

"Ted Wilson."

"How did he find you?"

"Looked in the phone book."

When Taylor finished, Lavine again tried to repair some of the damage. He asked several bewildering questions about the difference in accents between the north and south of France and then, in a tone that invited, if not begged, her to agree with him said: "You spoke to my office last night. We asked you to come here."

"You asked me if I was coming here," she replied. "I said yes. You said, 'I will see you here in the morning.'"

"But we subpoenaed you," Lavine shot back before sitting down.

Taylor jumped to his feet.

"Where were you when you got the subpoena?"

"In the district attorney's office."

Outside the courtroom, reporters swarmed around Janine, asking her if she had ever testified at a murder trial before. "No," she replied, admitting that she had been flabbergasted by the calls. Indulging his black sense of humour, John Makeig of the *Chronicle* asked how tall she was. She replied that she was five feet, one inch, and he looked disappointed. Still, like Jeannine, Janine had blue eyes and light brown hair. Makeig smiled, lit up a smoke and wandered off to chew on what oblique angle he could use to enter this bizarre story.

Janine's testimony had completed the defence's case. The trial had now been under way for almost two weeks.

The following morning, Densen read out instructions to the jury. He told them that Pat was considered, under Texas law, an "accomplice witness," and that they could not therefore convict Ray unless they, first, believed Pat beyond a reasonable doubt and, second, believed that her evidence was corroborated by other evidence that connected the defendant with the commission of the offence. Finally he added that the state wasn't obliged to prove its case beyond all possible doubt, only beyond all reasonable doubt.

If Lavine had been rattled by the events of the day before, he didn't show it that morning. He delivered his closing address with eloquence and conviction.

"This is a twenty-four-year-old case based on faded, perhaps confabulated memories." Lavine drew a mental picture for the jurors of Frenchy and Lady Justice standing on one side of a "great big ravine." He spoke of the bridge that had been thrown across that ravine by the state of Texas. "You have to walk over that bridge. You have to ensure you will not hesitate to step on each plank of that bridge, to be sure that a plank will not break and plunge you to the abyss below."

Bucklin, Lavine said, had testified that 68-500 was not Jeannine Durand because 68-500 had normal Fallopian tubes and brown eyes. Bucklin said it wasn't likely that he missed the tubal. "So don't step on that plank because it will break and you will fall to the abyss below."

The identification of 68-500 was based on medical evidence and the photo, he said. The photo identification was suspect. Nadeau got some information from Wingo about an unknown body with a scar, brown eyes, dark brown hair, five feet, seven inches tall, 144 pounds. Nadeau told Wingo that Jeannine weighed 144, stood five feet, seven inches and had brown eyes and reddish-brown hair. Where did he get his information? From Denis, Anne and Reggy, Lavine said. "Think of the circular nature of this and why we are here."

After these "false descriptions" had been given to the medical examiner's office, Wingo wrote to Béland, saying they had made "a presumptive ID" of the photo. "Michel Béland is not a lying witness. I'm not suggesting he is as I would if I were talking about Pat or Robert. But Béland saw Jeannine only once or twice after he was twenty or twenty-one years old. He does not remember."

Béland knew the family wanted "emotional closure, an end to this search." Lavine said Béland couldn't describe Jeannine's facial features and he testified that it was the only identification he had ever made of a decomposing body. Then Béland caused a very serious problem, Lavine said. Béland said that he told Denis and Reggy that he had identified the photo and then showed it to them so they wouldn't be shocked. "If he is wrong, then everybody else is wrong," Lavine then described what happened when Taylor showed Anne the photo. She began to cry. "Unless you are all dead," he said, "you felt the emotional pain of that moment, as I did. Why was that necessary? She couldn't identify her. She said she did not have a clear picture of her mother. For that emotional play, you can take them [Lavine pointed to Taylor and Wilson] to task."

As for Robert, Lavine asked: "What hate is welling in that man?...He is here because he got his dream crushed."

Then Lavine turned to Denis, reminding the jurors that Denis said that in 1974 his dad told him: "I know where Jeannine is. When she is ready to talk, I'll tell you." Denis visited the police with a journalist in 1972. Did the journalist plant the suggestion that his mother had been murdered? And, he added, Denis "knows something about Reggy that we don't know. When we asked him [Réginald] what he does for work, he said 'None of your business.' What does he have to hide?"

Réginald said Jeannine called home six times in a matter of days. "What was going on? Was she planning to leave Ray?" Lavine asked.

Finally, Lavine said, the stories don't make sense. "You have not heard any solid evidence that allows you to step on each plank. Each one is rotten. It will crack. Don't fall into the abyss," he concluded.

Zimmermann was the voice of reason when he began his address. He started in a soft, low voice and slowly wound himself up. "This case is probably the most clear example of reasonable doubt that you will ever find. If you don't know what happened, you have a reasonable doubt."

He urged them to look again at the morgue photo. "Is that Jeannine? If you are not convinced, you have no more work to do. He is not guilty. You can be out of here in ten minutes."

"Do you believe Pat Holben?" he asked. "If you don't beyond a reasonable doubt, then you don't have to consider anything further. Pat is the only witness that came before you and told you anything incriminating....If you don't believe the story of the newscast, then you can acquit."

Now he was reaching his stride, his voice taking on a sense of urgency. But just at that moment Densen interrupted and called for an emergency break. One of the jurors, who was taking medication, needed to rush to the washroom. Zimmermann was visibly frustrated. Ten minutes later, he attempted to reignite the momentum of his closing address.

We don't know what happened to Jeannine, Zimmermann told the jury as he paced back and forth in front of them. It was a rotten marriage; Jeannine left him once in Canada; Pat held the baby at the christening; Jeannine left him again in Florida; Jeannine and Pat were sharing a husband in Houston. Our suggestion, Zimmermann said, is that "at some point it becomes so obvious what is going on that even an eleven-year-old can see. Jeannine says to Pat, 'I've had it. I'm leaving.' The same day or the next, Pat takes the children and Frenchy to her apartment. She doesn't go to live in the house. Jeannine had told her she was leaving. She takes the family and moves with them to a rental house. Would she have done that if she had known that Jeannine was coming back?"

Who is telling the truth? Zimmermann asked, plaintively. The police officers were truthful and the four expert witnesses were truthful, he said.

Dr Jachimczyk was truthful as a pathologist but he made statements not in his field. "We brought you a real, live surgeon. He was truthful. They were honest witnesses, but they were mistaken," he said.

Denis and Anne were honest as well, he said, but also mistaken. "Anne said thirty-seven times in forty-eight minutes, 'I don't remember' or 'I don't know.' And Denis. You saw the looks he gave his dad, the hate in his eyes. We don't hold him at fault. He's just wrong."

Robert Durand, he said, wasn't worthy of belief and Pat "was a woman scorned who had lived with [Ray] for eighteen years and still loved him when he left. She told you she was scared when the police came. She made up a story that she thought they wanted to hear. You saw her. She said they'd been drinking."

Now he turned to his colour graphic of the female reproductive system. Pointing to the Fallopian tubes, he said, "It's a different body. The state is attacking its own witness's findings. The state is saying you should not believe what their own witness said he found in 1968."

He pulled out a chart he had drawn up:

68-500	JD
5'7"	5'3"
144 pounds	?
brown eyes	blue eyes
dark brown hair	blonde hair
normal tubes	Pomeroy
no contacts	wore contacts
no birthmark	birthmark on forehead
full dentures	don't know: witness saw upper bridge
Cdn clothing	?

Zimmermann invited the jurors to note the differences. He said that in one of his statements Denis had said that his mother had a faint birthmark on her forehead. No mention had been made in the autopsy of such a birthmark. The rest of it didn't match, he said.

Zimmermann said Frenchy had not run from the investigation and that none of the false stories had come from Frenchy. In addition, if Frenchy hadn't told the kids where Jeannine had gone, maybe it was because his wife had left him and he was embarrassed or frustrated or didn't know how to explain it to the kids.

Now he was hitting his stride again, his voice was rising with indignation. He said that when Labelle told Grandmother Durand about the phone call, that story had spread through the family.

"Is that the same kind of thing that would lead Denis to conclude that she was in an insane asylum?" he asked.

What about the clothes? he asked. None of the witnesses were able to say the clothes in the morgue pictures were Jeannine's clothes. "Did Pat say, 'That's the bedspread?' Denis said my mother only wore dresses. That's not a dress in the photo."

Why would Frenchy kill her anyway? "If Jeannine had wanted to leave, all she had to do was buy a ticket. The state doesn't have to prove motive. But you can ask. She had left before and she could leave again. She did."

Now Zimmermann was in high dudgeon. "Think of the resources arrayed against Frenchy—the sheriff's department, the Texas Rangers, the Texas Department of Public Safety, the Gatineau police, the Hull police, the RCMP. And what did Frenchy have? A three-lawyer law firm. Where are the fingerprints, blood type, clothes, instrument of death, bedspread, Canadian clothing?"

Zimmermann moved to stand beside his client, his hand on Frenchy's shoulder. "Frenchy should not pay the price because of human error. How can you prove a negative? We don't know where she is….Mr Lavine and I may have done a lot of things you didn't like. Don't hold it against Frenchy.

"I'll leave you with this. You are going on with your lives. All of us in this court are going on to other things. What about Frenchy? What would be the effect on him if you make a decision based on circumstantial evidence?"

Taylor opened for the prosecution. He was scornful and methodical. He began by striking out at Labelle's testimony, the defence's most vulnerable point.

The defence would have you believe, he said, that Jeannine Durand was in Houston in 1975 by virtue of a telephone listing and that she fled after the phone call. "The only assumption you can make is that their evidence is not accurate."

Ray's brother Gerry said Jeannine had a partial plate. "Recall what the oldest son said. Mother had upper and lower dentures….There is nothing there for you to consider."

Corpse number 68-500, he said, had "a clear indication of surgery. Dr Bucklin failed to account for the scar. It's supposed to be identified but it wasn't. Dr Jachimczyk concluded that it did account for a tubal." The experts agreed that the tube ends are placed together after surgery and then retract, said Taylor. As a person decomposes, it becomes more difficult to spot the results of a tubal. "There is not a doctor in the world who will admit that he has made a mistake. The evidence is that this doctor [Bucklin] made a mistake."

As for eye colour, when Bucklin said the eyes appeared brown, he was saying that he was not sure. "If he had been satisfied, he would have said blue or brown."

And what about Béland's identification of the photo, he asked. "Do you really believe that someone, under pain of perjury, would come in and tell you prosecution exhibit 1 was a loved one just to put Frenchy in jail? Do you really believe Michel Béland would jeopardize his standing in life merely for vengeance against this defendant?...He has a mental image of the deceased. He has no motive whatsoever to mislead you. And do you think a young woman who has loved her father for years and years and years would identify this photo as her mother? She testified she got along with her father, loved her father, but wanted answers."

"And by the way," Taylor paused, "I don't apologize for showing the photo to that woman. It is cruel. Nobody wants to relive that day. But I would also have been criticized for not showing it because the implication would have been that she couldn't identify the photo. No way to get around it. I hurt for her but I don't apologize."

Taylor tugged at some heartstrings, but for the most part he hung his address on the contradictions and weaknesses of the defence's theory. Wilson, when he finally rose, waded in on a note of sheer outrage.

"God help us," he thundered, "if a man can get away with murdering his wife and raising his children as he likes based on the mistake of an assistant medical examiner." Think of how difficult it must have been for Dr Jachimczyk to come before you, Wilson demanded, "and admit that one of his people had botched the autopsy. He's been the chief medical examiner for thirty-two years. He knows what happens when you tell family that this woman with six ribs broken, and her head hit so hard that it would be consistent with an automobile accident, the body laid out in potter's field, 'Well, you can come and get it, that's your mother.'"

Wilson reached for Zimmermann's comparison chart, which was

still staring at the jurors. He pointed at Zimmermann's notation of Jeannine's height, 5'3". Reaching over, Wilson picked up a group photo that Zimmermann had introduced into evidence during the trial. It was Jeannine and Ray's wedding photo.

Standing now in front of the jurors with the photo, Wilson pointed to Jeannine and Ray. "They put into evidence this photo of their client standing next to his wife. She's taller."

The birthmark, he asked, again pointing to the photo. "Where do the pictures show a birthmark?"

And the Canadian clothing. "How many women would have been in a field off the Barker-Clodine Road that would have had Canadian clothing on?"

As for their witnesses, Wilson said, let's deal with Hubert Labelle. Ray's brother-in-law came down here to "suggest to you that Jeannine was living in Houston in 1976. We caught them in that lie. [Labelle's] testimony was absolutely meaningless. He came here for one reason—to get his brother-in-law off the hook."

And why would this defendant want to kill? Wilson asked. "I don't understand what he saw in Pat. But he hung around her for eighteen years. Why did Pat beat Denis and Anne as badly as she did? Pat believed Ray was going to divorce his wife and that she [Jeannine] would leave with the kids. Suddenly, she [Pat] finds herself with the kids because of what he did. Reassess her treatment of Denis and Anne. She didn't want them in the first place. Martine— I can understand her wanting the baby. Suddenly she finds herself in a whole different predicament."

"Who could have killed Jeannine? Who knew her? The defendant and Pat. Fair to say none of the kids killed her. She couldn't speak English. She had no social contacts. Pat could have killed her but Jeannine was bigger. And if Pat had wanted to kill Jeannine, she would have known: I'm going to have to raise these kids."

Wilson told the jurors that there was sufficient evidence to corroborate Pat's testimony—Ray returning with the suitcase, the lies he told the children, the questions he put to Robert about decomposing bodies and his visit to the Boissonneault home in 1970. "He shows up at the in-laws. That's the epitome of gall. He shows up where his wife's brother and father live and tells them Jeannine is in Vancouver. Can you believe that gall?"

Wilson recalled one of Lavine's closing comments, the remark

Lavine had made about the family's felt need for emotional closure. "Closure is needed in this case. For twenty-four years this family has wondered. He stole from his family. He stole the mother from those kids. Twenty-four Mother's Days have gone by….Sooner or later everybody pays. Pay-day has taken twenty-four years. The state of Texas has awaited payment. It's your duty to make sure he does [pay]."

Chapter Twenty-Seven

+—❈—+

Houston, Texas, 1992: Part 5—To the Jury

The jury began its deliberations at 2:20 P.M. on Friday, August 28. Zimmermann and Lavine paced, Ray's brother Gerry stretched out on a bench at the back of the courtroom, and Frenchy and Gloria sat in the hallway talking quietly to each other.

The closing arguments by Lavine and Zimmermann had been masterful. They had piled contradiction upon questionable assumption upon doubtful witness and had provoked a host of questions about what had happened and why. During the course of the trial Ray's brother Gerry had told Gratton that Zimmermann's fee for Frenchy's defence was in the neighbourhood of $250,000. Cash. Zimmermann just laughed when asked to confirm the figure and said that he only wished he had been able to charge that much.

Still, whatever Ray had ended up paying, he had got his money's worth. Zimmermann and Lavine were adept, quick on their feet and impressively well prepared. They had given Frenchy just about the best defence money could buy. The only element absent from their closing arguments was moral authority. What they hadn't been able to do was to present Ray as a sympathetic character. It was Wilson who pointed out, after it was all over, that in most murder trials what the jury is shown is a thin slice of the defendant's life, an hour's or an evening's activity. But here a good stretch of Frenchy's life had been exposed and none of it was very attractive. The jury had been told about the callousness with which he had treated the kids, about his betrayals, about his brazen and heartless lies to his in-laws. And, on top of that, Lavine had made the mistake of mentioning, in his closing address, Denis's testimony that Ray had once told him, "I know where Jeannine is. When she's good and ready to see you, I'll take you." If that were the case, why hadn't Ray coughed up her whereabouts and saved himself from a murder charge? What sort of heartless man would tell his kid that and then never follow through? What was he hiding? The law prohibited the jury from holding against Ray the fact that he had not testified. But if the jurors believed Denis, then it seemed inescapable that they would ask themselves how that remark could be explained.

The closing addresses of Taylor and Wilson hadn't seemed as well organized. But they had moral authority and had worked the emotions of the jurors. The two prosecutors had the children on their side, a Mountie, a Texas Ranger, a legendary forensic pathologist and, perhaps most compelling of all, the memory of a gentle, loving mother. If Ray was going to be acquitted, the jurors would have to make a decision that wasn't based on their feelings. The defence had emphasized the importance of doing what was legally right. Taylor and Wilson had underlined the need for a decision that was morally appropriate.

At 3:05, less than an hour after they had begun deliberating, the jury buzzed once. (Two buzzes meant they had reached a decision.) The buzzer was sharp, loud and unexpected, and everyone in the court jumped. The jury asked for a transcript of the entire trial. They were told that wasn't possible, that a full transcript would take months to prepare. They could, however, have the court reporter read, from her notes, portions of the transcript. They went back to their discussions for another hour and three-quarters and buzzed again. This time they asked to be allowed to break for the weekend. So Densen released them until Monday at 10 A.M., and Frenchy went off to spend what was possibly the most nerve-racking weekend of his life.

On Monday morning, at 10 A.M., Frenchy and Gloria were back in court, as were the jury members.

At 2:30 that afternoon, Zimmermann filed the first of what was to be a stack of motions for the judge to declare a mistrial. He told Densen that the jury had been deliberating for five hours and thirty-five minutes, that the testimony had amounted to only nineteen hours and that "it should be obvious by now that the jury has reasonable doubts." Densen denied the motion and everyone went back to a jittery wait.

Less than an hour later, the jury buzzed once and sent out a note that they wanted to have read out to them that portion of Pat's testimony in which she was being re-examined by Wilson for the last time. Zimmermann immediately demanded that the jury be read his cross-examination as well. But Densen denied his request. The jury filed in and, as court reporter Glenda Blackmon began reading out the testimony from her notes, a violent storm broke outside, making it difficult to hear. Ten minutes later the jury filed back into chambers and the waiting resumed.

By now Gratton and I had discovered that Ted Wilson and John Makeig of the *Chronicle* were biding their time in bailiff Manuel Moreno's office, smoking and playing chess. To get to the bailiff's office we had to go through a door marked, "NO UNAUTHORIZED ENTRY." We sat around talking about the case while Moreno listened closely for sounds coming from the other side of a wall in his office. He said that on the other side were the washrooms used by the jurors and that he could always tell when the jury was ready to come out by the number of flushes he heard. Asked to explain, he said that whenever he heard a quick succession of toilet flushes—say, eight or ten in a row—that meant the jurors were rushing to relieve themselves before filing out. We kept our ears to the wall all afternoon and at one point got up to five flushes in a row but no buzzes.

I asked Wilson why he hadn't called Pat's ex-husband, Bert Matheis, to testify about the story she had told him. Wilson said he had considered it but felt it wouldn't be necessary. As the day wore it, I wondered if he was reconsidering.

By 5 P.M. the jury still hadn't reached a decision and were sent home. They were back at it the next morning, and Zimmermann was gearing up to file another motion for a mistrial.

Back in Moreno's office Wilson kept us entertained with stories about cases he had worked on and his own observations of Frenchy's trial. He said that for Reggy the trip to Houston was extraordinarily difficult, about the "same as me walking to Ottawa." Wilson talked about the case of a midget who had killed his grandfather, also a midget, whose name was Shorty. He told a story about the murderer of a ten-year-old girl who sent the police riddle clues and threatened to kill again every time they failed to solve one of his riddles.

The deliberations ended again on Tuesday without a verdict. The jury had now been at it since Friday afternoon, and the tension was making everyone jumpy. We all agreed that if the jury managed to conclude that 68-500 was Jeannine Durand, then Ray was sunk. But what was taking them so long?

On Wednesday morning, September 2, the jury filed in at 9:00 and at 10:30 buzzed once. They wanted to have two portions of

Denis's testimony read to them. An hour later they listened to Glenda Blackmon read to them Denis's account of the family's moves after Jeannine disappeared and of Ray's angry outburst in the car while they were driving by the Astrodome.

That afternoon, they buzzed again and this time asked to hear the story of Ray's comment to Denis: "I know where your mom is."

Immediately afterwards, Zimmermann called for a mistrial and again Densen denied his request. For some reason the lawyers now all sensed that the tide had turned and that it didn't look good for Ray.

At 4:38, another buzzer sounded and this time the note from the jury read: "Please do not interrupt the jury. We are very close to a verdict." And exactly twenty-one minutes later, on the fourth day of their deliberations, two buzzers sounded. Ray kissed Gloria and took a seat between his lawyers. She plucked a handful of tissues from her bag in preparation for a good cry.

The jury filed in at 5:04, and not one of them looked at Ray. Zimmermann and Lavine began whispering frantically to Ray. Moments later Densen asked Ray to stand. Then he read out the fateful words: "We, the jury, find the defendant, Raymond Durand, guilty of murder, as charged in the indictment."

Zimmermann rose, furious, and demanded that each juror be polled to indicate whether he or she found the defendant guilty beyond a reasonable doubt. All twelve jurors, polled individually, answered, without hesitation, in the affirmative.

Ray looked impassive, his eyes flat. But something seemed to have gone out of him. He suddenly appeared small and pitiful. Gloria was weeping loudly. Zimmermann asked that Ray be allowed to remain free until sentencing but Densen refused. Manuel Moreno moved behind Ray to usher him into the cells. Ray turned to Gloria just before he left and silently formed the words, "I love you."

Under Texas law juries not only determine guilt or innocence but are responsible for sentencing as well. The punishment phase of the trial begins immediately after a verdict has been reached, and during the punishment phase both prosecution and defence can call witnesses and introduce evidence.

The trial was, by now, in its third week. The jury deliberations had been so draining, had taken so long, that the attorneys and veteran court observers were convinced that the jury would fix a sentence in a matter of hours. Wilson was evidently eager to move on as well.

On Thursday morning, when Ray was led in from the cells, looking gaunt, and the punishment phase began, Wilson simply offered all the prosecution evidence that had already been presented.

Zimmermann, for his first witness, called Ray's brother Gerry, who asked that Ray be given probation and not sent to jail.

In cross-examination Wilson asked Gerry if he believed that "a man who beats his wife, breaks all her ribs and busts open her head and leaves her in a field should not go to jail?"

"He should but that's not Ray that did it."

Gerry's wife, Louise, appeared next. She, too, asked that Ray be given probation.

Wilson asked her if she knew Jeannine. She said she did and she agreed that Jeannine was a good mother.

"And you liked her?"

"Yes," she said. Then she added quickly before Wilson could object, "We don't know if she is dead."

"Let's assume that's her. You don't think Jeannine deserved to die that way?"

"I know the jury thinks it's her. But we think it isn't. That wasn't Jeannine in the photo."

And finally, after sitting for three weeks on a courtroom bench, prim and attractive and stoic, Gloria was called to the stand. Lavine intended to ask her questions that would have challenged Anne's testimony about the conversation she had had in Tex Ritter's office and the second conversation on the phone in which Frenchy remarked from the background that Jeannine had died of cancer. But Wilson objected and Densen instructed Lavine to steer clear of references to those conversations. He said that Gloria had been in the courtroom throughout the trial, had heard everything and could not now be called upon to impeach a witness's testimony. So Gloria was allowed to say little more than that she loved Ray.

In his closing argument Zimmermann hectored the jurors, saying he disagreed with the verdict. "You were out for twenty-one hours. There was twenty-one hours of testimony. I have never had that happen in eighteen years of practice. Somebody had a reasonable doubt....Whatever is in your heart is right. You stand strong. Don't let anybody stampede your judgment."

In his closing argument, Wilson told the jury that they had a choice that ranged from five years to life. And he invoked the gods of justice, insisting the jurors consider what they knew about Ray. "Did he finally get religion and tell his family what really happened? He's here because an investigator in Riverside listened to Anne and did something about it. He has lied to everybody about it. What kind of family did he give the kids? Anne got her nose busted. He left his son in Canada. Lied to his daughter [Martine] till she was sixteen. Had the audacity to knock on the door of his in-laws two years after he beat her to death....What's he done since then? Pounded out a few fenders. Would we be talking about this if we had caught him the day after? Does he get bonus points for what he's done since then?

"What in the world did Jeannine do to deserve that? She never saw her children grow up; they never saw their mother. She never saw her grandchildren. She doesn't know how good her children turned out in spite of him."

Wilson suggested the sentence be "on the high side of forty-five years."

The jury retired and continued their deliberations until 8 P.M. that evening. They buzzed then and sent out a note that threw the conviction into doubt: "All twelve jurors agree that we are hopelessly deadlocked on the punishment phase. All jurors stand firm on their extremely diverse positions. We unanimously feel that future deliberations are futile."

Zimmermann was elated; Wilson chilled to the bone. If the jury couldn't agree on punishment, Zimmermann could win a mistrial or, in the best-case scenario for Wilson, a new jury would be sworn in just to consider punishment. Densen thought for a moment and decided to sequester the jury for the night. He said he would instruct them in the morning on the consequences of their inability to set punishment. And, indeed, the following morning when he made clear to them that the hard work they had put into arriving at a verdict would be in vain if they couldn't agree on punishment, brows went up across the jury box. Later one juror said that they hadn't understood, had thought that if they couldn't make a decision on sentencing, that the judge would.

An hour later the jurors buzzed twice. Gloria misunderstood, thought the buzzers meant they had given up and smiled. She became sober and grim after Zimmermann whispered in her ear. The jury filed in and moments later Ray heard the judge read out his sentence: thirty years in a Texas penitentiary. Ray remained impassive. Asked if he had anything to say, he uttered the first, last and only words he was to pronounce at his own trial: "I'm not guilty."

Epilogue

+—※※—+

After Frenchy was sentenced, I arranged for an interview with Sheriff Johnny Klevenhagen, whose office is on the ground floor of a twelve-storey county jail. In the lobby about fifty people were milling about, waiting for afternoon visiting hours to begin. Only one of the visitors was white and dressed in silks. Seeing me, Gloria Durand called out. She looked lonely and distressed and began to cry as we talked. She said Ray had been sleeping on the floor because there was a shortage of beds and that he had been given a pair of coveralls with the crotch torn out. With her assistance, he had bought from a fellow inmate a mattress and a decent pair of coveralls. She said she was going to move to Houston, find a job and wait for him.

"God is in our hearts," she told me. "I didn't know Ray before. I love him. So I have to believe him."

It struck me that Ray must have felt blessed as he approached his sixties. He had bought a sprawling new home in Myrtle Beach, had a new business, an attractive young wife and enough money to retire on. Pat and the rest of his past were long behind him. There hadn't been a cloud in his sky until Talton and Madeira showed up with a warrant for his arrest.

Frenchy has always been astoundingly resilient, though. Immediately after his sentencing his lawyers filed a motion for a new trial, which was denied. He declared he was broke, and the state appointed a lawyer to handle his appeal, which began winding its way through the courts. He hasn't given up and, with luck, could be out of prison within seven years, possibly less. Prisons in Texas are overcrowded, and Ray is an ideal candidate for parole. The stereotypical murderer in Houston is a crazed crackhead doing time for stabbing his sister-in-law in the eye with an ice-pick. By comparison, Ray seems like an upstanding citizen. He's a businessman who has never before been charged with a felony. He's got a loyal and supportive wife.

Because of the problem of prison overcrowding, Frenchy would spend almost a year in county jail before being moved. Wilson said that when Frenchy does make it into prison, his skills will be much in demand. Penitentiary inmates in Texas repair and paint school buses for school boards across the state. Texas is going to give Frenchy a chance to work at his old trade.

Leaving Gloria, I met Klevenhagen in his office. He said he wasn't fooled by Frenchy's act in court. He viewed Frenchy as "cold, very calculating. He's got a very arrogant outlook on authority."

Klevenhagen estimated that Frenchy would end up serving about five years if the conviction wasn't overturned on appeal. The possibility that Frenchy might serve only five years clearly irked him. When I asked why Frenchy was sleeping on the floor, he vented his frustration. He said the "easy solution to not being uncomfortable [in jail] is to follow the law." And then he added a remark that was chilling and final. The "sweetest victory," he said, would have been a sentence for Ray of "death by injection."

Denis had endured the four-day return train journey and was back at work in his body shop by the time the verdict came in. The first day he returned to the shop he had found his answering machine choked with calls from reporters—more than three dozen of them. He erased the tape and refused to return any of the calls. But the press interest in the story had, to Denis's astonishment, attracted the interest of a number of movie producers. A deal for a movie was eventually struck with a Los Angeles-based company. When it was clear to Denis that he was going to make some money from the rights to his story, he decided to set up a charitable foundation in Jeannine's name. He arranged to funnel all of the income into it and he decided that the funds from the foundation would be used to support battered women's shelters in the Hull area. Denis had always believed that if his mother had had a place to go, someone to help her, she would not have joined Raymond in Houston. His mother's memory kept him sane, he said, and he hoped that the money might help other women in need.

Denis eventually heard about Pat's testimony about her recollection that Ray had met them at her apartment the day after Jeannine's disappearance and about the fact that she didn't remember Ray coming in with suitcases. It bothered him that he couldn't account for the discrepancy between Pat's recollections and his own. He could remember the hallway he had been in when his father had entered and could even remember seeing the door open. But Pat had said they were at her apartment when Ray returned and that he hadn't been carrying suitcases.

About six months after the trial Denis and Line were in a restaurant one night and Denis was gazing, idly, at a young mother reaching into a large bag for a diaper for her baby. A thought struck him like a thunderbolt. Diapers. Pat had sent him back to the house for diapers for Martine. That's why he was at the house. He thought about it constantly for the following week, trying to remember more, but in the end he remembered less. Maybe, he said, he was just imagining that he had been sent home for diapers. He had never doubted what he knew, what he testified to at the trial, but now that his father was in jail he began, like his siblings, trying to imagine the rest of it. Were the diapers part of the imagining? He'd always said that it didn't matter to him how it had happened, that nothing Ray could say about the circumstances of Jeannine's death would excuse what he had done. Now, though, Denis wondered how it had occurred. He'd never know. He'd always live with that question.

In San Jacinto, Anne had mixed feelings about the verdict and sentence. She felt great anguish for her father but now, also, great anger. The trial had, in her mind, settled the question of whether her father had killed her mother. But she felt an acute need to know why. A month after the trial, she sat down and wrote Frenchy a letter:

Father,

Why? Why did the search for our mother have to end up that you killed her? Have you any idea the pain that you put your children through? The hardest thing I ever had to do was get on that stand in Texas and testify against my own father, whom I loved so much.

Growing up, things were not good at all but I tried to forget all the hurt that you caused us....

I hope one day that you will tell us the truth once and for all why you did this to our mother. If we mean anything to you, then you need to come out straight with us. I don't want to hear from you if it's going to be more lies. By the way, was Pat worth it all? Anne

Frenchy's arrest and trial were cathartic experiences for Denis and Anne as well as many others. So many people had had their lives or livelihoods ruined by Ray Durand that after his arrest and conviction many of them understood, for the first time, that it wasn't their weakness but Ray's cunning that had done them in. The most crippling effect Ray had had on his victims was the lingering doubt about themselves and about humanity that he left them with. For years afterwards many of them found themselves unable to trust others. Most of them never knew just how accomplished a predator Ray was.

I found Lori Wells, now Lori Gooldrup, in a small town in British Columbia. She hadn't heard of or seen Ray Durand since 1970, when he had made off with her father's life savings. She hadn't forgotten him, though, and was immediately deeply suspicious when I mentioned his name. I told her what had happened and she was silent.

"Ray Durand killed my father," she said finally. "I always blamed myself." Lori said her father had never gotten over the loss of his savings. "It broke his heart and his health," she said of her father, Robert, who had died, a bitter man, some years later.

"I felt so responsible," she said, because she had been eager to meet Denis and the kids, and had then brought the families together. She said the burden she had carried since 1970 was the notion that she had brought her father together with Ray. She said she remembered her sister walking into her parents' bedroom and seeing her father, sitting on the bed, crying. Hearing about Ray, about the life he had led and what he had done to others, made her "knees shake," she said. But it also helped ease the guilt she had packed around for so long.

In Pointe Gatineau, I found Gilles Paquin in the same house he had been living in when Ray set him up on the forgery bust in January of 1966. I tracked down Paquin in January, 1992, and when I walked into his office and introduced myself and said I was writing about Ray Durand, he stared at me, dumbfounded.

"Yesterday was the twenty-sixth anniversary of my arrest," he said, when he got over his surprise. He said he had read that Ray had been charged with murder and he hoped that Ray was going to get what he deserved.

In California, I found Arlene Knight, who had lived next to Ray at the ranch and had once put a gun to his head when he broke into her house. She and her husband, Daniel, now live on a quiet street on the outskirts of Los Angeles.

"I've been waiting for you to call," she said when I rang. She explained that she had visions and had sensed someone would be contacting her about Ray, one of the most malevolent men she said she had ever met. She was eager to share what she knew and encouraged me to pursue the story. Unlike many others I met in California who had known Ray and had done business with him, she wanted to be quoted, wanted to set the record straight and expose Ray for what he was.

I knocked on Pat's door, too, while I was in California. She no longer goes by her maiden name, Holben, and lives in anonymity in a trailer park in a small town. She has never bothered to explain to the children what happened. The police had to pry the story of the newscast out of her. And now, she told me, she doesn't want to talk to anyone, under any circumstances, about her life with Ray. I drove off thinking about Pat's stony silence and about how characteristic it was. At her own arson trial she never defended herself, never explained herself. She'd done the same this time around. She won't defend her actions, even to the children, won't explain why she treated them as she did. And for that, they cannot forgive her, cannot forget her. (Ten months after my visit Pat died of complications related to leukemia. Her brother Harold said she had known for more than a year that she was suffering from the disease. When she testified, she apparently knew she was dying.)

I thought as well about Jeannine. Anne was nine and Denis twelve when she disappeared. In the short years that they knew her she managed to pass on to them indelible memories, memories that could be manipulated but not erased. When you ask Denis and Anne about their mother, they remember not so much the specifics but the feelings, many of them no doubt evoked by her piano recitals for her children and neighbours. Just as they remember Pat's hatred, Denis and Anne remember Jeannine's love. They remember the qualities of her character—patience, understanding, kindness. Because Denis and Anne could not forget her—even if there were long years in which they did not actively pursue the mystery of what had happened—they were eventually driven to confirm the truth of their memories and the truth about themselves. Ray and Pat did a great deal to undermine Anne and Denis's sense of identity. Slapping Denis around and calling him a big dummy, and telling Anne that her mother had thrown her in front of a car and didn't love her, were corrosive, debilitating actions. Their memories of Jeannine told them that they were deserving of the respect and love of others. Jeannine's death was the central misfortune of their lives. Misfortune's gift was their ability to draw strength from her memory and to use the tragedy of her disappearance to assert their identities and, as Cormac McCarthy put it, to "make their way back into the common enterprise of man."

Acknowledgments

S eeing the gaunt face of Ray Durand on television as he was being hauled, in handcuffs, to jail was what engaged me initially in this story of murder. I happened to be in Houston when he was arraigned. At first I simply wanted to know how and why this fellow countryman of mine had come to be charged with murder in Texas. I'm still not certain that I understand the why or even, for that matter, the how. Only Ray Durand can answer those questions, but even if he now offered me or his children an account of what actually happened, I wouldn't believe him, couldn't believe him. The only truth that could be drawn from a statement from Ray would be the fact that the statement would be untruthful. That much I've learned from my study of his character and his life.

Although it was Ray who sparked my interest, it was his children who sustained it. Denis Durand and Anne Hallberg are remarkable people who told me a story of pain and loss and, ultimately, of redemption. I found their story inspiring and hope that I have managed to convey in this book a measure of the admiration I feel for them. I'd like to thank them and their families for putting up with my endless questions, my often indelicate probing of their feelings and my intrusions into the privacy of their family life.

Martine Durand trusted me enough to tell me about her childhood and adolescence. She has all my sympathy. I hope this account helps her to understand something of the circumstances that provoked the despair she has been grappling with for most of her life.

Marc Durand, evasive but nonetheless helpful, gave me a fleeting glimpse into his life. It was as much as I wanted to see. I hope he, too, finds a way to make peace with his past.

Molly Kane, Jasper Boychuk and Claire Boychuk deserve thanks and a thousand blessings for the loyal support they extended to an angst-ridden, first-time author.

I am grateful to Barbara Moon, my editor at *Saturday Night,* for commissioning the story on Jeannine Durand's murder.

My agent, Denise Bukowski, helped package this project, and

her guidance was invaluable in chasing it through to completion. Penguin Books publisher Cynthia Good edited the first draft and was generous with her praise. I'm still not certain whether she arranged for the cameraman to capture my smiling mug for the Jumbotron at the Jays' game we attended or whether it was mere happenstance. Whatever, I was impressed.

Among the more than 100 people I interviewed for the book I'd like to thank, in particular, Jean Nadeau, who took me up to the ranch and kept me on my toes by pointing out all the snakeholes; Michel Béland, who was frank and forthcoming in recounting his mother's family's history; Ted Wilson, who was the epitome of calm professionalism throughout the trial and who always had time to answer my queries; Lieutenant Roch Menard, who tried to smoke me out of his office with his cigarettes, cigars and his pipe and who helped me understand the *demi-monde* Ray inhabited in Hull in the 1950s and 1960s; Lieutenant François Cloutier, who helped orient some of my research; Arlene and Daniel Knight, who were hospitable and encouraging; "Jane," who, despite her embarrassment, told me about her marriage to Frenchy; Gayle Wigmore, who never threw anything out; Judge John Kane Jr., who made helpful suggestions that improved the trial portion of the text; and John Makeig of the Houston *Chronicle* and Barbara Linkin of the Houston *Post,* both of whom were kind enough to share with me their expert knowledge of the workings of the Harris County judicial system.

Finally, I wish to thank C.T. Dornan and David Wimhurst for their companionship and for the morale-boosting sessions.

Index